THE QUEEN'S KNIGHT

The Queen's Knight Vol. 6
Created by Kim Kang Won

Translation - Sora Han
English Adaptation - Anina Bennett
Retouch and Lettering - Alyson Stetz
Production Artist - Alyson Stetz
Cover Design - Mona Lisa De Asis

Editor - Troy Lewter
Digital Imaging Manager - Chris Buford
Managing Editor - Lindsey Johnston
Editor-in-Chief - Rob Tokar
VP of Production - Ron Klamert
Publisher - Mike Kiley
President and C.O.O. - John Parker
C.E.O. and Chief Creative Officer - Stuart Levy

A **TOKYOPOP** Manga

TOKYOPOP Inc.
5900 Wilshire Blvd. Suite 2000
Los Angeles, CA 90036

E-mail: info@TOKYOPOP.com
Come visit us online at www.TOKYOPOP.com

ISBN: 1-59532-262-0

First TOKYOPOP printing: June 2006
10 9 8 7 6 5 4 3 2 1
Printed in the USA

THE QUEEN'S KNIGHT

VOLUME 6

BY KIM KANG WON

HAMBURG // LONDON // LOS ANGELES // TOKYO

LAST TIME IN...

THE QUEEN's KNIGHT

YUNA IS A NORMAL GIRL WHO VISITS HER MOTHER IN GERMANY AND ENDURES A TERRIBLE DISASTER. AFTER SHE RETURNS HOME FROM HER ACCIDENT, SHE BEGINS TO HAVE STRANGE DREAMS. IN HER DREAM, A KNIGHT WHO CALLS HIMSELF "RIENO" TELLS YUNA THAT SHE IS HIS QUEEN AND THAT HE IS HER KNIGHT. YUNA'S BROTHERS SEND HER BACK TO GERMANY, WHERE SHE MEETS THE KNIGHT FROM HER DREAMS--WHO THEN PROMPTLY KIDNAPS HER, TAKING HER TO PHANTASMA.

PHANTASMA IS A WORLD COVERED ENTIRELY WITH SNOW, AND YUNA IS FORCED TO LIVE WITH RIENO. BUT JUST WHEN YUNA WAS GETTING USED TO BEING WITH HIM, SPRING ARRIVES, AND YUNA IS TAKEN TO ELYSIAN TO BE PROPERLY INSTALLED AS THE QUEEN OF PHANTASMA. ONCE THERE, YUNA BEFRIENDS THE QUEEN'S GUARDIAN KNIGHTS, EHREN, LEON AND SCHILLER, AND MEETS THE HATEFUL CHANCELLOR KENT AS WELL AS THE QUEEN'S RIVAL, PRINCESS LIBERA.

YUNA IS FURIOUS WHEN SHE REALIZES SHE WAS TRICKED BY CHANCELLOR KENT INTO SIGNING AN EXECUTION DECREE. THAT NIGHT, RIENO CATCHES EHREN IN YUNA'S ROOM AND IMMEDIATELY GETS JEALOUS. YUNA ANGRILY TELLS HIM THAT HE CAN GO BE LIBERA'S KNIGHT. LATER, YUNA, SCHILLER AND LEON SECRETLY LEAVE THE CASTLE, ONLY TO BE ROBBED AND BRANDED AS FUGITIVES. ON THE RUN, THEY ALL SPEND SOME TIME AT THE HAMLET OF EHREN, AND YUNA IS TOLD THAT THE EARLY ARRIVAL OF SPRING MEANS THAT SHE IS INDEED IN LOVE. MEANWHILE, LEON "FIGHTS" EVA IN A CONTEST TO TRY AND WIN HER AS HIS MATE, BUT HE DOESN'T REALIZE THAT HE IS IN FACT FATED TO BE THE QUEEN'S CONSORT. LATER, LEON EXPRESSES HIS LOVE FOR YUNA...HOWEVER, MUCH TO HIS DISMAY, SHE TELLS HIM THAT SHE CANNOT LOVE HIM. LEON THEN GOES TO VISIT HIS GRANDMOTHER, WHO KNOWS A DARK SECRET...

THE QUEEN's KNIGHT

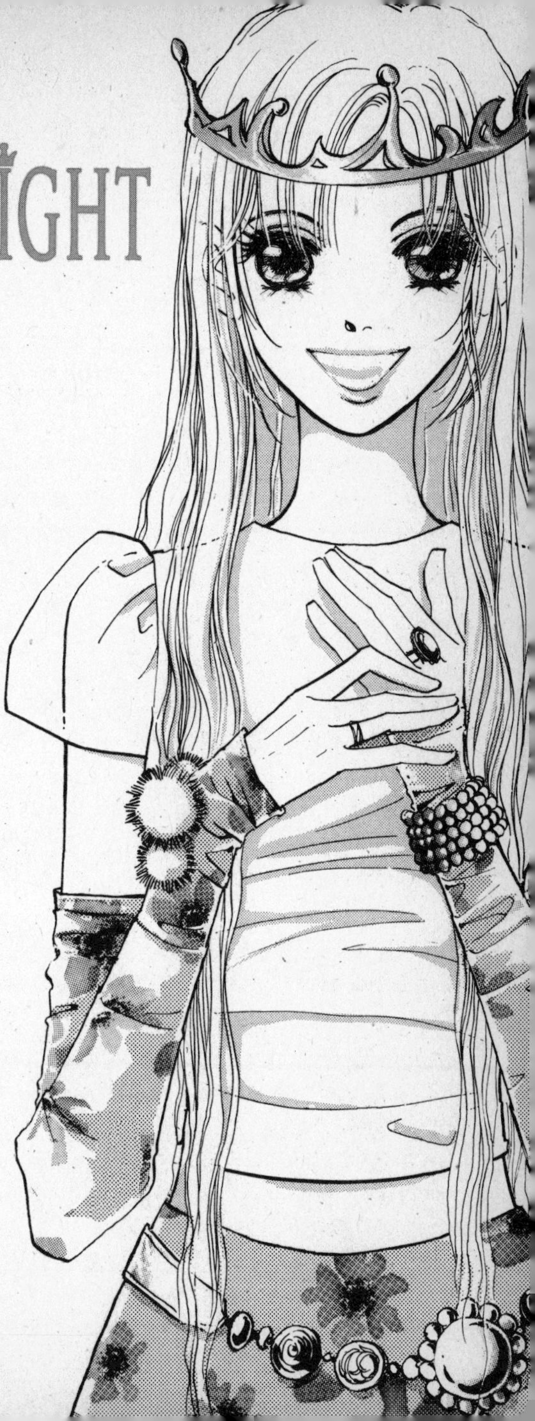

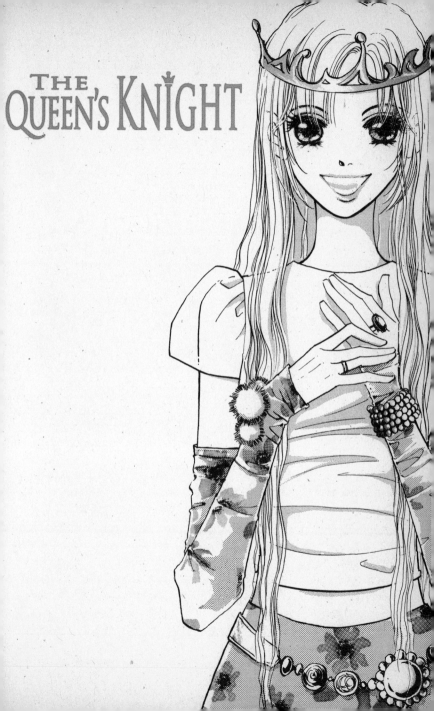

A MAP OF PHANTASMA

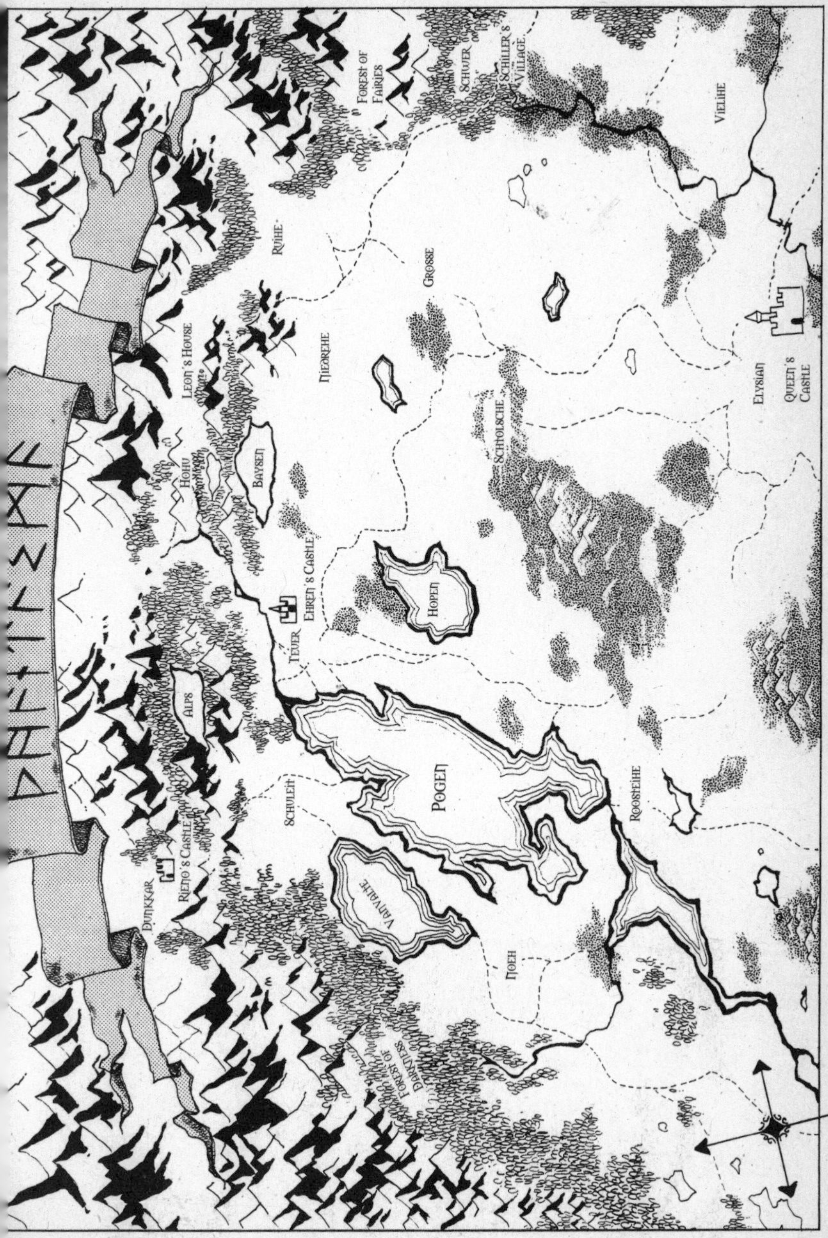
Forest of Fairies
Schiller's Village
Vielihe
Ruhe
Grosse
Niedrehe
Leon's House
Hohu
Baysen
Ehren's Castle
Teuer
Hopen
Elysian
Queen's Castle
Alps
Pogen
Schulen
Roosteihe
Rieno's Castle
Dunkkar
Noeh
Forest of Darkness

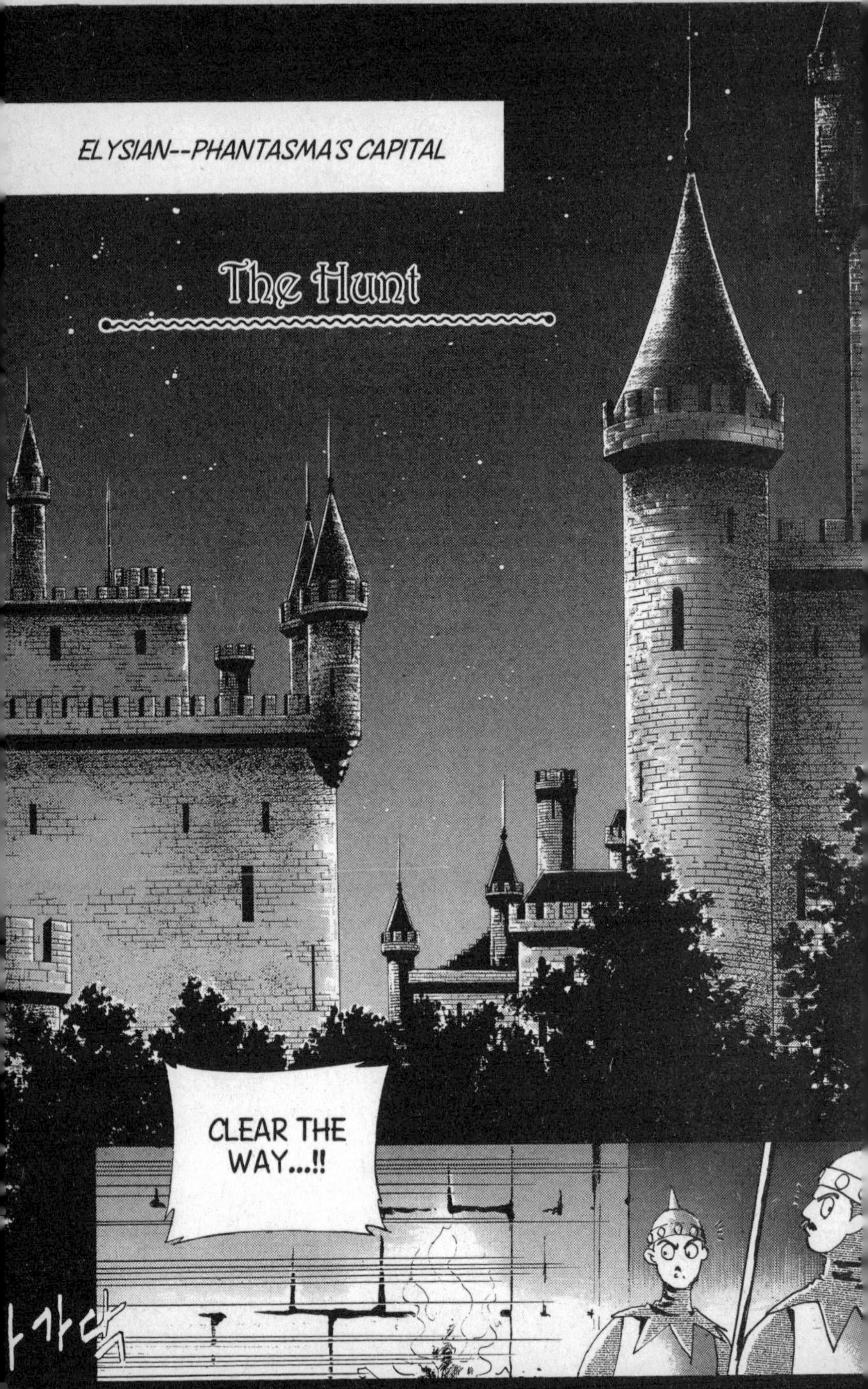
ELYSIAN--PHANTASMA'S CAPITAL
The Hunt
CLEAR THE WAY...!!

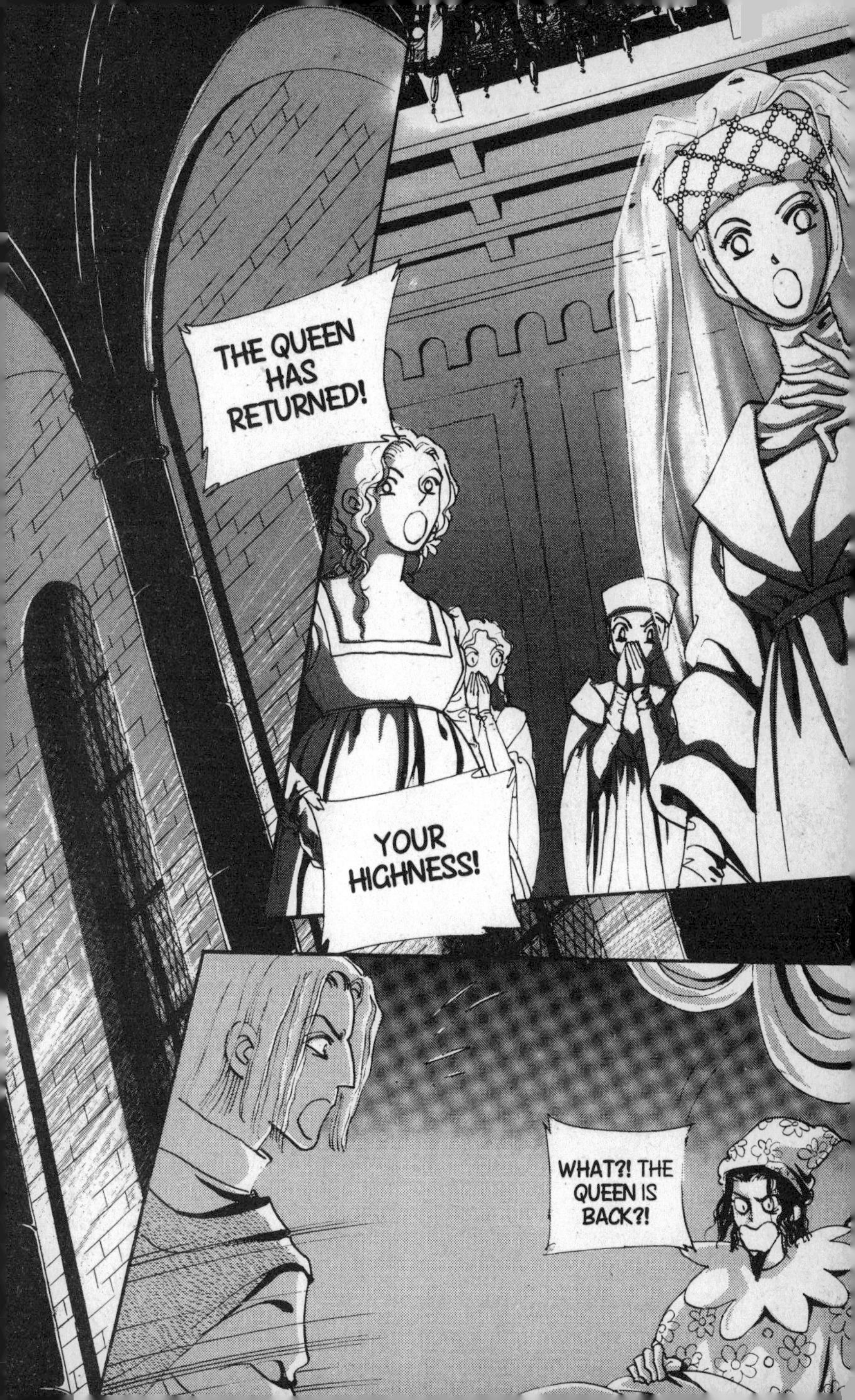
THE QUEEN HAS RETURNED!
YOUR HIGHNESS!
WHAT?! THE QUEEN IS BACK?!

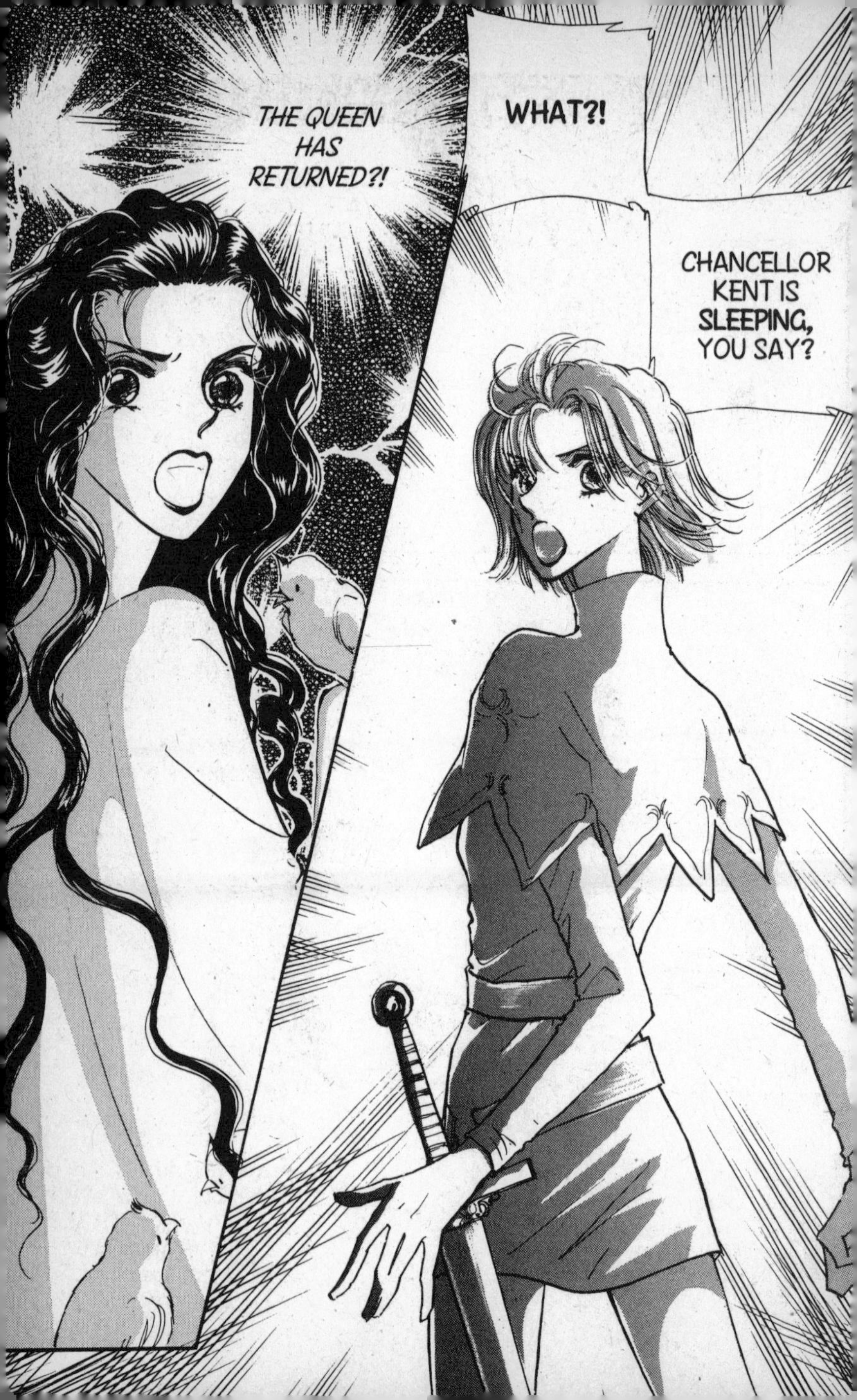
THE QUEEN HAS RETURNED?!
WHAT?!
CHANCELLOR KENT IS SLEEPING, YOU SAY?

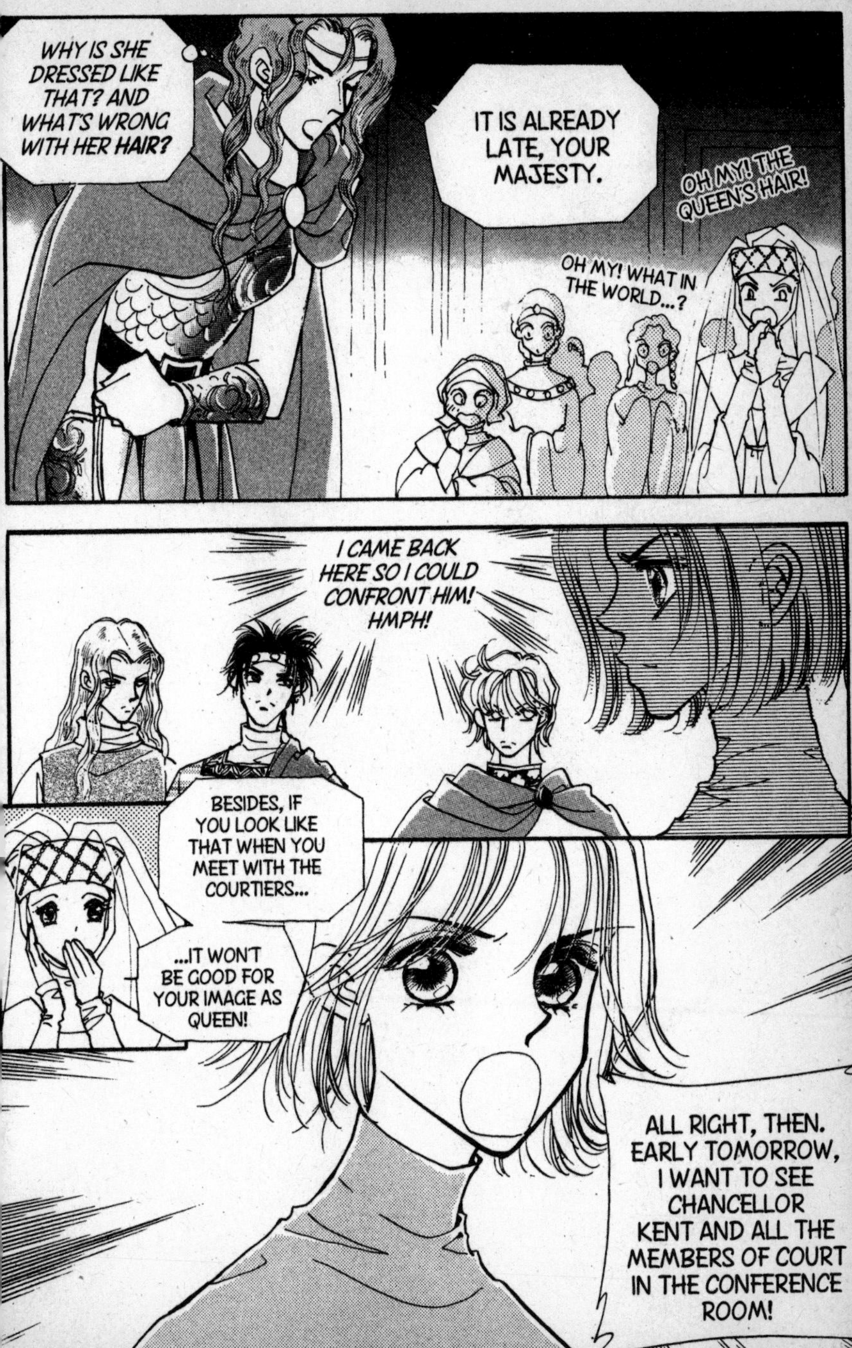
WHY IS SHE DRESSED LIKE THAT? AND WHAT'S WRONG WITH HER HAIR?
IT IS ALREADY LATE, YOUR MAJESTY.
OH MY! THE QUEEN'S HAIR!
OH MY! WHAT IN THE WORLD...?
I CAME BACK HERE SO I COULD CONFRONT HIM! HMPH!
BESIDES, IF YOU LOOK LIKE THAT WHEN YOU MEET WITH THE COURTIERS...
...IT WON'T BE GOOD FOR YOUR IMAGE AS QUEEN!
ALL RIGHT, THEN. EARLY TOMORROW, I WANT TO SEE CHANCELLOR KENT AND ALL THE MEMBERS OF COURT IN THE CONFERENCE ROOM!

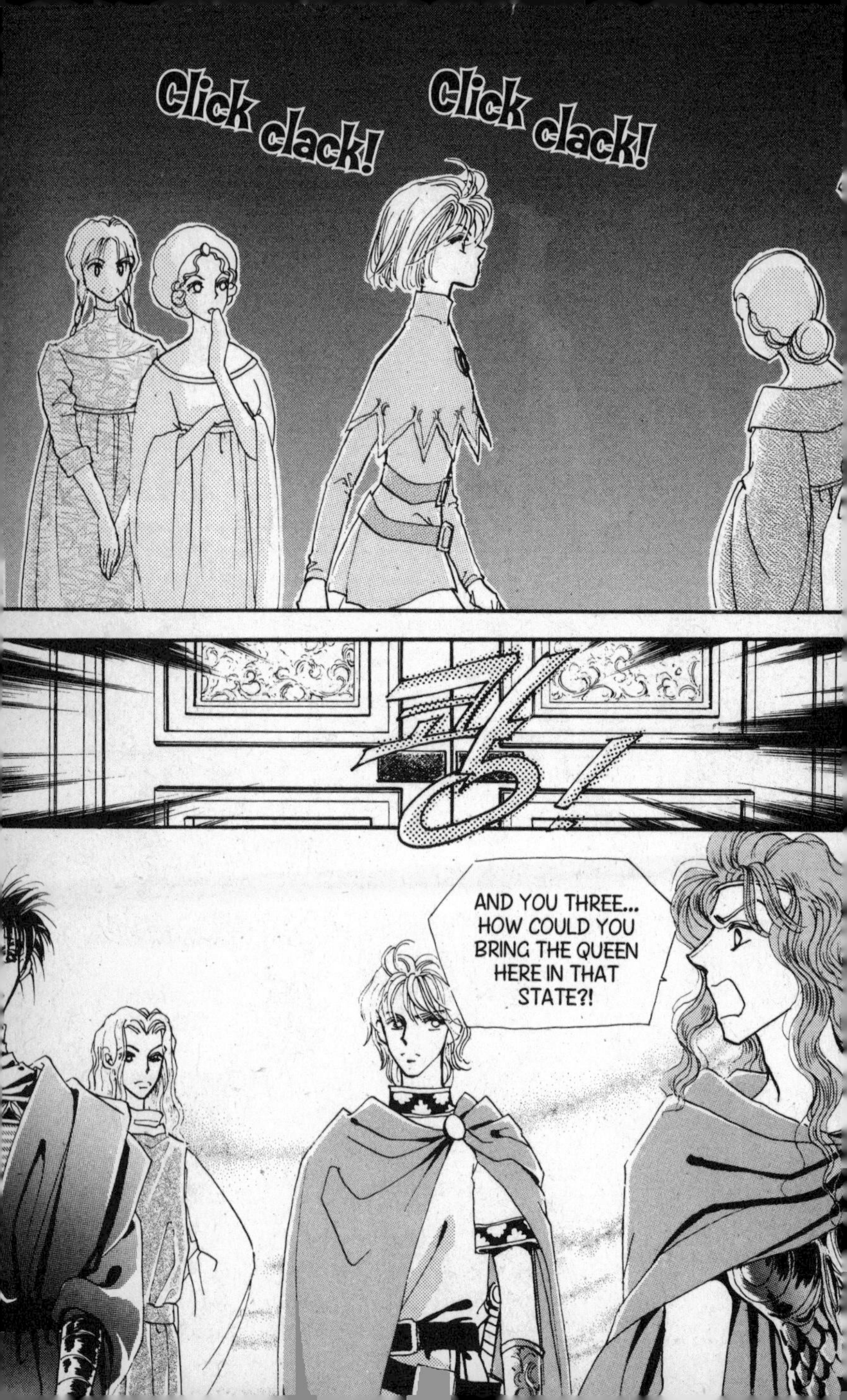
Click clack!
Click clack!
AND YOU THREE... HOW COULD YOU BRING THE QUEEN HERE IN THAT STATE?!

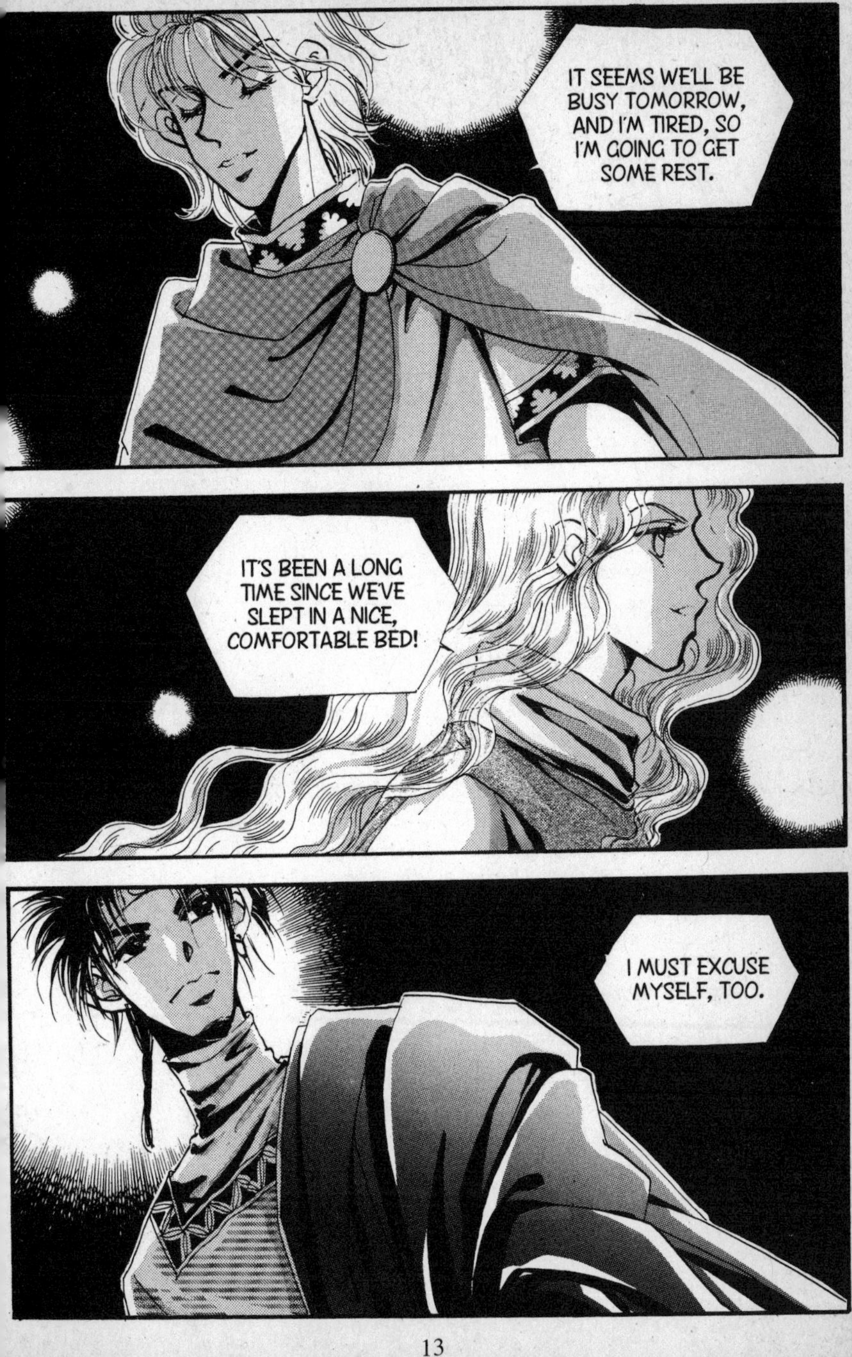
IT SEEMS WE'LL BE BUSY TOMORROW, AND I'M TIRED, SO I'M GOING TO GET SOME REST.
IT'S BEEN A LONG TIME SINCE WE'VE SLEPT IN A NICE, COMFORTABLE BED!
I MUST EXCUSE MYSELF, TOO.

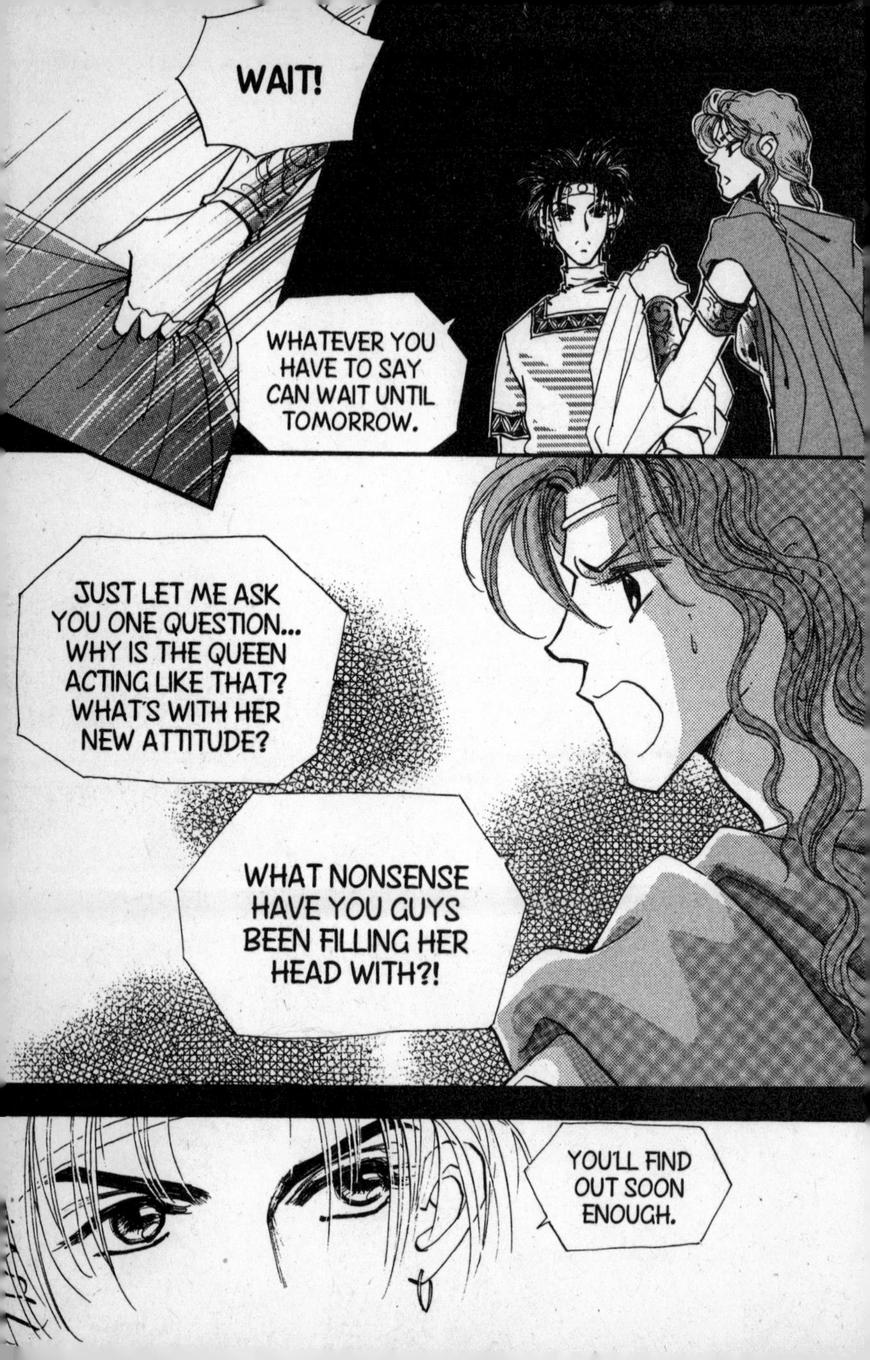
WAIT!
WHATEVER YOU HAVE TO SAY CAN WAIT UNTIL TOMORROW.
JUST LET ME ASK YOU ONE QUESTION... WHY IS THE QUEEN ACTING LIKE THAT? WHAT'S WITH HER NEW ATTITUDE?
WHAT NONSENSE HAVE YOU GUYS BEEN FILLING HER HEAD WITH?!
YOU'LL FIND OUT SOON ENOUGH.

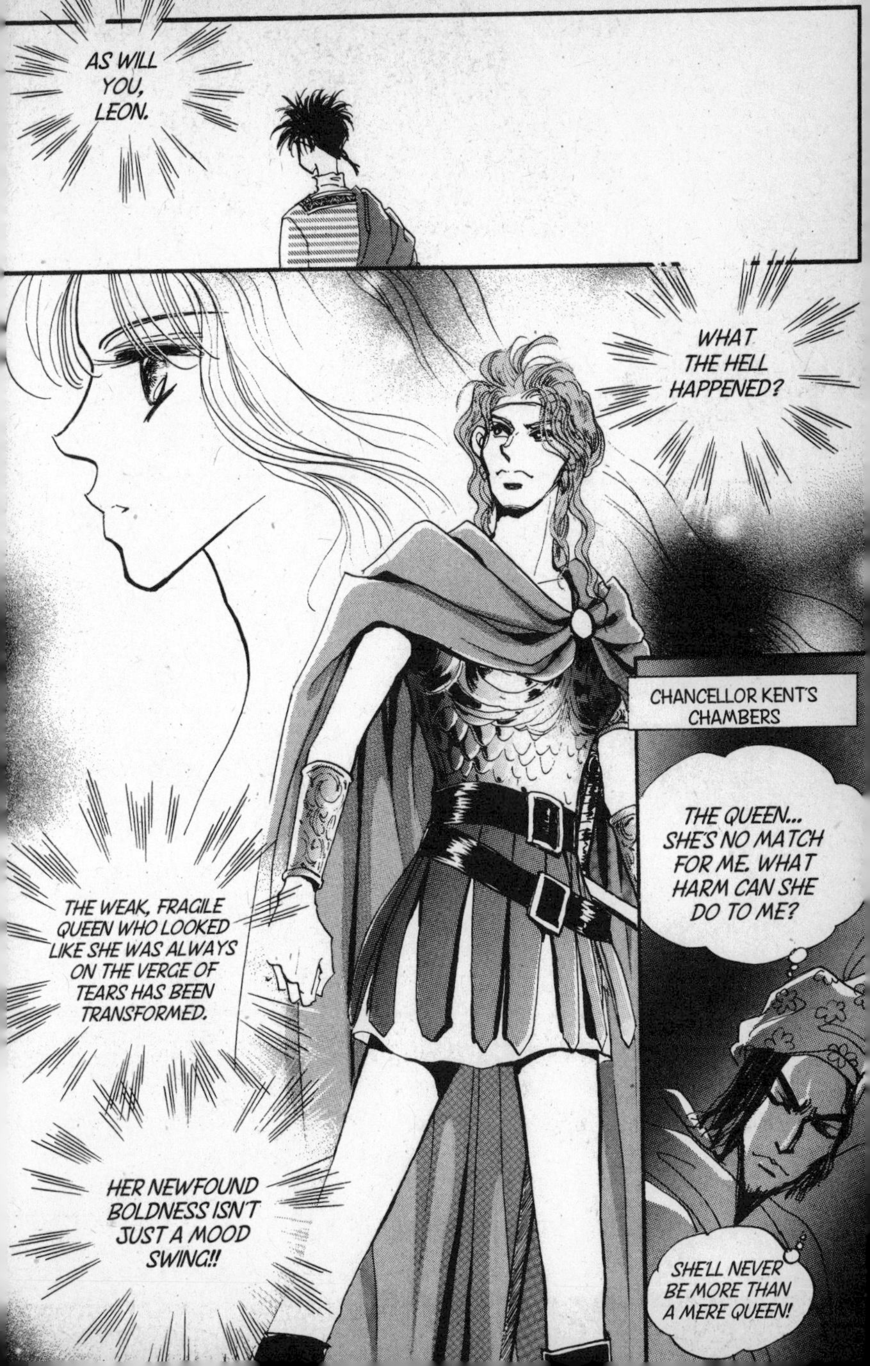
AS WILL YOU, LEON.
WHAT THE HELL HAPPENED?
THE WEAK, FRAGILE QUEEN WHO LOOKED LIKE SHE WAS ALWAYS ON THE VERGE OF TEARS HAS BEEN TRANSFORMED.
HER NEWFOUND BOLDNESS ISN'T JUST A MOOD SWING!!
CHANCELLOR KENT'S CHAMBERS
THE QUEEN... SHE'S NO MATCH FOR ME. WHAT HARM CAN SHE DO TO ME?
SHE'LL NEVER BE MORE THAN A MERE QUEEN!

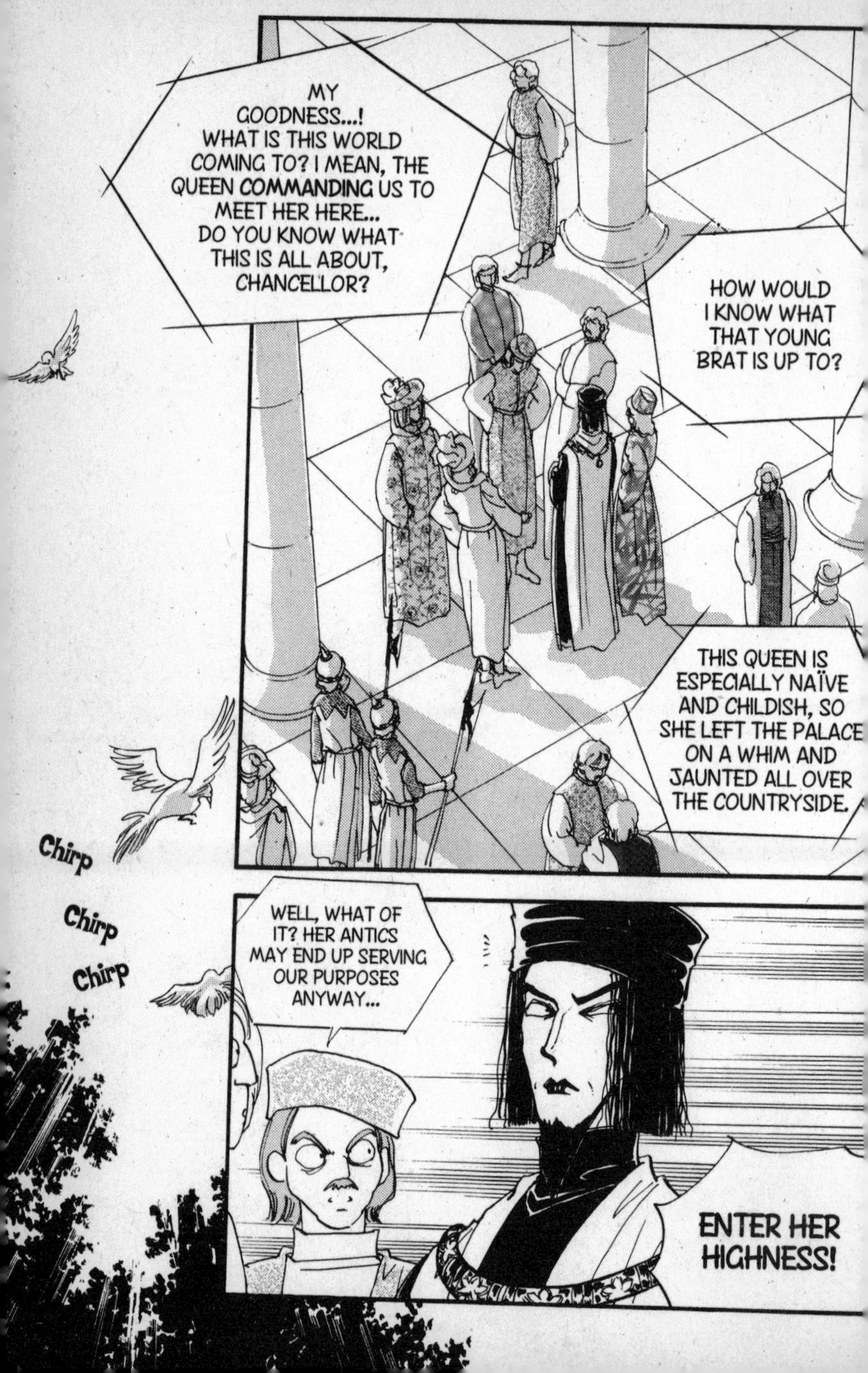
MY GOODNESS...! WHAT IS THIS WORLD COMING TO? I MEAN, THE QUEEN COMMANDING US TO MEET HER HERE... DO YOU KNOW WHAT THIS IS ALL ABOUT, CHANCELLOR?
HOW WOULD I KNOW WHAT THAT YOUNG BRAT IS UP TO?
THIS QUEEN IS ESPECIALLY NAÏVE AND CHILDISH, SO SHE LEFT THE PALACE ON A WHIM AND JAUNTED ALL OVER THE COUNTRYSIDE.
Chirp
Chirp
Chirp
WELL, WHAT OF IT? HER ANTICS MAY END UP SERVING OUR PURPOSES ANYWAY...
ENTER HER HIGHNESS!

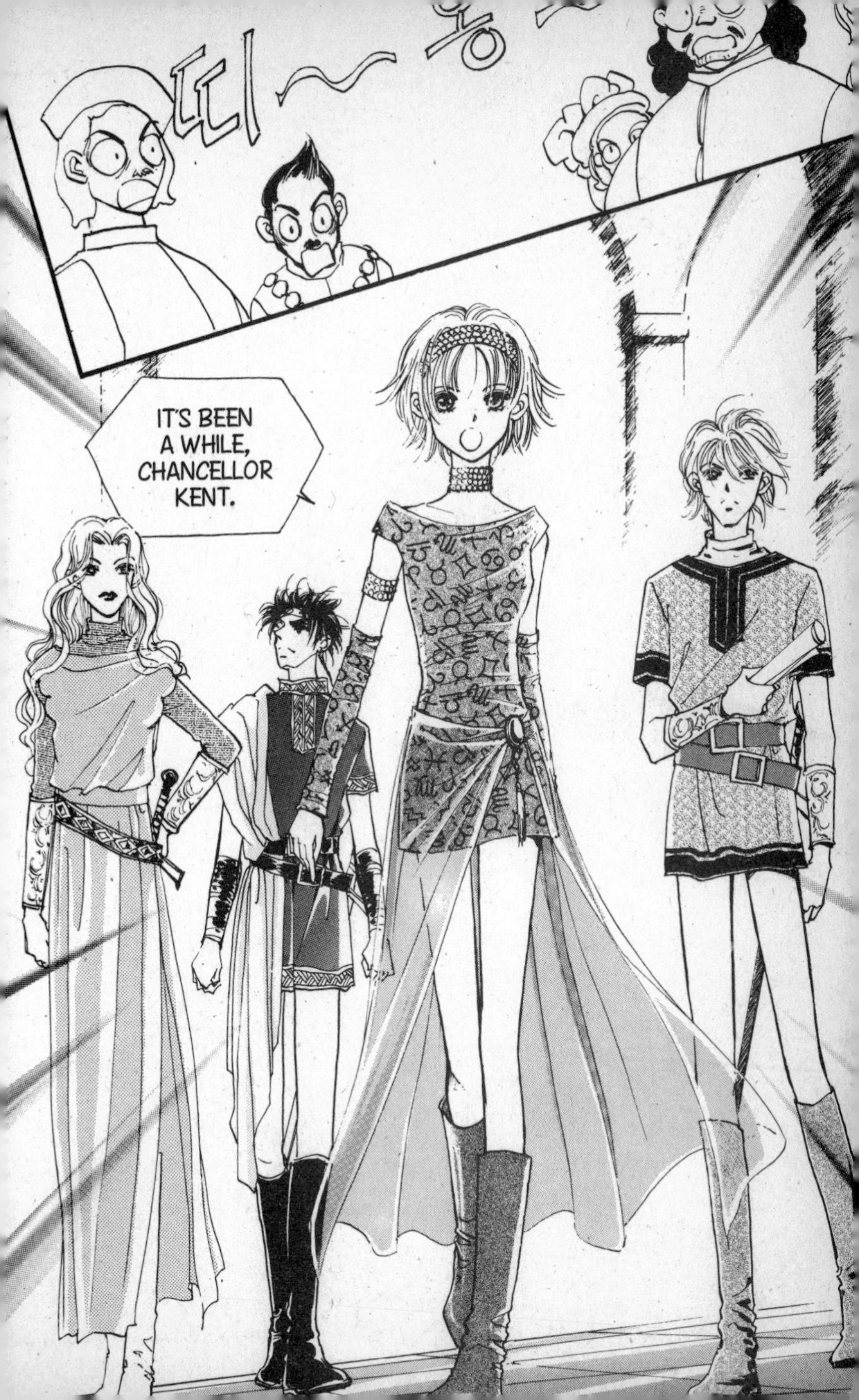
띠~용~
IT'S BEEN A WHILE, CHANCELLOR KENT.

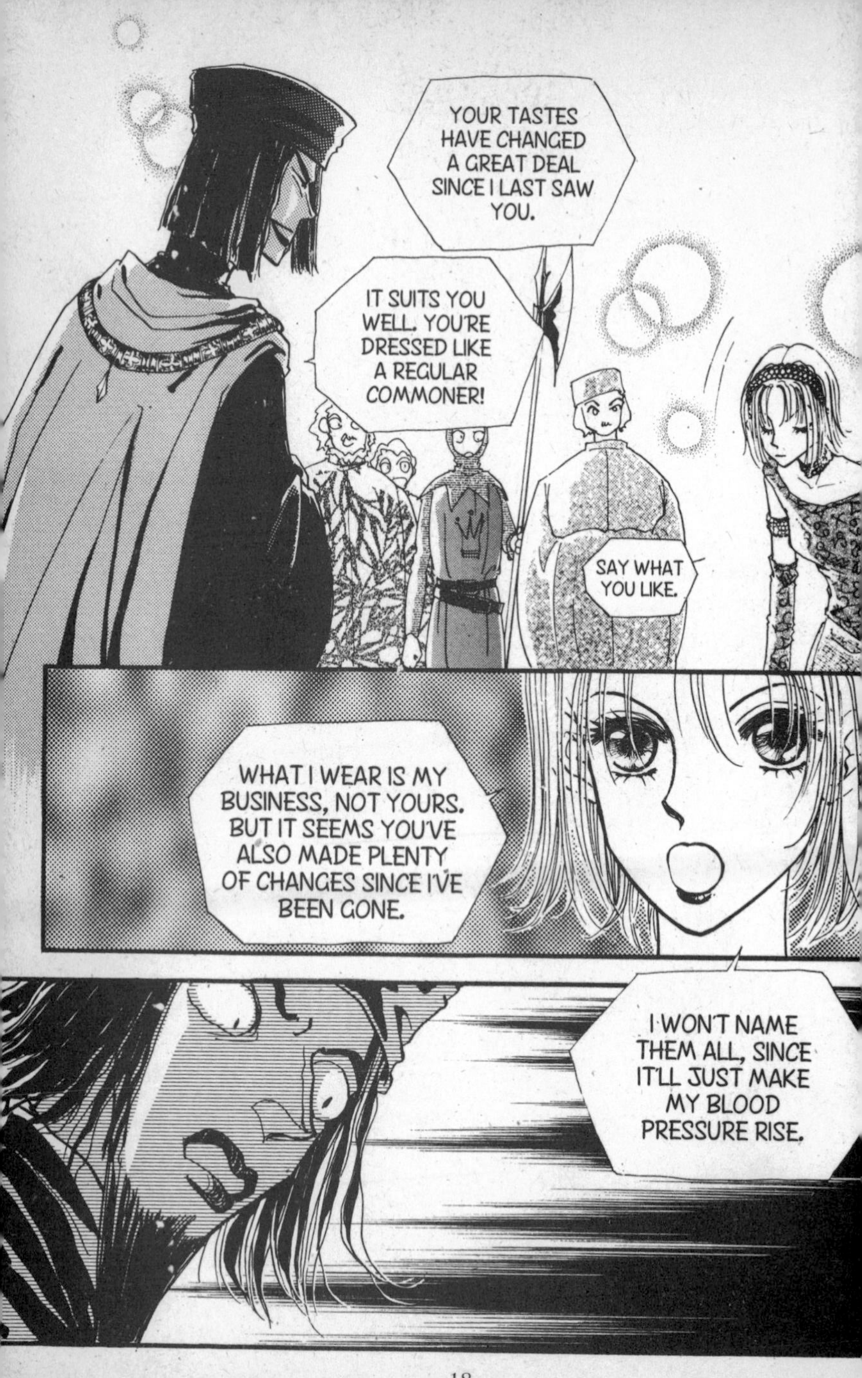
YOUR TASTES HAVE CHANGED A GREAT DEAL SINCE I LAST SAW YOU.
IT SUITS YOU WELL. YOU'RE DRESSED LIKE A REGULAR COMMONER!
SAY WHAT YOU LIKE.
WHAT I WEAR IS MY BUSINESS, NOT YOURS. BUT IT SEEMS YOU'VE ALSO MADE PLENTY OF CHANGES SINCE I'VE BEEN GONE.
I WON'T NAME THEM ALL, SINCE IT'LL JUST MAKE MY BLOOD PRESSURE RISE.

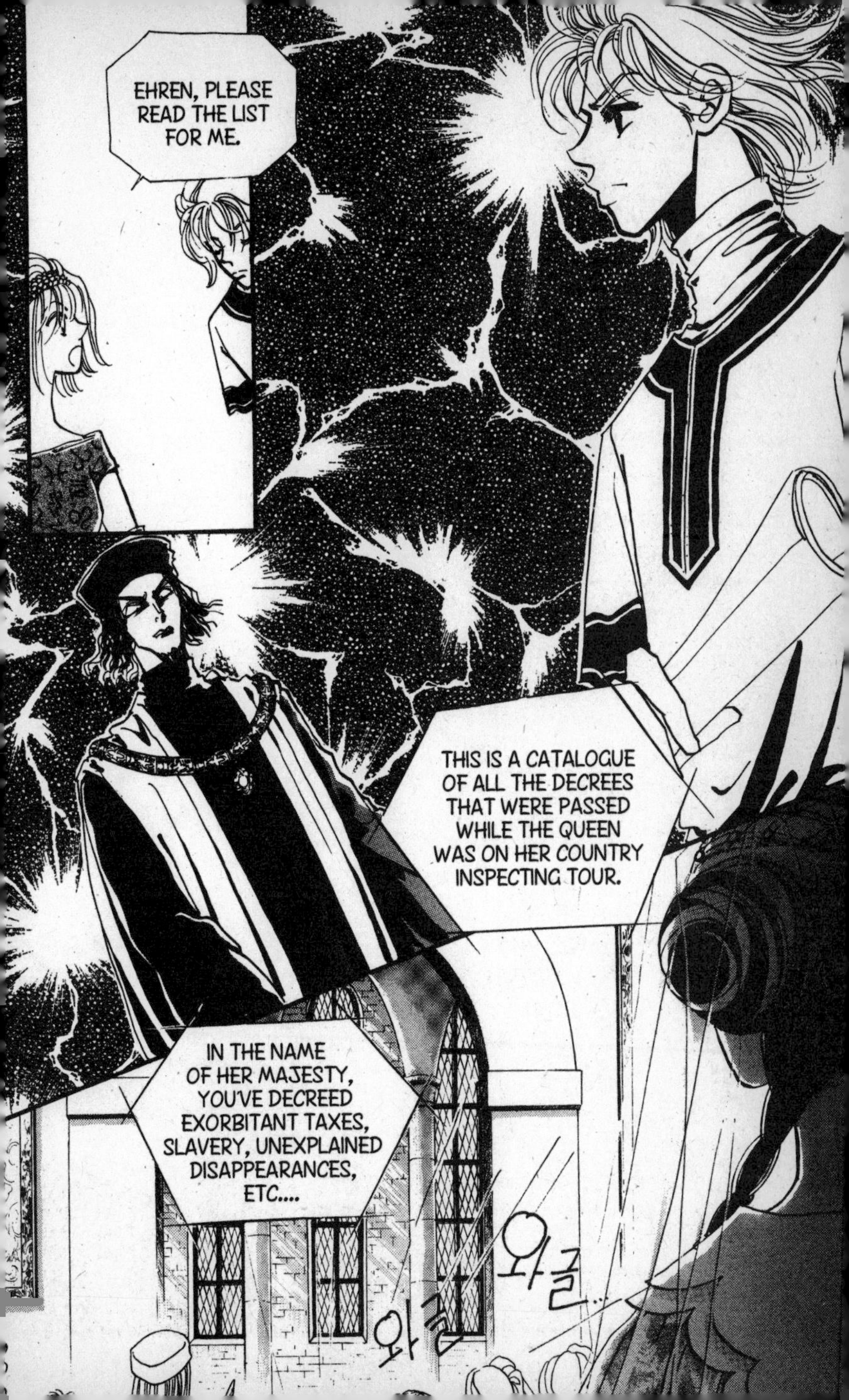
EHREN, PLEASE READ THE LIST FOR ME.
THIS IS A CATALOGUE OF ALL THE DECREES THAT WERE PASSED WHILE THE QUEEN WAS ON HER COUNTRY INSPECTING TOUR.
IN THE NAME OF HER MAJESTY, YOU'VE DECREED EXORBITANT TAXES, SLAVERY, UNEXPLAINED DISAPPEARANCES, ETC....
와글...
와글

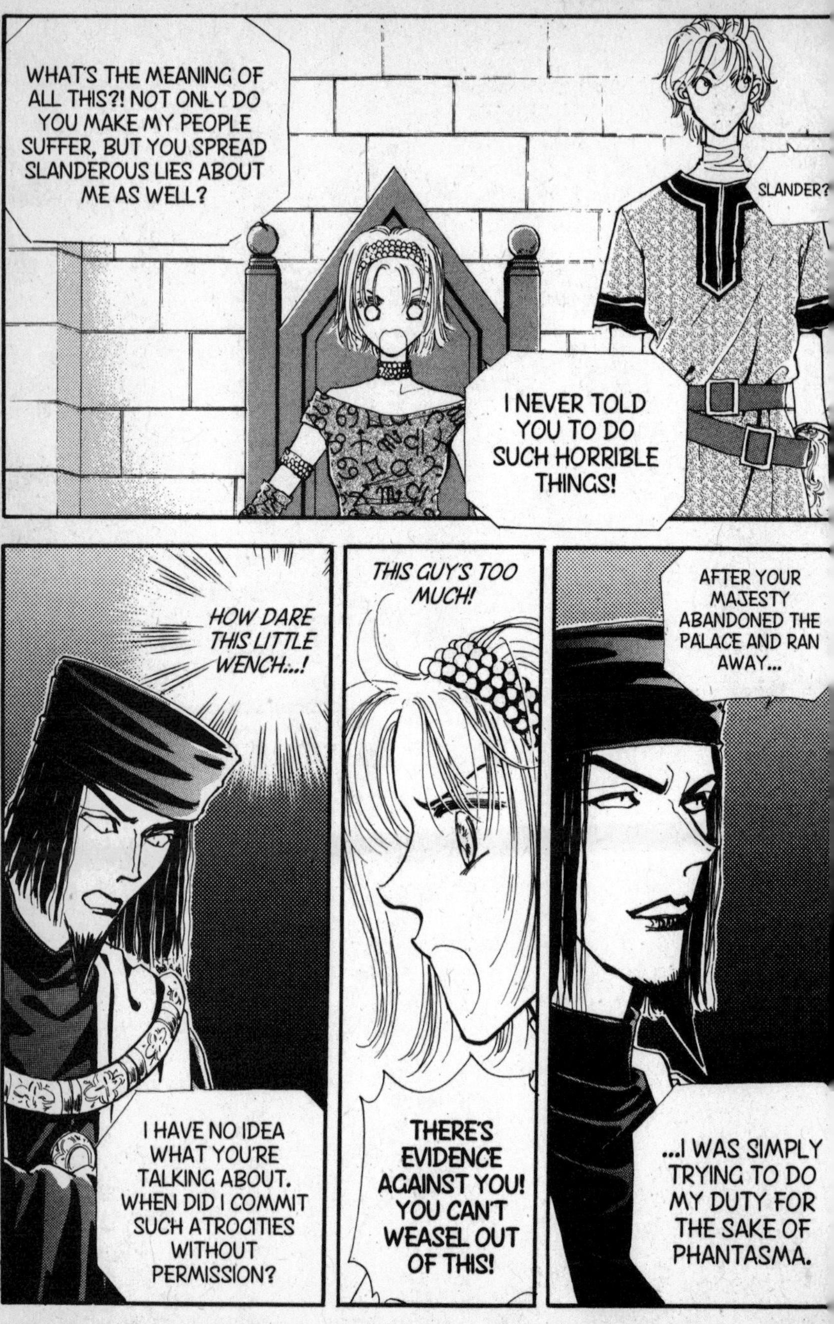
WHAT'S THE MEANING OF ALL THIS?! NOT ONLY DO YOU MAKE MY PEOPLE SUFFER, BUT YOU SPREAD SLANDEROUS LIES ABOUT ME AS WELL?
SLANDER?
I NEVER TOLD YOU TO DO SUCH HORRIBLE THINGS!
HOW DARE THIS LITTLE WENCH...!
I HAVE NO IDEA WHAT YOU'RE TALKING ABOUT. WHEN DID I COMMIT SUCH ATROCITIES WITHOUT PERMISSION?
THIS GUY'S TOO MUCH!
THERE'S EVIDENCE AGAINST YOU! YOU CAN'T WEASEL OUT OF THIS!
AFTER YOUR MAJESTY ABANDONED THE PALACE AND RAN AWAY...
...I WAS SIMPLY TRYING TO DO MY DUTY FOR THE SAKE OF PHANTASMA.

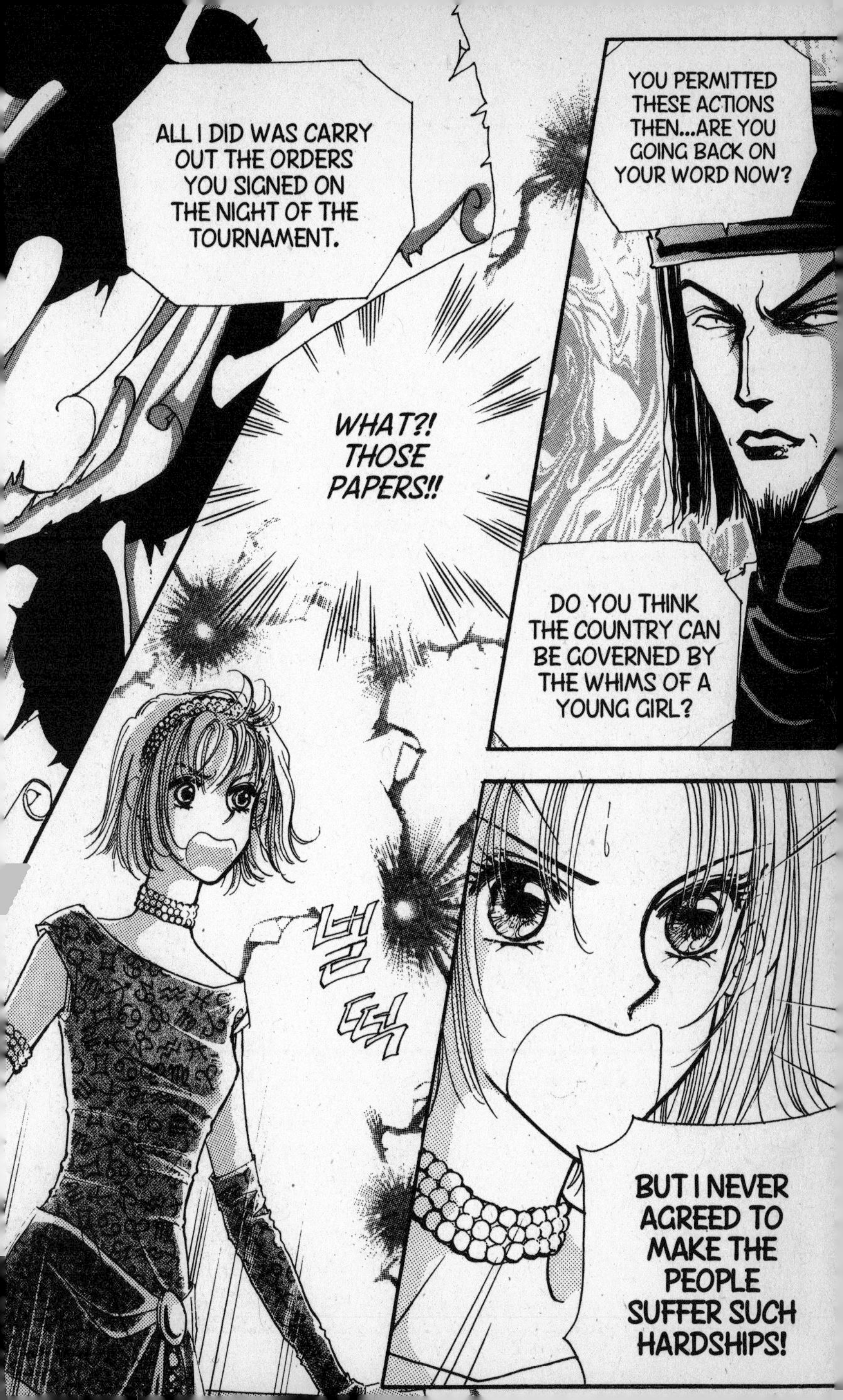
ALL I DID WAS CARRY OUT THE ORDERS YOU SIGNED ON THE NIGHT OF THE TOURNAMENT.
YOU PERMITTED THESE ACTIONS THEN...ARE YOU GOING BACK ON YOUR WORD NOW?
DO YOU THINK THE COUNTRY CAN BE GOVERNED BY THE WHIMS OF A YOUNG GIRL?
WHAT?! THOSE PAPERS!!
BUT I NEVER AGREED TO MAKE THE PEOPLE SUFFER SUCH HARDSHIPS!

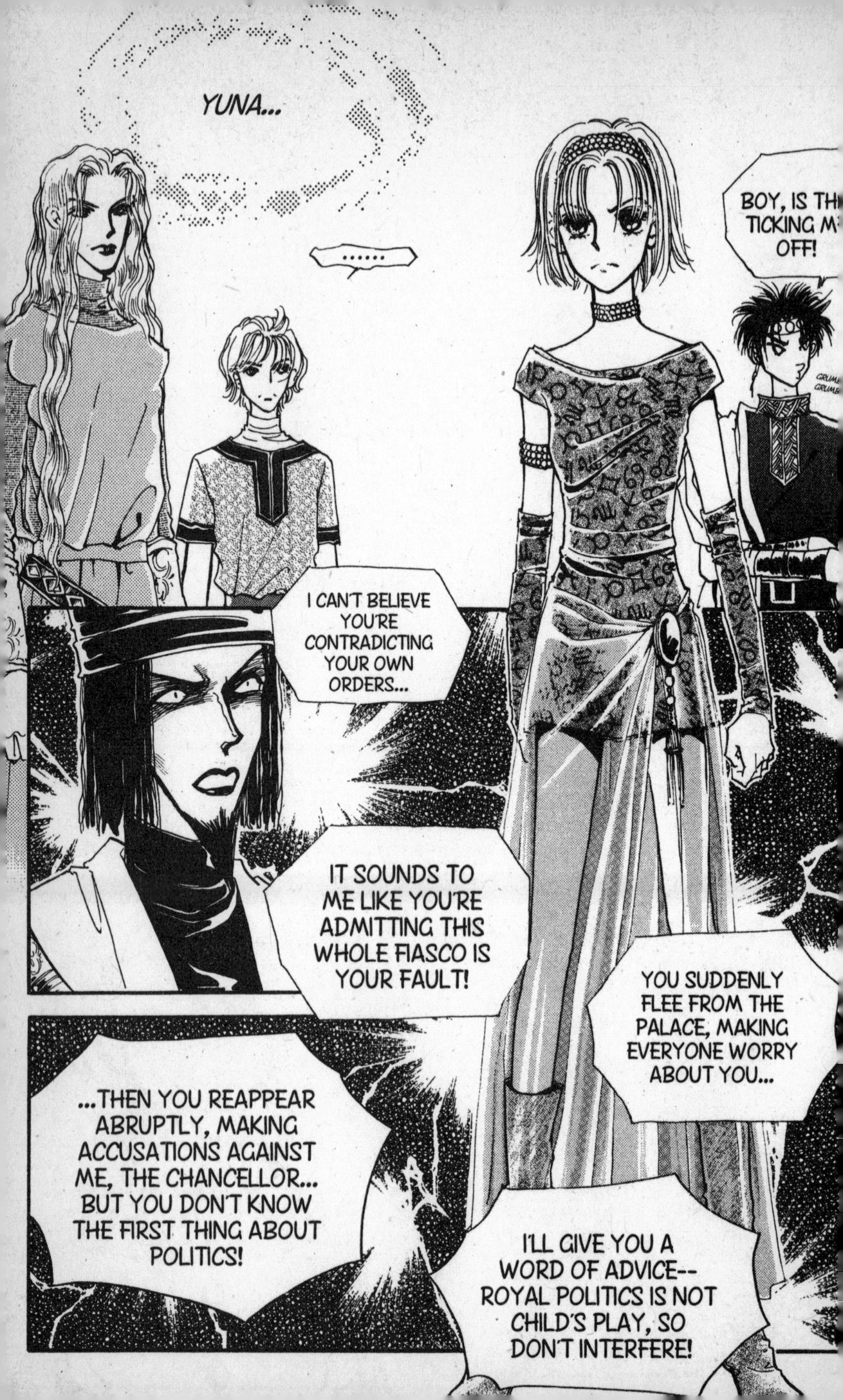
YUNA...
......
BOY, IS TH TICKING M OFF!
I CAN'T BELIEVE YOU'RE CONTRADICTING YOUR OWN ORDERS...
IT SOUNDS TO ME LIKE YOU'RE ADMITTING THIS WHOLE FIASCO IS YOUR FAULT!
YOU SUDDENLY FLEE FROM THE PALACE, MAKING EVERYONE WORRY ABOUT YOU...
...THEN YOU REAPPEAR ABRUPTLY, MAKING ACCUSATIONS AGAINST ME, THE CHANCELLOR... BUT YOU DON'T KNOW THE FIRST THING ABOUT POLITICS!
I'LL GIVE YOU A WORD OF ADVICE-- ROYAL POLITICS IS NOT CHILD'S PLAY, SO DON'T INTERFERE!

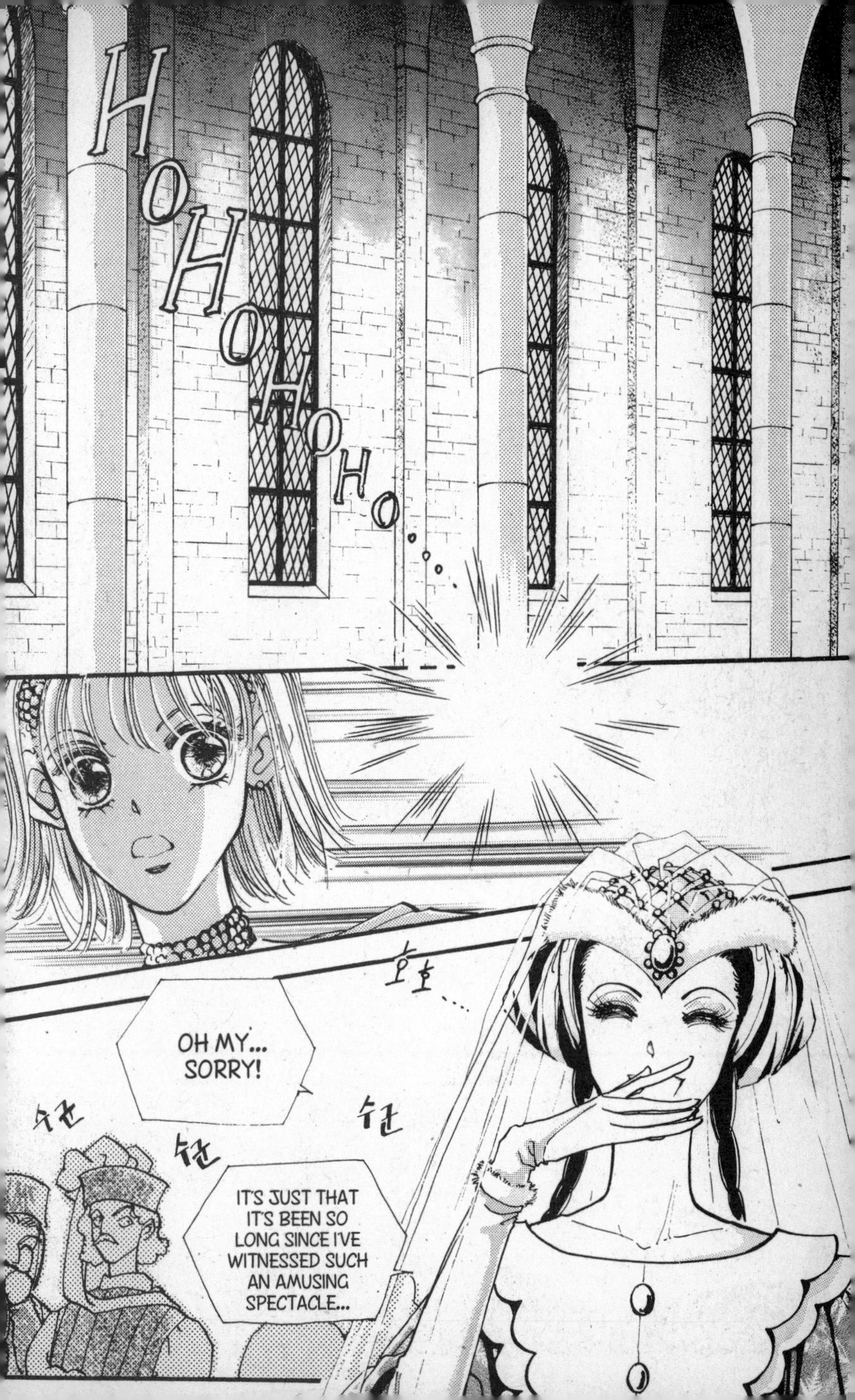
HOHOHOHO...
호호...
OH MY... SORRY!
수군
수군
수군
IT'S JUST THAT IT'S BEEN SO LONG SINCE I'VE WITNESSED SUCH AN AMUSING SPECTACLE...

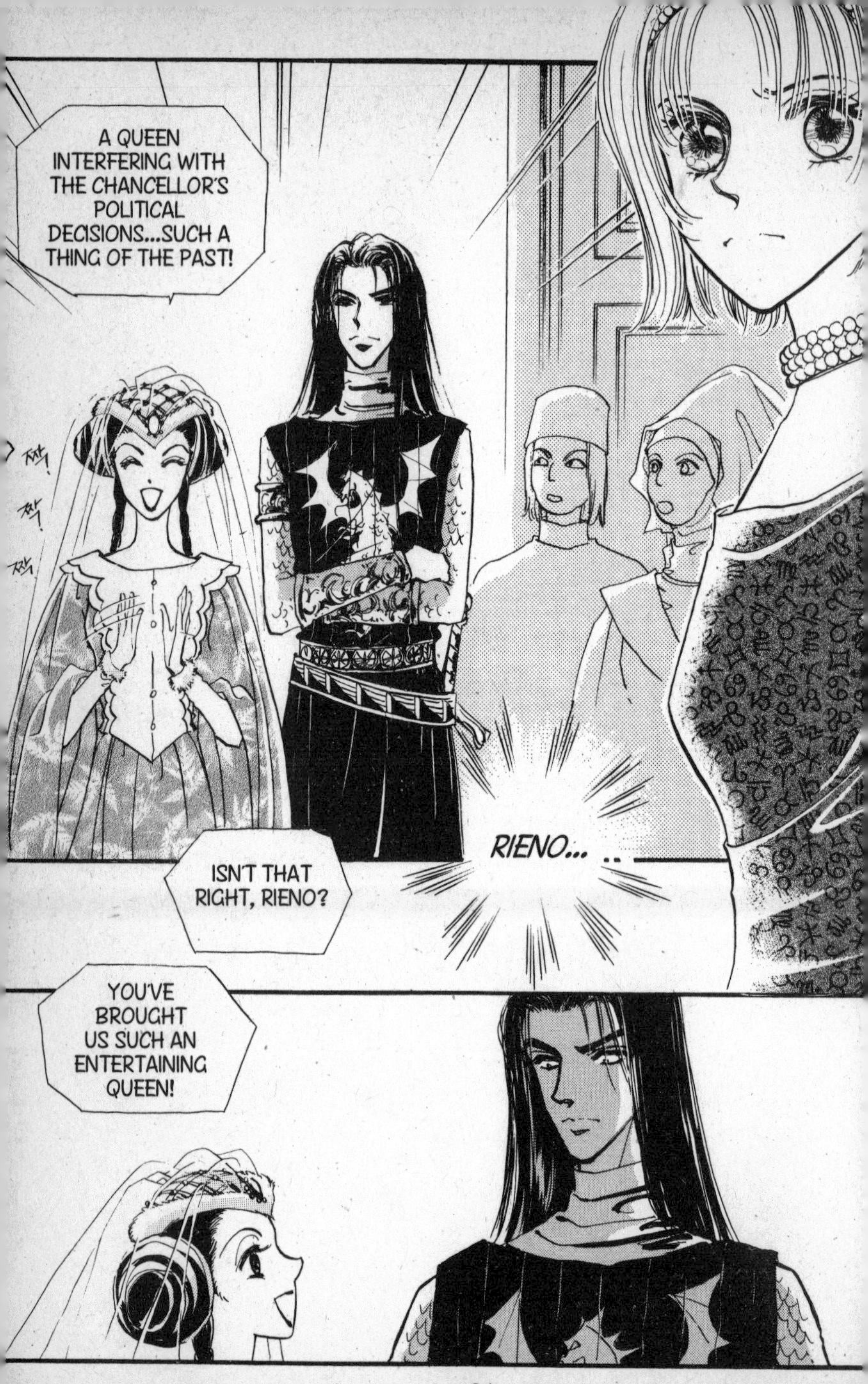
A QUEEN INTERFERING WITH THE CHANCELLOR'S POLITICAL DECISIONS...SUCH A THING OF THE PAST!
짝!
짝!
짝
ISN'T THAT RIGHT, RIENO?
RIENO... ..
YOU'VE BROUGHT US SUCH AN ENTERTAINING QUEEN!

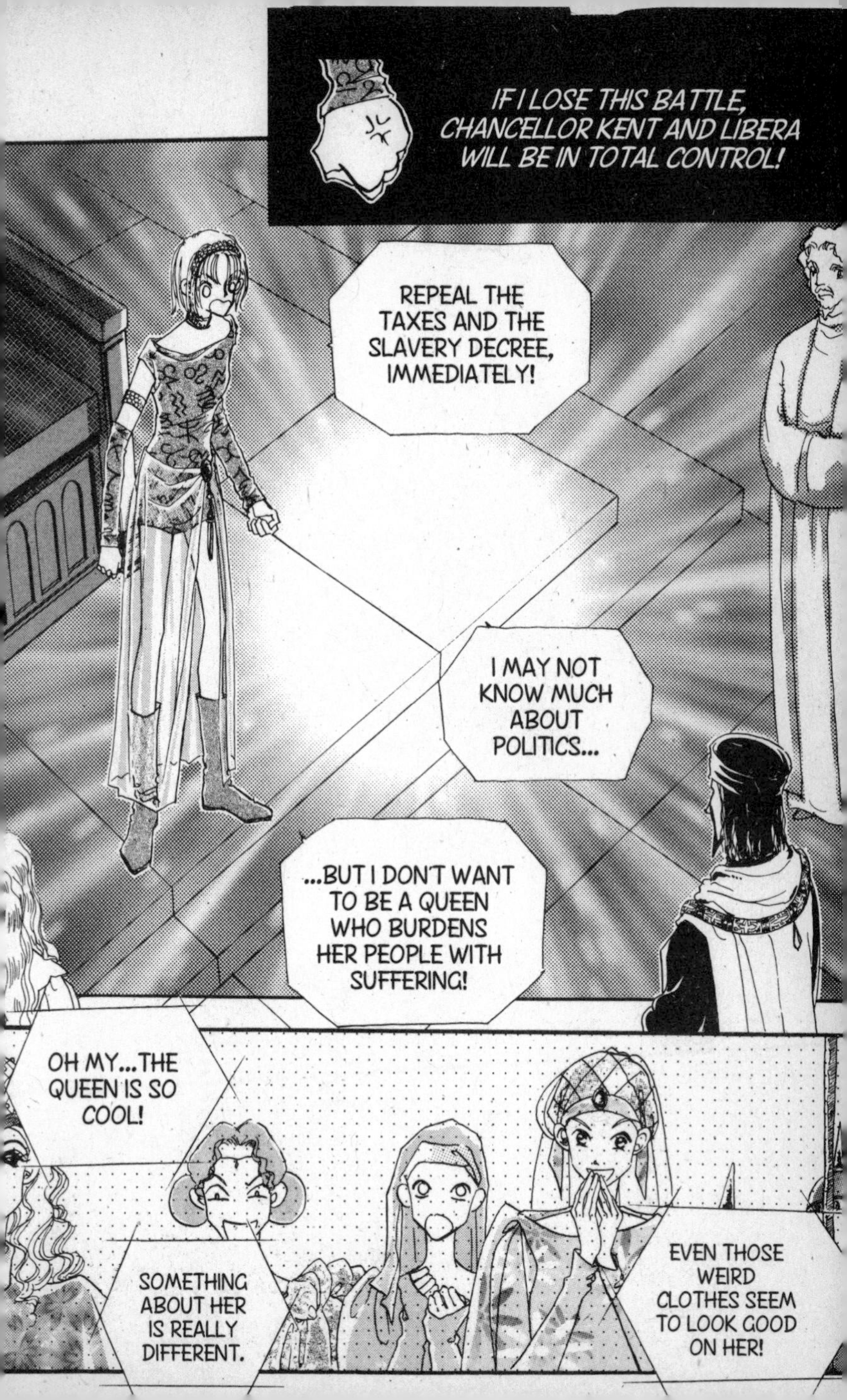
IF I LOSE THIS BATTLE, CHANCELLOR KENT AND LIBERA WILL BE IN TOTAL CONTROL!
REPEAL THE TAXES AND THE SLAVERY DECREE, IMMEDIATELY!
I MAY NOT KNOW MUCH ABOUT POLITICS...
...BUT I DON'T WANT TO BE A QUEEN WHO BURDENS HER PEOPLE WITH SUFFERING!
OH MY...THE QUEEN IS SO COOL!
SOMETHING ABOUT HER IS REALLY DIFFERENT.
EVEN THOSE WEIRD CLOTHES SEEM TO LOOK GOOD ON HER!

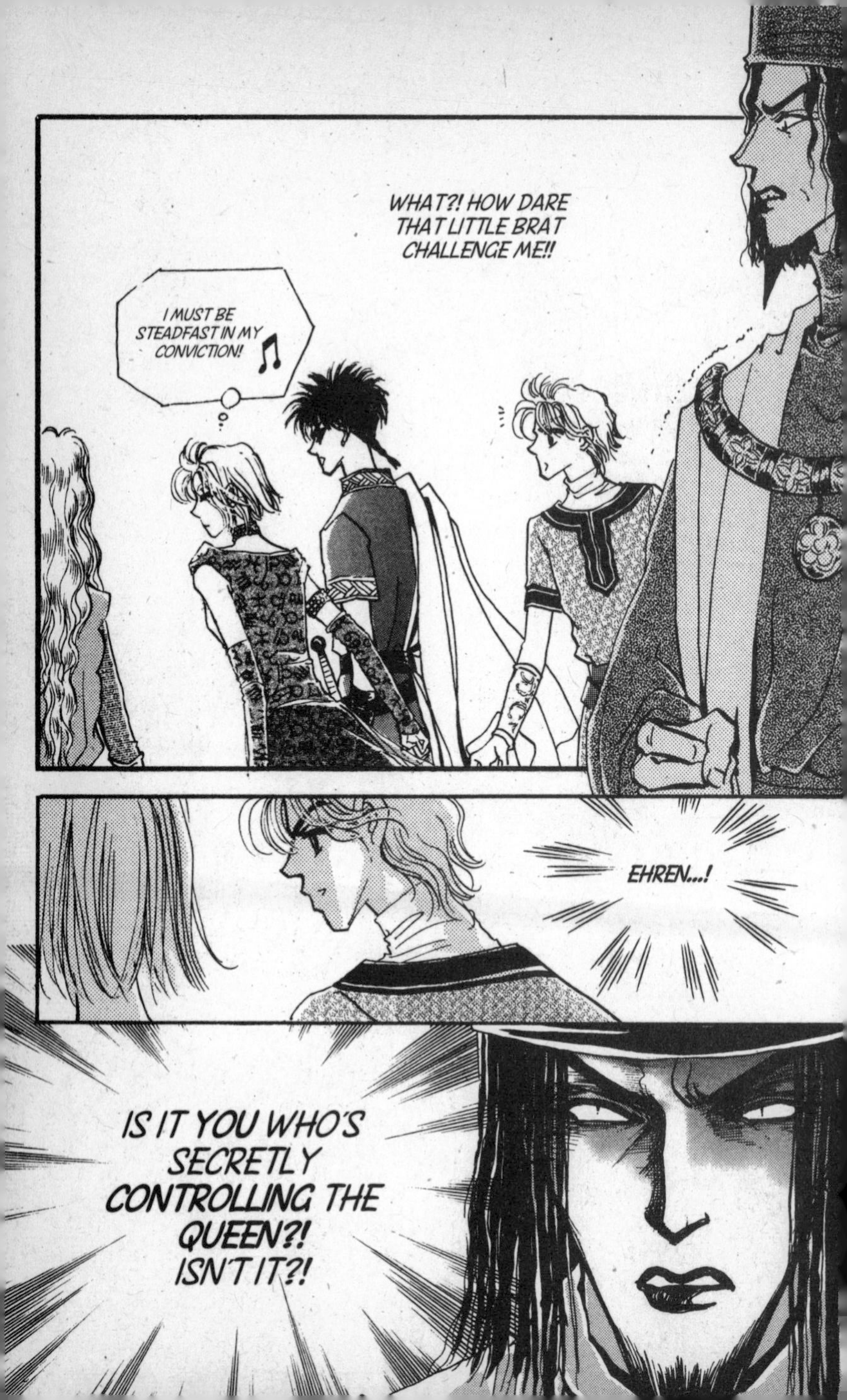
I MUST BE STEADFAST IN MY CONVICTION! ♫
WHAT?! HOW DARE THAT LITTLE BRAT CHALLENGE ME!!
EHREN...!
IS IT YOU WHO'S SECRETLY CONTROLLING THE QUEEN?! ISN'T IT?!

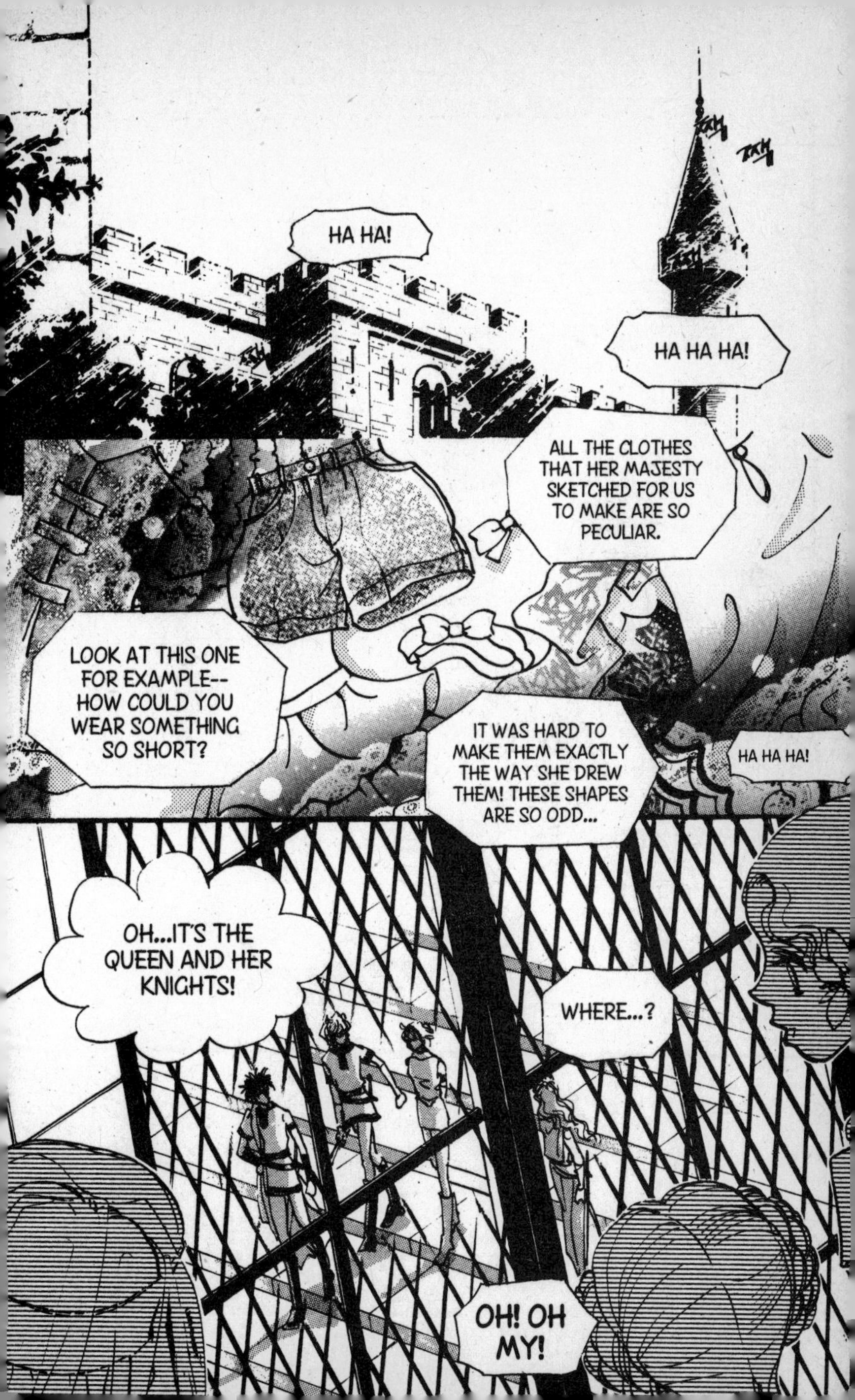
HA HA!
HA HA HA!
ALL THE CLOTHES THAT HER MAJESTY SKETCHED FOR US TO MAKE ARE SO PECULIAR.
LOOK AT THIS ONE FOR EXAMPLE-- HOW COULD YOU WEAR SOMETHING SO SHORT?
IT WAS HARD TO MAKE THEM EXACTLY THE WAY SHE DREW THEM! THESE SHAPES ARE SO ODD...
HA HA HA!
OH...IT'S THE QUEEN AND HER KNIGHTS!
WHERE...?
OH! OH MY!

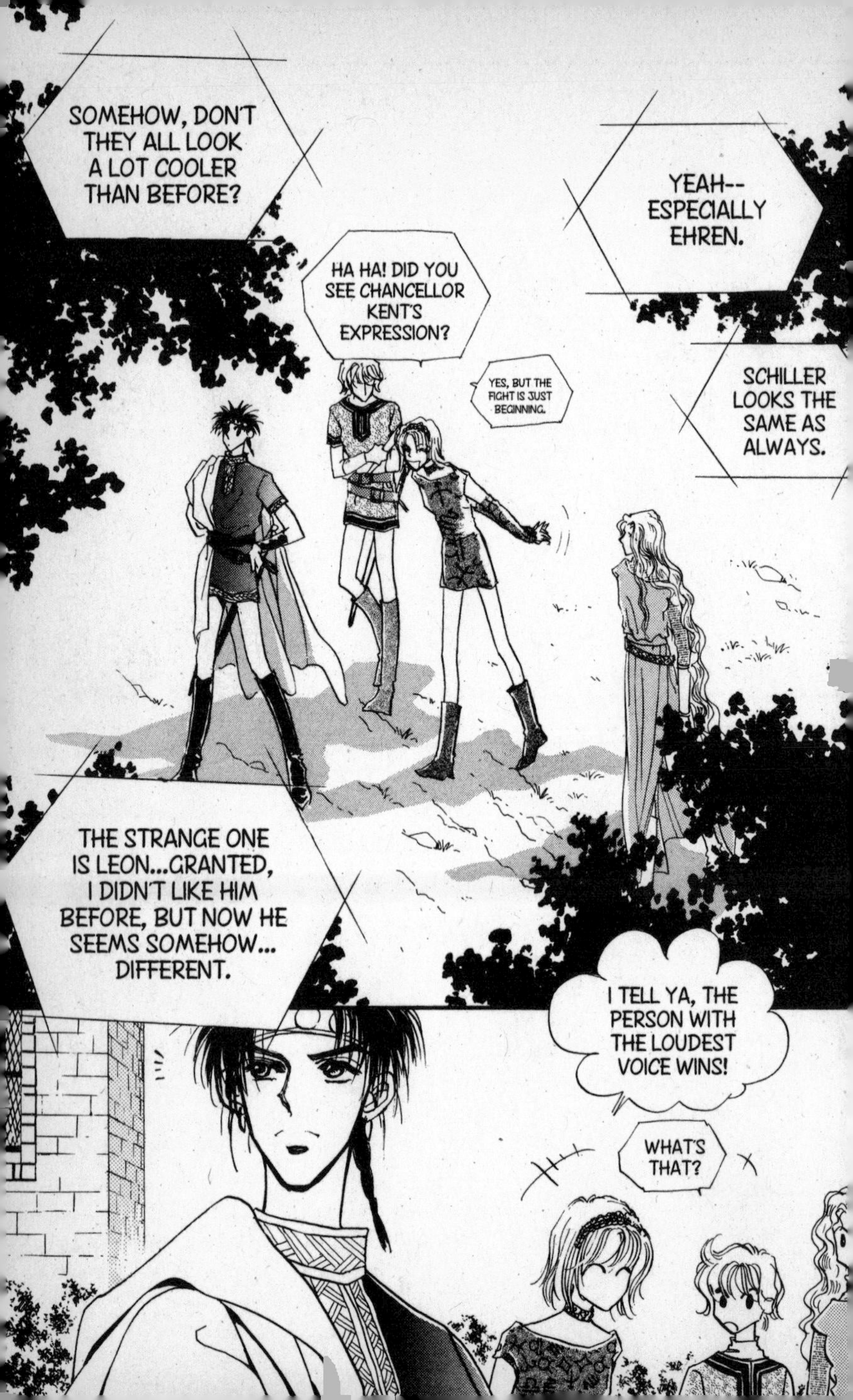
SOMEHOW, DON'T THEY ALL LOOK A LOT COOLER THAN BEFORE?
HA HA! DID YOU SEE CHANCELLOR KENT'S EXPRESSION?
YEAH-- ESPECIALLY EHREN.
YES, BUT THE FIGHT IS JUST BEGINNING.
SCHILLER LOOKS THE SAME AS ALWAYS.
THE STRANGE ONE IS LEON...GRANTED, I DIDN'T LIKE HIM BEFORE, BUT NOW HE SEEMS SOMEHOW... DIFFERENT.
I TELL YA, THE PERSON WITH THE LOUDEST VOICE WINS!
WHAT'S THAT?

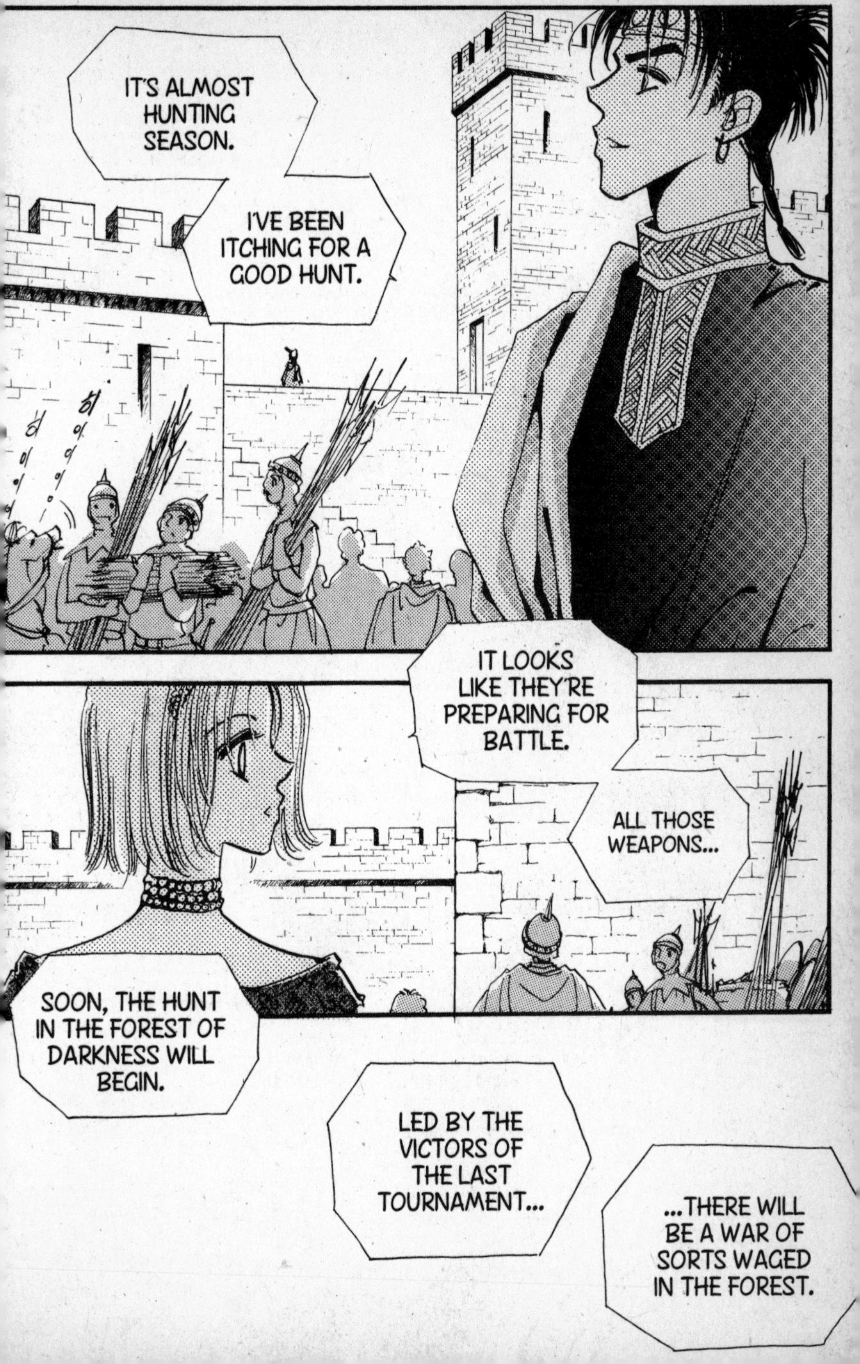
IT'S ALMOST HUNTING SEASON.
I'VE BEEN ITCHING FOR A GOOD HUNT.
IT LOOKS LIKE THEY'RE PREPARING FOR BATTLE.
ALL THOSE WEAPONS...
SOON, THE HUNT IN THE FOREST OF DARKNESS WILL BEGIN.
LED BY THE VICTORS OF THE LAST TOURNAMENT...
...THERE WILL BE A WAR OF SORTS WAGED IN THE FOREST.

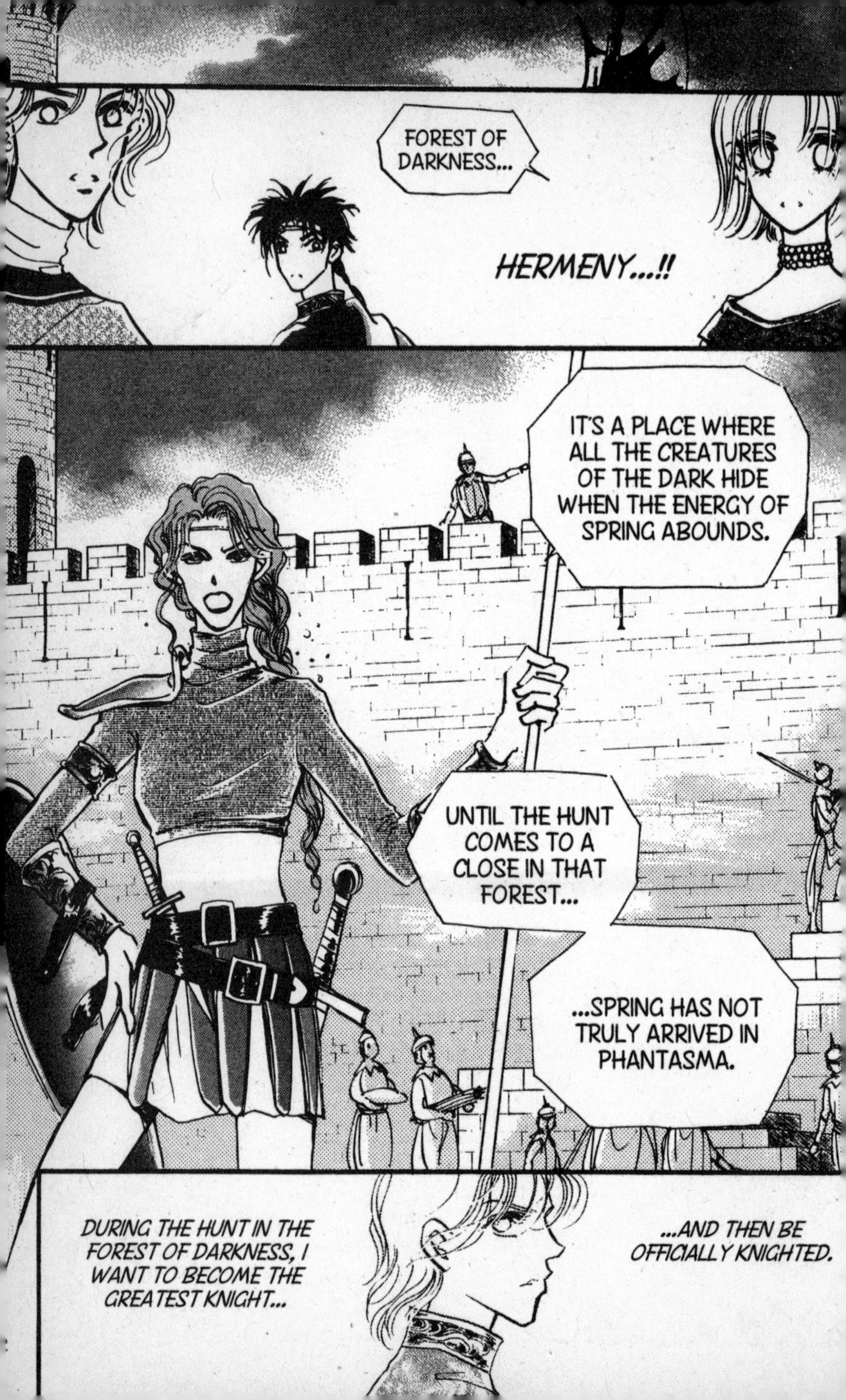
FOREST OF DARKNESS...
HERMENY...!!
IT'S A PLACE WHERE ALL THE CREATURES OF THE DARK HIDE WHEN THE ENERGY OF SPRING ABOUNDS.
UNTIL THE HUNT COMES TO A CLOSE IN THAT FOREST...
...SPRING HAS NOT TRULY ARRIVED IN PHANTASMA.
DURING THE HUNT IN THE FOREST OF DARKNESS, I WANT TO BECOME THE GREATEST KNIGHT...
...AND THEN BE OFFICIALLY KNIGHTED.

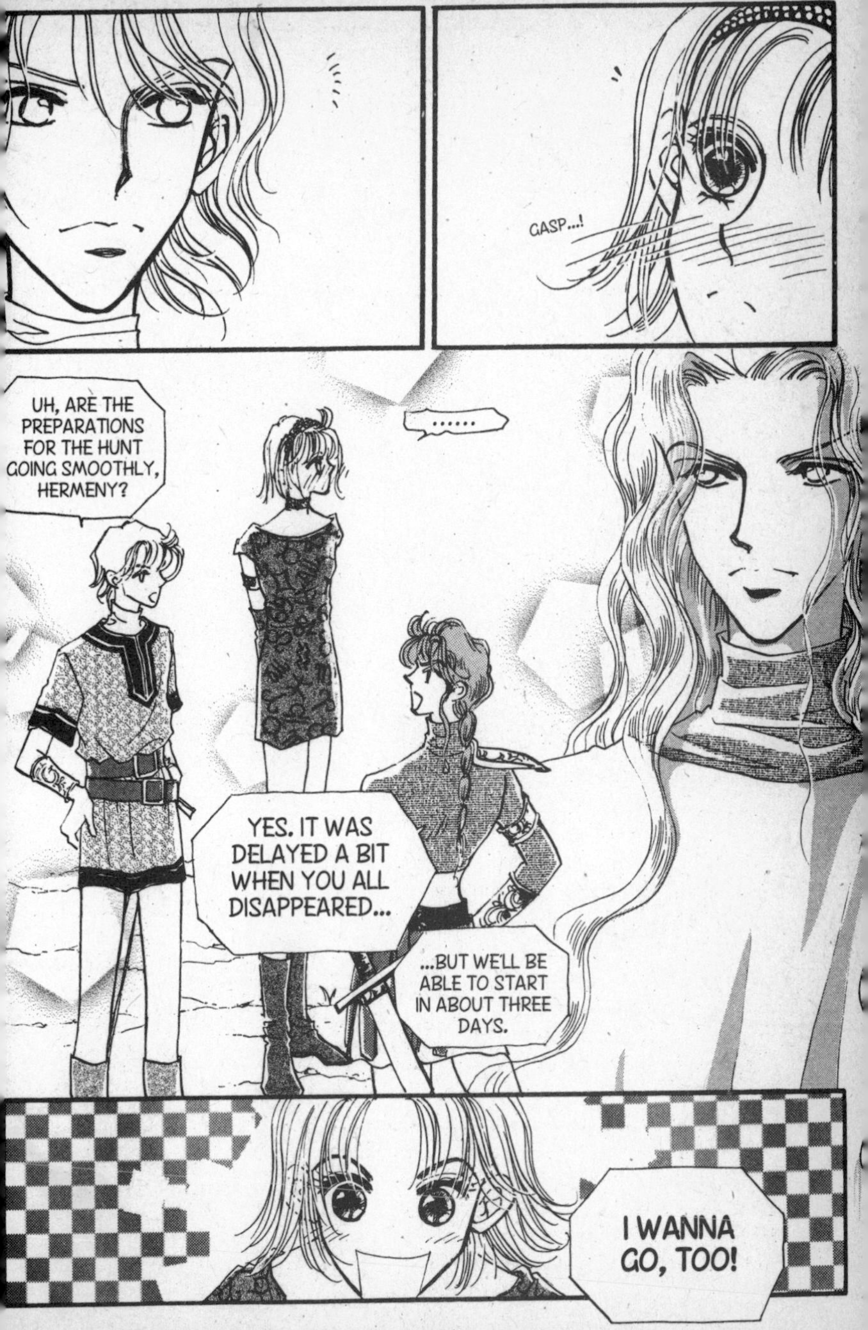
GASP...!
UH, ARE THE PREPARATIONS FOR THE HUNT GOING SMOOTHLY, HERMENY?
......
YES. IT WAS DELAYED A BIT WHEN YOU ALL DISAPPEARED...
...BUT WE'LL BE ABLE TO START IN ABOUT THREE DAYS.
I WANNA GO, TOO!

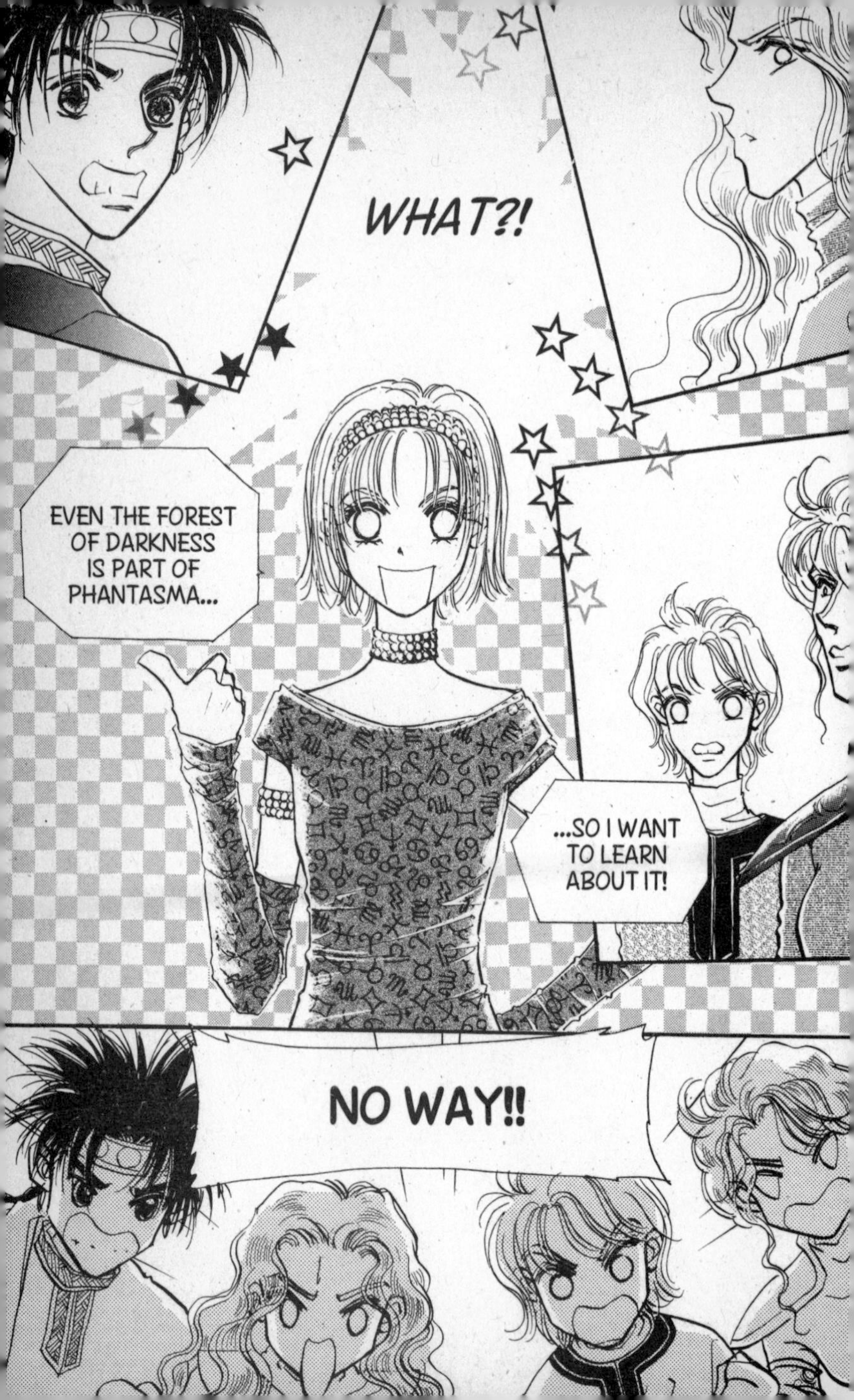
WHAT?!
EVEN THE FOREST OF DARKNESS IS PART OF PHANTASMA...
...SO I WANT TO LEARN ABOUT IT!
NO WAY!!

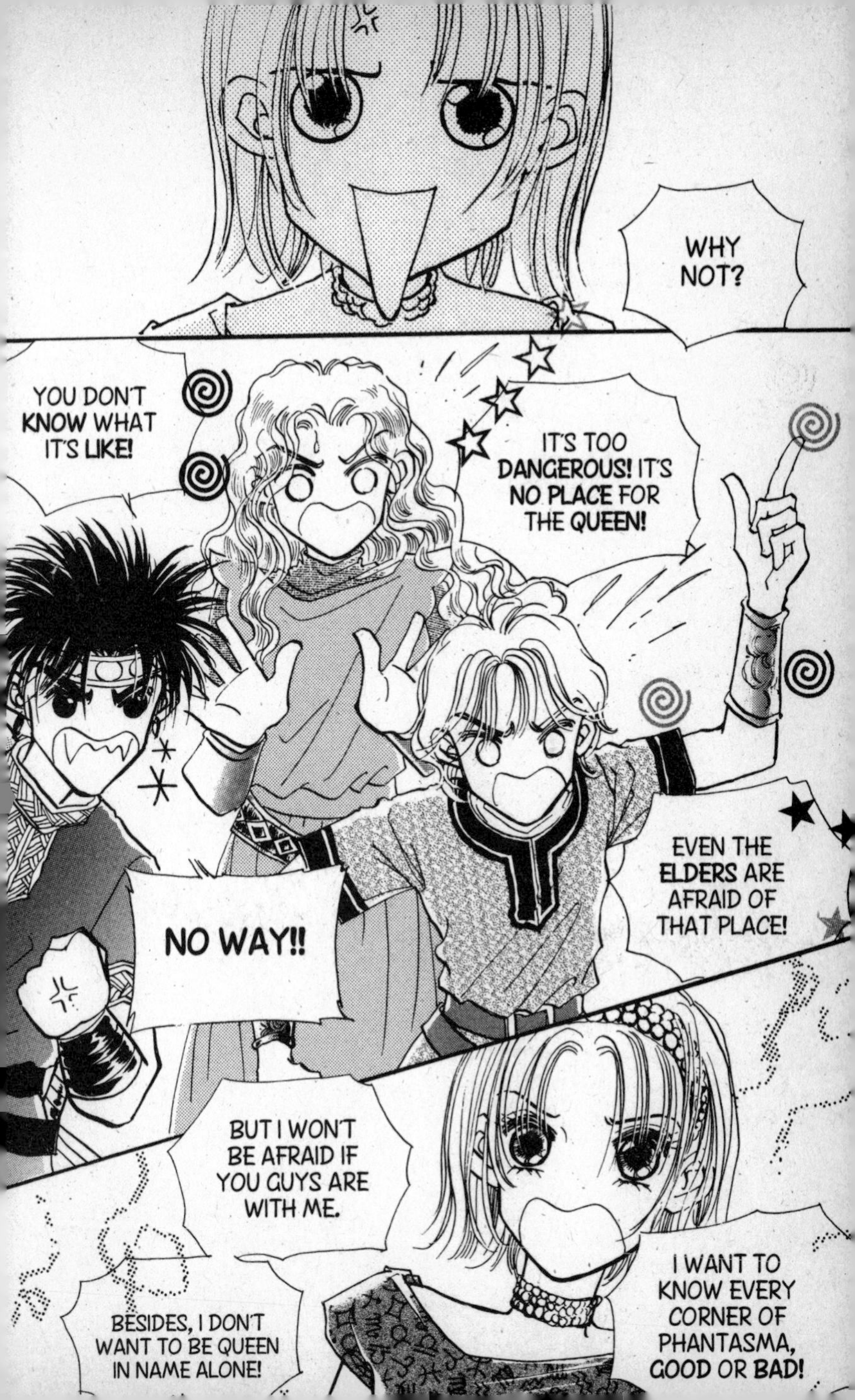
WHY NOT?
YOU DON'T KNOW WHAT IT'S LIKE!
IT'S TOO DANGEROUS! IT'S NO PLACE FOR THE QUEEN!
NO WAY!!
EVEN THE ELDERS ARE AFRAID OF THAT PLACE!
BUT I WON'T BE AFRAID IF YOU GUYS ARE WITH ME.
BESIDES, I DON'T WANT TO BE QUEEN IN NAME ALONE!
I WANT TO KNOW EVERY CORNER OF PHANTASMA, GOOD OR BAD!

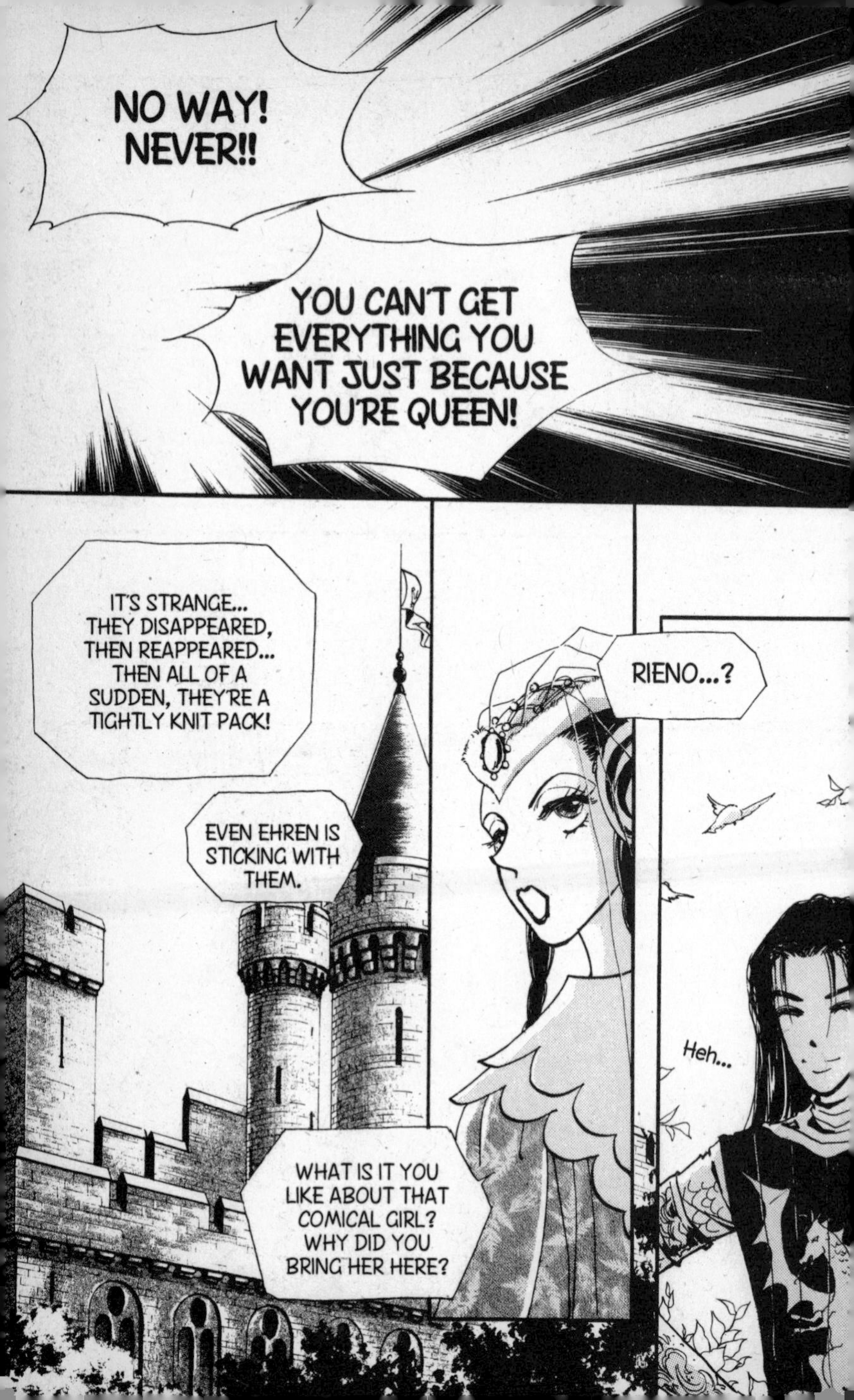
NO WAY! NEVER!!
YOU CAN'T GET EVERYTHING YOU WANT JUST BECAUSE YOU'RE QUEEN!
IT'S STRANGE... THEY DISAPPEARED, THEN REAPPEARED... THEN ALL OF A SUDDEN, THEY'RE A TIGHTLY KNIT PACK!
EVEN EHREN IS STICKING WITH THEM.
WHAT IS IT YOU LIKE ABOUT THAT COMICAL GIRL? WHY DID YOU BRING HER HERE?
RIENO...?
Heh...

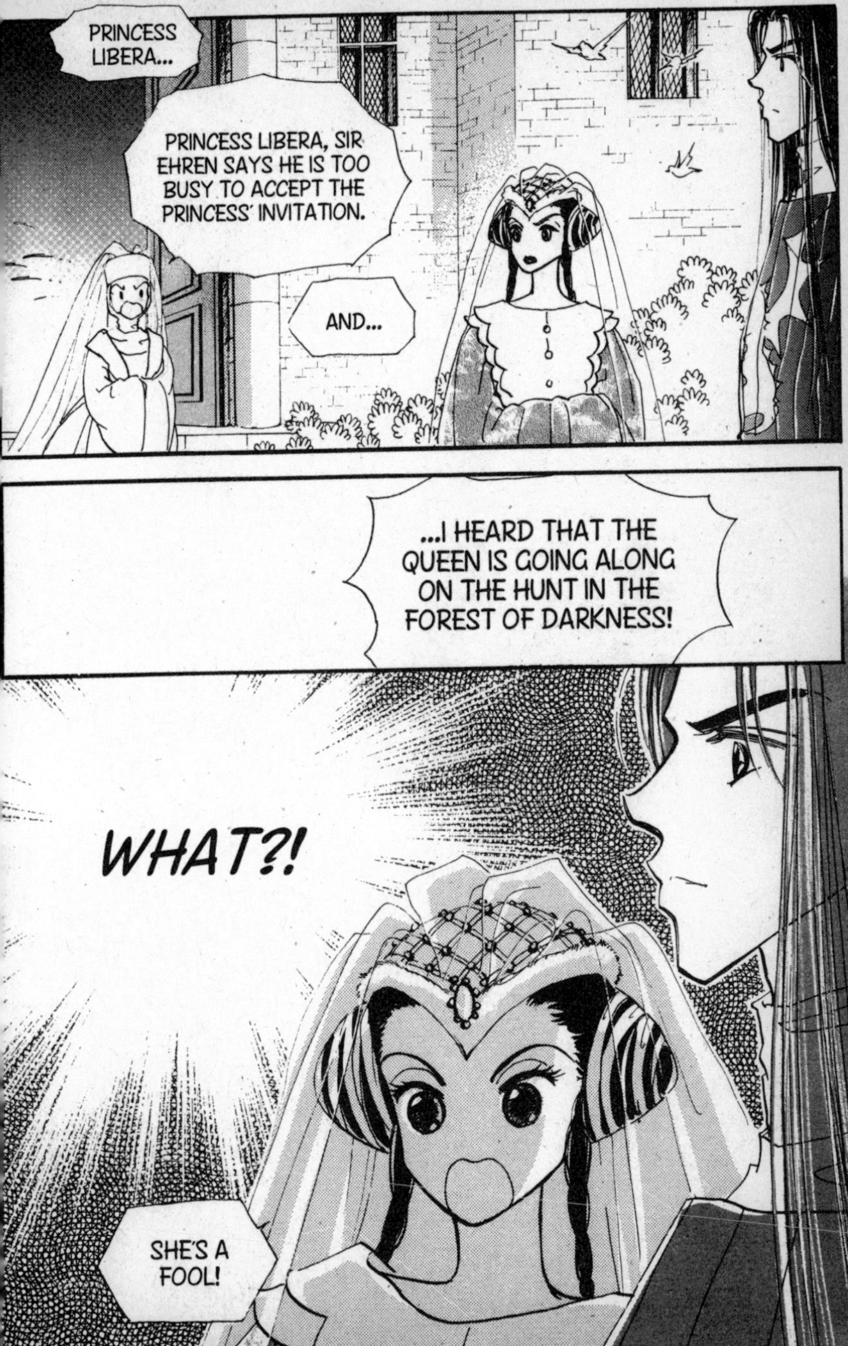
PRINCESS LIBERA...
PRINCESS LIBERA, SIR EHREN SAYS HE IS TOO BUSY TO ACCEPT THE PRINCESS' INVITATION.
AND...
...I HEARD THAT THE QUEEN IS GOING ALONG ON THE HUNT IN THE FOREST OF DARKNESS!
WHAT?!
SHE'S A FOOL!

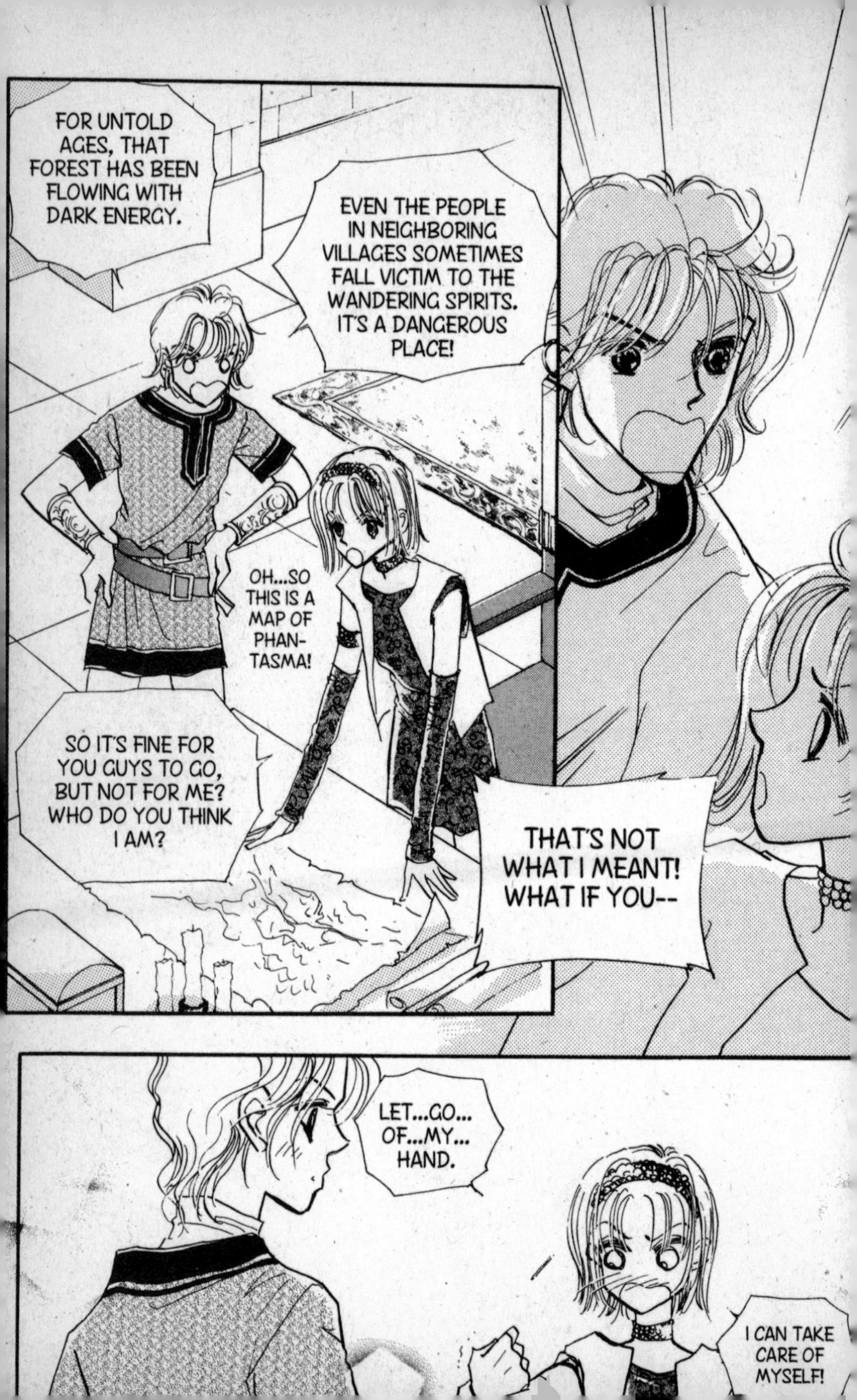
FOR UNTOLD AGES, THAT FOREST HAS BEEN FLOWING WITH DARK ENERGY.
EVEN THE PEOPLE IN NEIGHBORING VILLAGES SOMETIMES FALL VICTIM TO THE WANDERING SPIRITS. IT'S A DANGEROUS PLACE!
OH...SO THIS IS A MAP OF PHAN-TASMA!
SO IT'S FINE FOR YOU GUYS TO GO, BUT NOT FOR ME? WHO DO YOU THINK I AM?
THAT'S NOT WHAT I MEANT! WHAT IF YOU--
LET...GO... OF...MY... HAND.
I CAN TAKE CARE OF MYSELF!

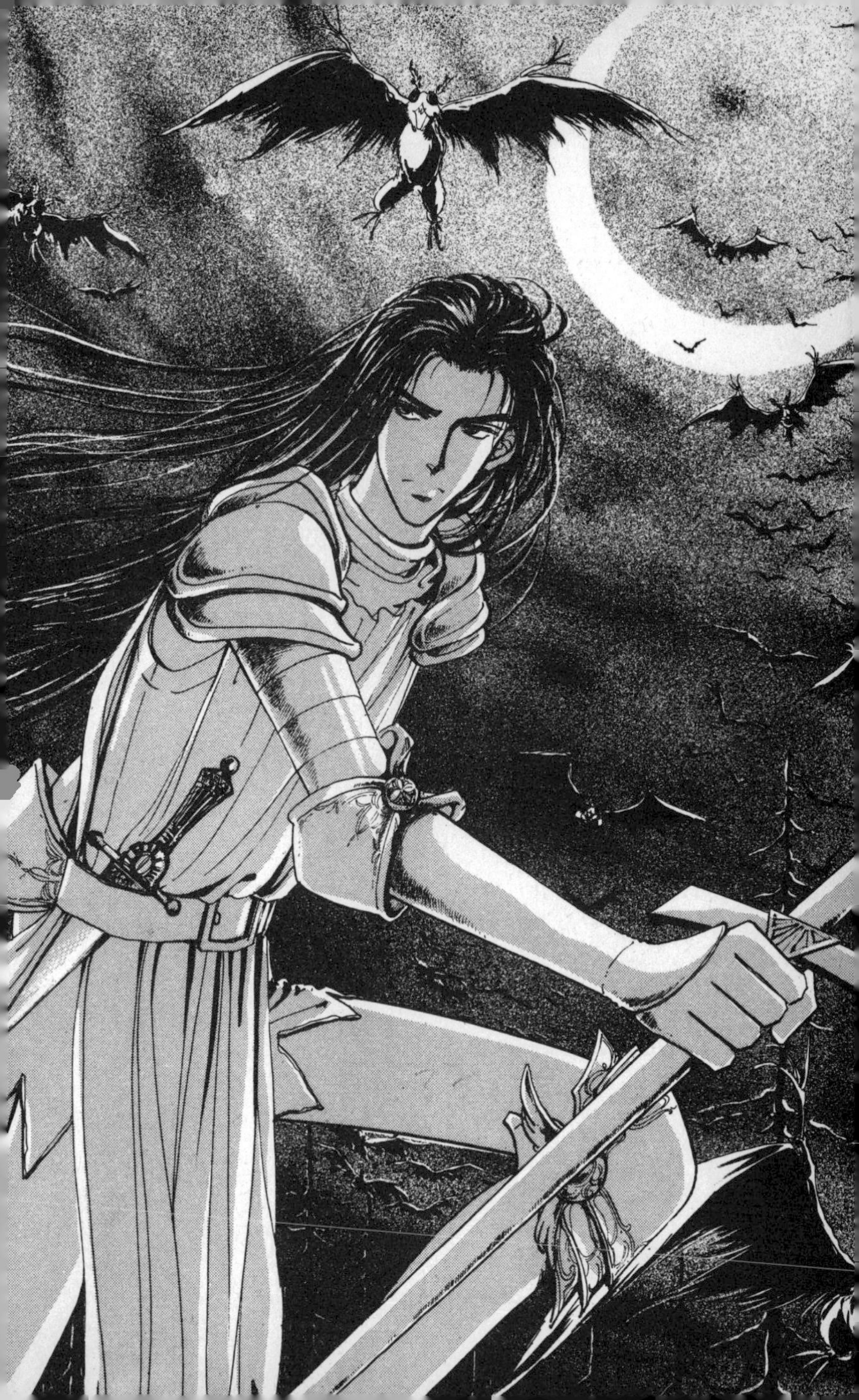

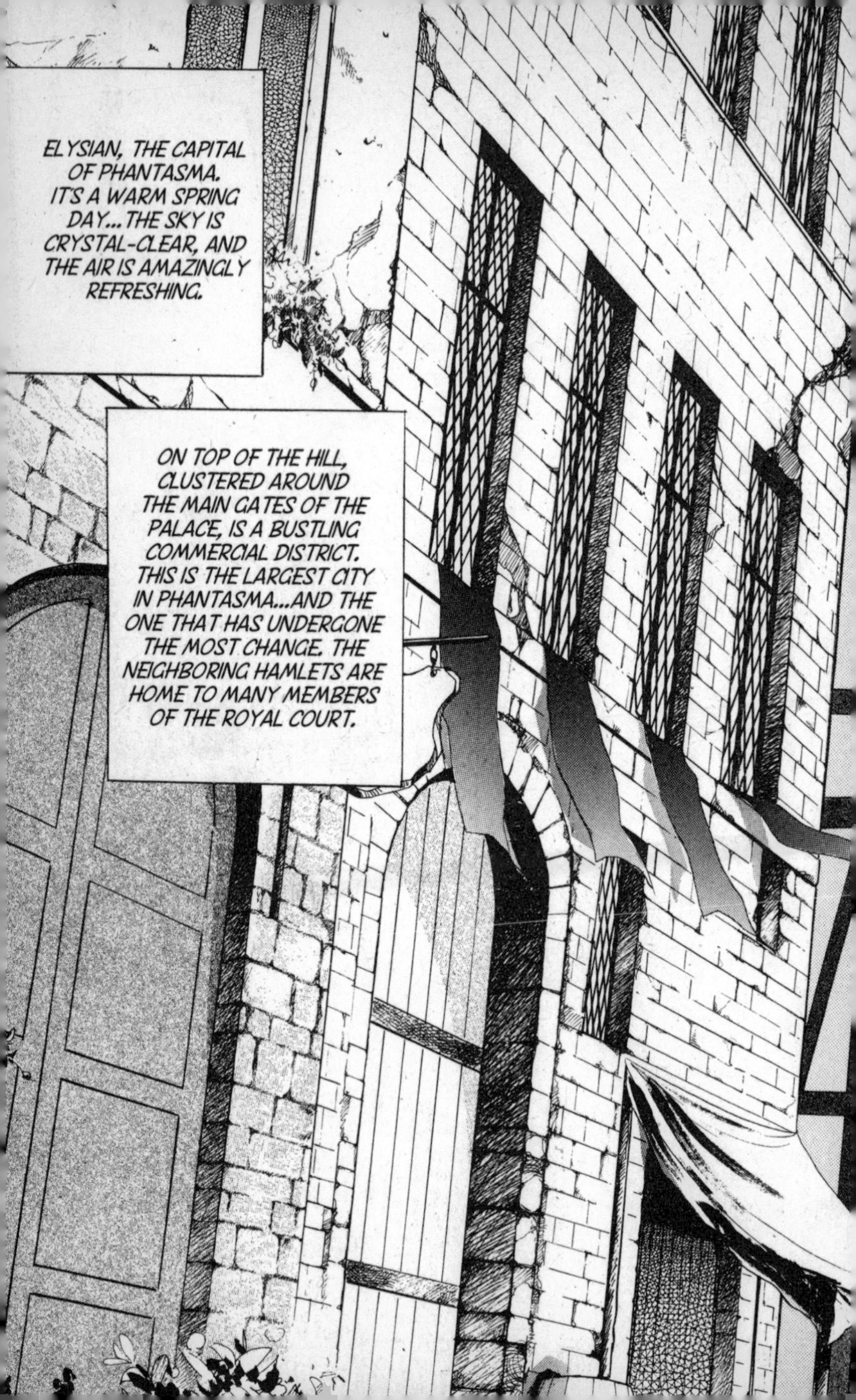
ELYSIAN, THE CAPITAL OF PHANTASMA. IT'S A WARM SPRING DAY...THE SKY IS CRYSTAL-CLEAR, AND THE AIR IS AMAZINGLY REFRESHING.
ON TOP OF THE HILL, CLUSTERED AROUND THE MAIN GATES OF THE PALACE, IS A BUSTLING COMMERCIAL DISTRICT. THIS IS THE LARGEST CITY IN PHANTASMA...AND THE ONE THAT HAS UNDERGONE THE MOST CHANGE. THE NEIGHBORING HAMLETS ARE HOME TO MANY MEMBERS OF THE ROYAL COURT.

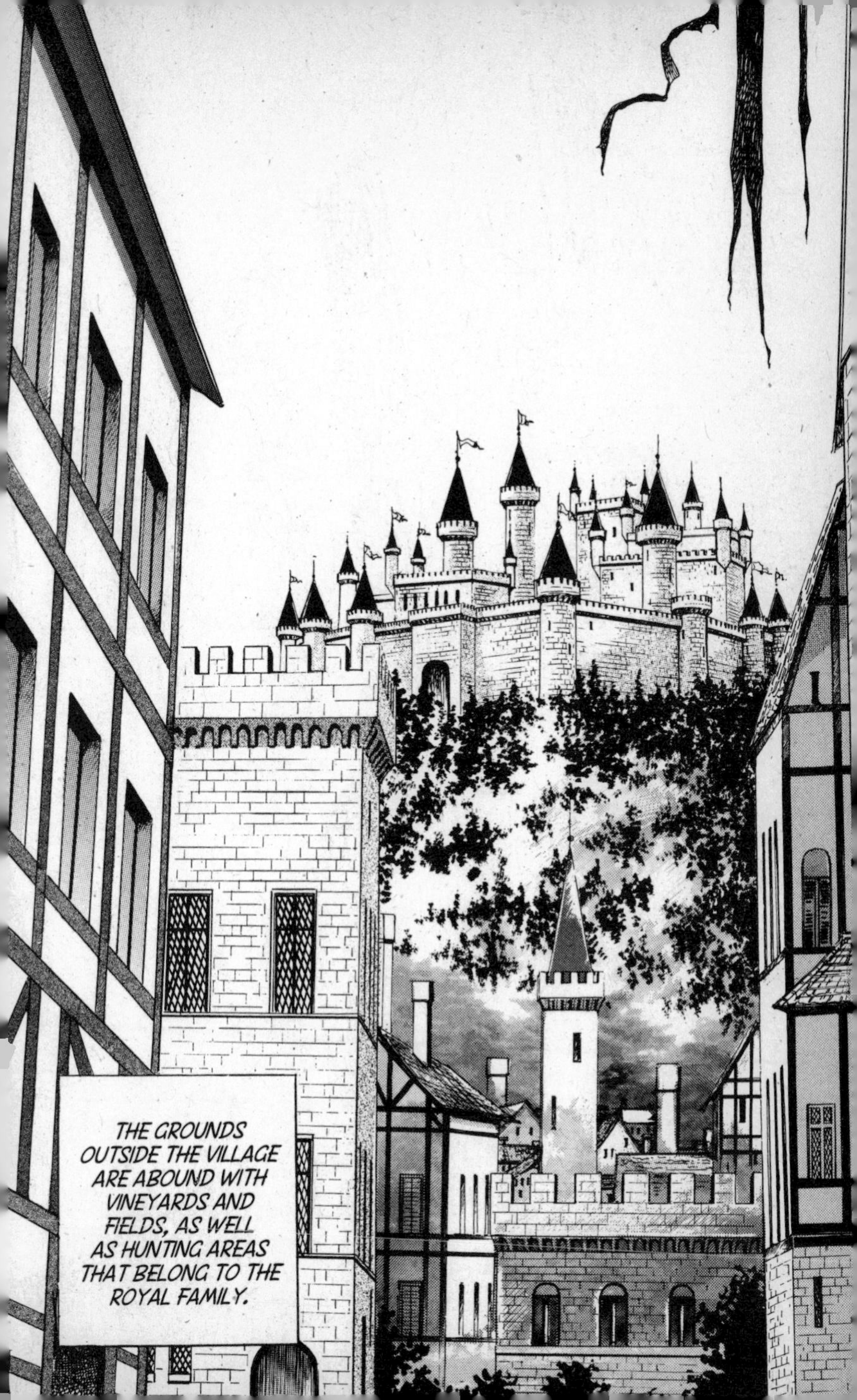
THE GROUNDS OUTSIDE THE VILLAGE ARE ABOUND WITH VINEYARDS AND FIELDS, AS WELL AS HUNTING AREAS THAT BELONG TO THE ROYAL FAMILY.

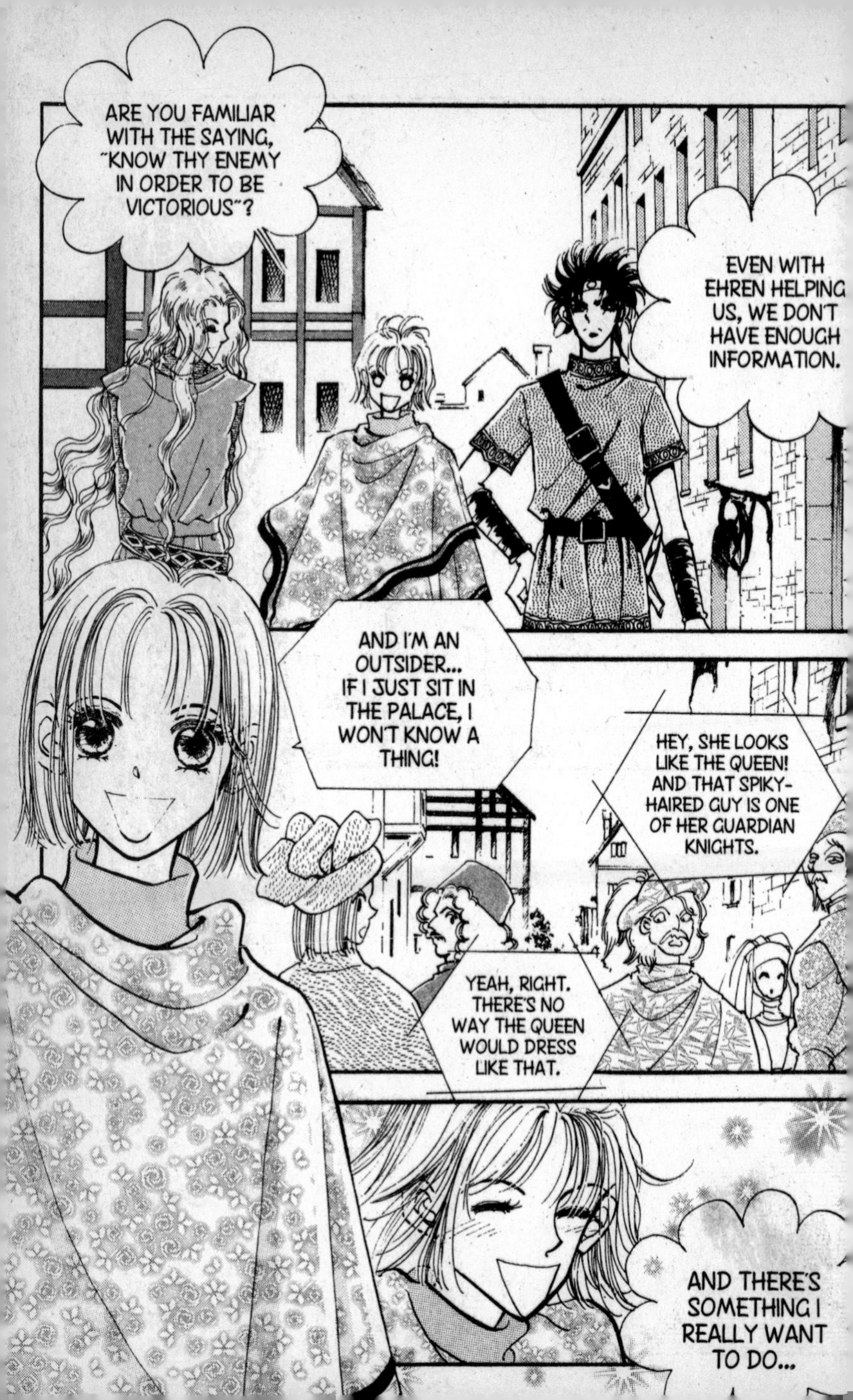
ARE YOU FAMILIAR WITH THE SAYING, "KNOW THY ENEMY IN ORDER TO BE VICTORIOUS"?
EVEN WITH EHREN HELPING US, WE DON'T HAVE ENOUGH INFORMATION.
AND I'M AN OUTSIDER... IF I JUST SIT IN THE PALACE, I WON'T KNOW A THING!
HEY, SHE LOOKS LIKE THE QUEEN! AND THAT SPIKY-HAIRED GUY IS ONE OF HER GUARDIAN KNIGHTS.
YEAH, RIGHT. THERE'S NO WAY THE QUEEN WOULD DRESS LIKE THAT.
AND THERE'S SOMETHING I REALLY WANT TO DO...

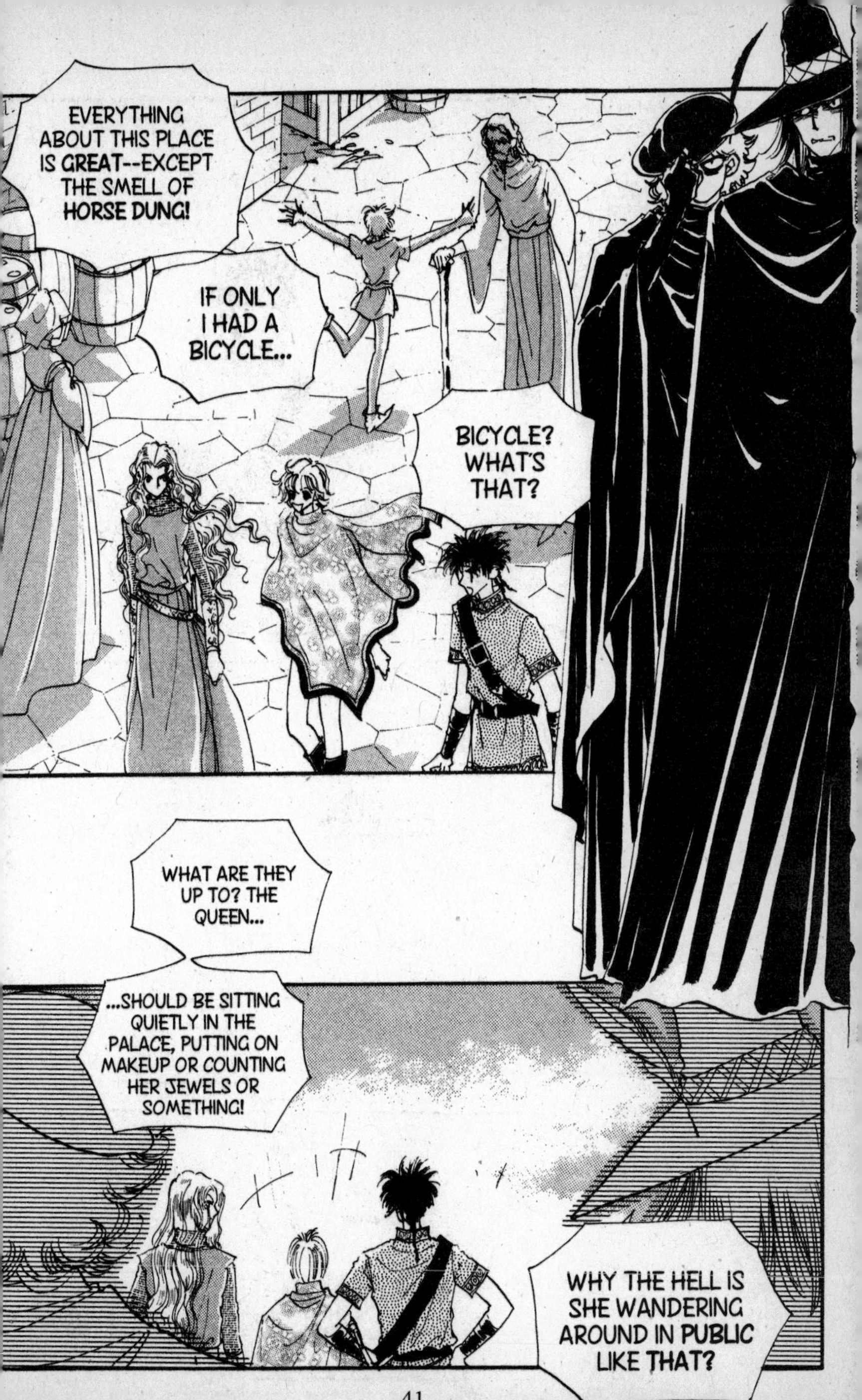
EVERYTHING ABOUT THIS PLACE IS GREAT--EXCEPT THE SMELL OF HORSE DUNG!
IF ONLY I HAD A BICYCLE...
BICYCLE? WHAT'S THAT?
WHAT ARE THEY UP TO? THE QUEEN...
...SHOULD BE SITTING QUIETLY IN THE PALACE, PUTTING ON MAKEUP OR COUNTING HER JEWELS OR SOMETHING!
WHY THE HELL IS SHE WANDERING AROUND IN PUBLIC LIKE THAT?

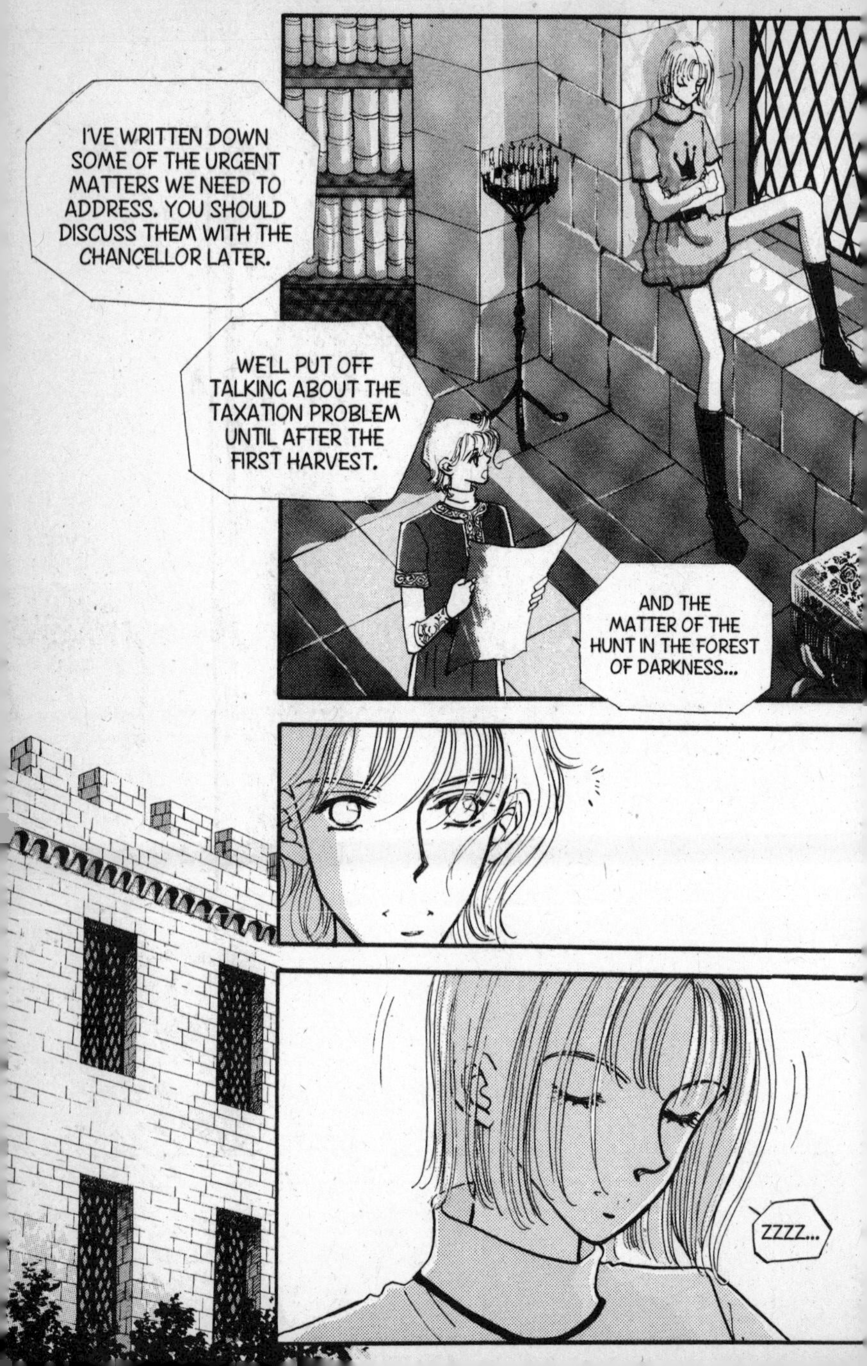
I'VE WRITTEN DOWN SOME OF THE URGENT MATTERS WE NEED TO ADDRESS. YOU SHOULD DISCUSS THEM WITH THE CHANCELLOR LATER.
WE'LL PUT OFF TALKING ABOUT THE TAXATION PROBLEM UNTIL AFTER THE FIRST HARVEST.
AND THE MATTER OF THE HUNT IN THE FOREST OF DARKNESS...
ZZZZ...

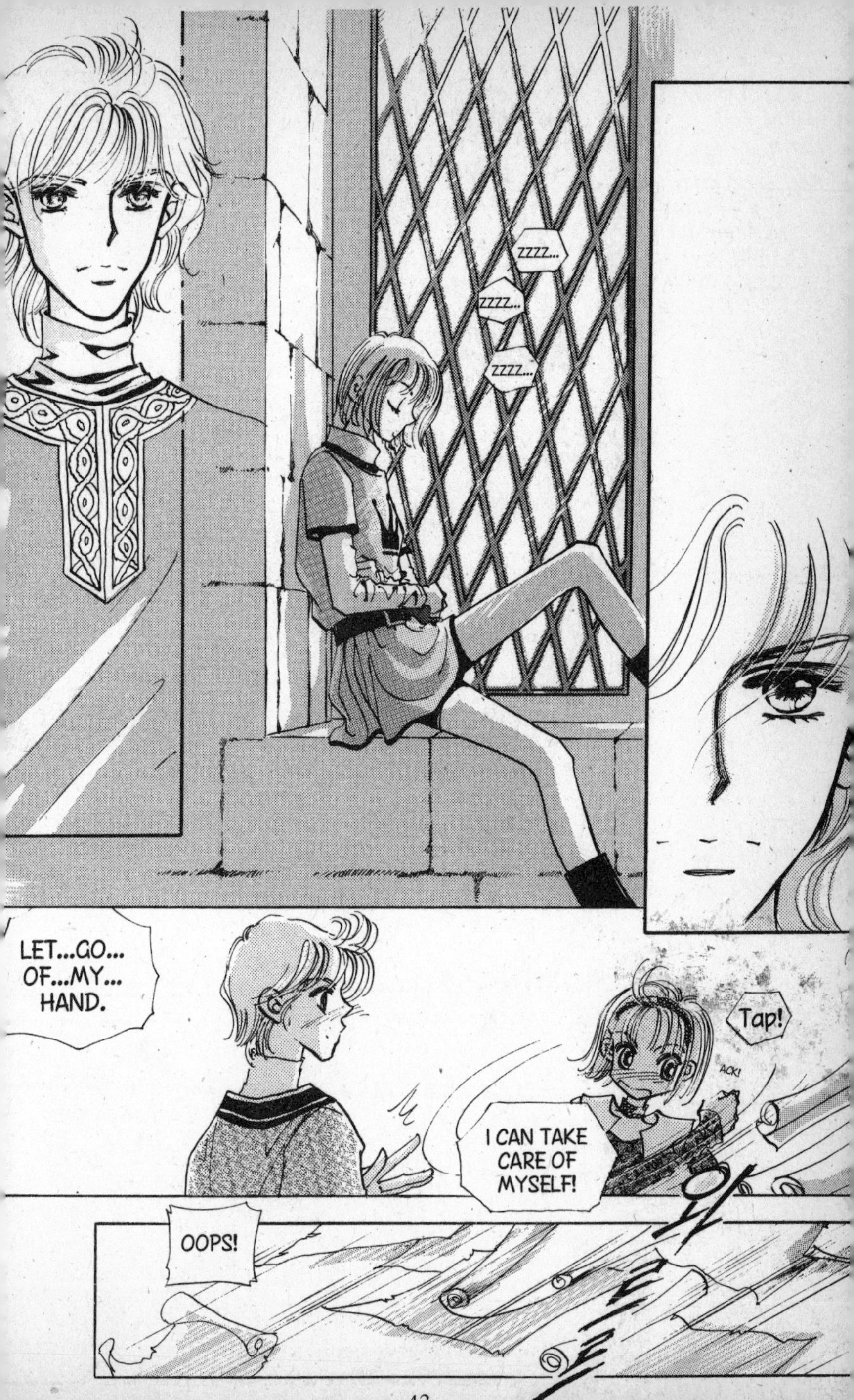
ZZZZ...
ZZZZ...
ZZZZ...
LET...GO... OF...MY... HAND.
Tap!
ACK!
I CAN TAKE CARE OF MYSELF!
OOPS!

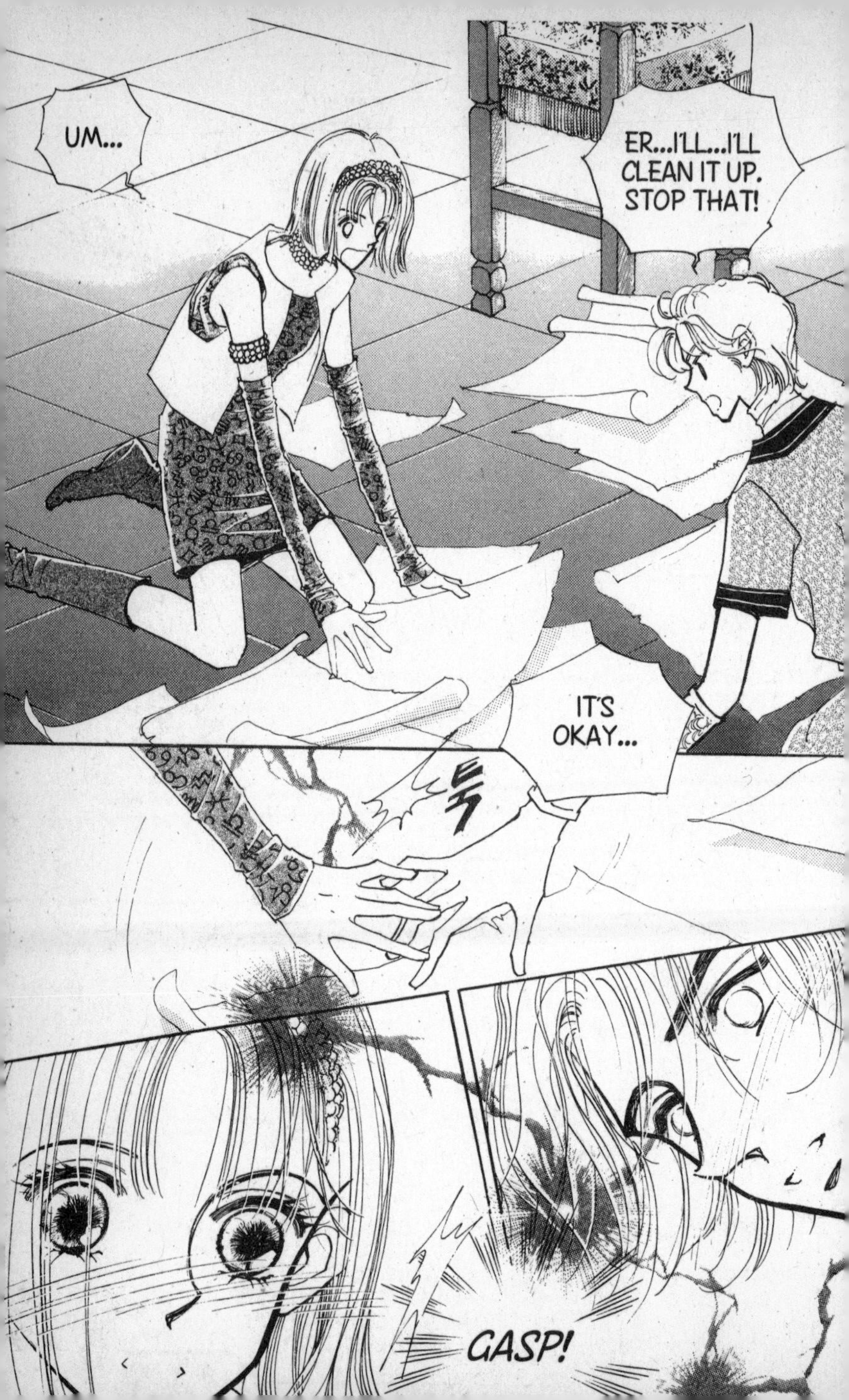
UM...
ER...I'LL...I'LL CLEAN IT UP. STOP THAT!
IT'S OKAY...
GASP!

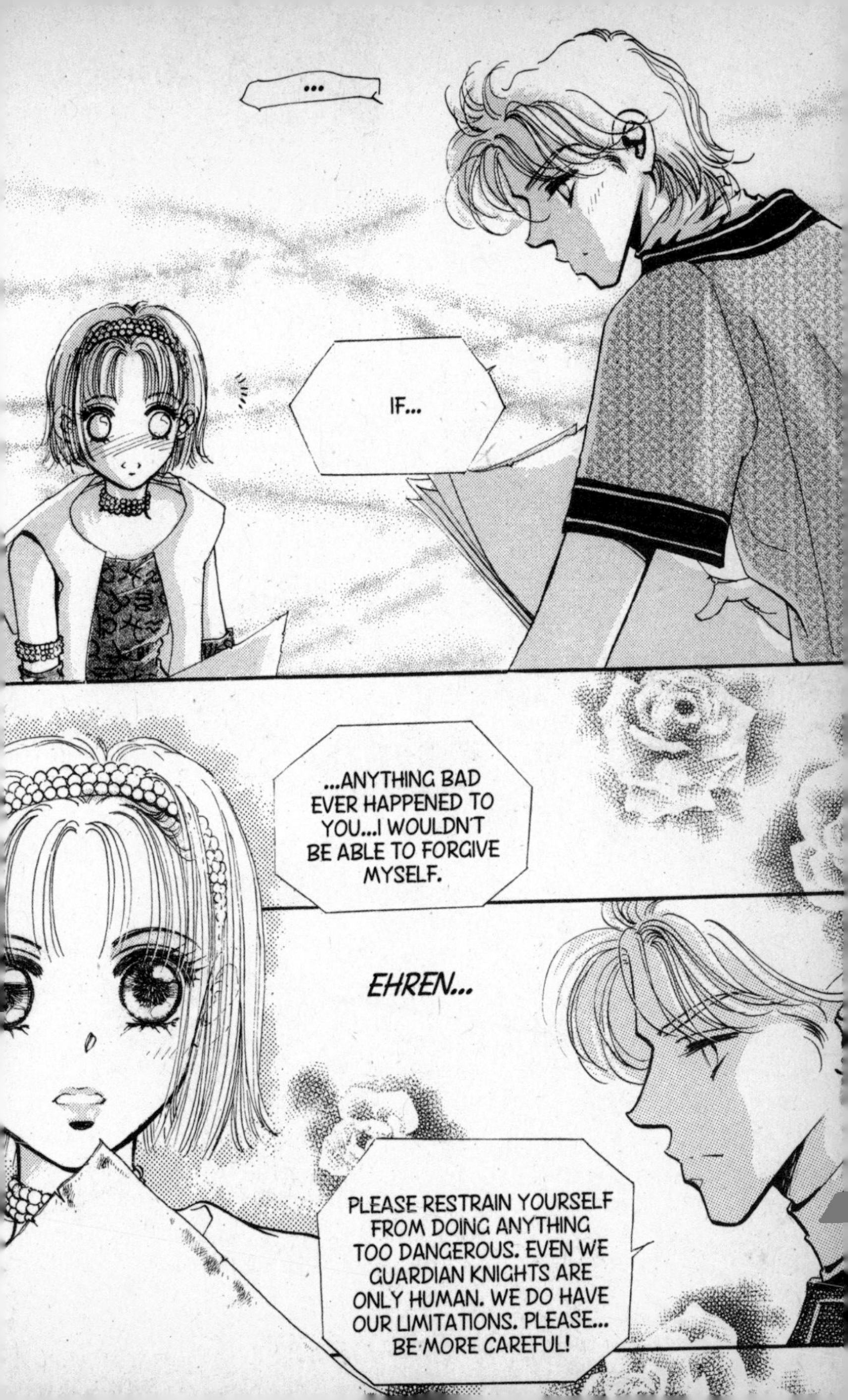
...
IF...
...ANYTHING BAD EVER HAPPENED TO YOU...I WOULDN'T BE ABLE TO FORGIVE MYSELF.
EHREN...
PLEASE RESTRAIN YOURSELF FROM DOING ANYTHING TOO DANGEROUS. EVEN WE GUARDIAN KNIGHTS ARE ONLY HUMAN. WE DO HAVE OUR LIMITATIONS. PLEASE... BE MORE CAREFUL!

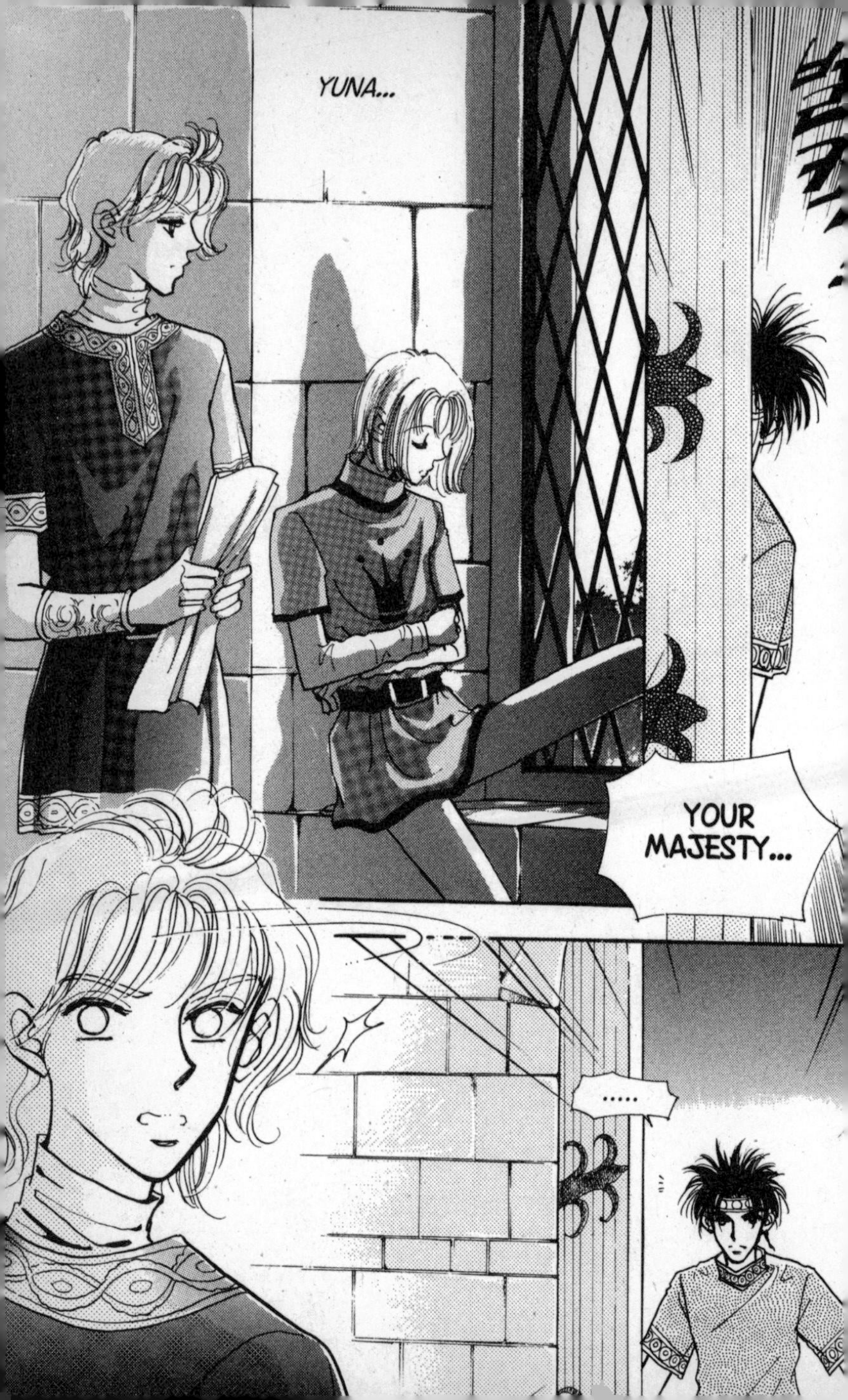

YUNA...
YOUR MAJESTY...
.....

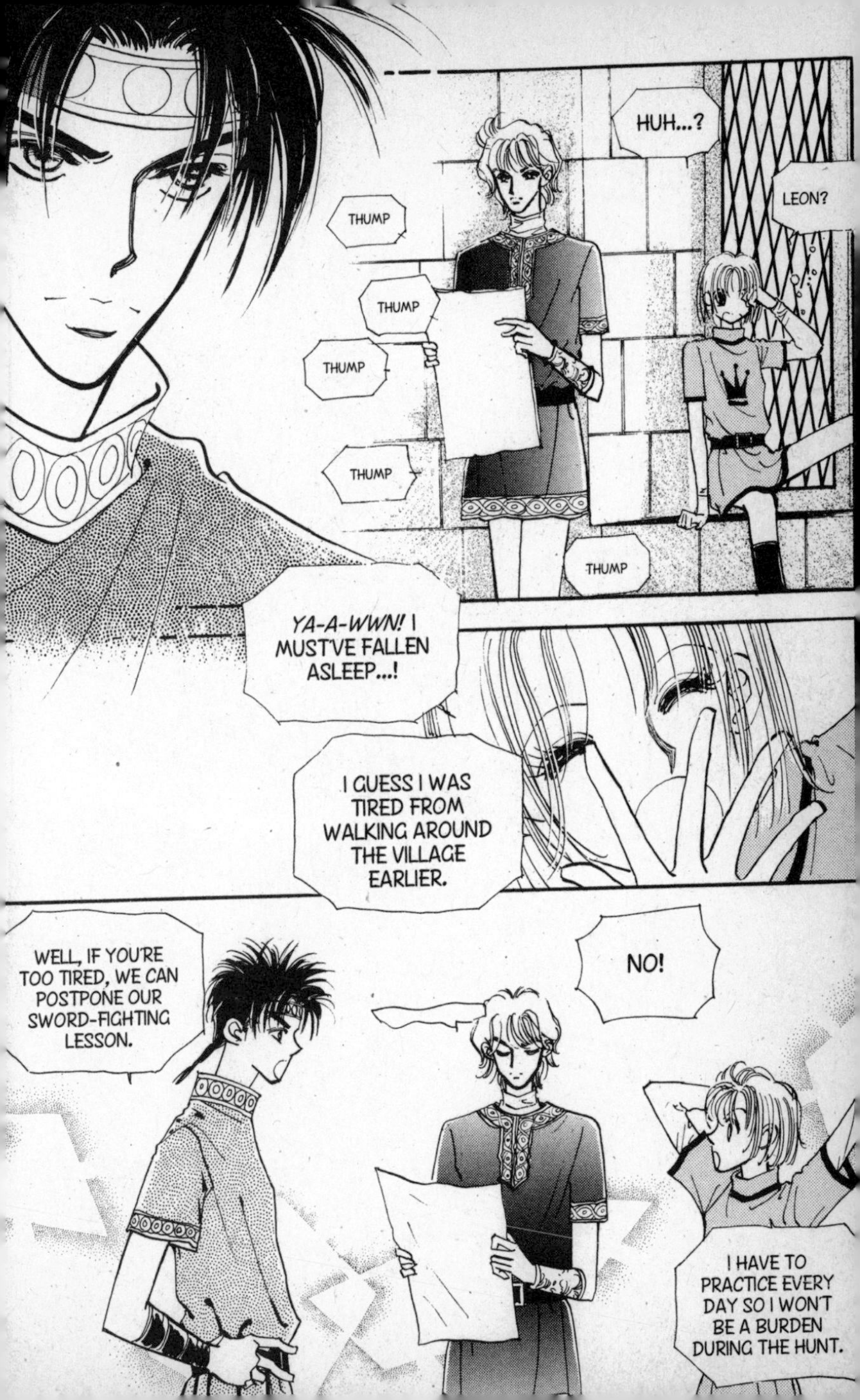

HUH...?
LEON?
THUMP
THUMP
THUMP
THUMP
THUMP
YA-A-WWN! I MUST'VE FALLEN ASLEEP...!
I GUESS I WAS TIRED FROM WALKING AROUND THE VILLAGE EARLIER.
WELL, IF YOU'RE TOO TIRED, WE CAN POSTPONE OUR SWORD-FIGHTING LESSON.
NO!
I HAVE TO PRACTICE EVERY DAY SO I WON'T BE A BURDEN DURING THE HUNT.

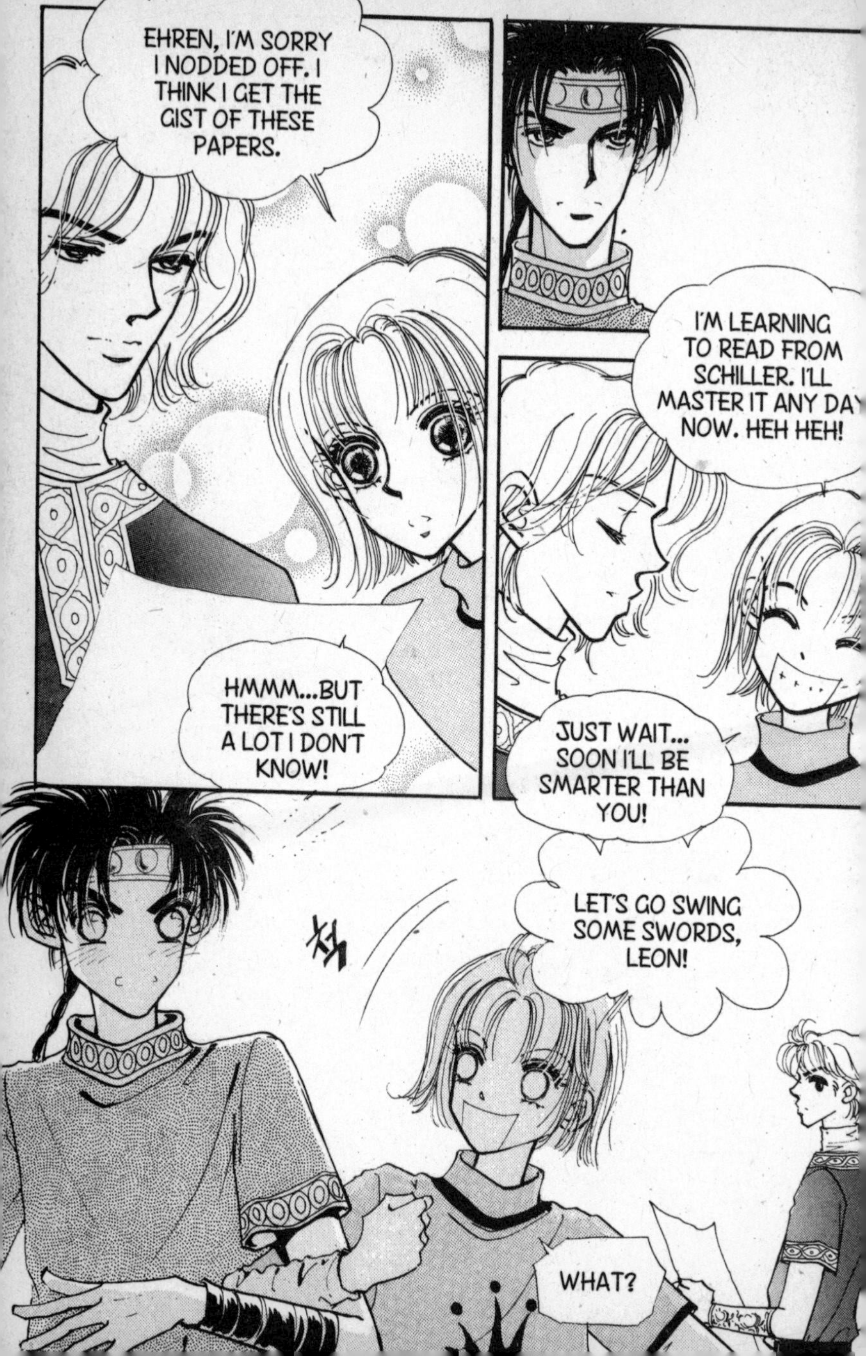
EHREN, I'M SORRY I NODDED OFF. I THINK I GET THE GIST OF THESE PAPERS.
HMMM...BUT THERE'S STILL A LOT I DON'T KNOW!
I'M LEARNING TO READ FROM SCHILLER. I'LL MASTER IT ANY DAY NOW. HEH HEH!
JUST WAIT... SOON I'LL BE SMARTER THAN YOU!
LET'S GO SWING SOME SWORDS, LEON!
WHAT?

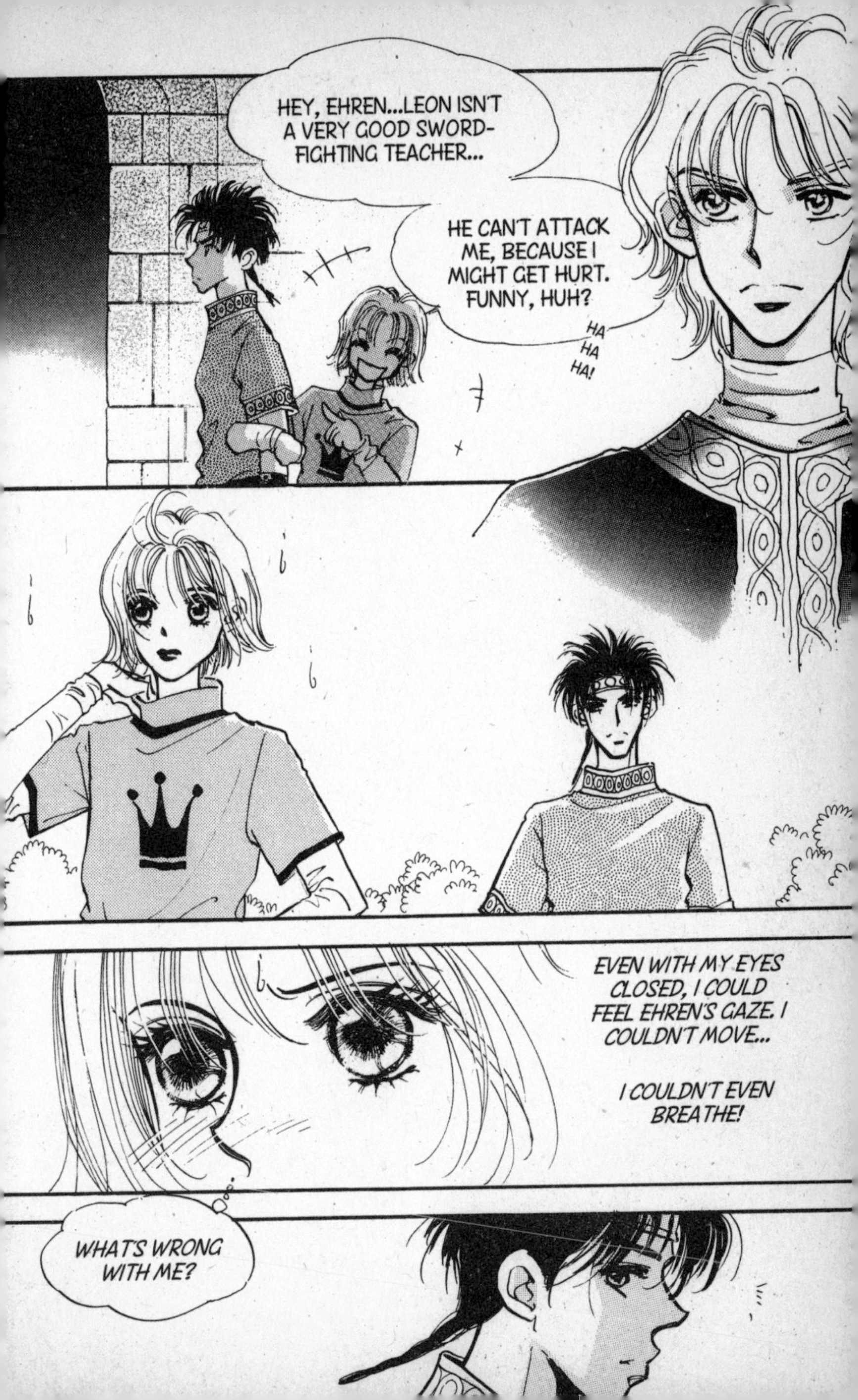

HEY, EHREN...LEON ISN'T A VERY GOOD SWORD-FIGHTING TEACHER...
HE CAN'T ATTACK ME, BECAUSE I MIGHT GET HURT. FUNNY, HUH?
HA HA HA!
EVEN WITH MY EYES CLOSED, I COULD FEEL EHREN'S GAZE. I COULDN'T MOVE...
I COULDN'T EVEN BREATHE!
WHAT'S WRONG WITH ME?

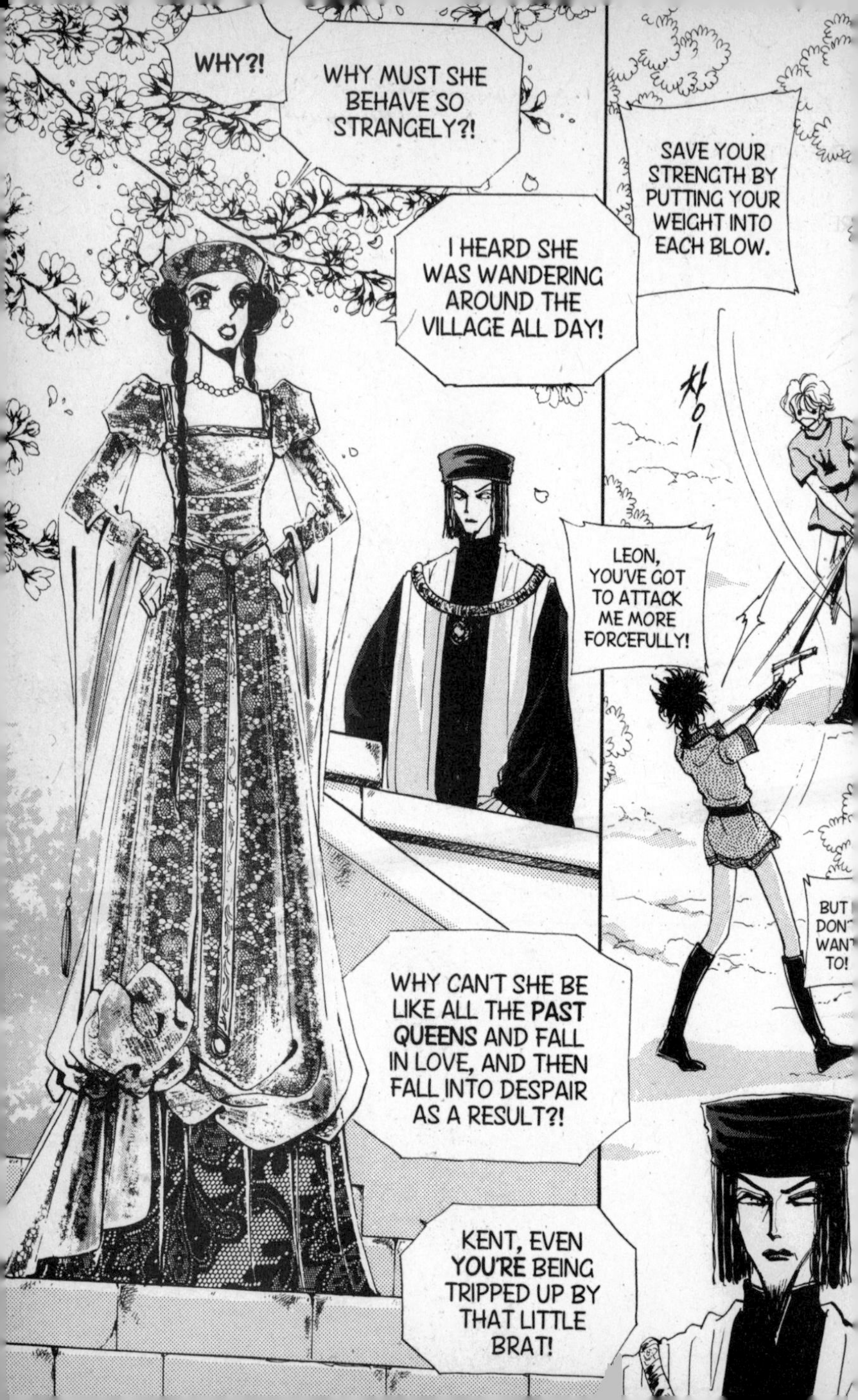

WHY?!
WHY MUST SHE BEHAVE SO STRANGELY?!
I HEARD SHE WAS WANDERING AROUND THE VILLAGE ALL DAY!
WHY CAN'T SHE BE LIKE ALL THE **PAST QUEENS** AND FALL IN LOVE, AND THEN FALL INTO DESPAIR AS A RESULT?!
KENT, EVEN YOU'RE BEING TRIPPED UP BY THAT LITTLE BRAT!
SAVE YOUR STRENGTH BY PUTTING YOUR WEIGHT INTO EACH BLOW.
창
LEON, YOU'VE GOT TO ATTACK ME MORE FORCEFULLY!
BUT I DON'T WANT TO!

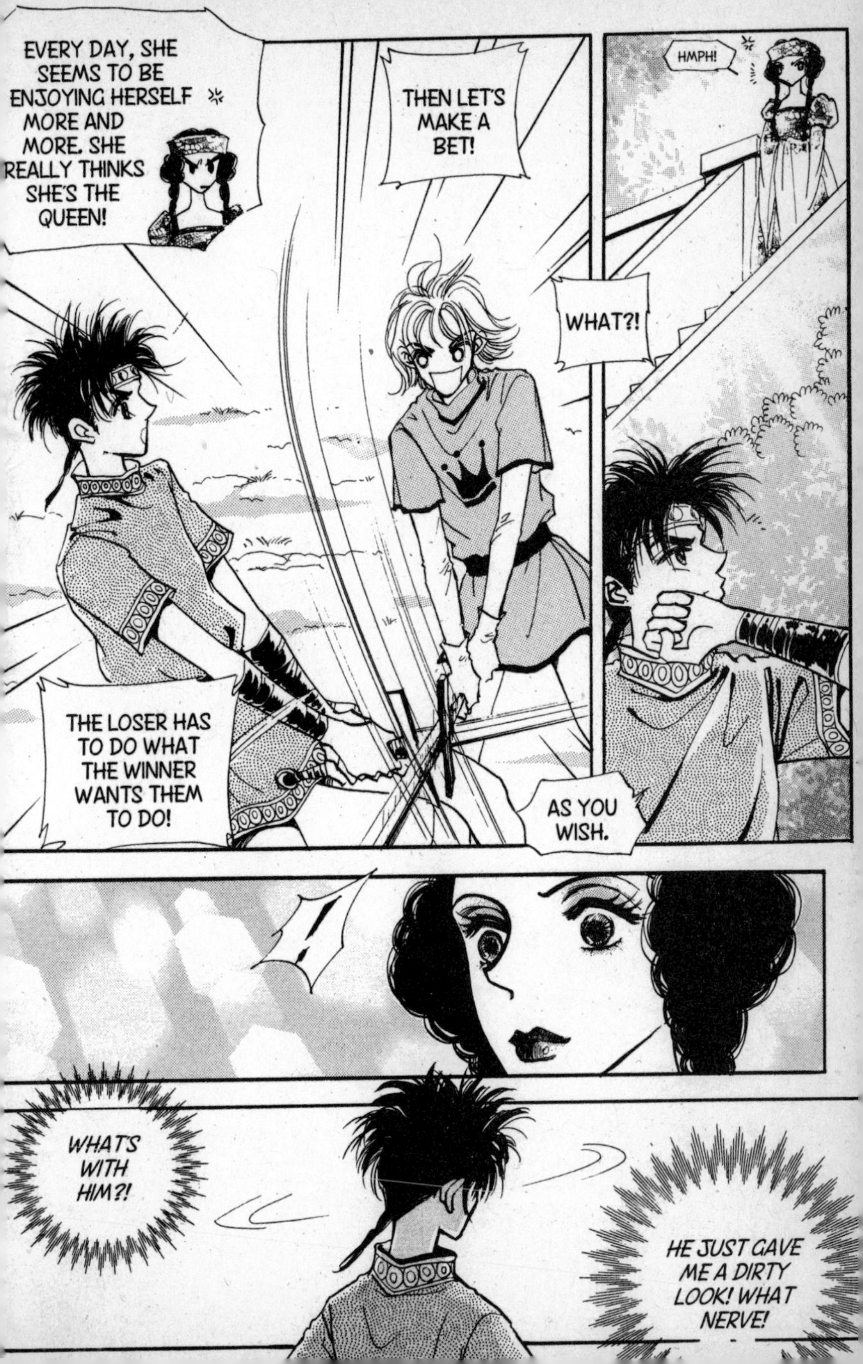
EVERY DAY, SHE SEEMS TO BE ENJOYING HERSELF MORE AND MORE. SHE REALLY THINKS SHE'S THE QUEEN!
THEN LET'S MAKE A BET!
THE LOSER HAS TO DO WHAT THE WINNER WANTS THEM TO DO!
HMPH!
WHAT?!
AS YOU WISH.
!
WHAT'S WITH HIM?!
HE JUST GAVE ME A DIRTY LOOK! WHAT NERVE!

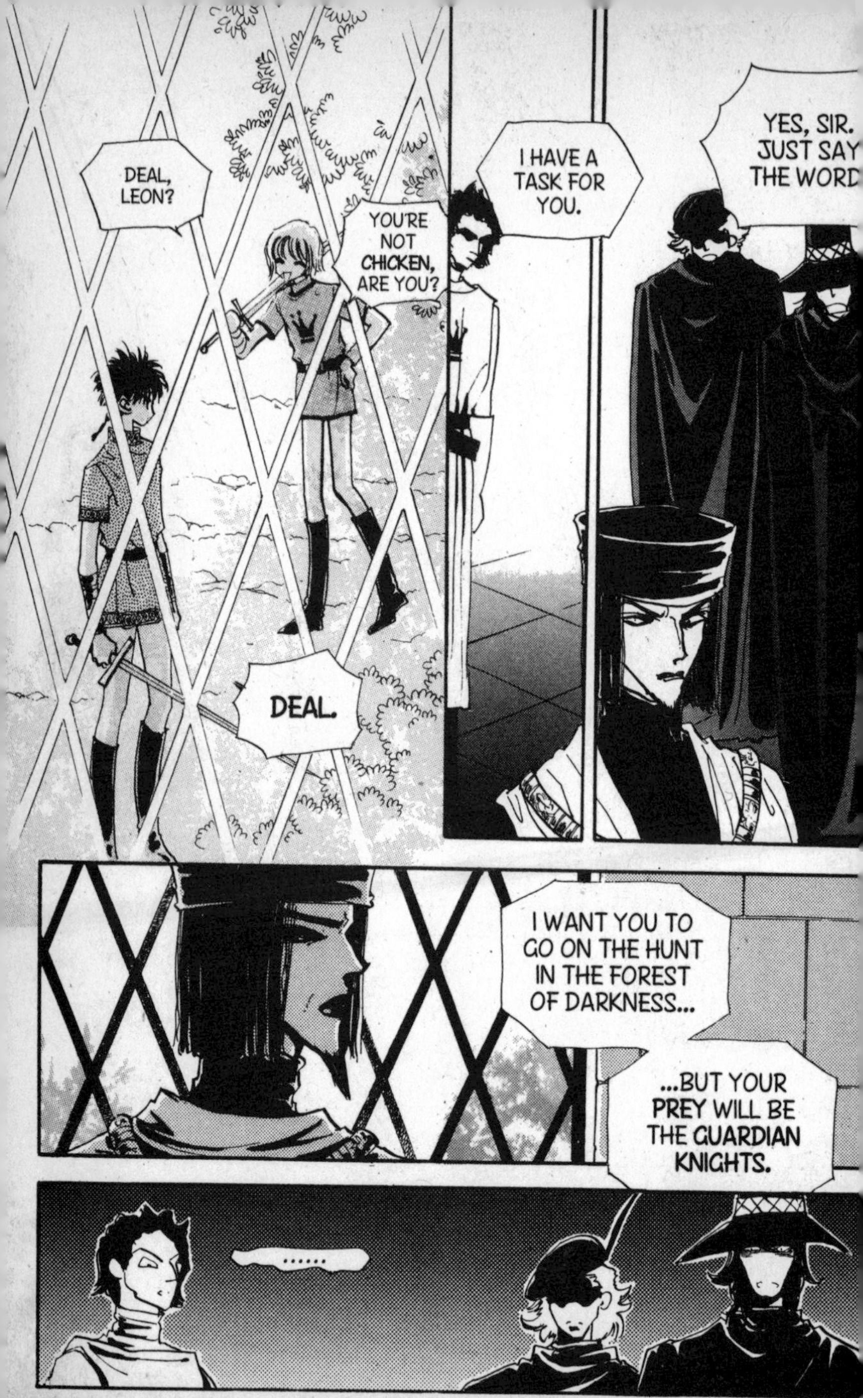
DEAL, LEON?
YOU'RE NOT CHICKEN, ARE YOU?
DEAL.
I HAVE A TASK FOR YOU.
YES, SIR. JUST SAY THE WORD
I WANT YOU TO GO ON THE HUNT IN THE FOREST OF DARKNESS...
...BUT YOUR PREY WILL BE THE GUARDIAN KNIGHTS.
......

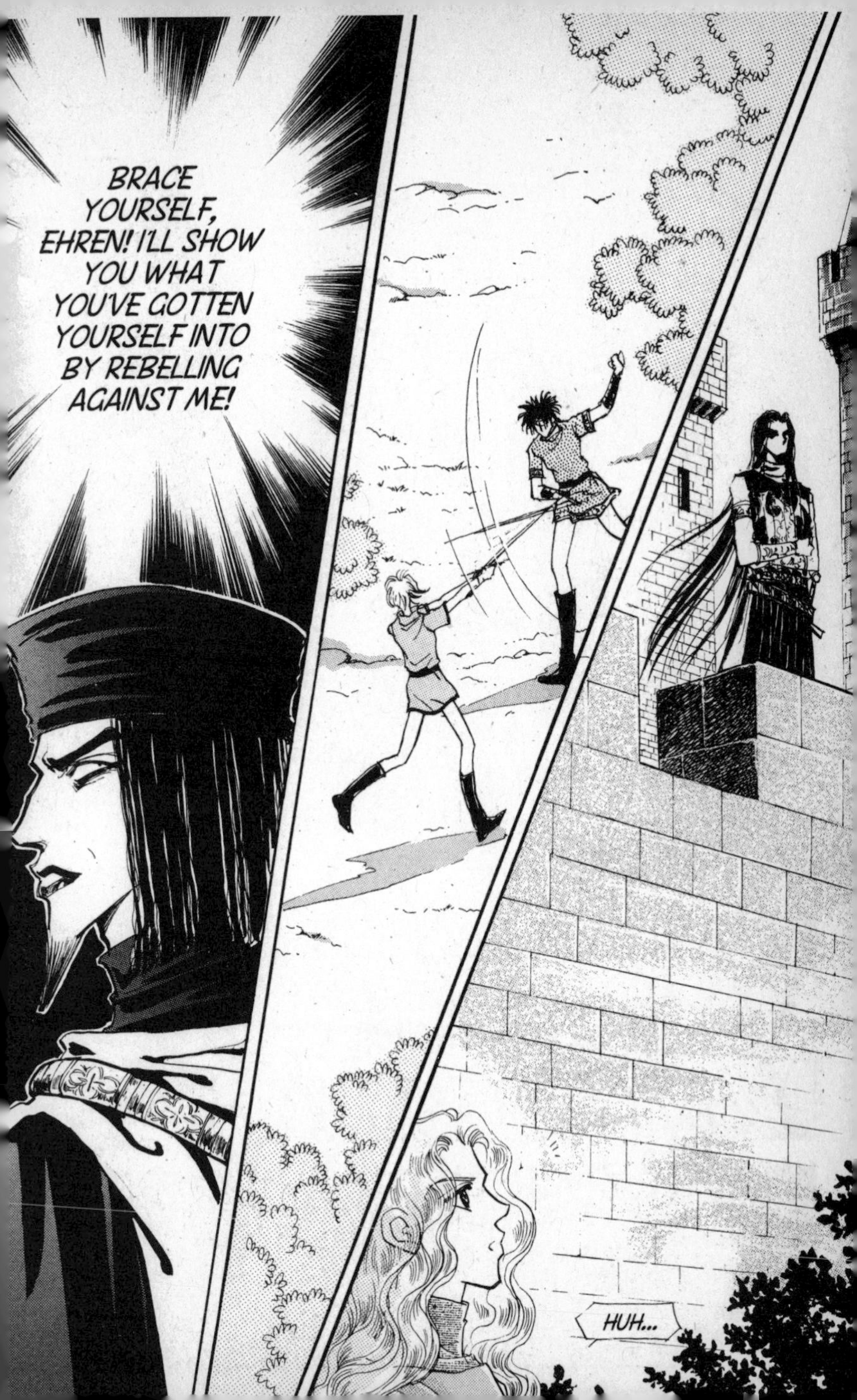
BRACE YOURSELF, EHREN! I'LL SHOW YOU WHAT YOU'VE GOTTEN YOURSELF INTO BY REBELLING AGAINST ME!
HUH...

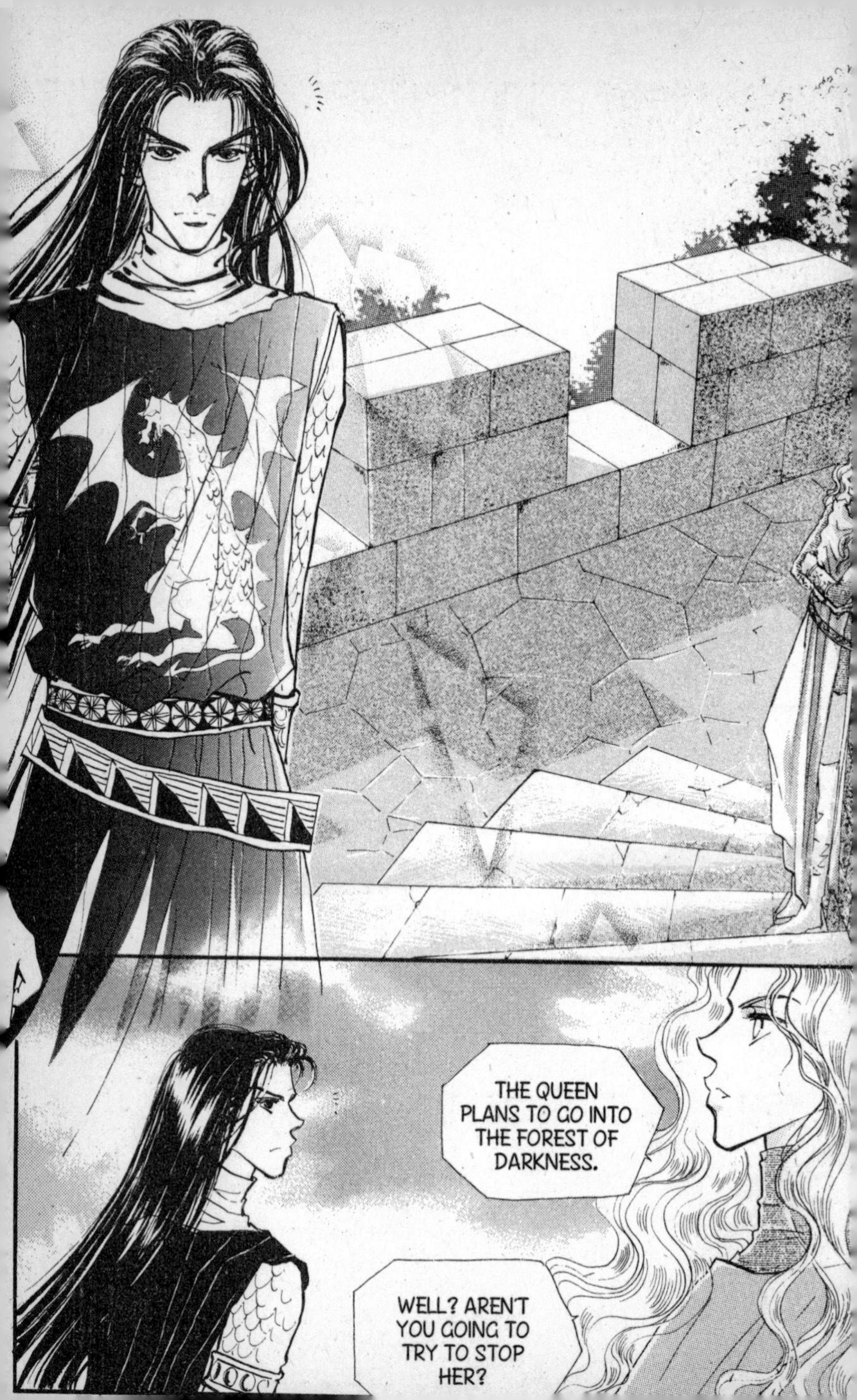
THE QUEEN PLANS TO GO INTO THE FOREST OF DARKNESS.
WELL? AREN'T YOU GOING TO TRY TO STOP HER?

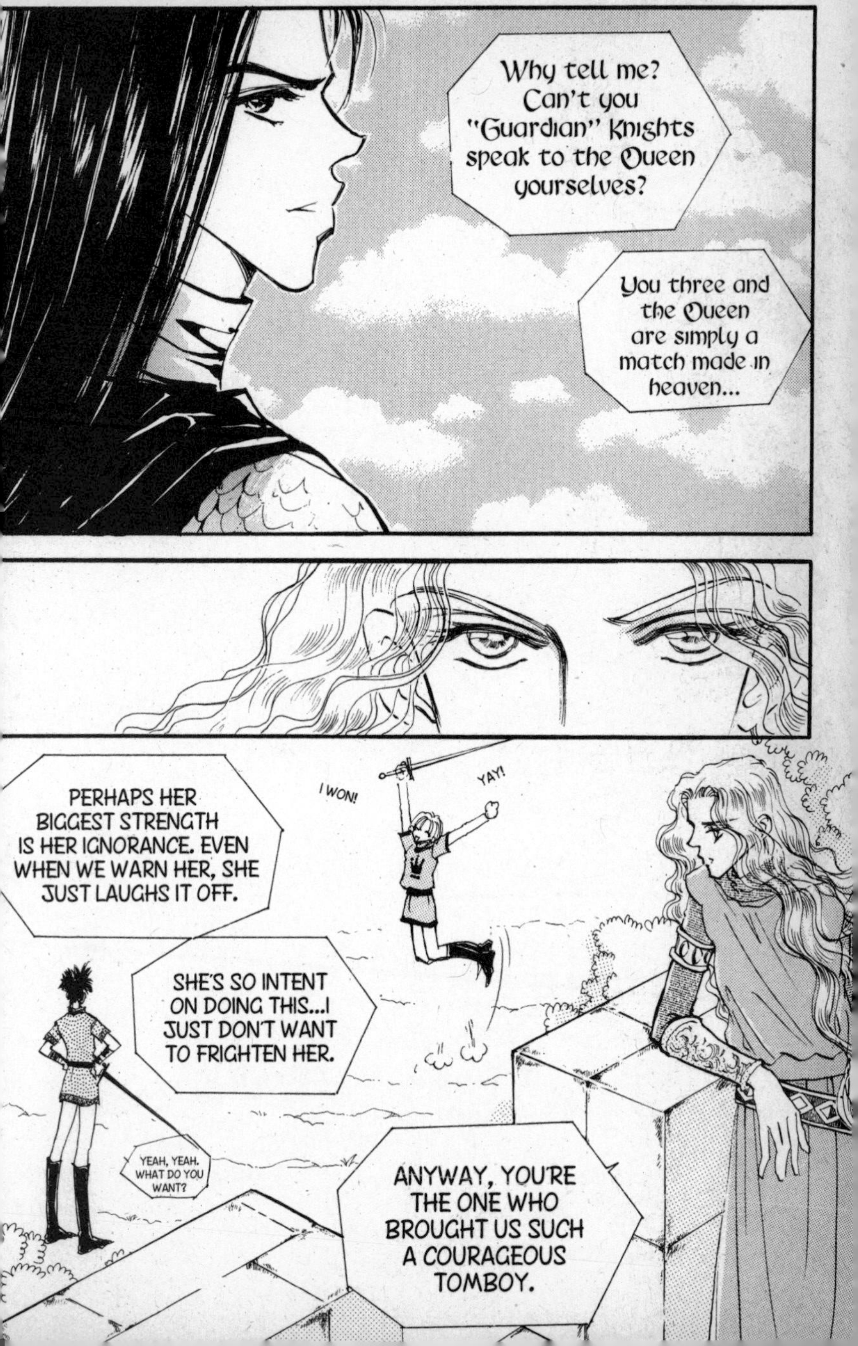
Why tell me? Can't you "Guardian" Knights speak to the Queen yourselves?
You three and the Queen are simply a match made in heaven...
PERHAPS HER BIGGEST STRENGTH IS HER IGNORANCE. EVEN WHEN WE WARN HER, SHE JUST LAUGHS IT OFF.
I WON!
YAY!
SHE'S SO INTENT ON DOING THIS...I JUST DON'T WANT TO FRIGHTEN HER.
YEAH, YEAH. WHAT DO YOU WANT?
ANYWAY, YOU'RE THE ONE WHO BROUGHT US SUCH A COURAGEOUS TOMBOY.

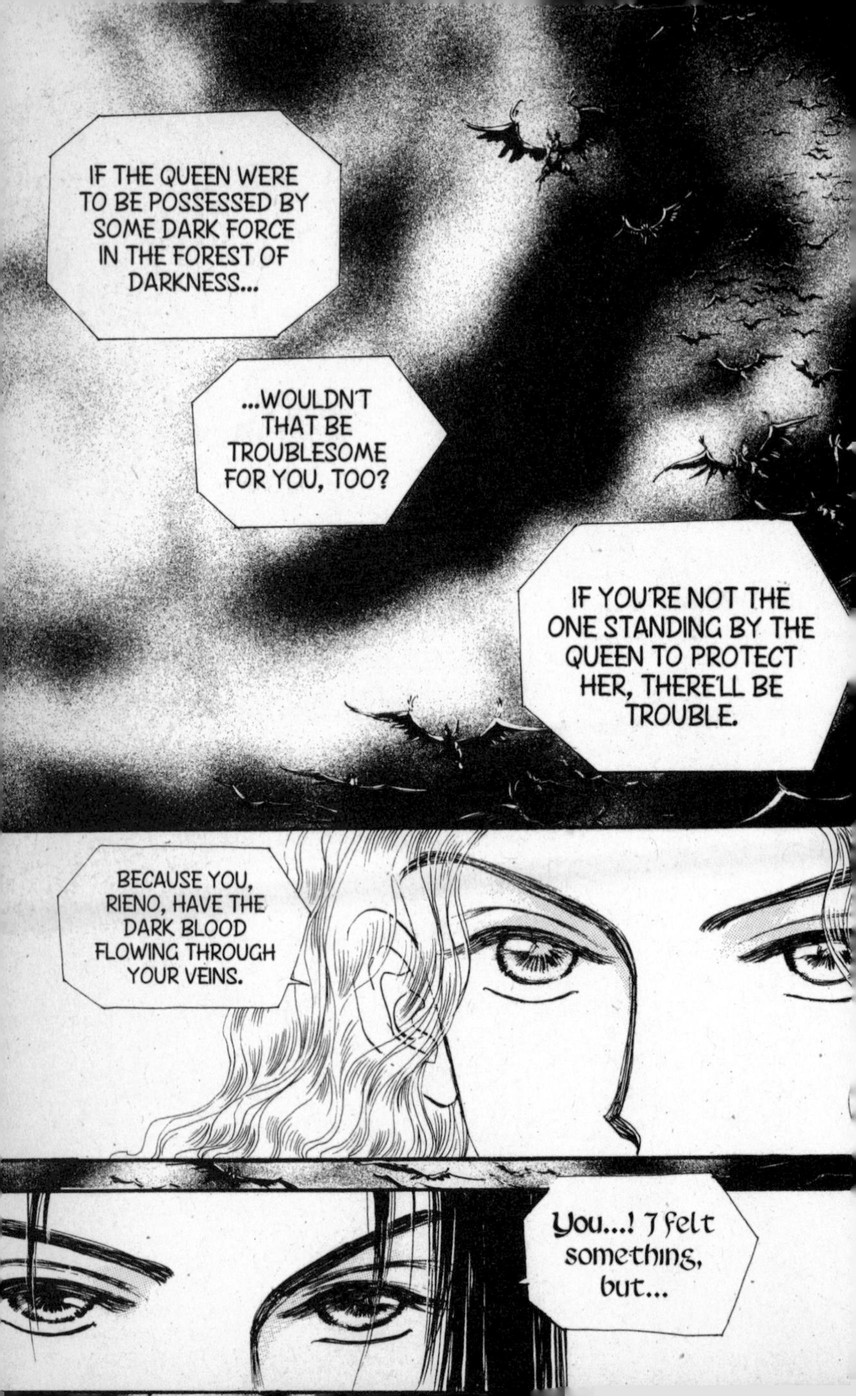
IF THE QUEEN WERE TO BE POSSESSED BY SOME DARK FORCE IN THE FOREST OF DARKNESS...
...WOULDN'T THAT BE TROUBLESOME FOR YOU, TOO?
IF YOU'RE NOT THE ONE STANDING BY THE QUEEN TO PROTECT HER, THERE'LL BE TROUBLE.
BECAUSE YOU, RIENO, HAVE THE DARK BLOOD FLOWING THROUGH YOUR VEINS.
You...! I felt something, but...

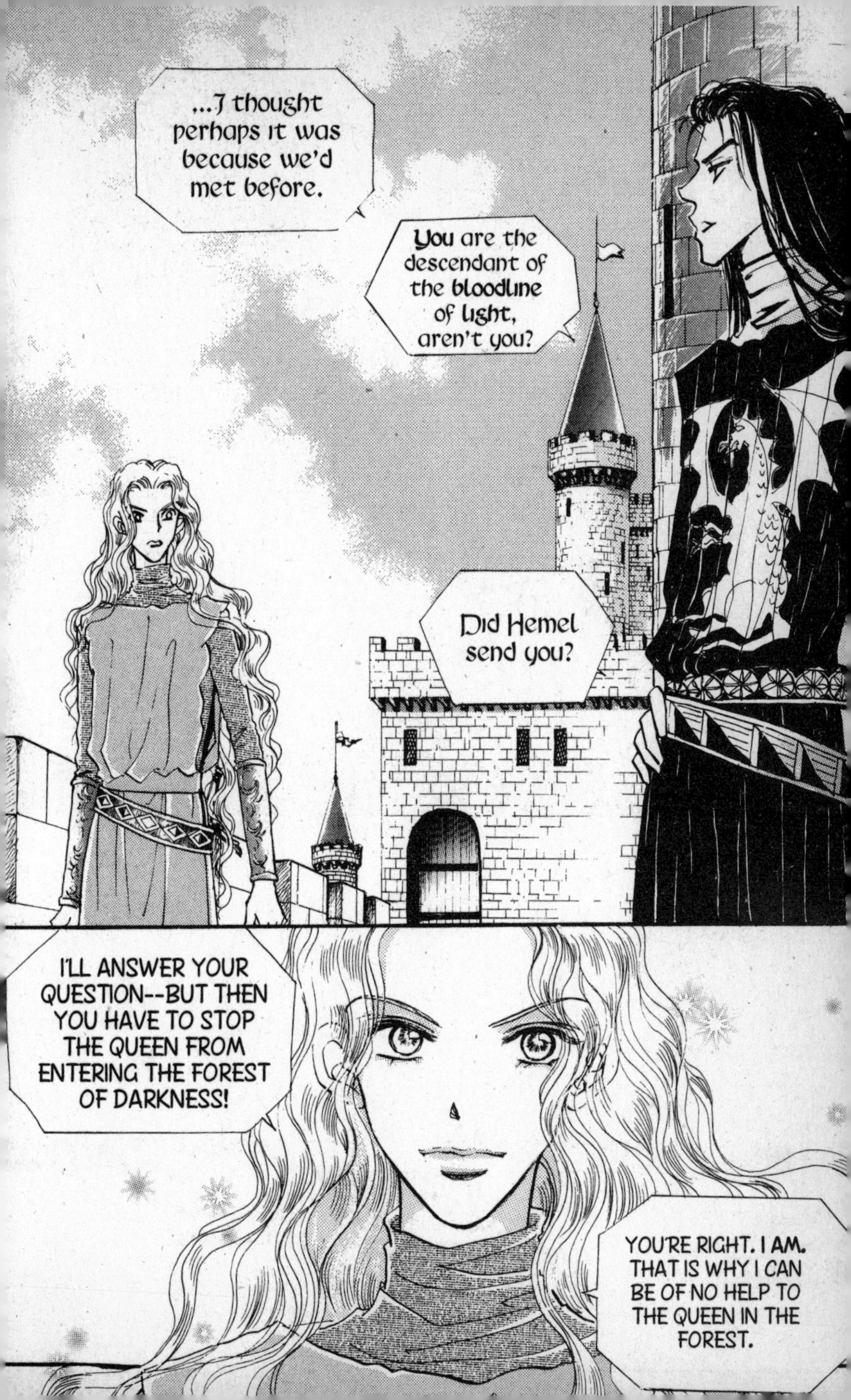
...I thought perhaps it was because we'd met before.
You are the descendant of the bloodline of light, aren't you?
Did Hemel send you?
I'LL ANSWER YOUR QUESTION--BUT THEN YOU HAVE TO STOP THE QUEEN FROM ENTERING THE FOREST OF DARKNESS!
YOU'RE RIGHT. I AM. THAT IS WHY I CAN BE OF NO HELP TO THE QUEEN IN THE FOREST.

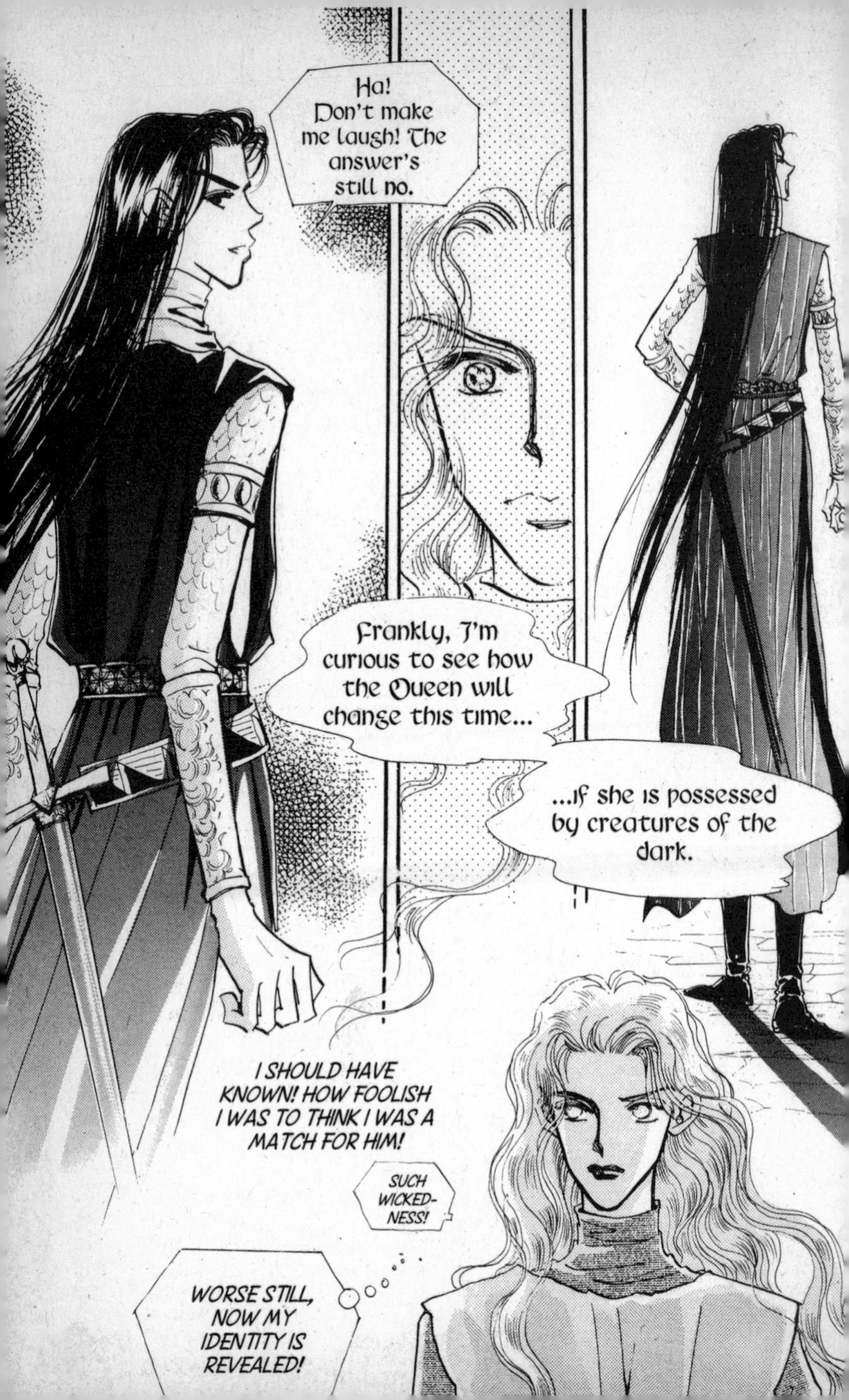
Ha! Don't make me laugh! The answer's still no.
Frankly, I'm curious to see how the Queen will change this time...
...if she is possessed by creatures of the dark.
I SHOULD HAVE KNOWN! HOW FOOLISH I WAS TO THINK I WAS A MATCH FOR HIM!
SUCH WICKED-NESS!
WORSE STILL, NOW MY IDENTITY IS REVEALED!

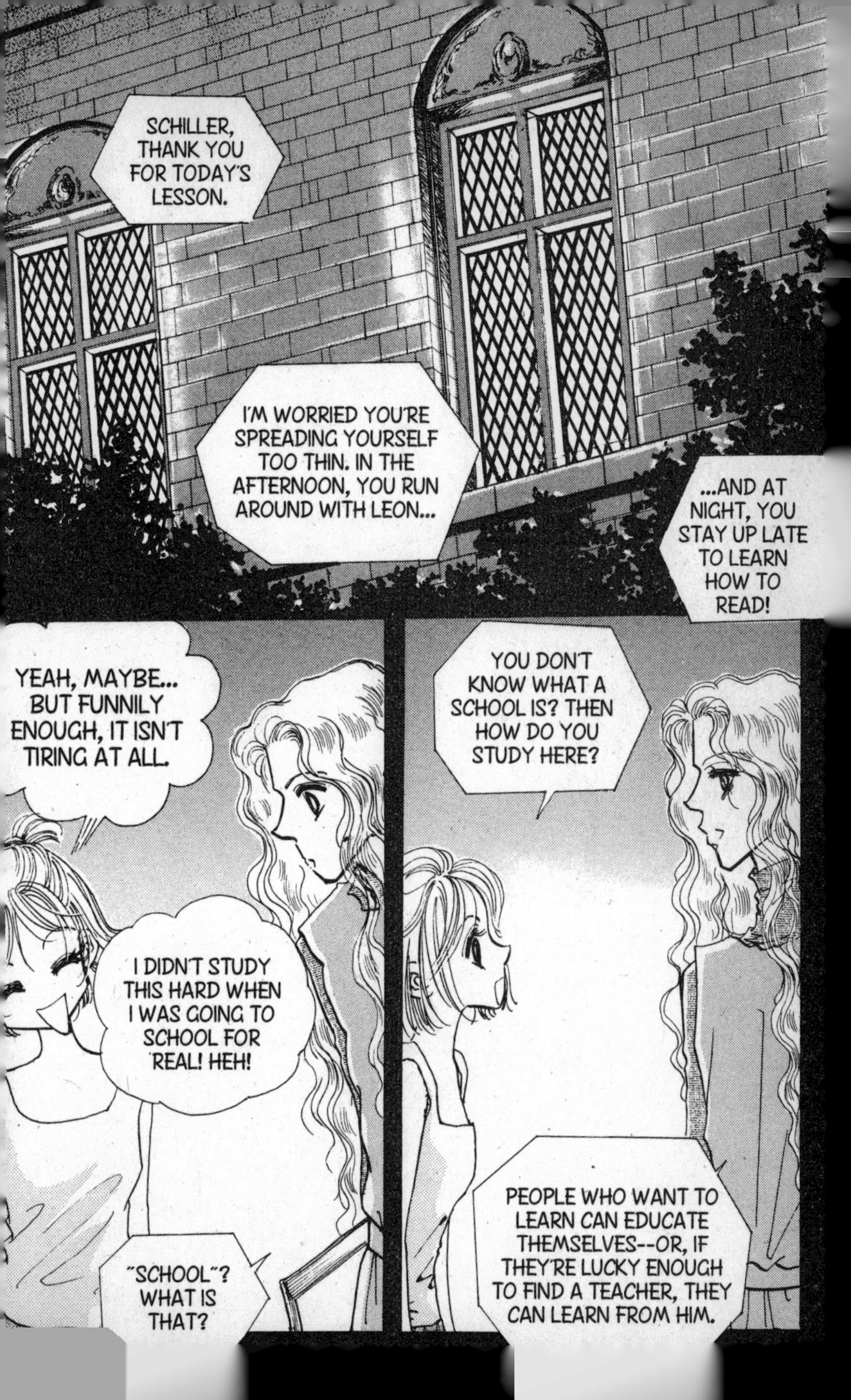
SCHILLER, THANK YOU FOR TODAY'S LESSON.
I'M WORRIED YOU'RE SPREADING YOURSELF TOO THIN. IN THE AFTERNOON, YOU RUN AROUND WITH LEON...
...AND AT NIGHT, YOU STAY UP LATE TO LEARN HOW TO READ!
YEAH, MAYBE... BUT FUNNILY ENOUGH, IT ISN'T TIRING AT ALL.
I DIDN'T STUDY THIS HARD WHEN I WAS GOING TO SCHOOL FOR REAL! HEH!
"SCHOOL"? WHAT IS THAT?
YOU DON'T KNOW WHAT A SCHOOL IS? THEN HOW DO YOU STUDY HERE?
PEOPLE WHO WANT TO LEARN CAN EDUCATE THEMSELVES--OR, IF THEY'RE LUCKY ENOUGH TO FIND A TEACHER, THEY CAN LEARN FROM HIM.

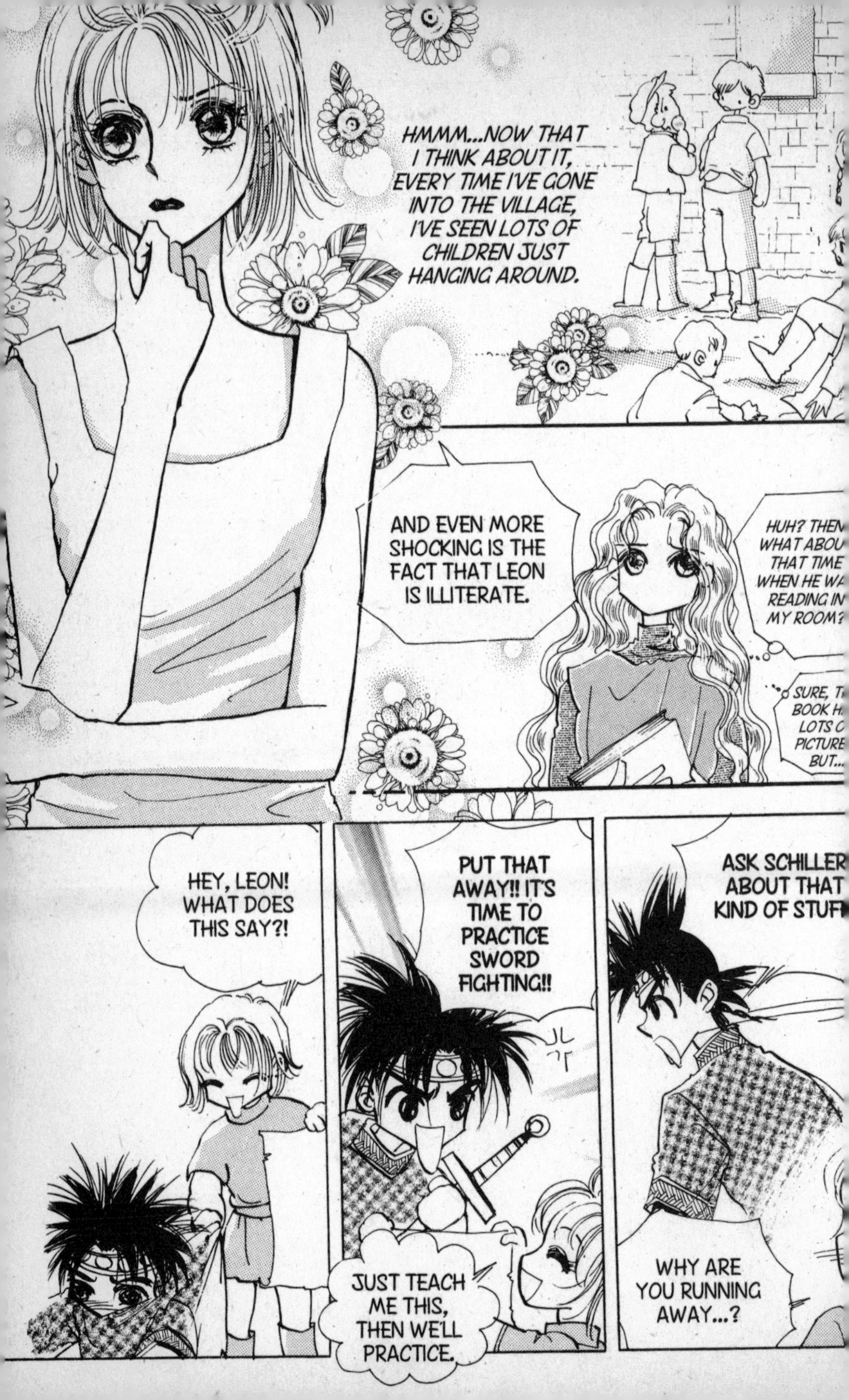
HMMM...NOW THAT I THINK ABOUT IT, EVERY TIME I'VE GONE INTO THE VILLAGE, I'VE SEEN LOTS OF CHILDREN JUST HANGING AROUND.
AND EVEN MORE SHOCKING IS THE FACT THAT LEON IS ILLITERATE.
HUH? THEN WHAT ABOU THAT TIME WHEN HE WA READING IN MY ROOM?
SURE, T BOOK H LOTS O PICTURE BUT...
HEY, LEON! WHAT DOES THIS SAY?!
PUT THAT AWAY!! IT'S TIME TO PRACTICE SWORD FIGHTING!!
JUST TEACH ME THIS, THEN WE'LL PRACTICE.
ASK SCHILLER ABOUT THAT KIND OF STUF
WHY ARE YOU RUNNING AWAY...?

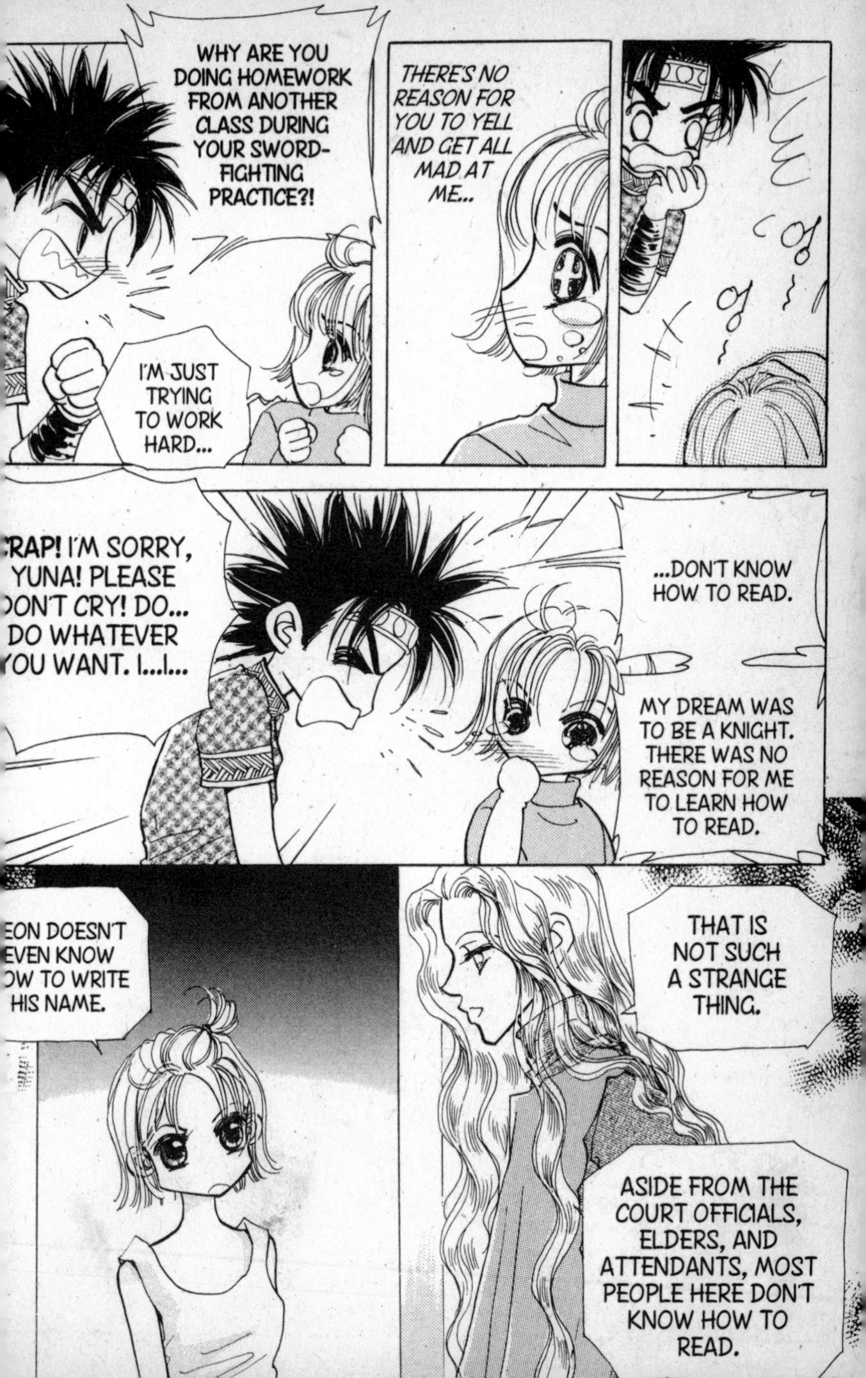
WHY ARE YOU DOING HOMEWORK FROM ANOTHER CLASS DURING YOUR SWORD-FIGHTING PRACTICE?!
I'M JUST TRYING TO WORK HARD...
THERE'S NO REASON FOR YOU TO YELL AND GET ALL MAD AT ME...
RAP! I'M SORRY, YUNA! PLEASE ON'T CRY! DO... DO WHATEVER OU WANT. I...I...
...DON'T KNOW HOW TO READ.
MY DREAM WAS TO BE A KNIGHT. THERE WAS NO REASON FOR ME TO LEARN HOW TO READ.
EON DOESN'T EVEN KNOW OW TO WRITE HIS NAME.
THAT IS NOT SUCH A STRANGE THING.
ASIDE FROM THE COURT OFFICIALS, ELDERS, AND ATTENDANTS, MOST PEOPLE HERE DON'T KNOW HOW TO READ.

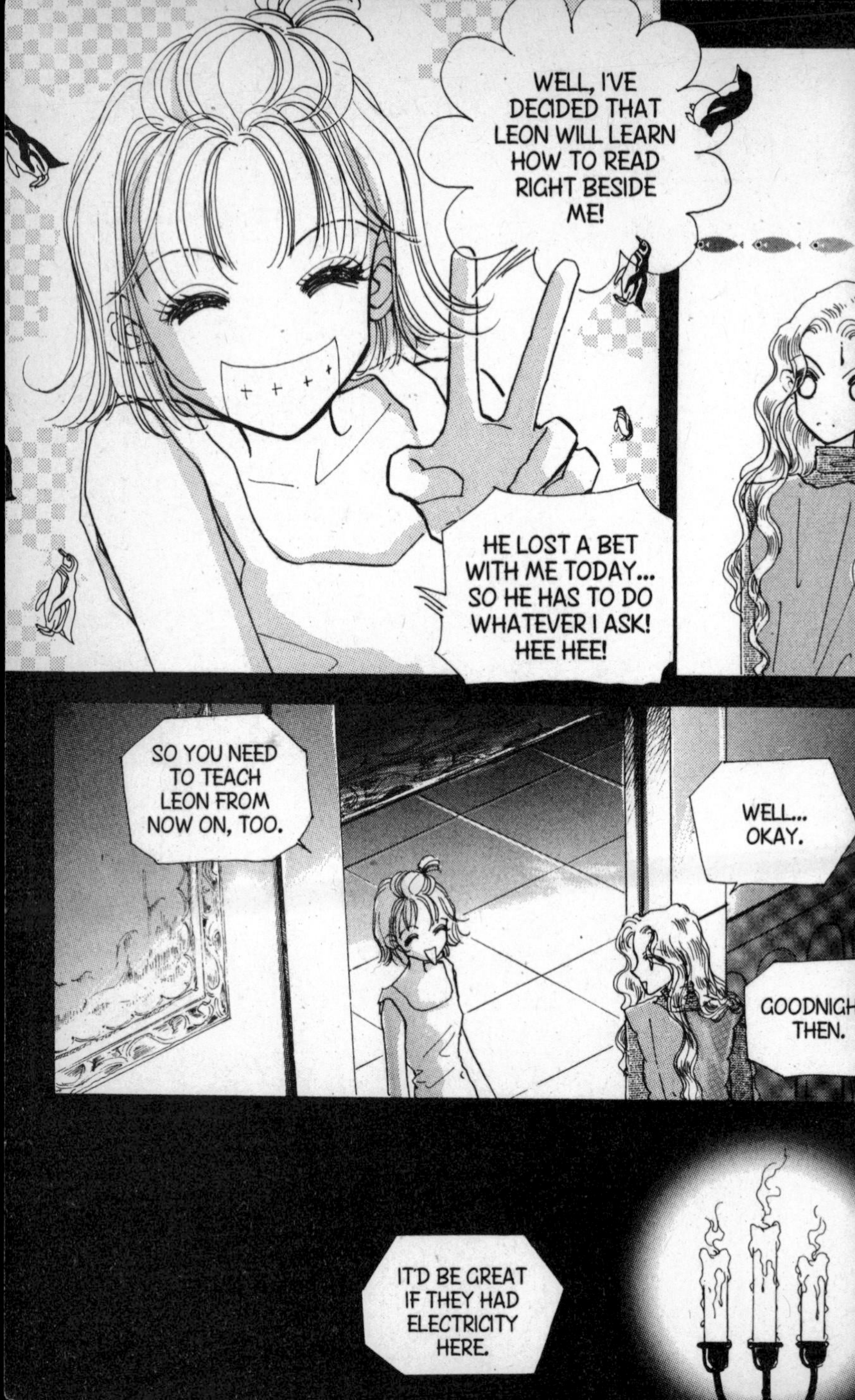
WELL, I'VE DECIDED THAT LEON WILL LEARN HOW TO READ RIGHT BESIDE ME!
HE LOST A BET WITH ME TODAY... SO HE HAS TO DO WHATEVER I ASK! HEE HEE!
SO YOU NEED TO TEACH LEON FROM NOW ON, TOO.
WELL... OKAY.
GOODNIGH
THEN.
IT'D BE GREAT IF THEY HAD ELECTRICITY HERE.

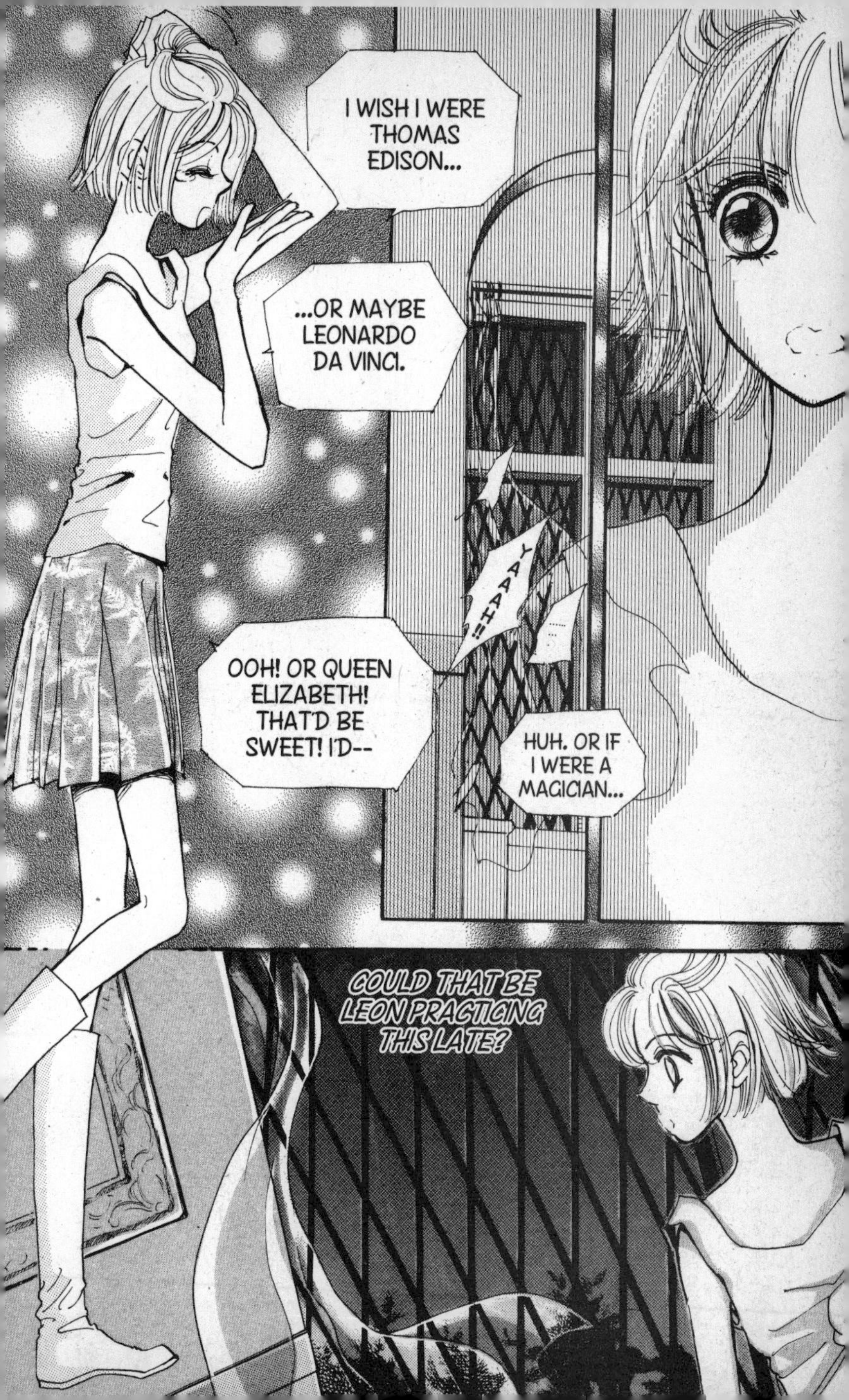
I WISH I WERE THOMAS EDISON...
...OR MAYBE LEONARDO DA VINCI.
OOH! OR QUEEN ELIZABETH! THAT'D BE SWEET! I'D--
YAAAH!!
......
...
HUH. OR IF I WERE A MAGICIAN...
COULD THAT BE LEON PRACTICING THIS LATE?

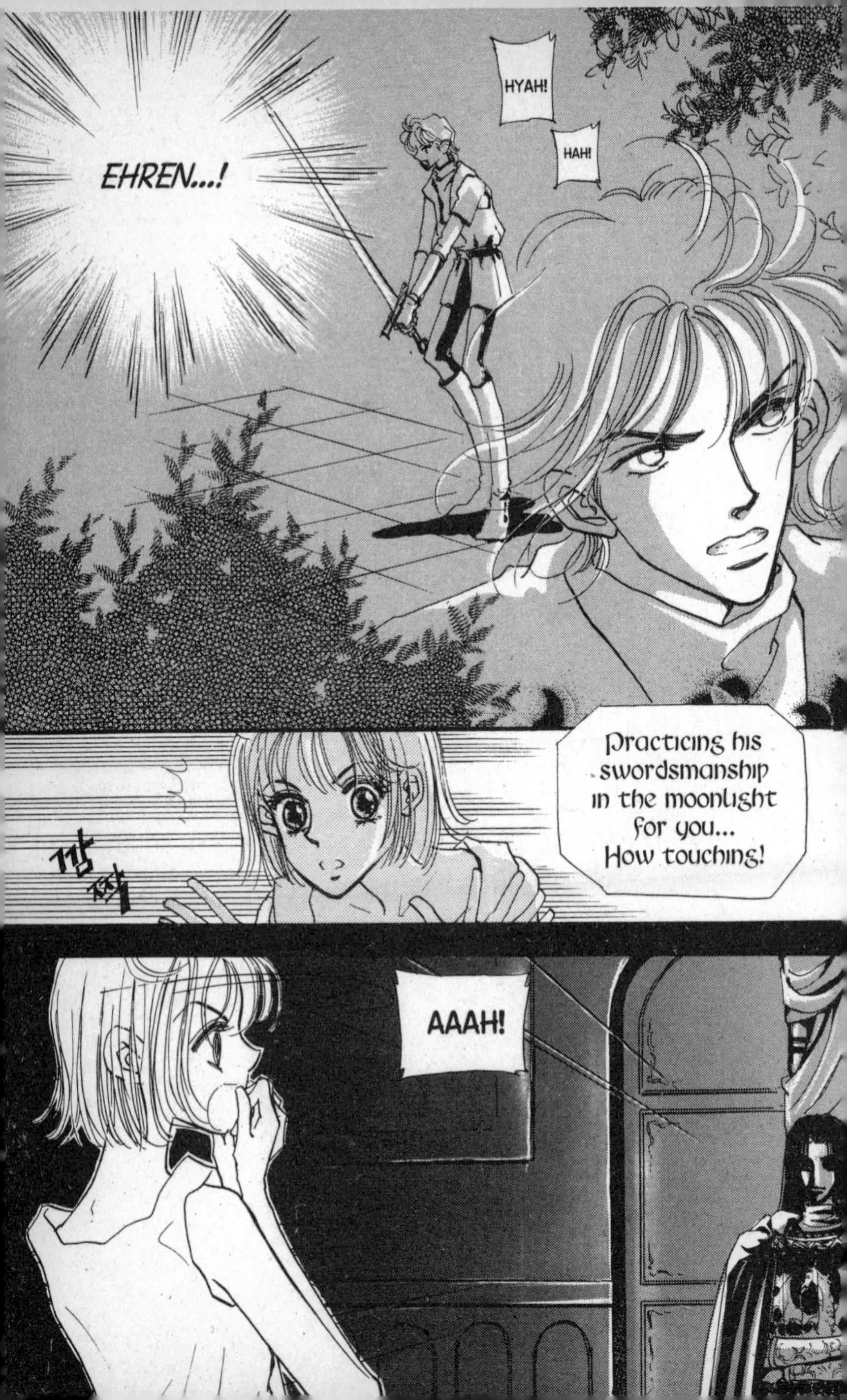
EHREN...!
HYAH!
HAH!
Practicing his swordsmanship in the moonlight for you... How touching!
AAAH!

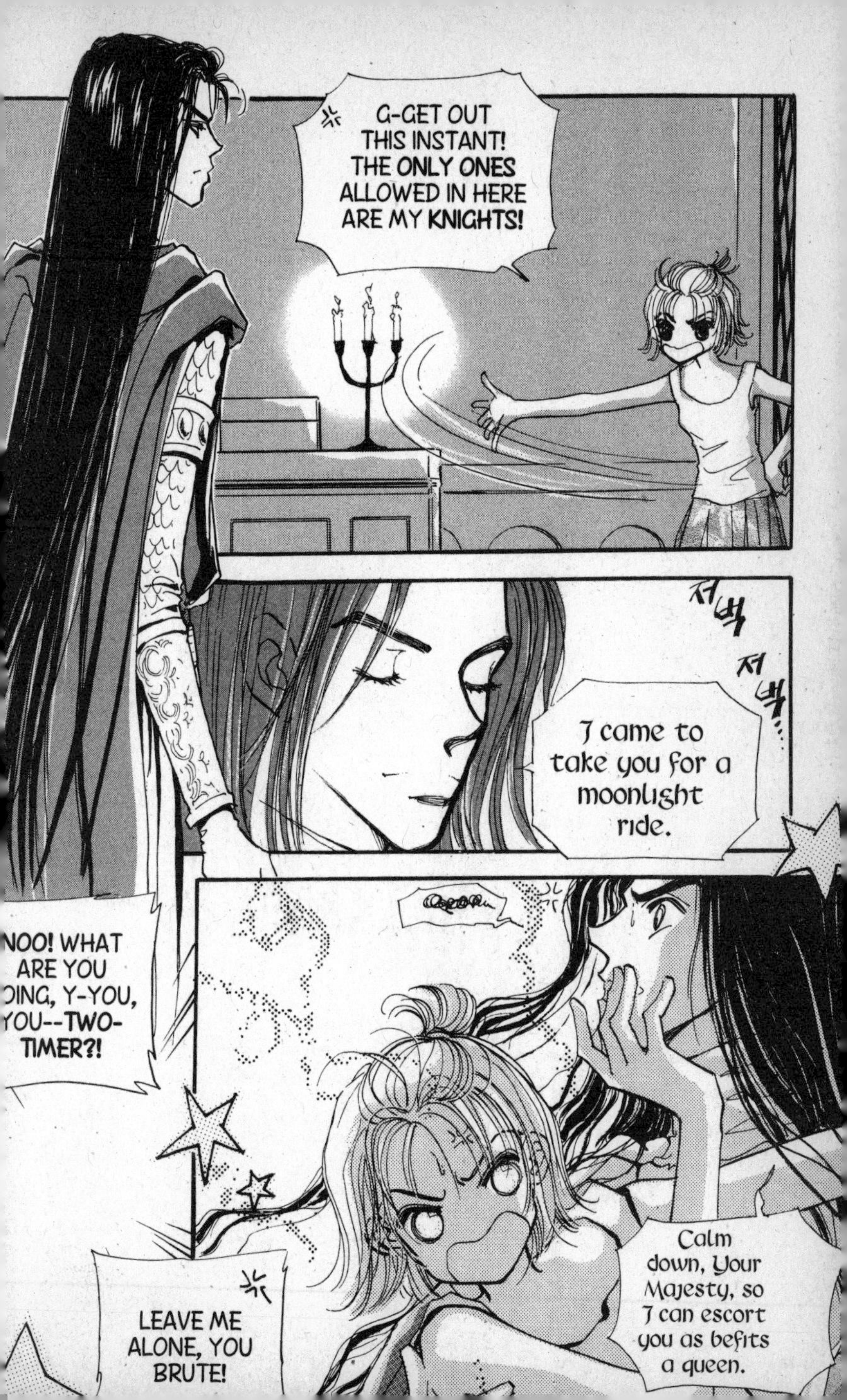
G-GET OUT THIS INSTANT! THE ONLY ONES ALLOWED IN HERE ARE MY KNIGHTS!
저벅 저벅...
I came to take you for a moonlight ride.
NOO! WHAT ARE YOU OING, Y-YOU, YOU--TWO-TIMER?!
LEAVE ME ALONE, YOU BRUTE!
Calm down, Your Majesty, so I can escort you as befits a queen.

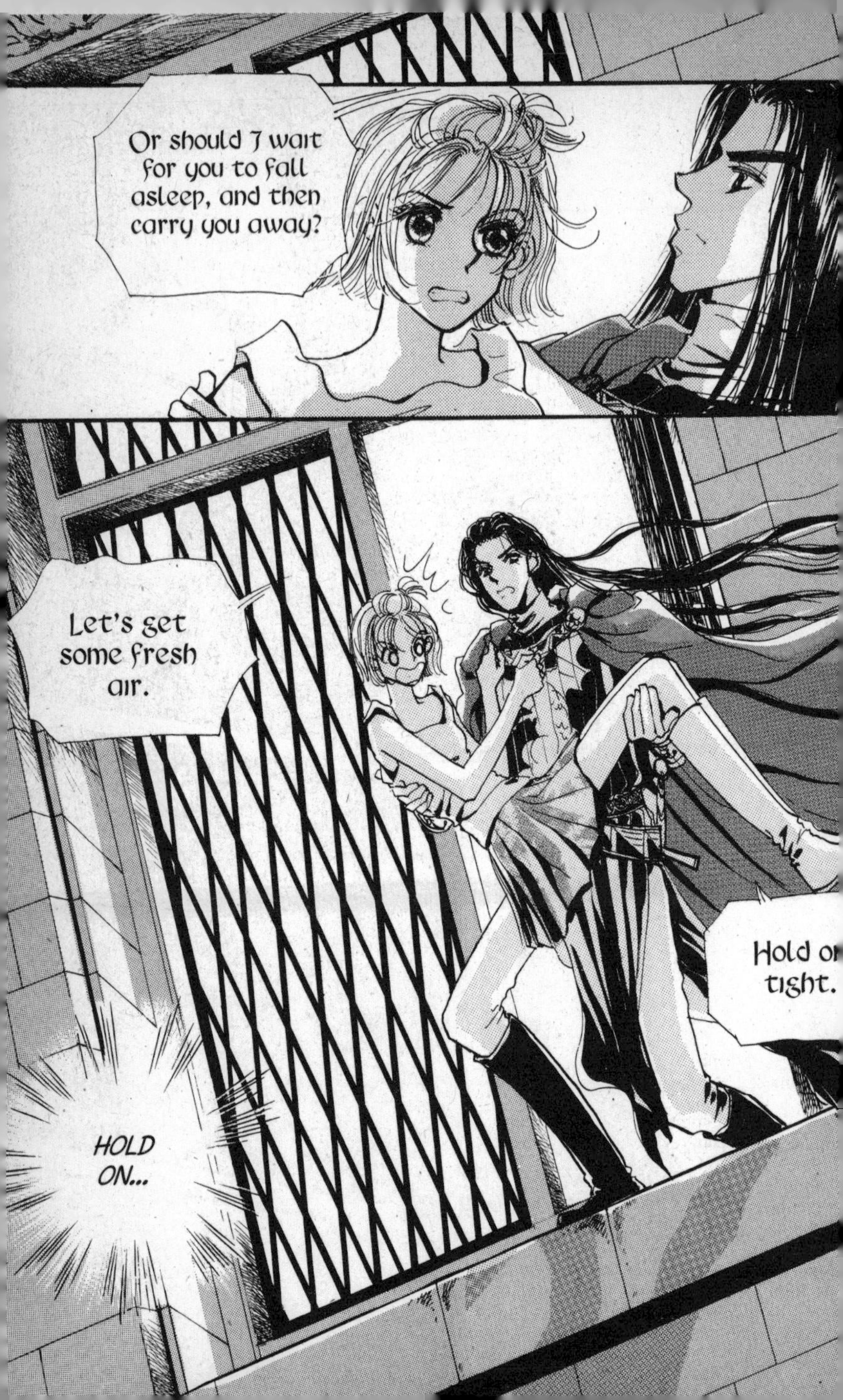
Or should I wait for you to fall asleep, and then carry you away?
Let's get some fresh air.
Hold on tight.
HOLD ON...

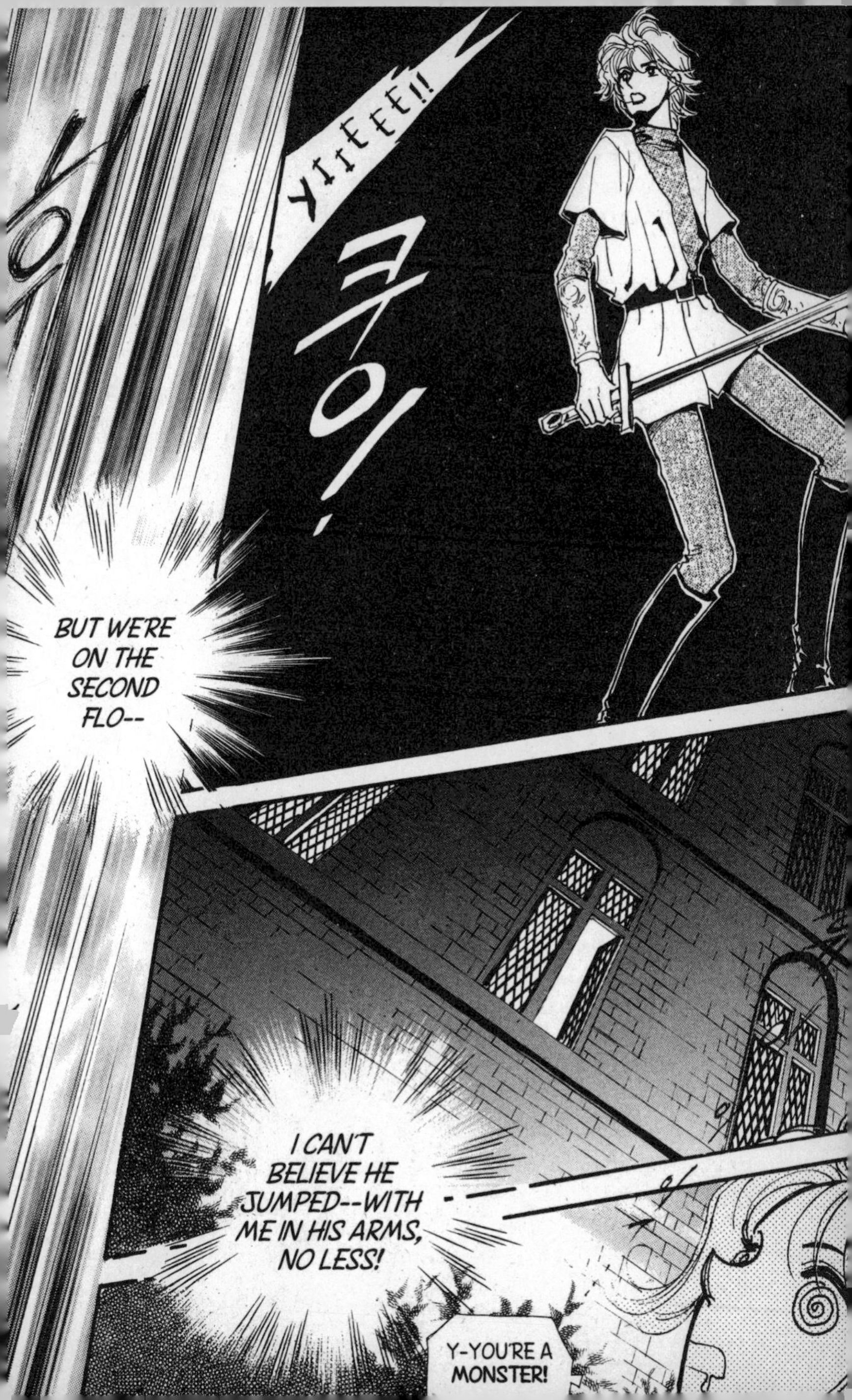
YIKEEE!!
BUT WE'RE ON THE SECOND FLO--
I CAN'T BELIEVE HE JUMPED--WITH ME IN HIS ARMS, NO LESS!
Y-YOU'RE A MONSTER!

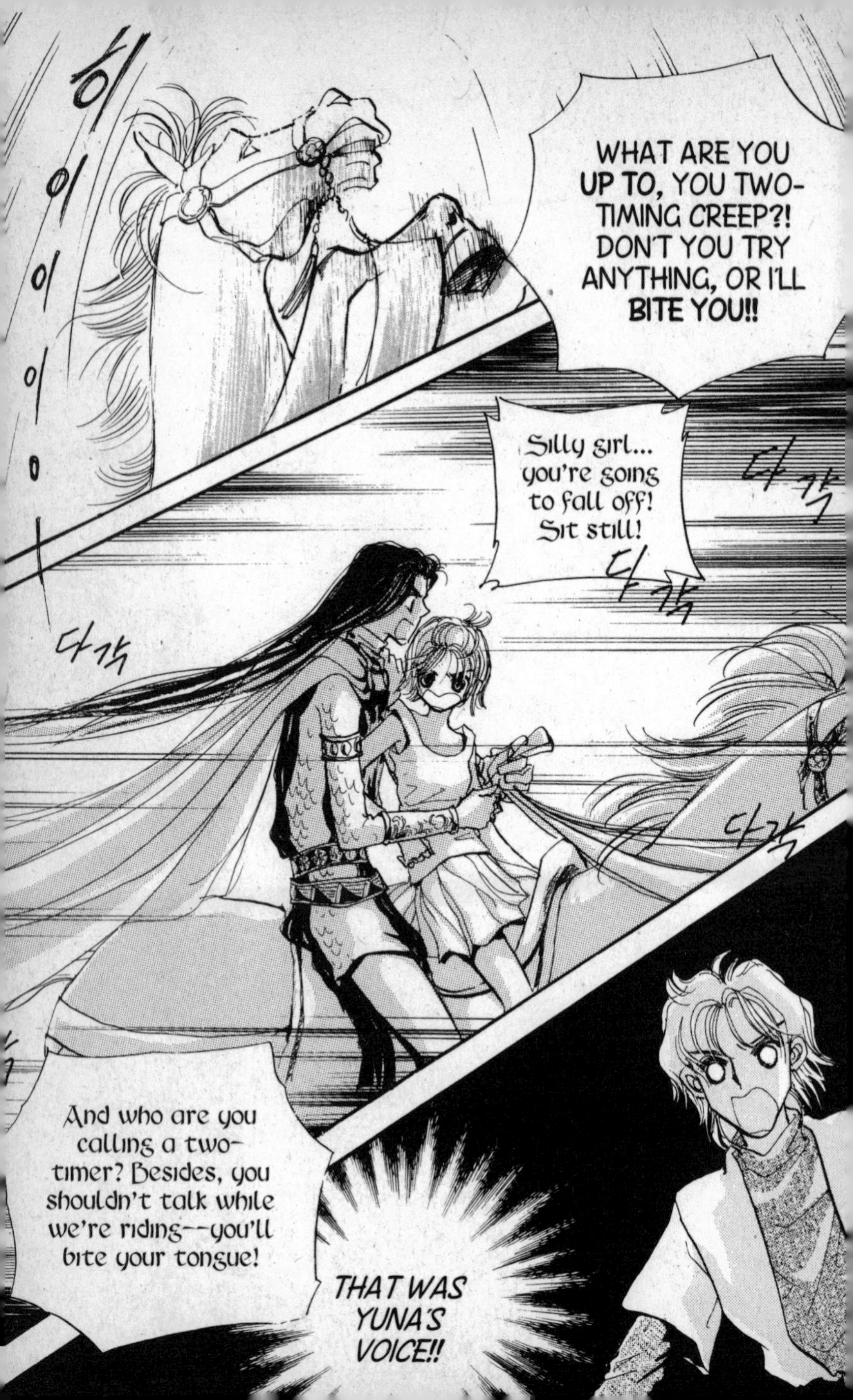
WHAT ARE YOU UP TO, YOU TWO-TIMING CREEP?! DON'T YOU TRY ANYTHING, OR I'LL BITE YOU!!
Silly girl... you're going to fall off! Sit still!
다각
다각
다각
다각
And who are you calling a two-timer? Besides, you shouldn't talk while we're riding--you'll bite your tongue!
THAT WAS YUNA'S VOICE!!

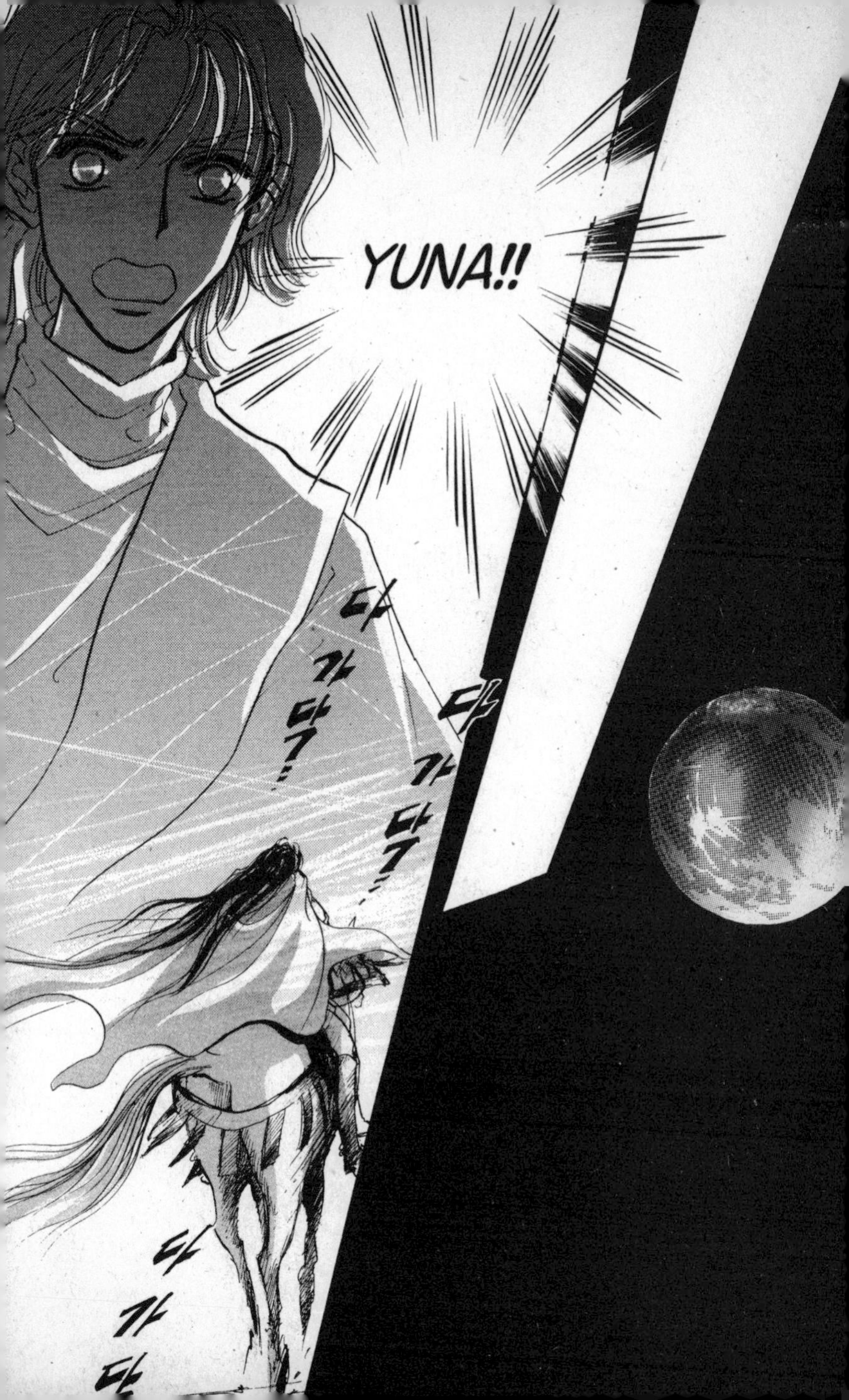
YUNA!!
다가닥..
다가닥..
다가닥

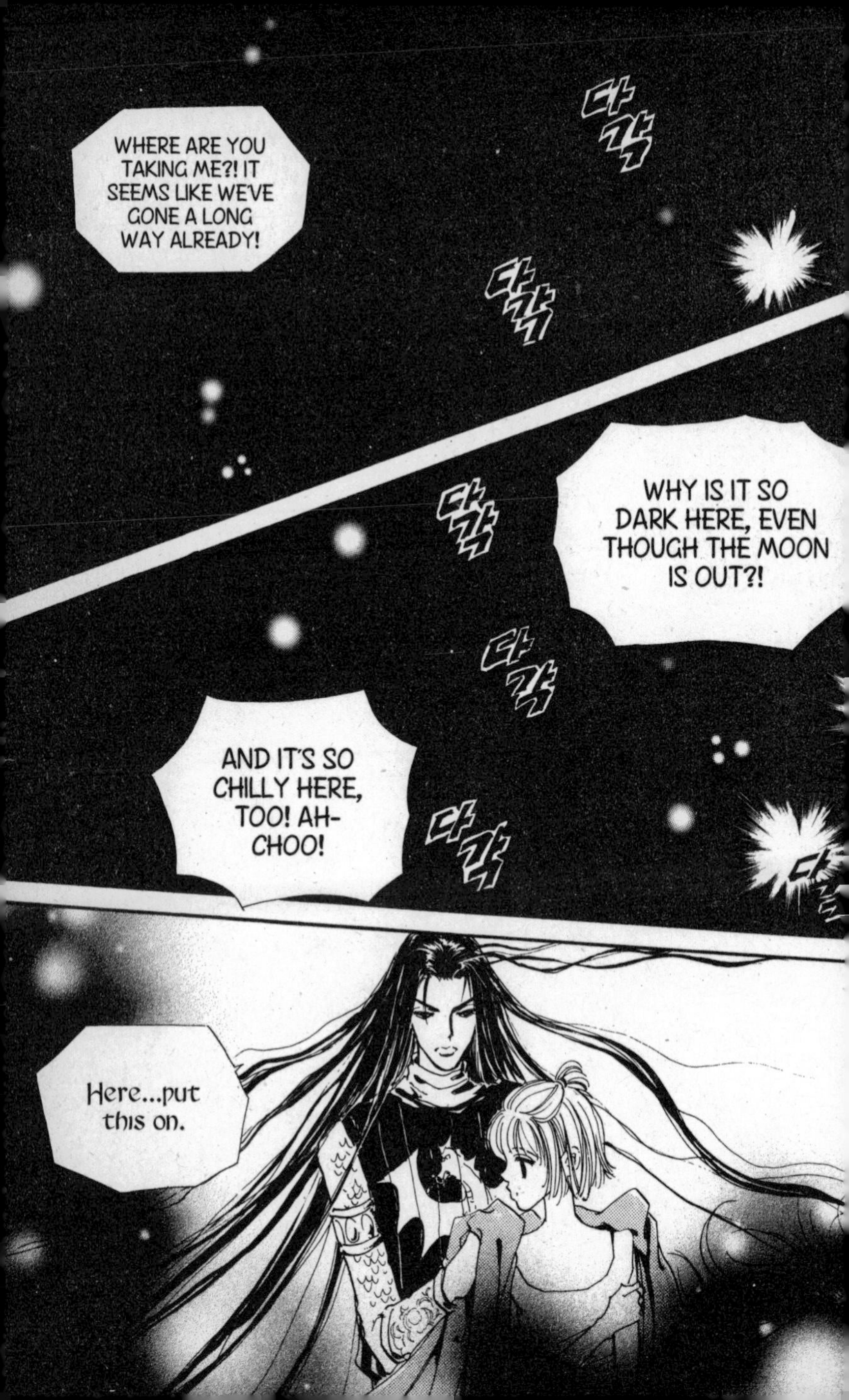
WHERE ARE YOU TAKING ME?! IT SEEMS LIKE WE'VE GONE A LONG WAY ALREADY!
WHY IS IT SO DARK HERE, EVEN THOUGH THE MOON IS OUT?!
AND IT'S SO CHILLY HERE, TOO! AH-CHOO!
Here...put this on.

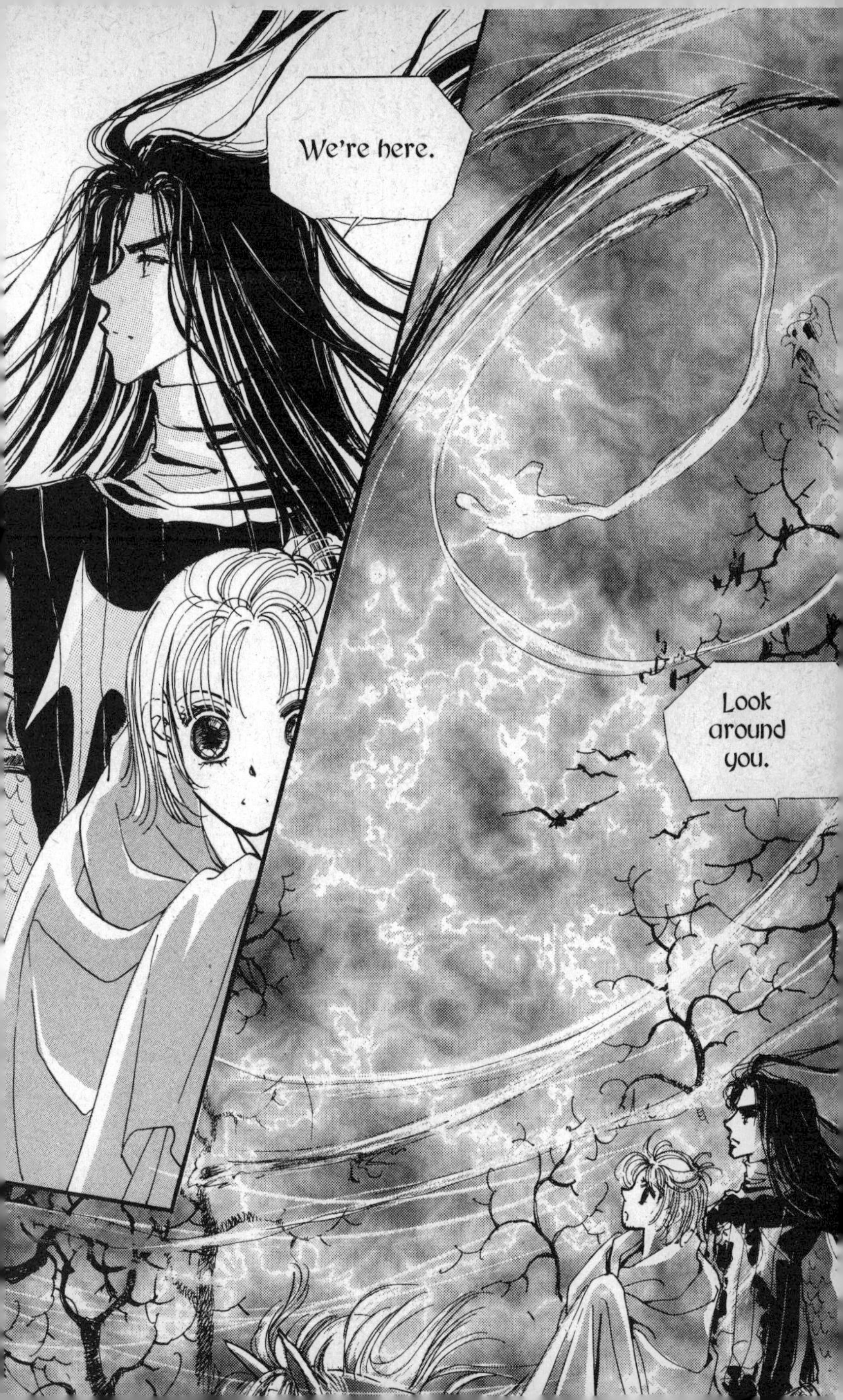
We're here.
Look around you.

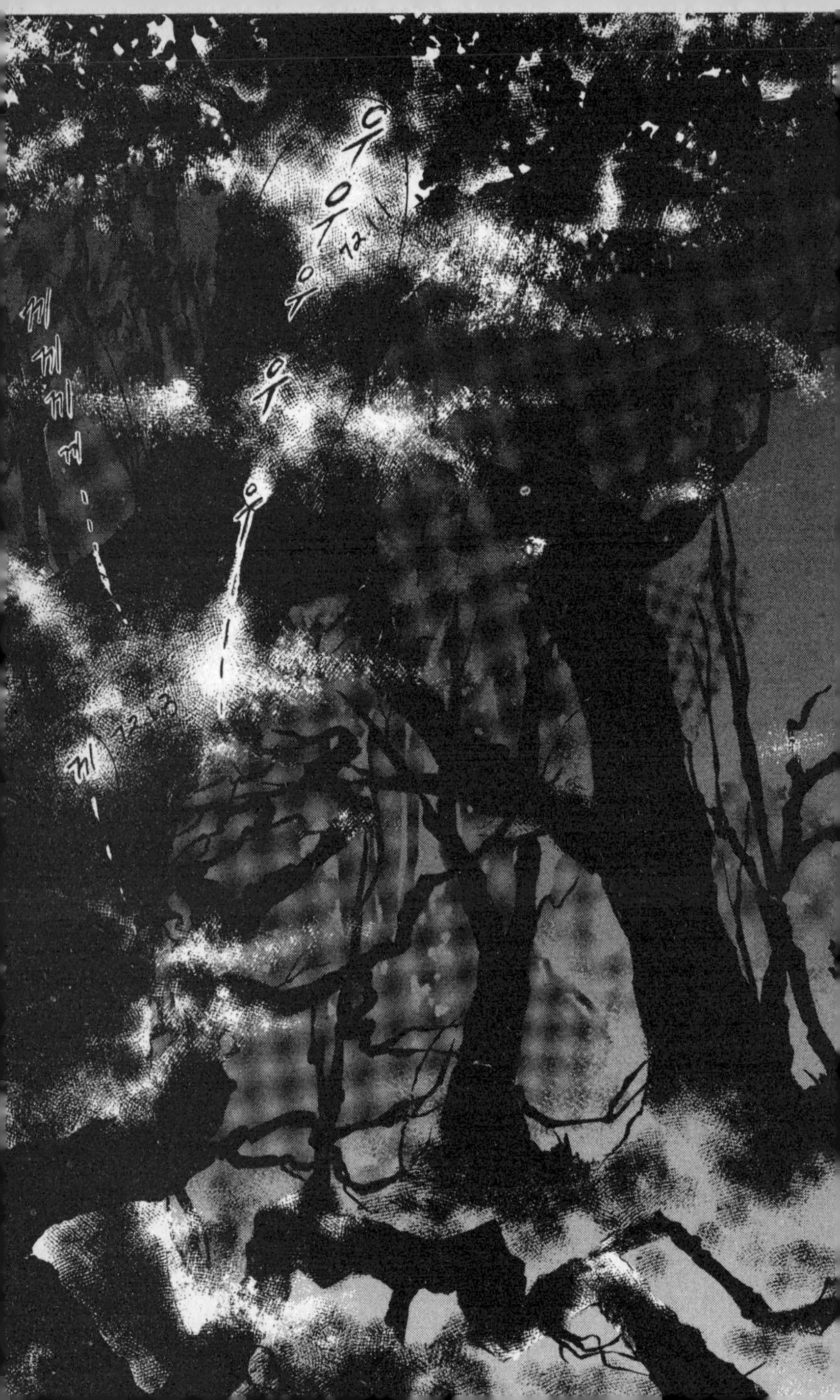

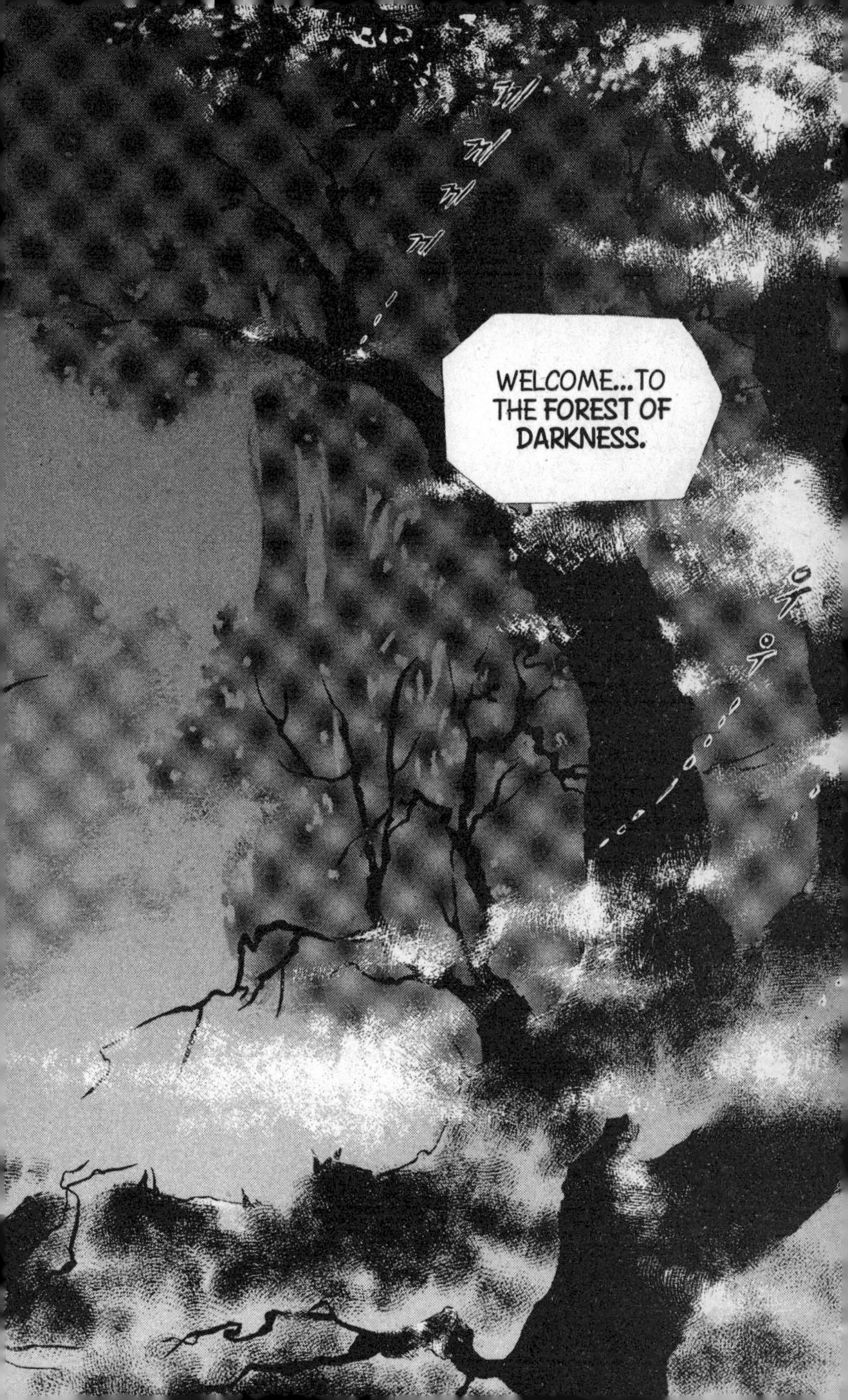
WELCOME...TO THE FOREST OF DARKNESS.

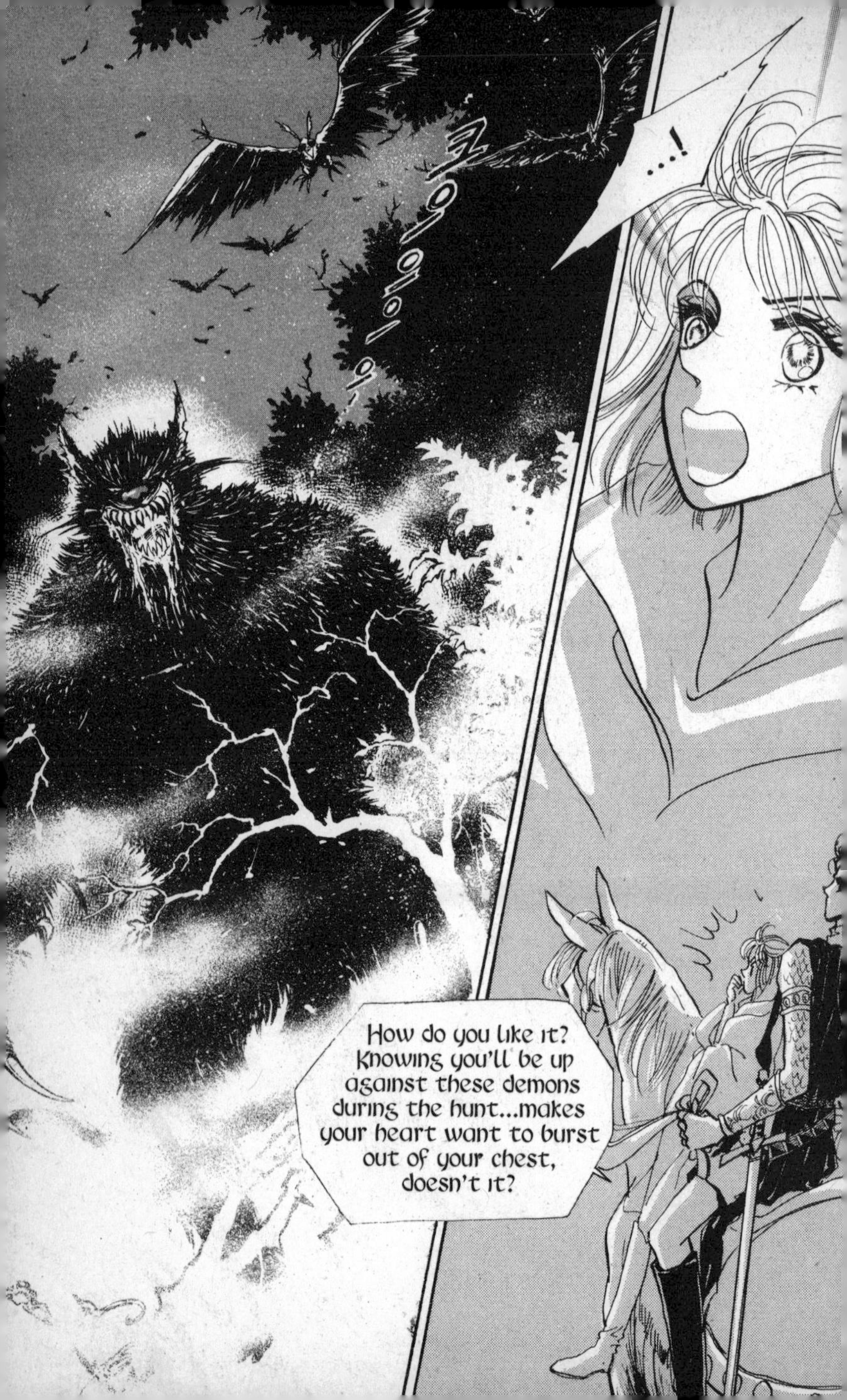
...!
How do you like it? Knowing you'll be up against these demons during the hunt...makes your heart want to burst out of your chest, doesn't it?

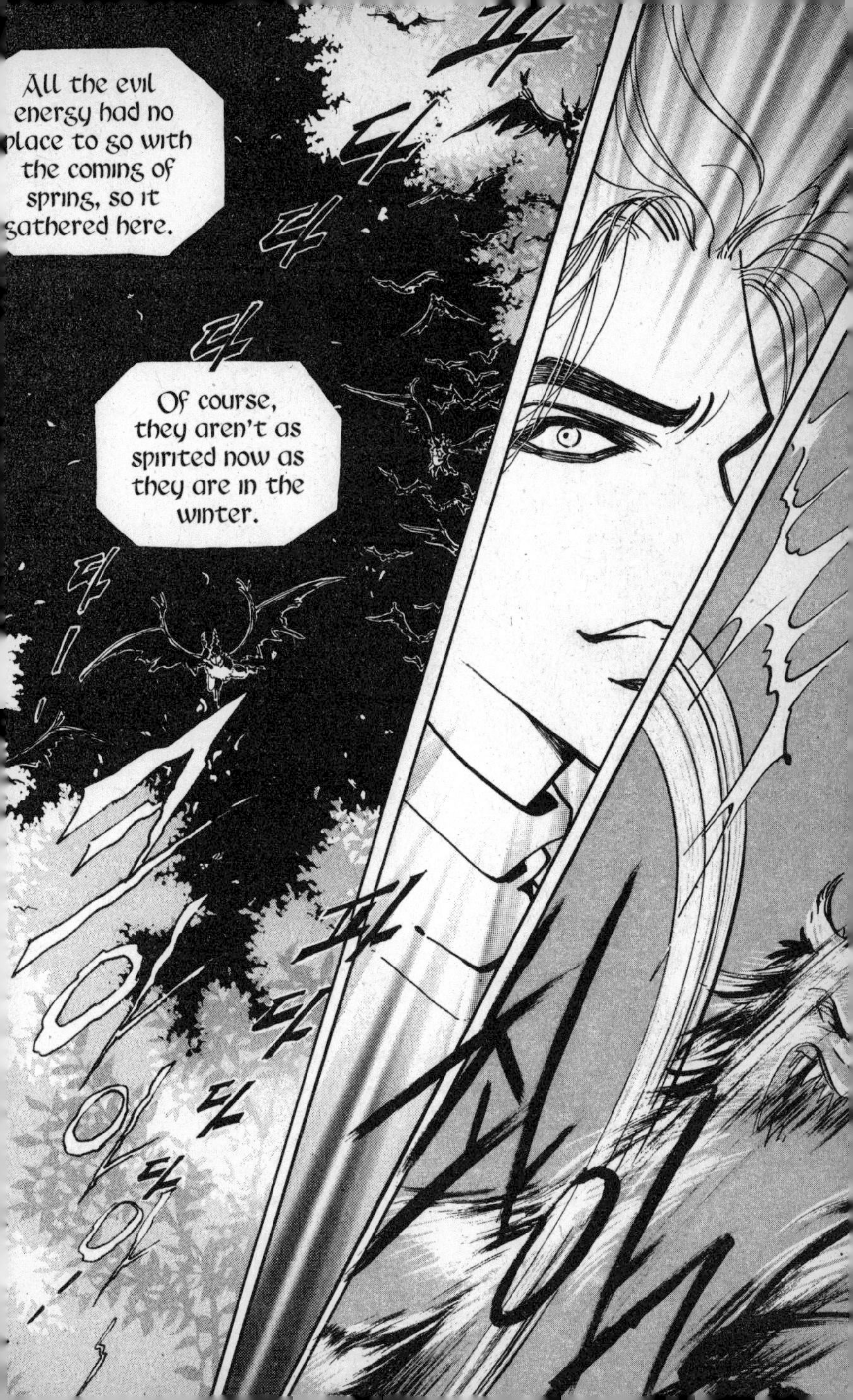
All the evil energy had no place to go with the coming of spring, so it gathered here.
Of course, they aren't as spirited now as they are in the winter.

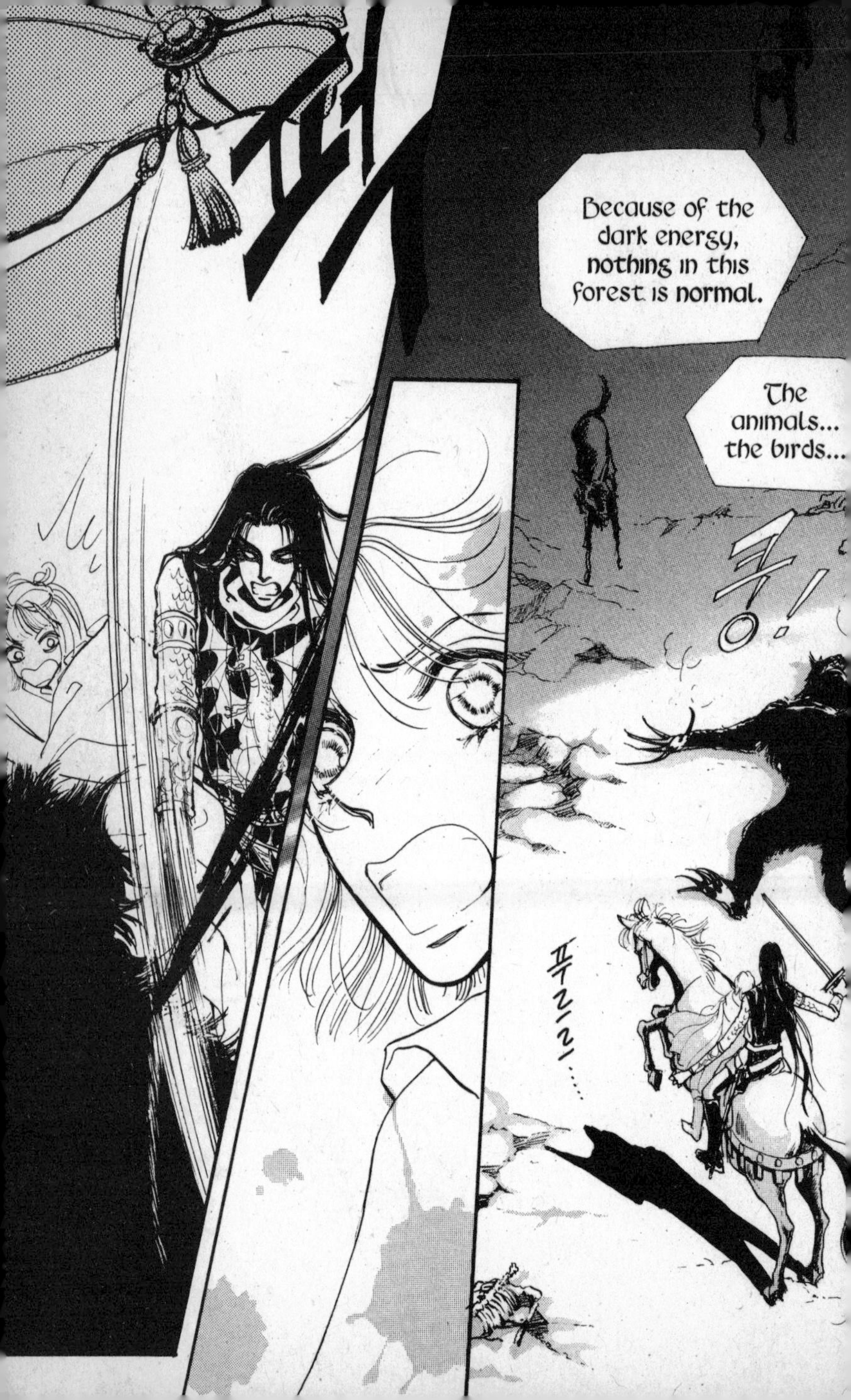
Because of the dark energy, nothing in this forest is normal.
The animals... the birds...

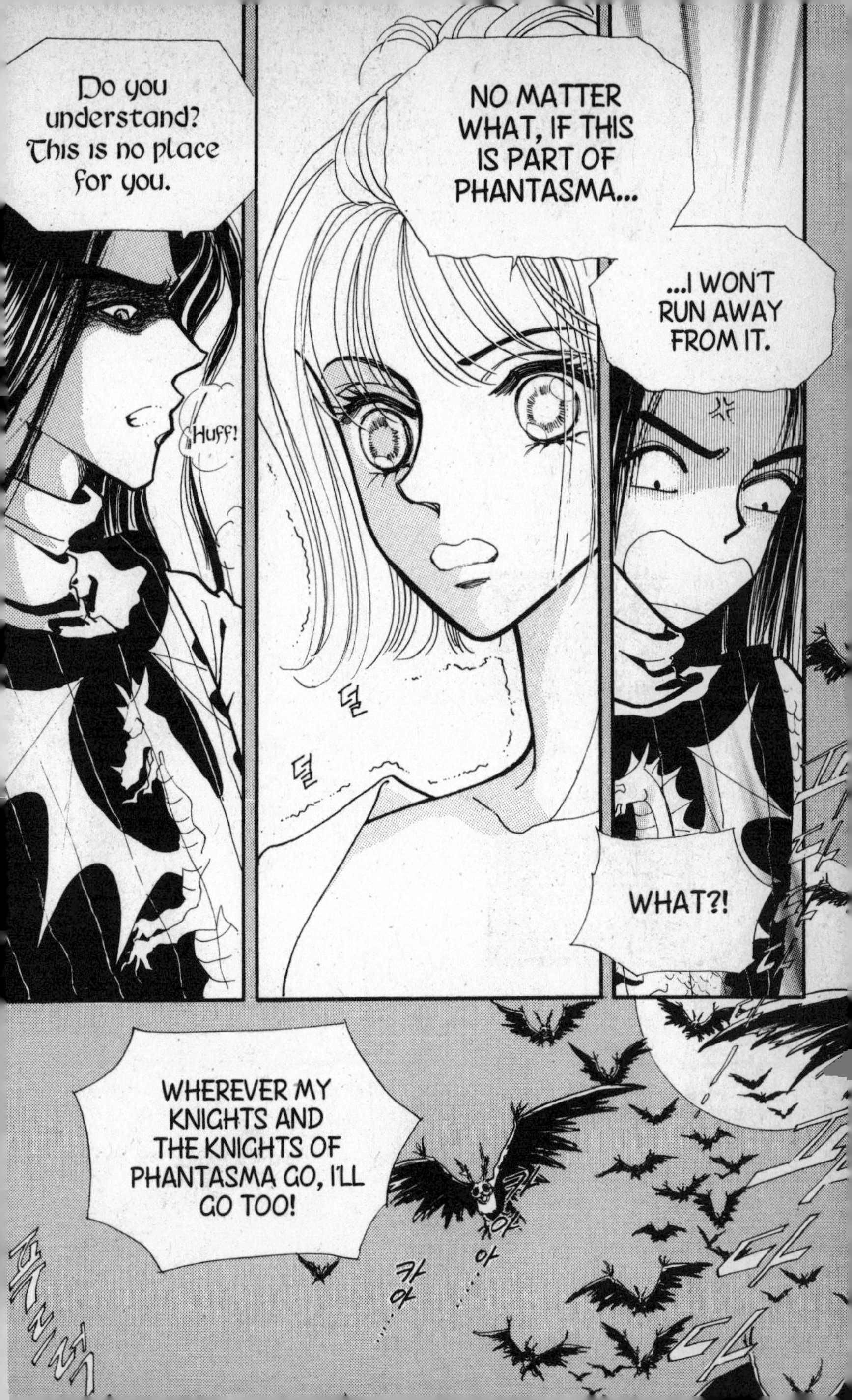
Do you understand? This is no place for you.
Huff!
NO MATTER WHAT, IF THIS IS PART OF PHANTASMA...
덜
덜
...I WON'T RUN AWAY FROM IT.
WHAT?!
WHEREVER MY KNIGHTS AND THE KNIGHTS OF PHANTASMA GO, I'LL GO TOO!

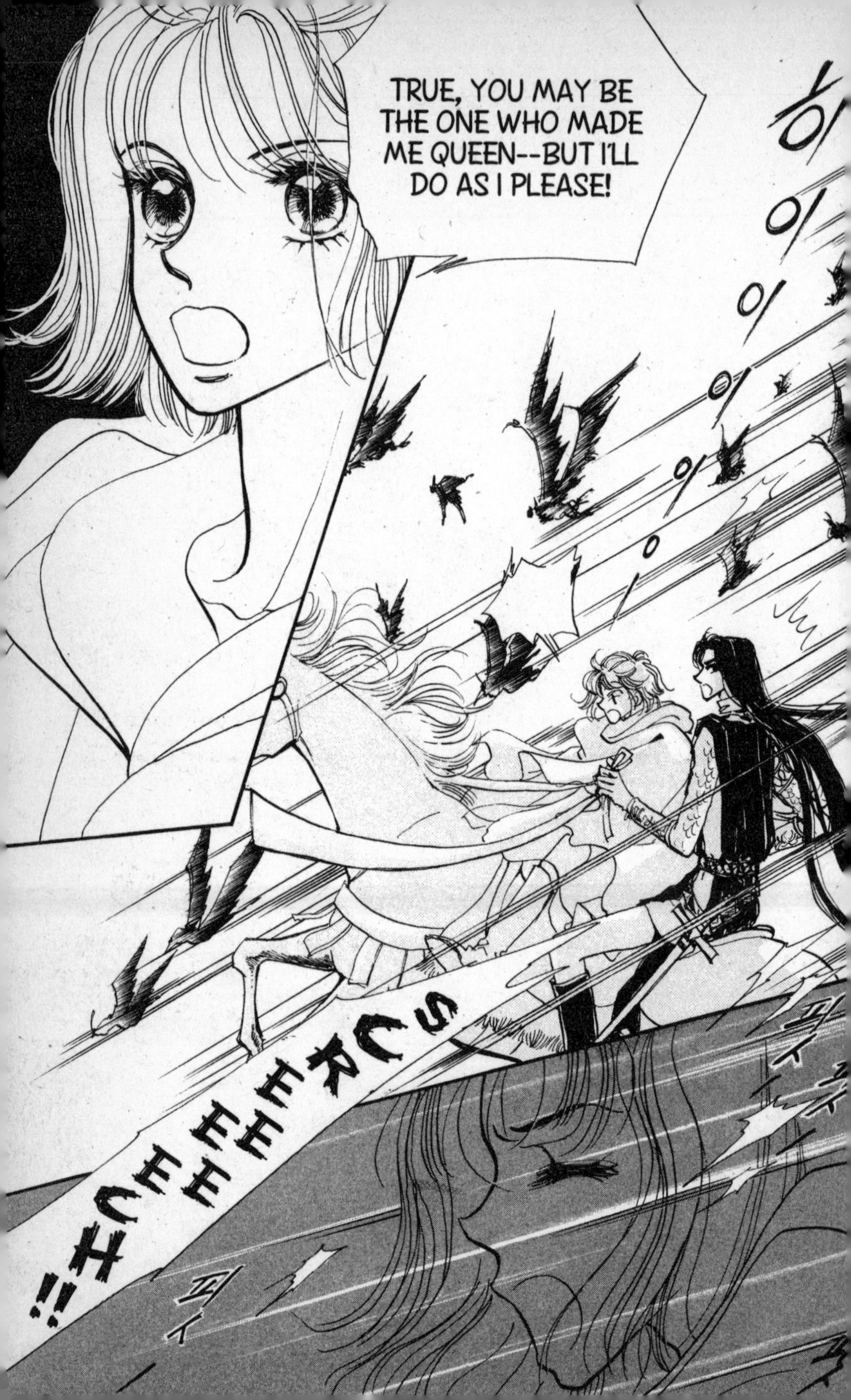
TRUE, YOU MAY BE THE ONE WHO MADE ME QUEEN--BUT I'LL DO AS I PLEASE!
SCREEEECH!!

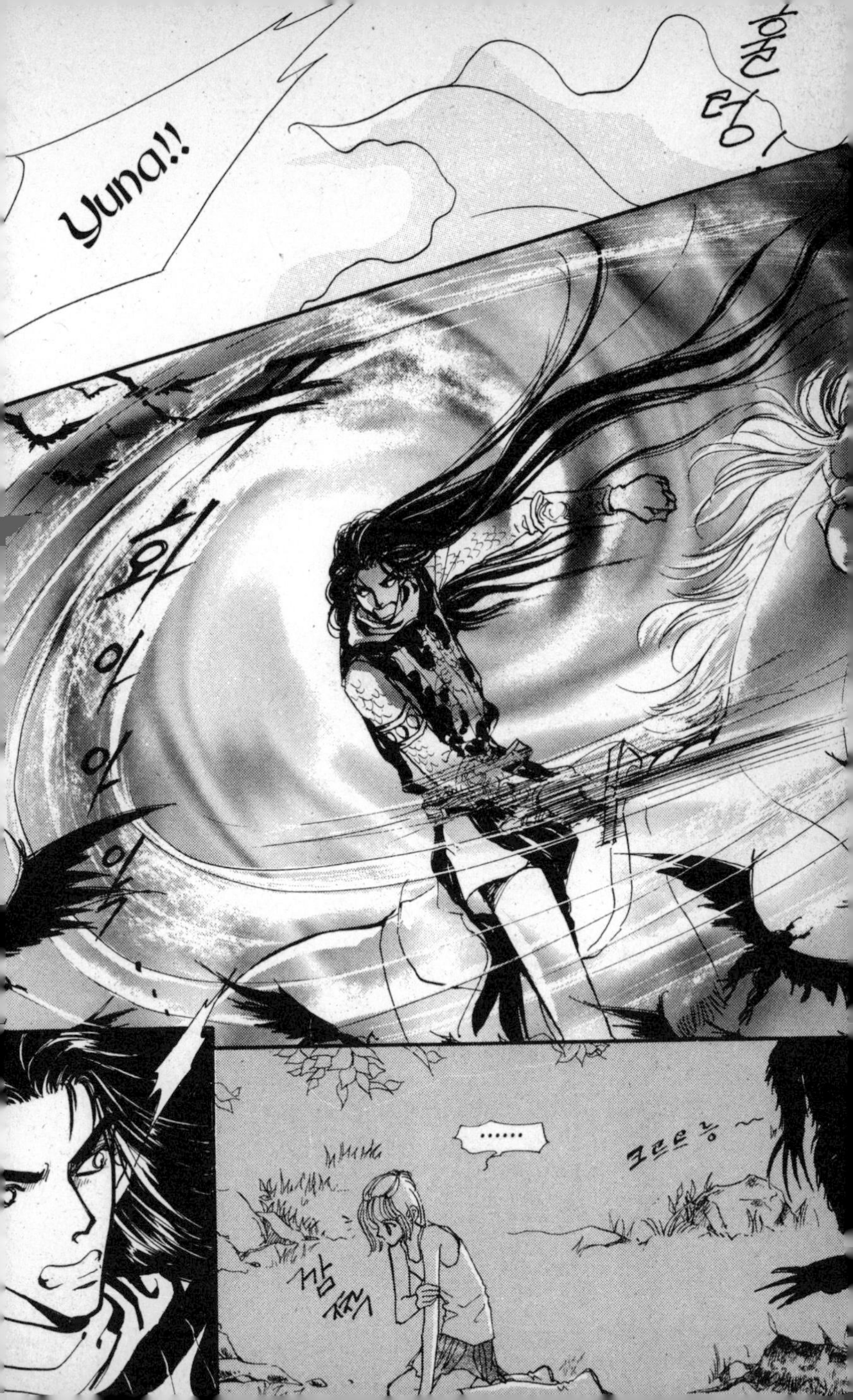
Yuna!!
훌렁!
......
크르르릉~
깜짝

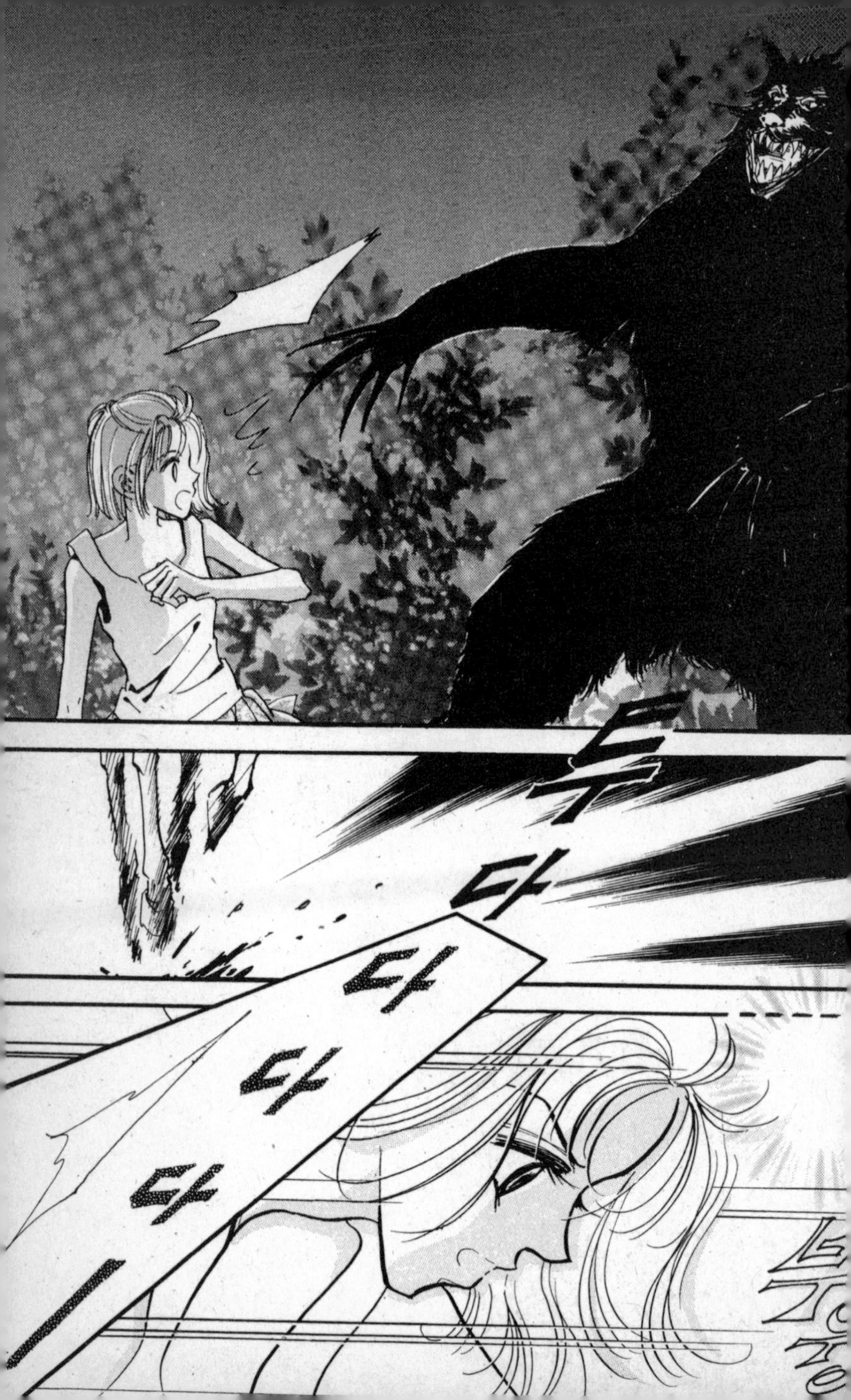
두다다다다ㅡ

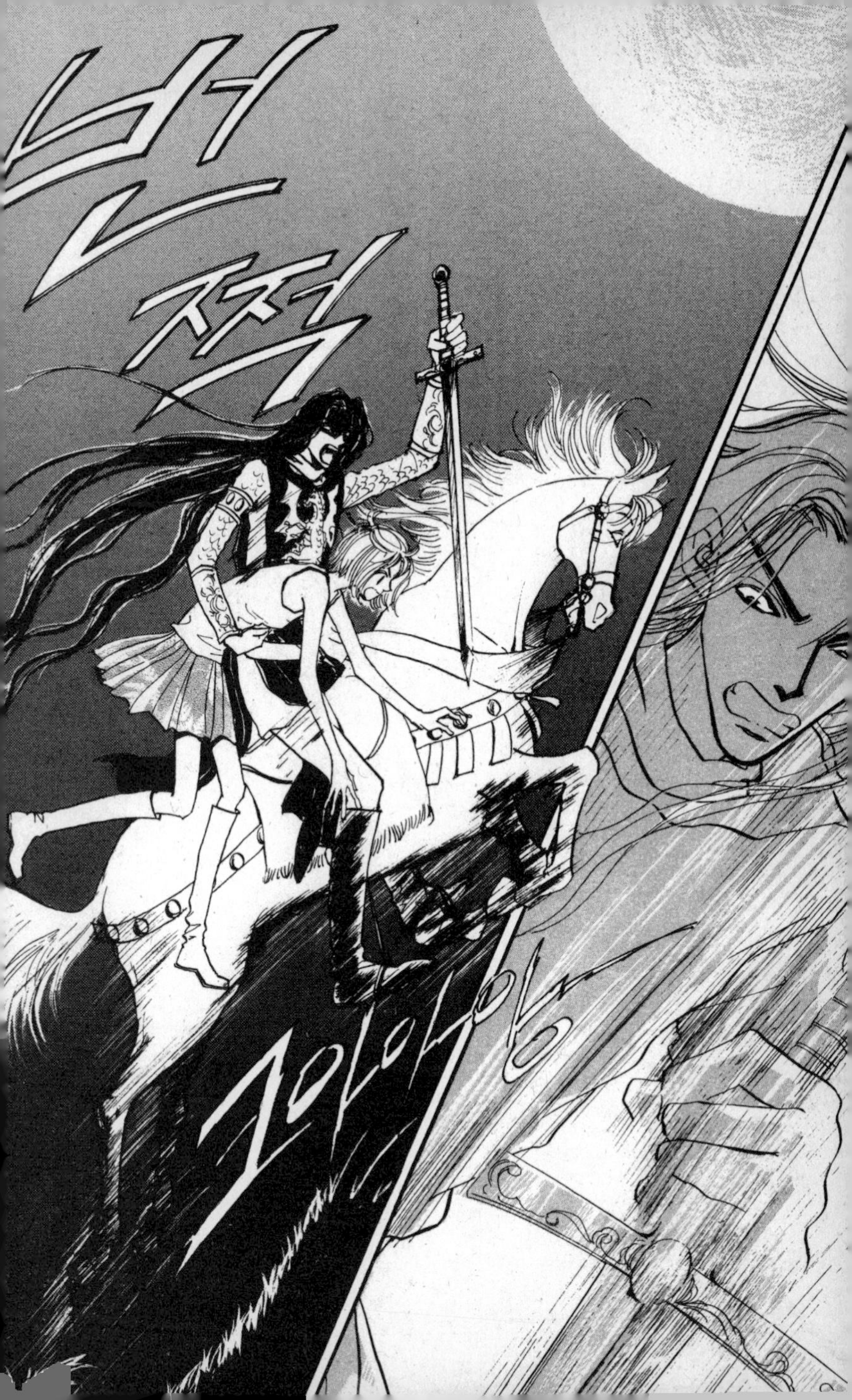

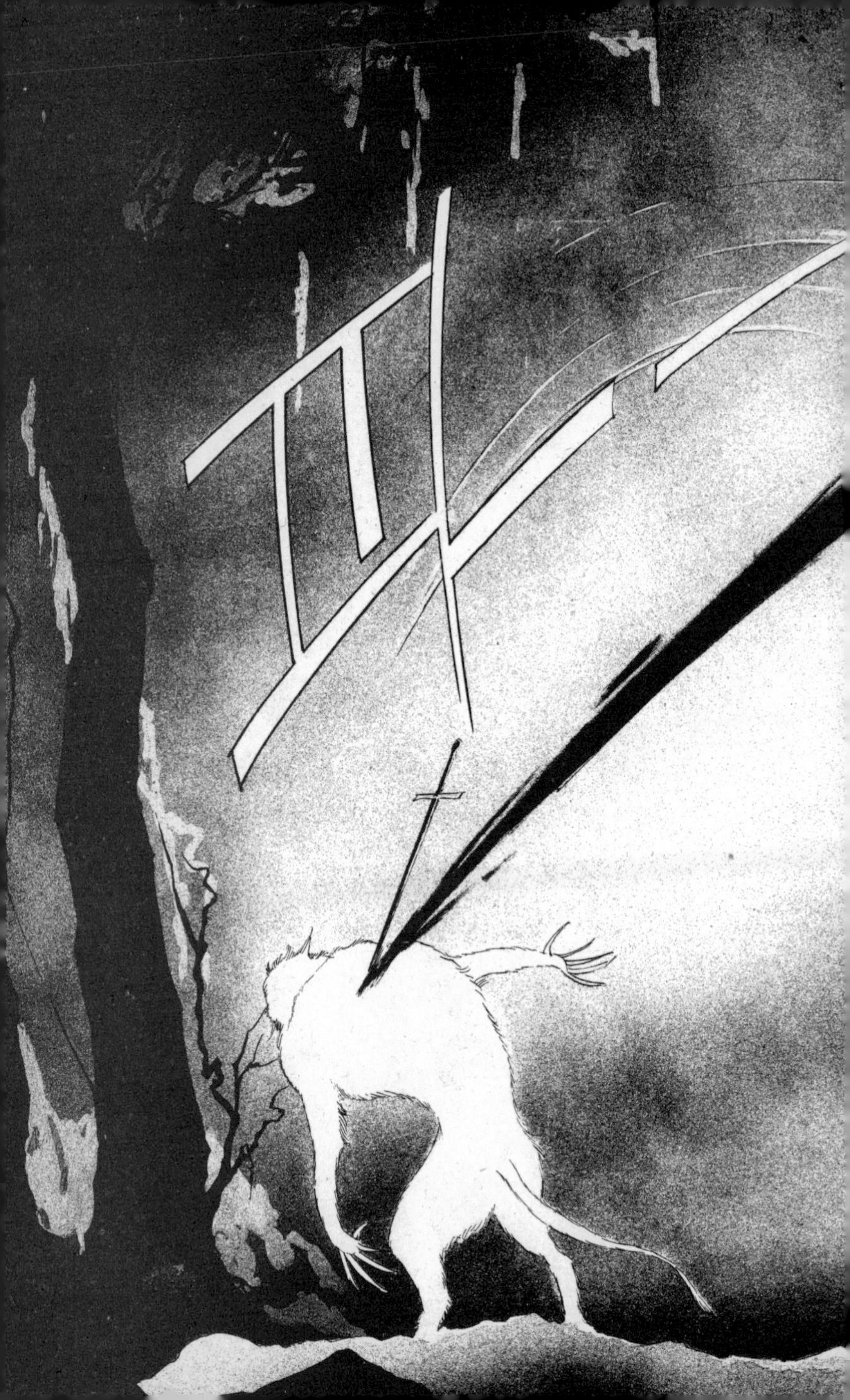

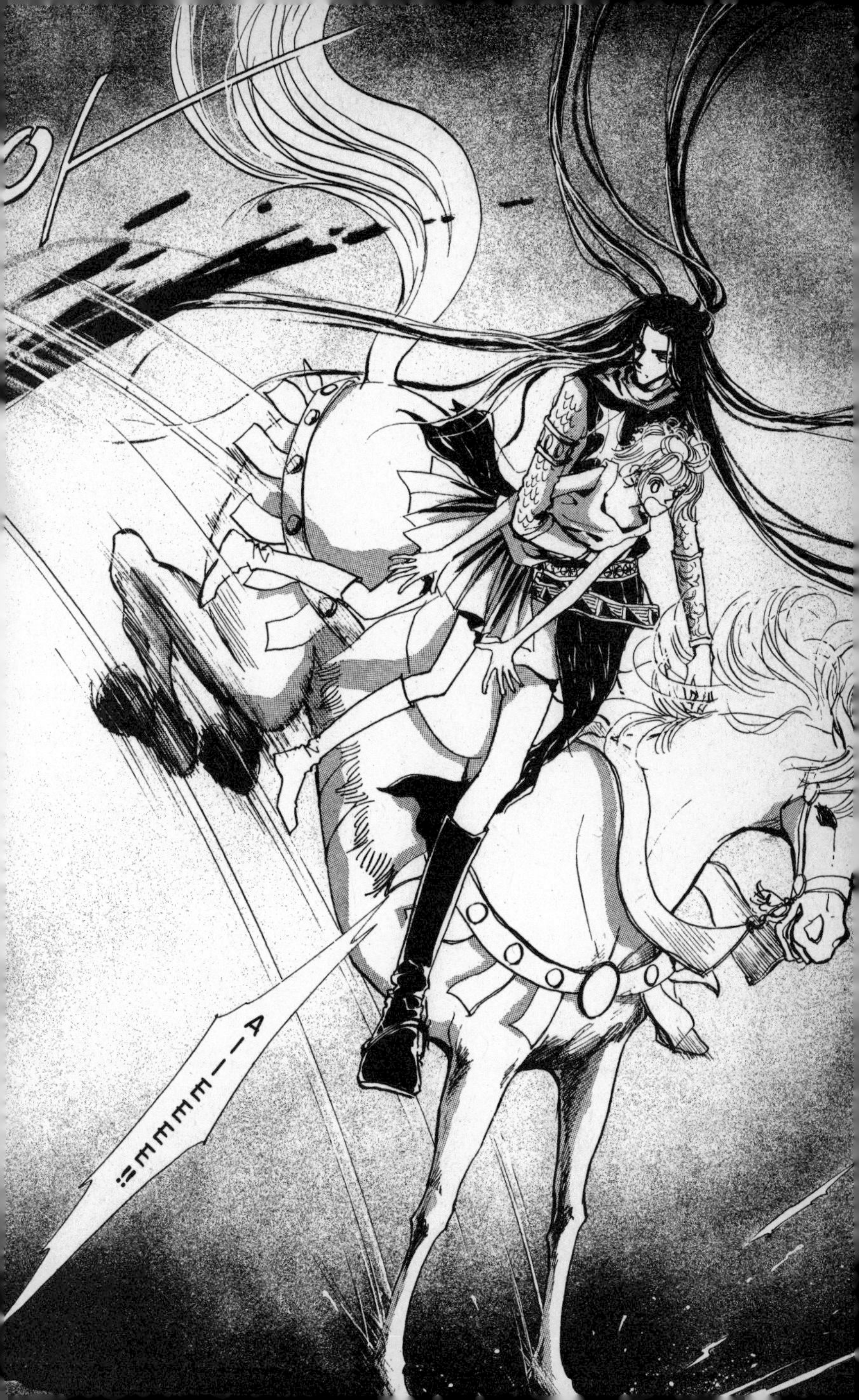
A—EEEEE!!

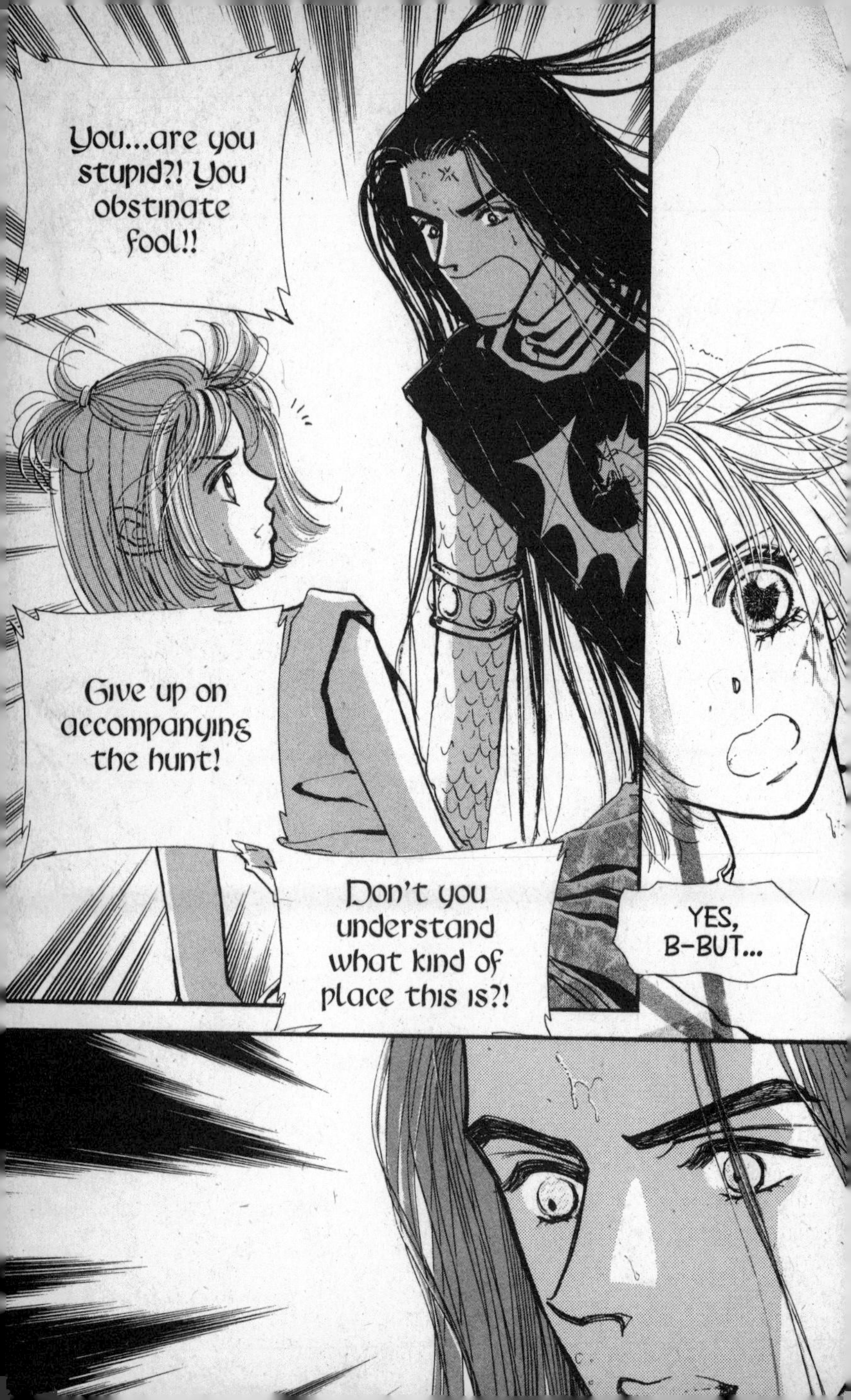
You...are you stupid?! You obstinate fool!!
Give up on accompanying the hunt!
Don't you understand what kind of place this is?!
YES, B-BUT...

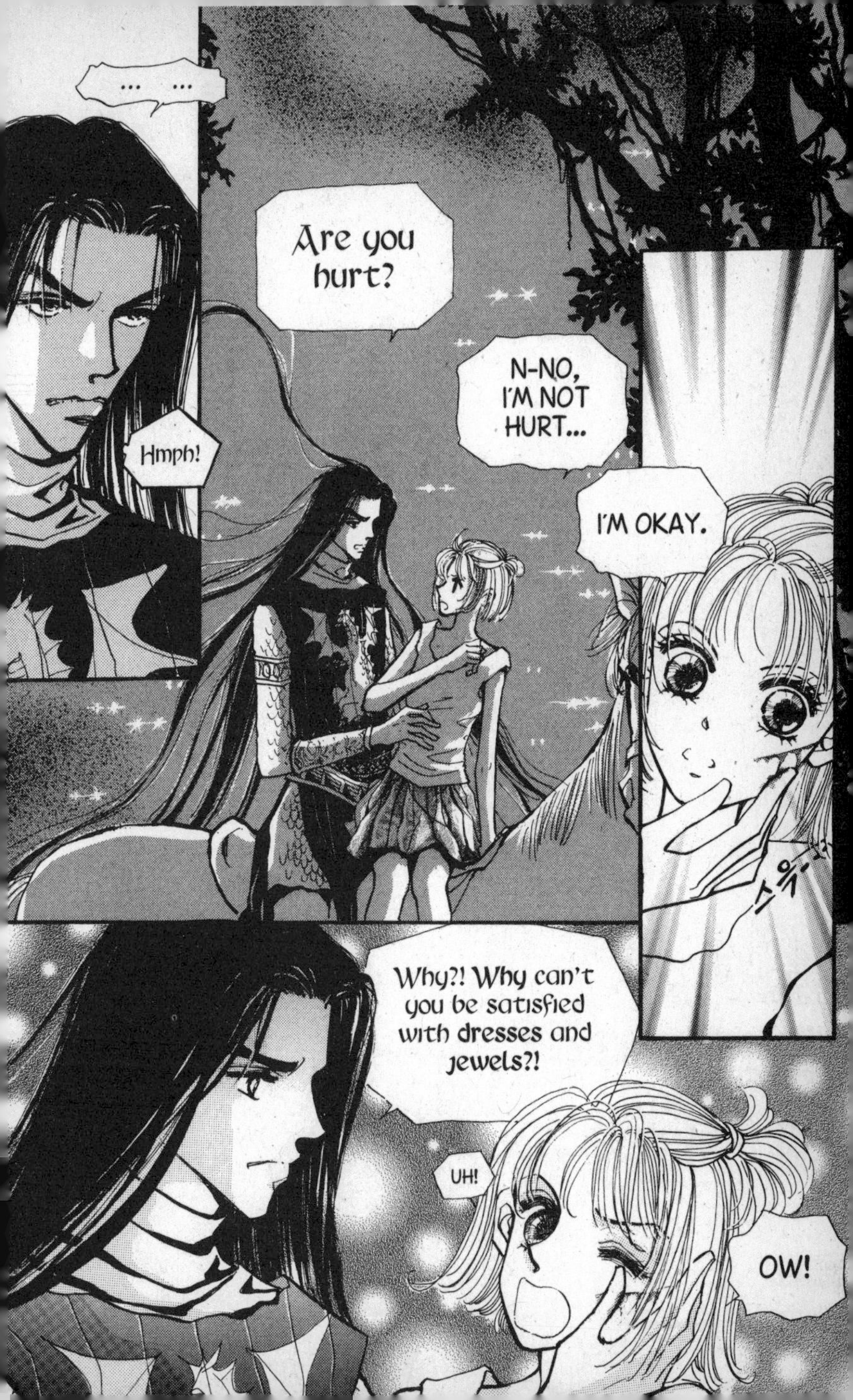
... ...
Hmph!
Are you hurt?
N-NO, I'M NOT HURT...
I'M OKAY.
Why?! Why can't you be satisfied with dresses and jewels?!
UH!
OW!

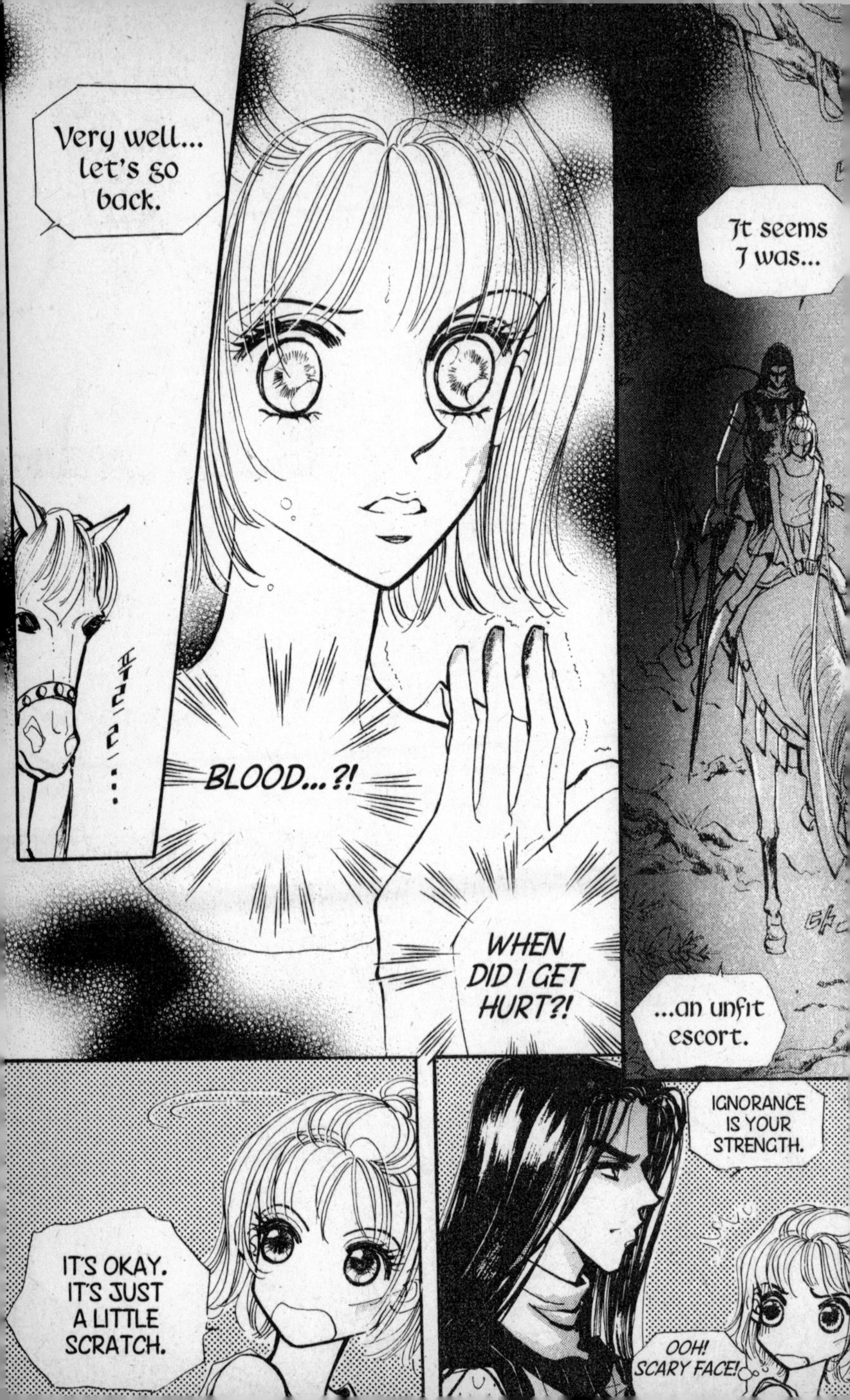
Very well... let's go back.
BLOOD...?!
WHEN DID I GET HURT?!
It seems I was...
...an unfit escort.
IT'S OKAY. IT'S JUST A LITTLE SCRATCH.
IGNORANCE IS YOUR STRENGTH.
OOH! SCARY FACE!

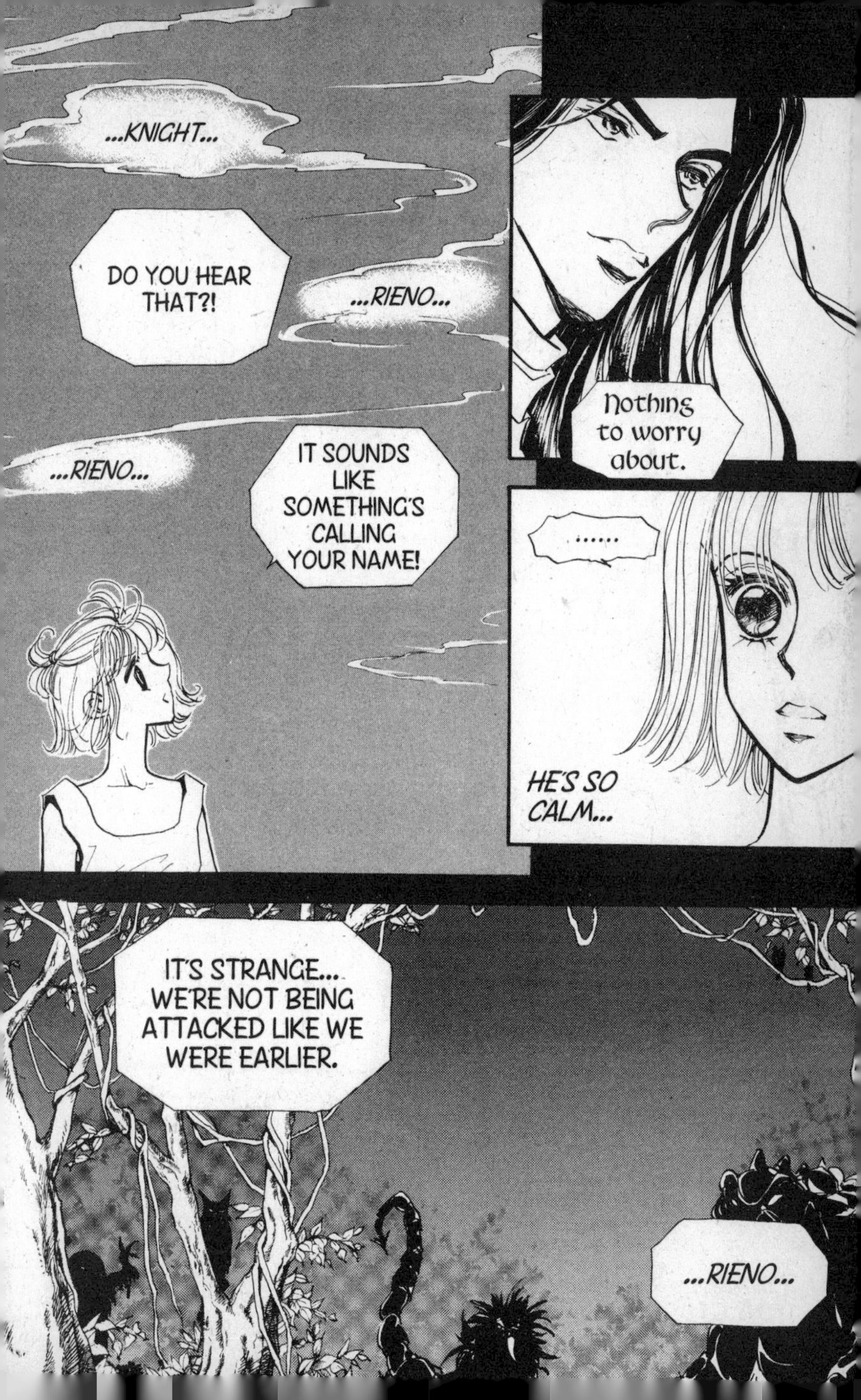
...KNIGHT...
DO YOU HEAR THAT?!
...RIENO...
...RIENO...
IT SOUNDS LIKE SOMETHING'S CALLING YOUR NAME!
Nothing to worry about.
......
HE'S SO CALM...
IT'S STRANGE... WE'RE NOT BEING ATTACKED LIKE WE WERE EARLIER.
...RIENO...

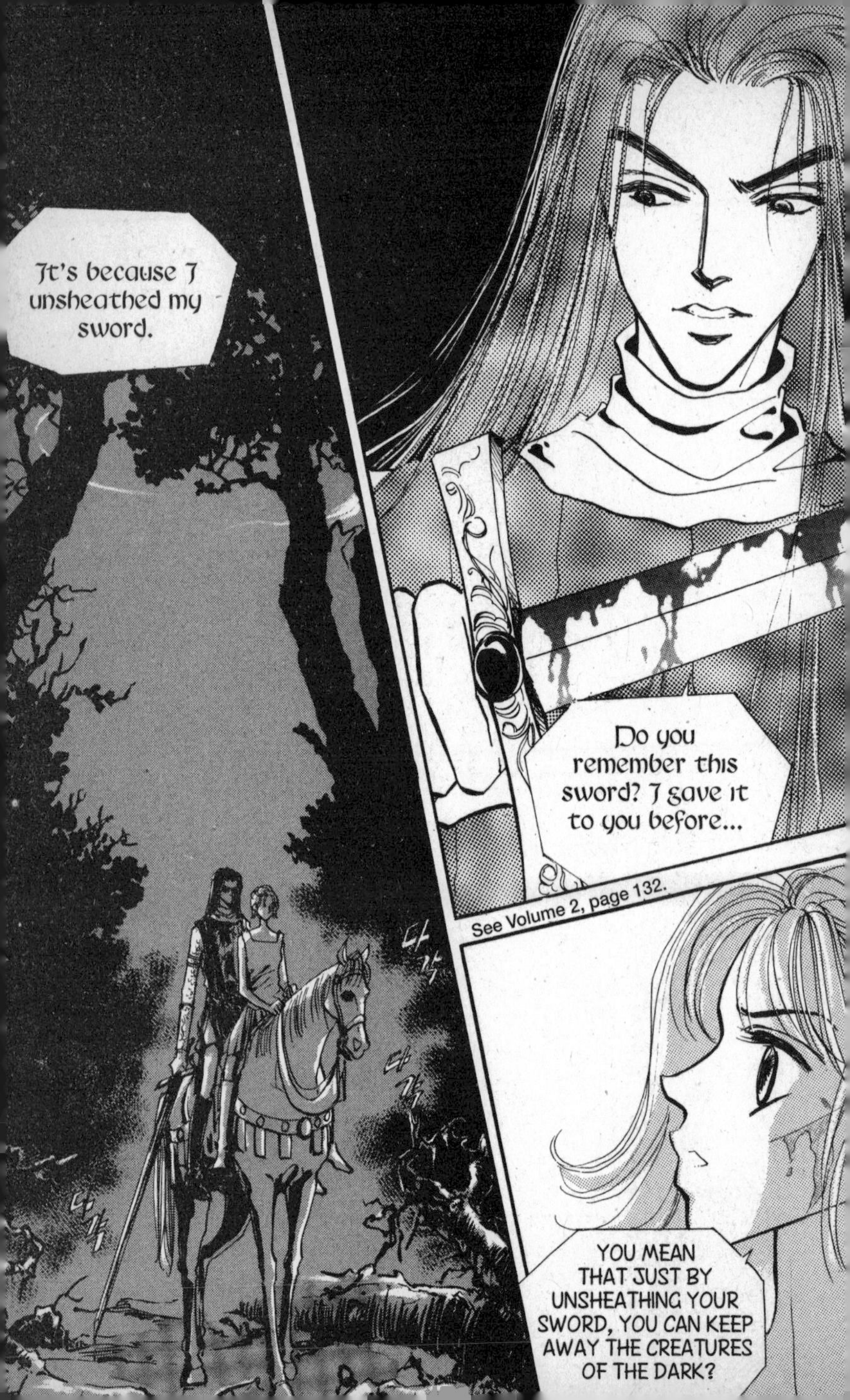
It's because I unsheathed my sword.
Do you remember this sword? I gave it to you before...
See Volume 2, page 132.
YOU MEAN THAT JUST BY UNSHEATHING YOUR SWORD, YOU CAN KEEP AWAY THE CREATURES OF THE DARK?

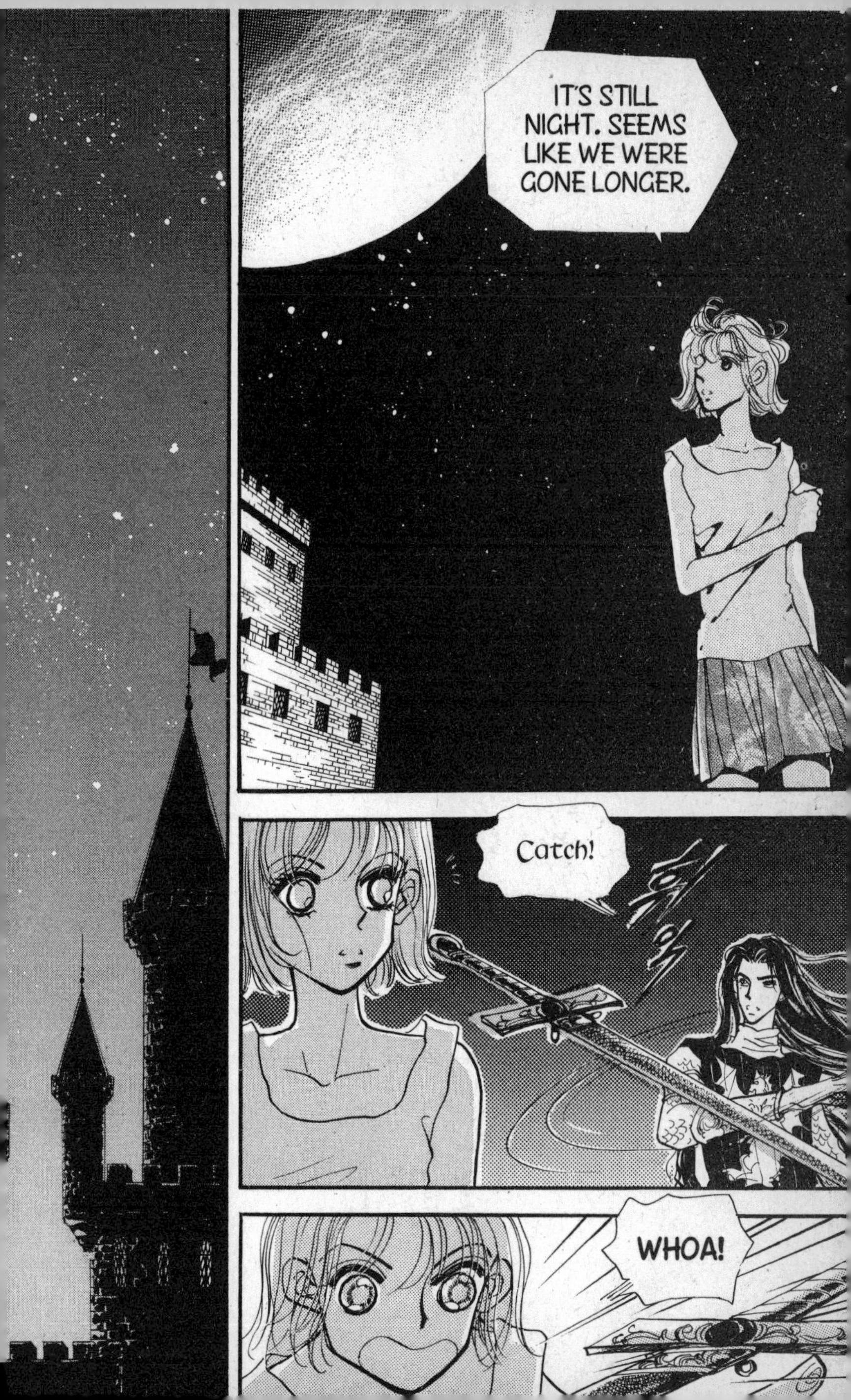
IT'S STILL NIGHT. SEEMS LIKE WE WERE GONE LONGER.
Catch!
WHOA!

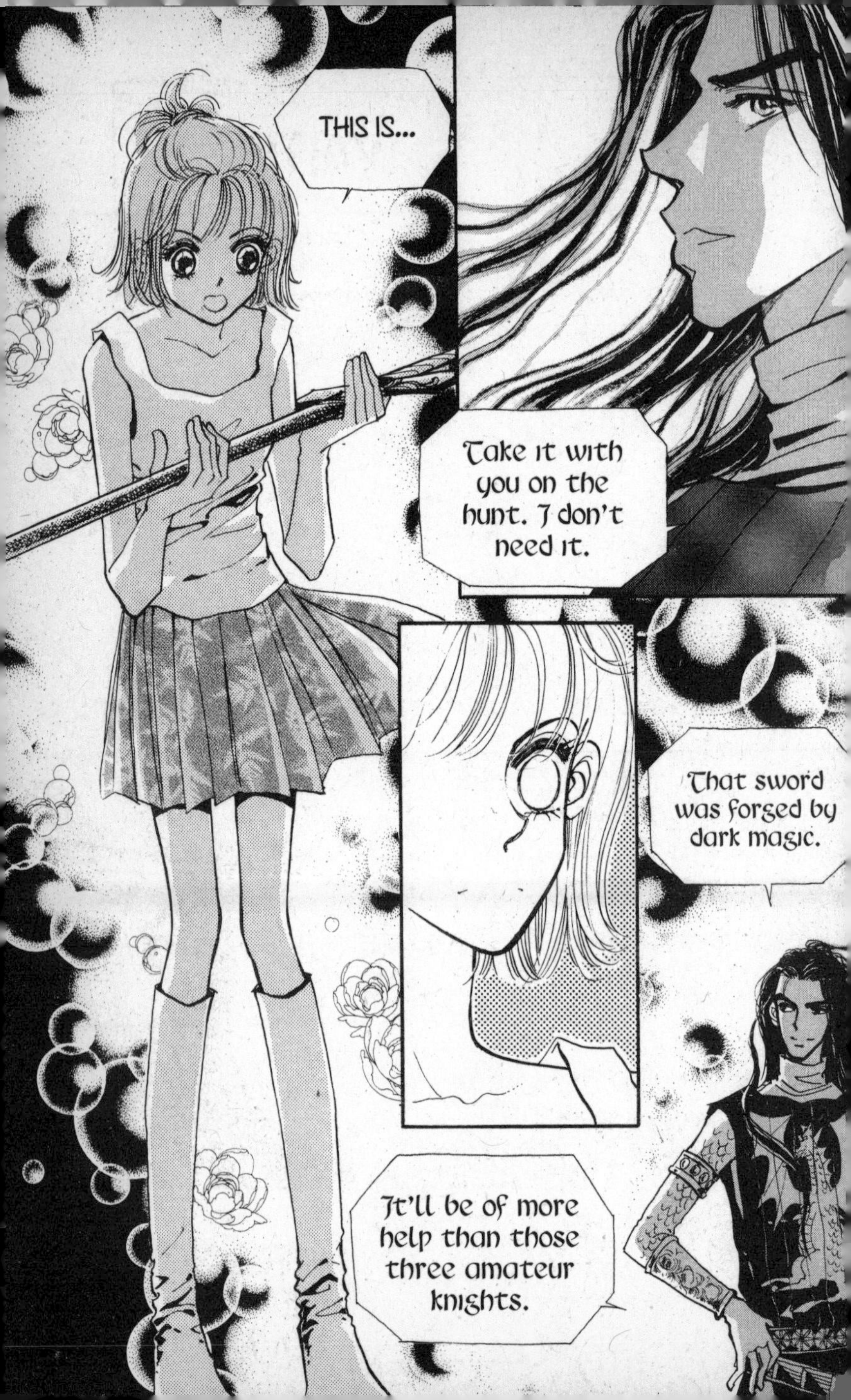
THIS IS...
Take it with you on the hunt. I don't need it.
That sword was forged by dark magic.
It'll be of more help than those three amateur knights.

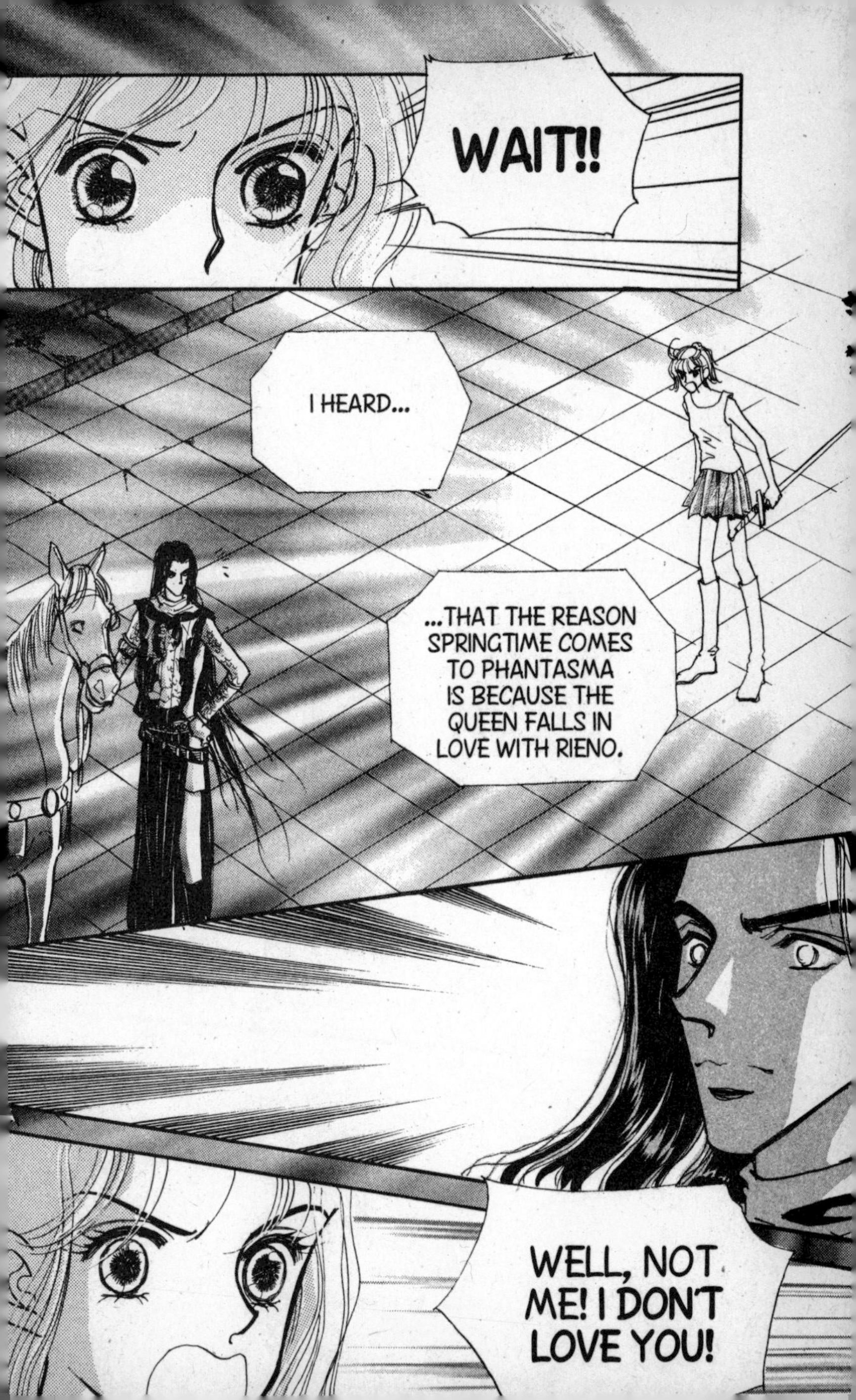
WAIT!!
I HEARD...
...THAT THE REASON SPRINGTIME COMES TO PHANTASMA IS BECAUSE THE QUEEN FALLS IN LOVE WITH RIENO.
WELL, NOT ME! I DON'T LOVE YOU!

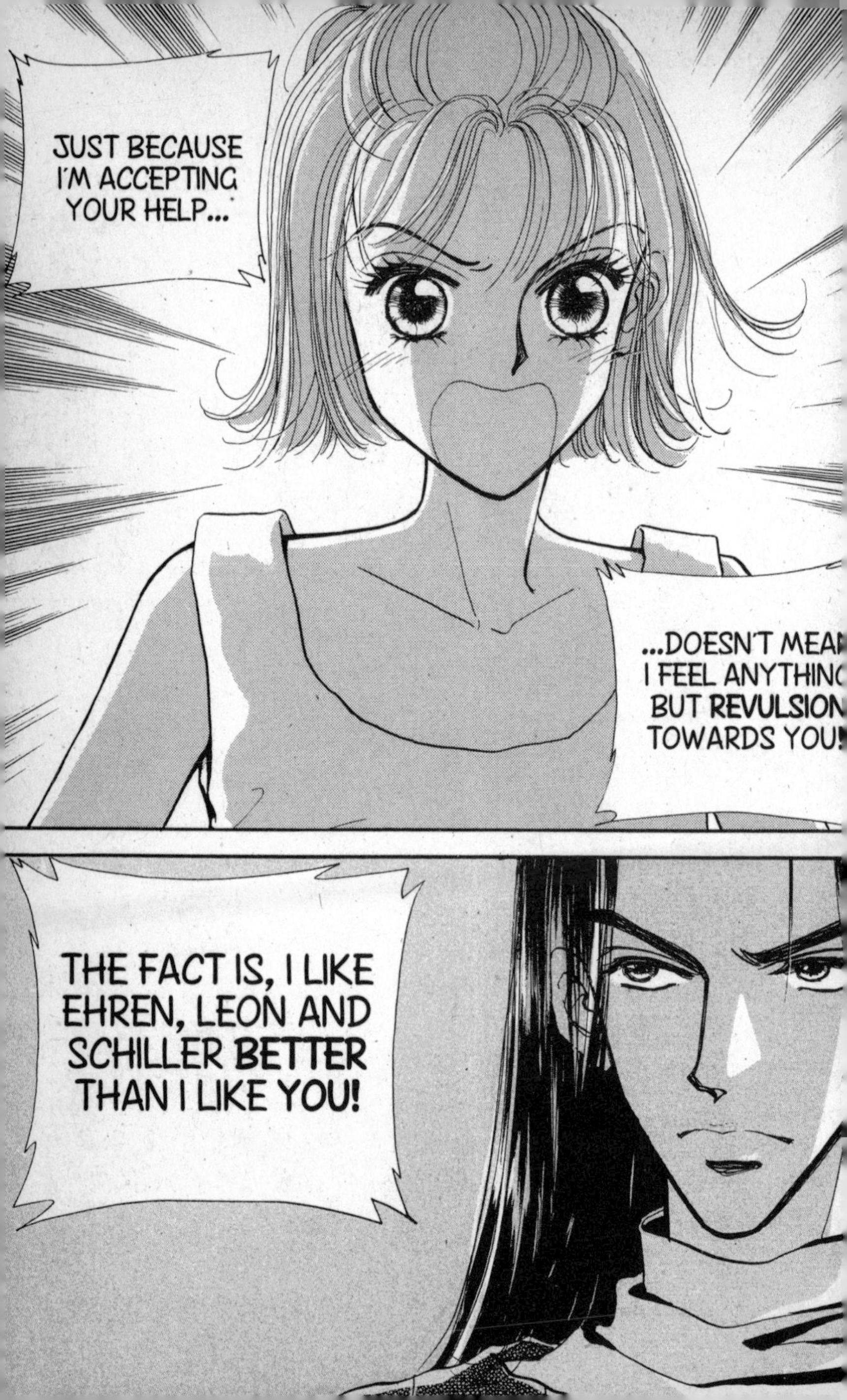
JUST BECAUSE I'M ACCEPTING YOUR HELP...
...DOESN'T MEAN I FEEL ANYTHING BUT REVULSION TOWARDS YOU!
THE FACT IS, I LIKE EHREN, LEON AND SCHILLER BETTER THAN I LIKE YOU!

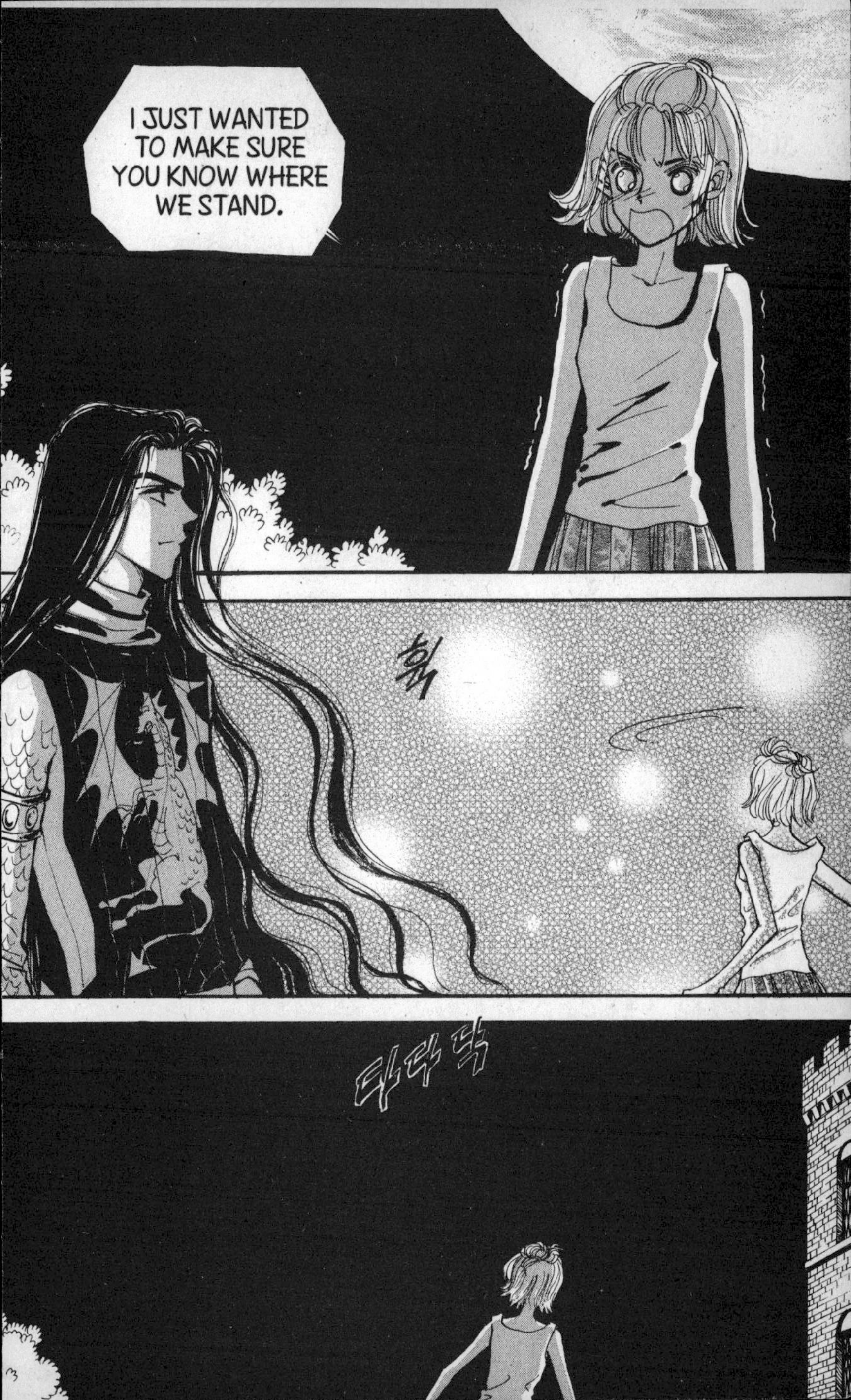
I JUST WANTED TO MAKE SURE YOU KNOW WHERE WE STAND.

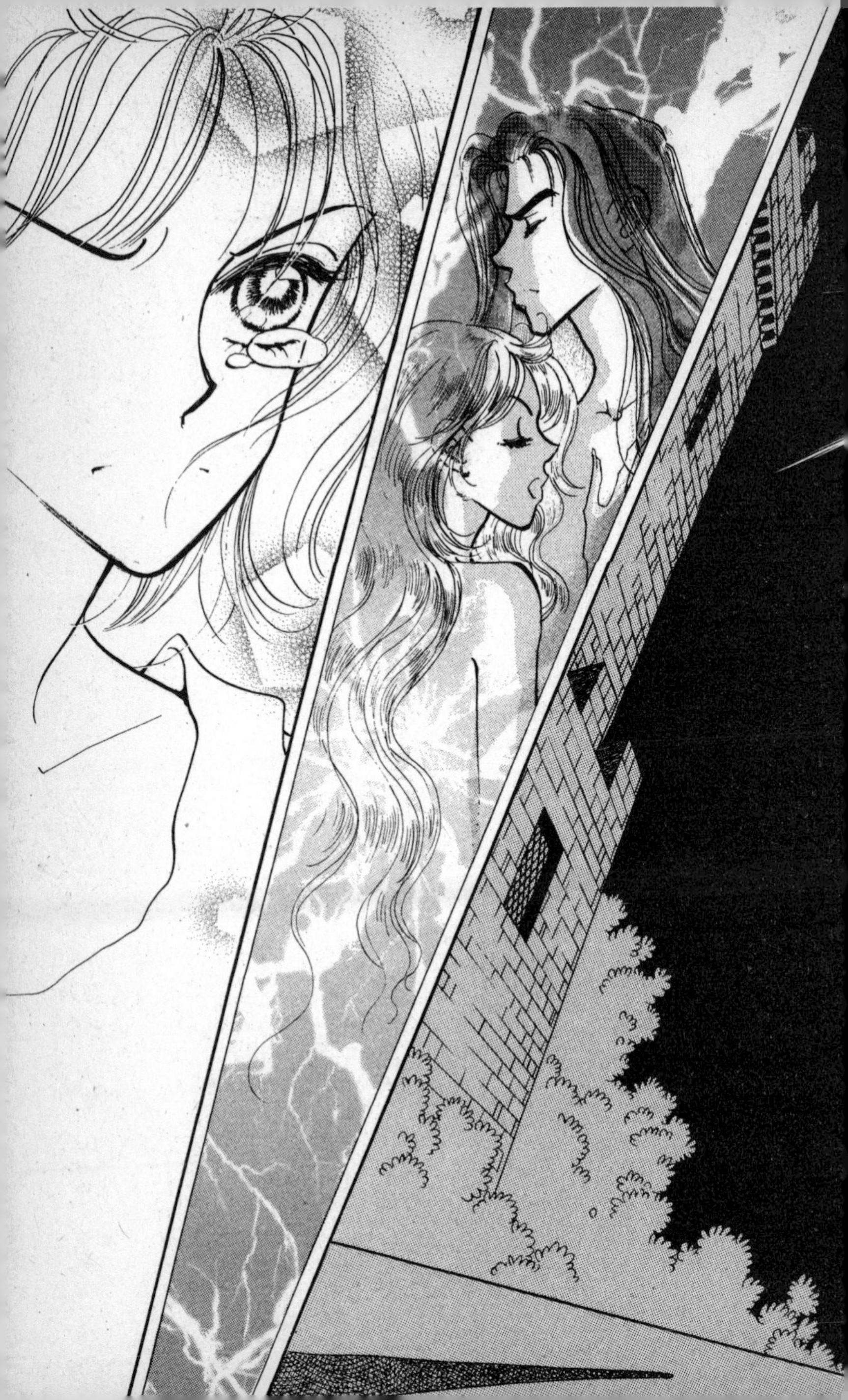

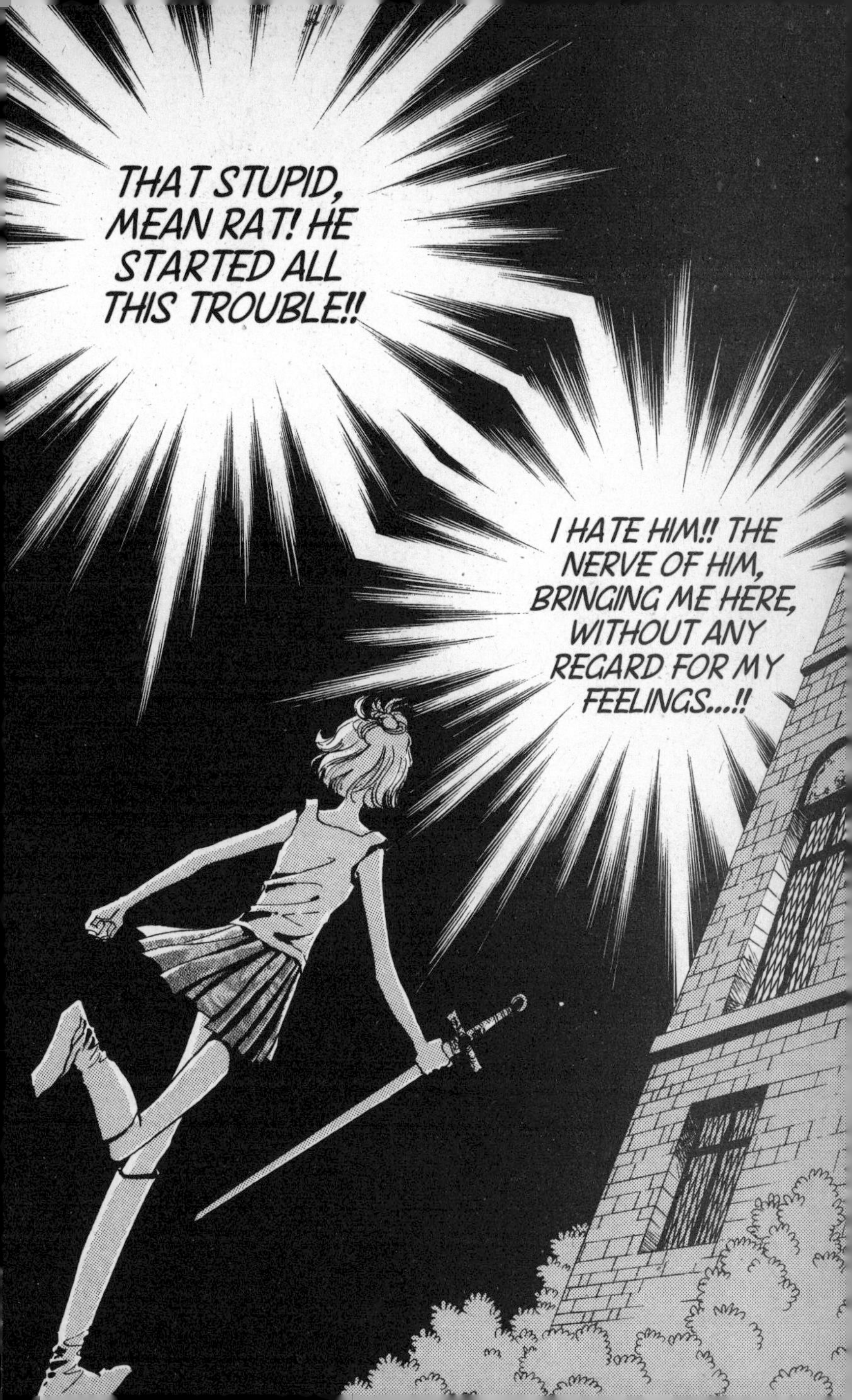
THAT STUPID, MEAN RAT! HE STARTED ALL THIS TROUBLE!!
I HATE HIM!! THE NERVE OF HIM, BRINGING ME HERE, WITHOUT ANY REGARD FOR MY FEELINGS...!!

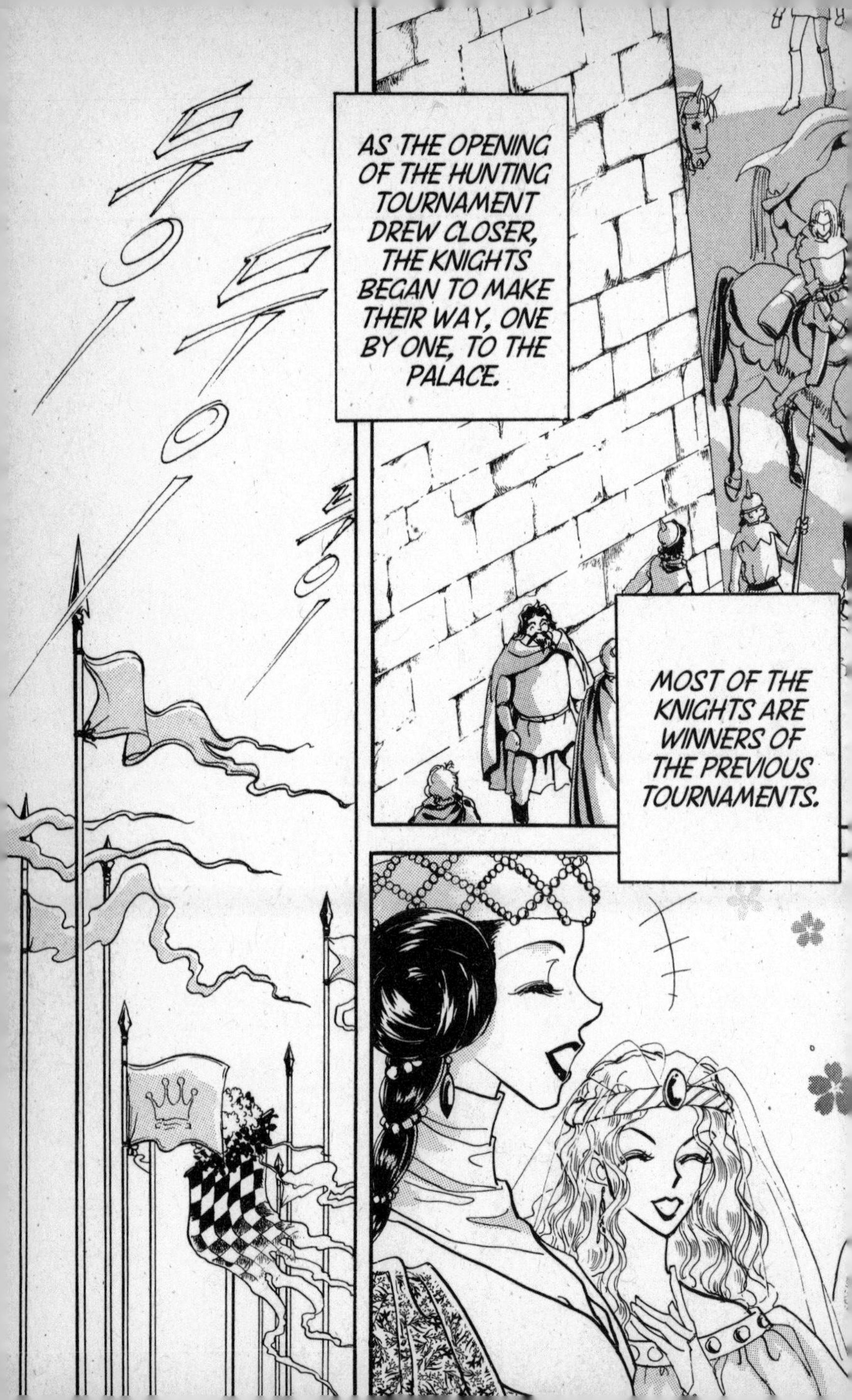
AS THE OPENING OF THE HUNTING TOURNAMENT DREW CLOSER, THE KNIGHTS BEGAN TO MAKE THEIR WAY, ONE BY ONE, TO THE PALACE.
MOST OF THE KNIGHTS ARE WINNERS OF THE PREVIOUS TOURNAMENTS.

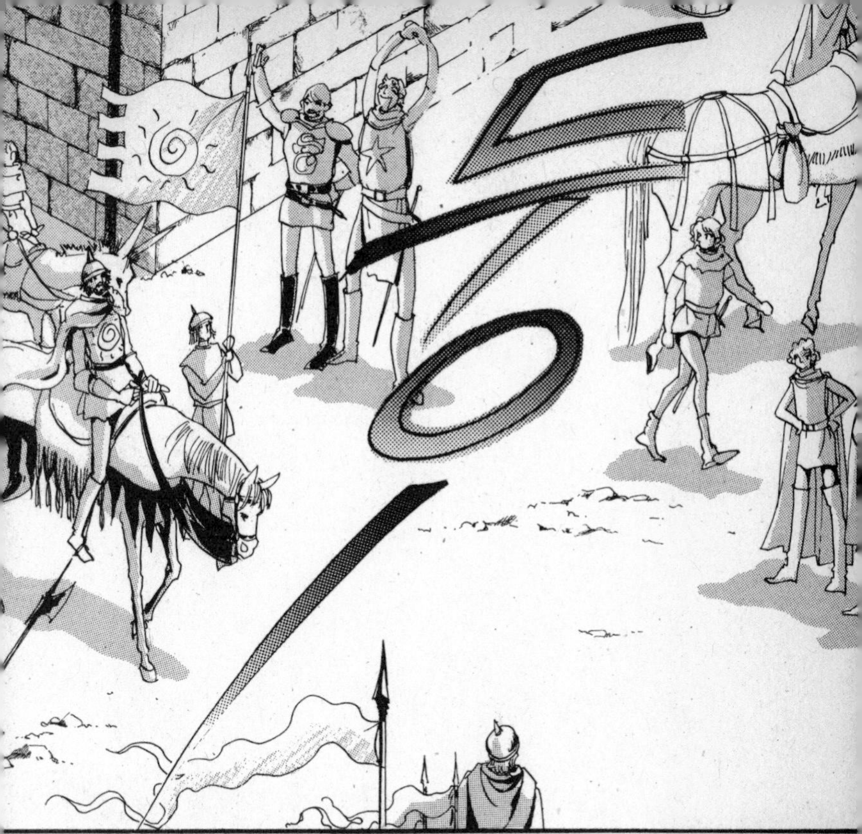
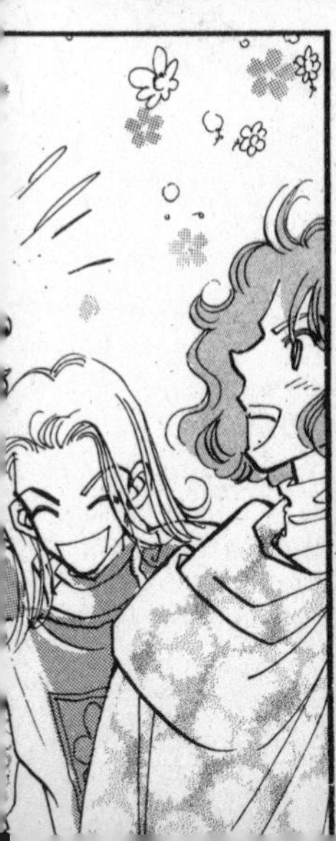
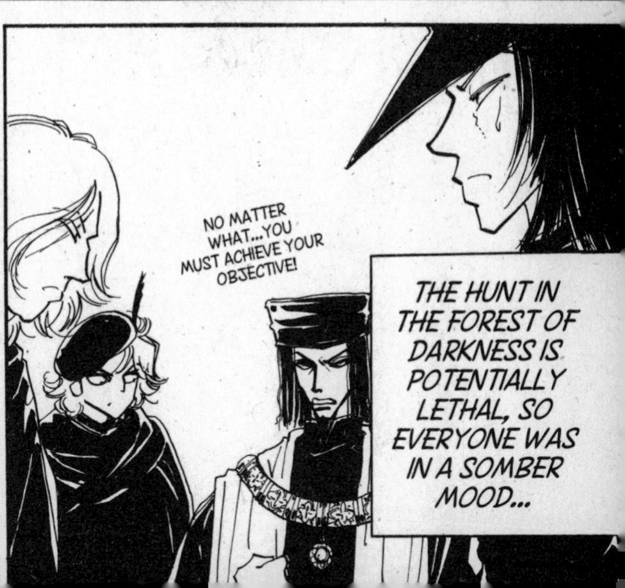
NO MATTER WHAT...YOU MUST ACHIEVE YOUR OBJECTIVE!
THE HUNT IN THE FOREST OF DARKNESS IS POTENTIALLY LETHAL, SO EVERYONE WAS IN A SOMBER MOOD...

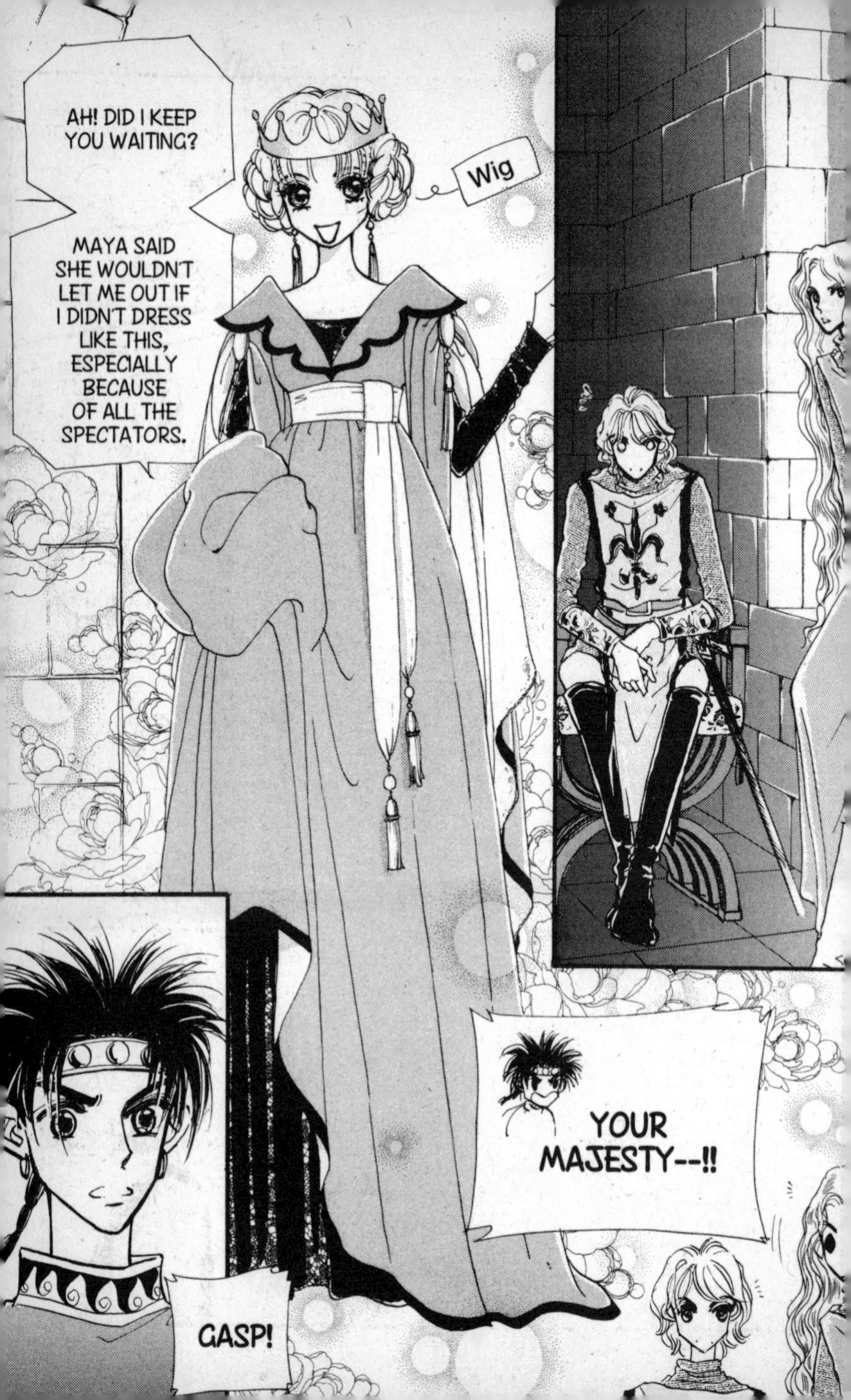
AH! DID I KEEP YOU WAITING?
MAYA SAID SHE WOULDN'T LET ME OUT IF I DIDN'T DRESS LIKE THIS, ESPECIALLY BECAUSE OF ALL THE SPECTATORS.
Wig
YOUR MAJESTY--!!
GASP!

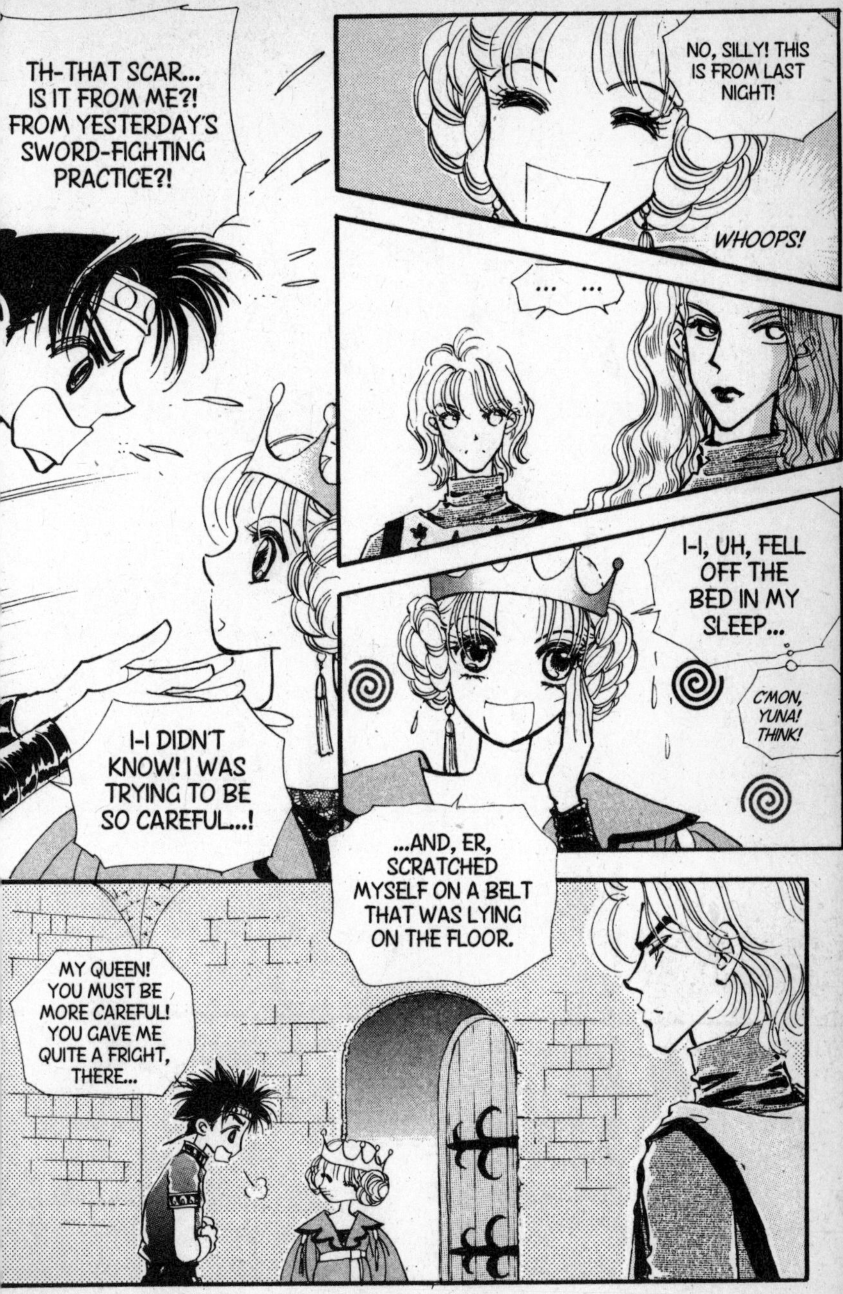
TH-THAT SCAR... IS IT FROM ME?! FROM YESTERDAY'S SWORD-FIGHTING PRACTICE?!
I-I DIDN'T KNOW! I WAS TRYING TO BE SO CAREFUL...!
NO, SILLY! THIS IS FROM LAST NIGHT!
WHOOPS!
... ...
I-I, UH, FELL OFF THE BED IN MY SLEEP...
C'MON, YUNA! THINK!
...AND, ER, SCRATCHED MYSELF ON A BELT THAT WAS LYING ON THE FLOOR.
MY QUEEN! YOU MUST BE MORE CAREFUL! YOU GAVE ME QUITE A FRIGHT, THERE...

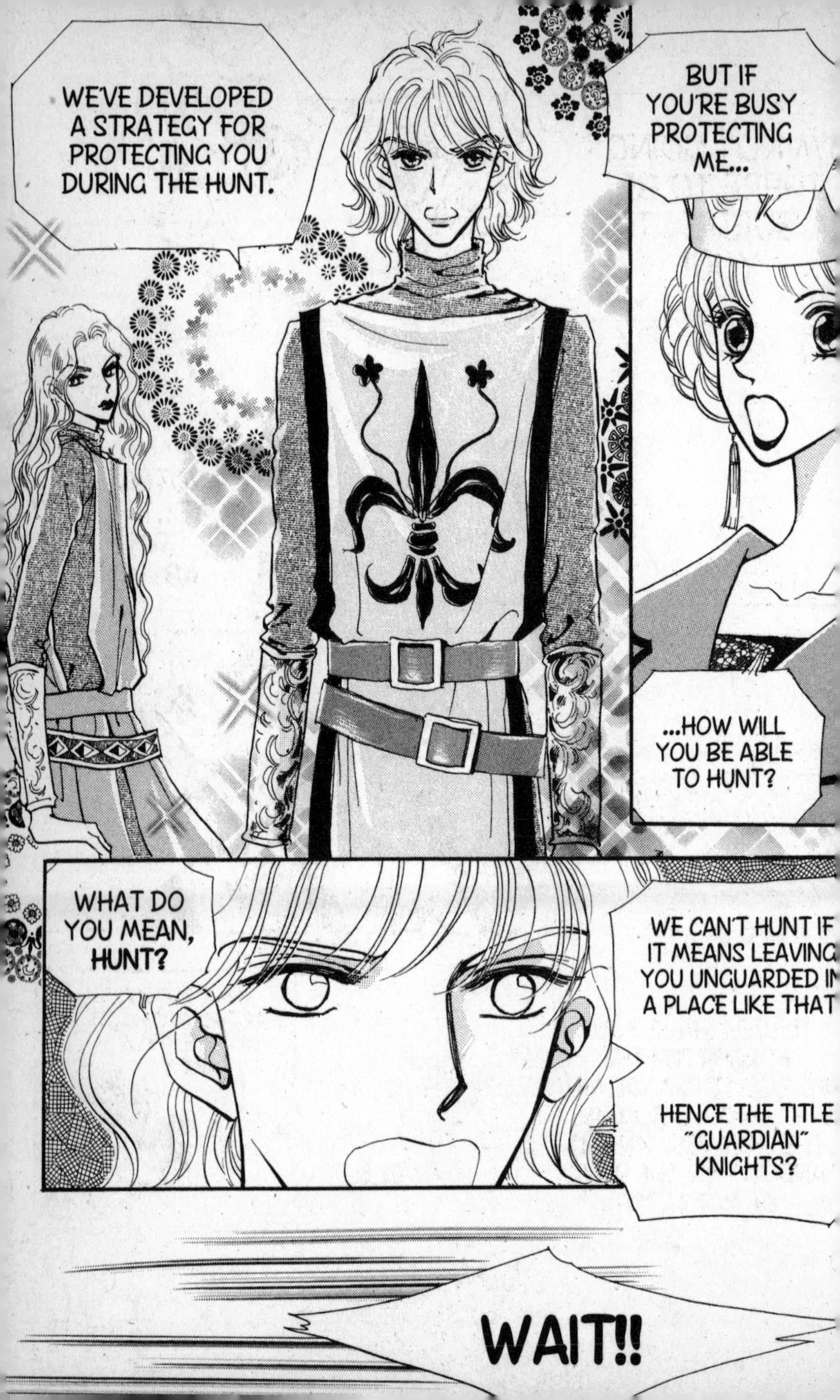
WE'VE DEVELOPED A STRATEGY FOR PROTECTING YOU DURING THE HUNT.
BUT IF YOU'RE BUSY PROTECTING ME...
...HOW WILL YOU BE ABLE TO HUNT?
WHAT DO YOU MEAN, HUNT?
WE CAN'T HUNT IF IT MEANS LEAVING YOU UNGUARDED IN A PLACE LIKE THAT
HENCE THE TITLE "GUARDIAN" KNIGHTS?
WAIT!!

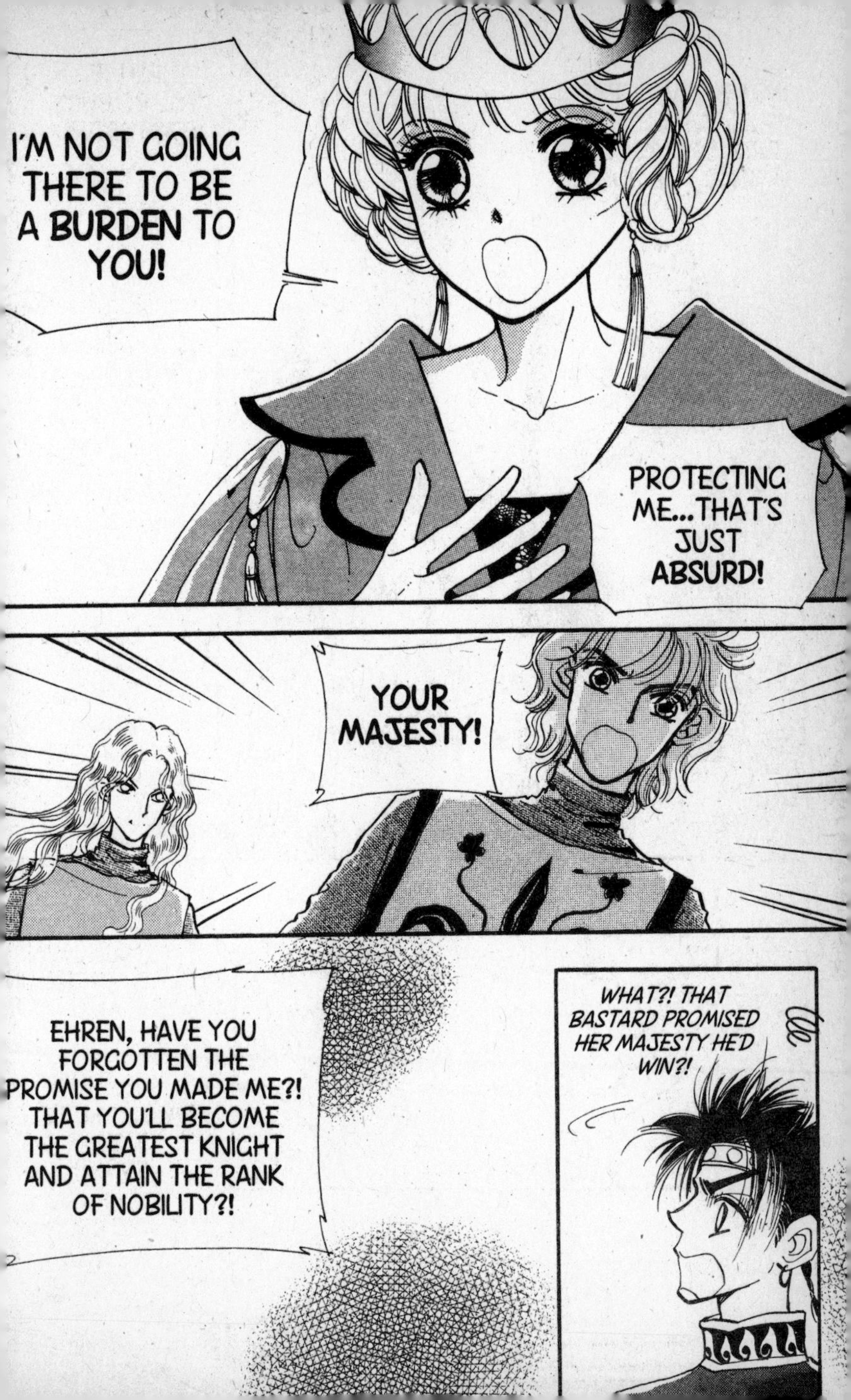
I'M NOT GOING THERE TO BE A BURDEN TO YOU!
PROTECTING ME...THAT'S JUST ABSURD!
YOUR MAJESTY!
EHREN, HAVE YOU FORGOTTEN THE PROMISE YOU MADE ME?! THAT YOU'LL BECOME THE GREATEST KNIGHT AND ATTAIN THE RANK OF NOBILITY?!
WHAT?! THAT BASTARD PROMISED HER MAJESTY HE'D WIN?!

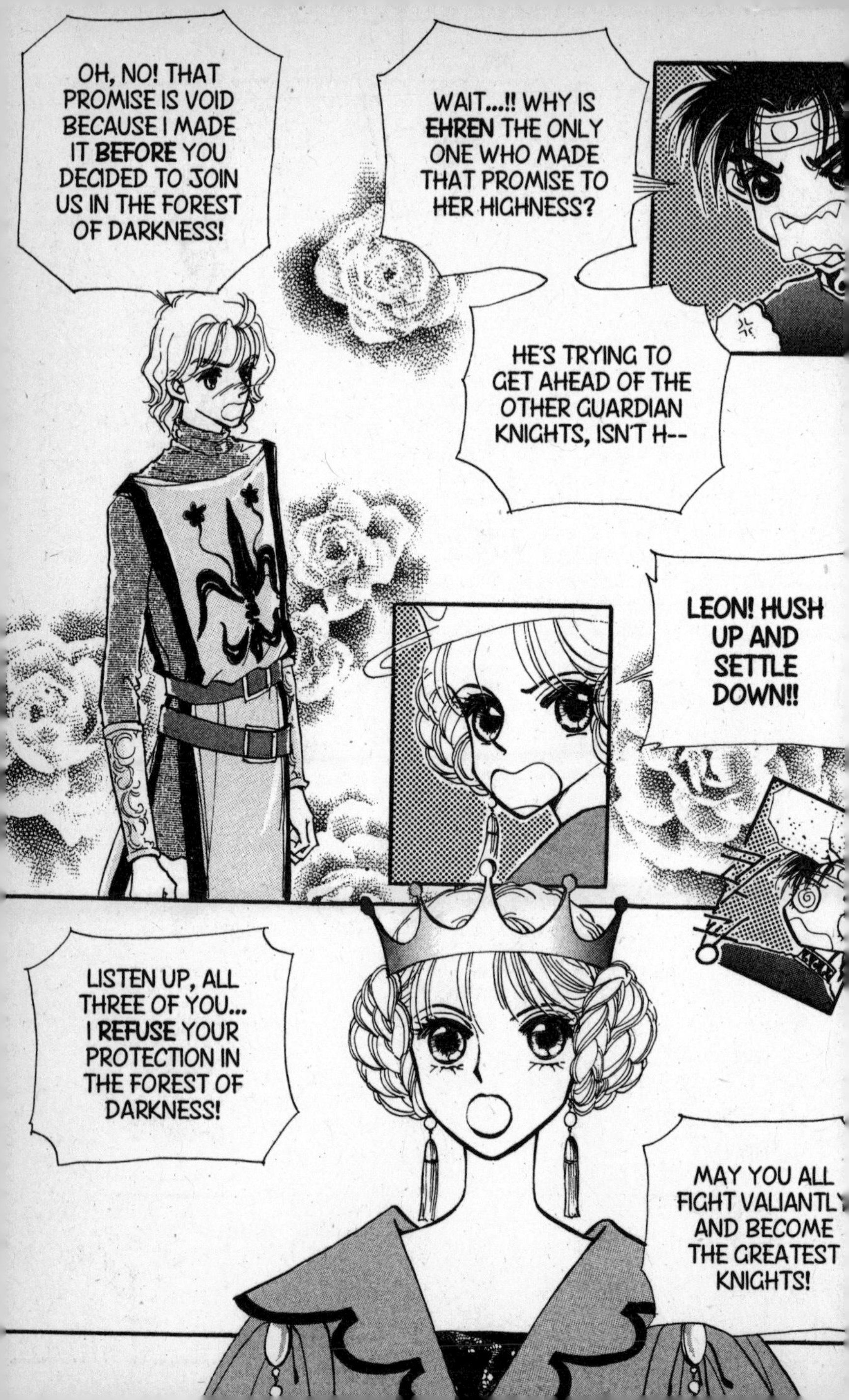
OH, NO! THAT PROMISE IS VOID BECAUSE I MADE IT BEFORE YOU DECIDED TO JOIN US IN THE FOREST OF DARKNESS!
WAIT...!! WHY IS EHREN THE ONLY ONE WHO MADE THAT PROMISE TO HER HIGHNESS?
HE'S TRYING TO GET AHEAD OF THE OTHER GUARDIAN KNIGHTS, ISN'T H--
LEON! HUSH UP AND SETTLE DOWN!!
LISTEN UP, ALL THREE OF YOU... I REFUSE YOUR PROTECTION IN THE FOREST OF DARKNESS!
MAY YOU ALL FIGHT VALIANTLY AND BECOME THE GREATEST KNIGHTS!

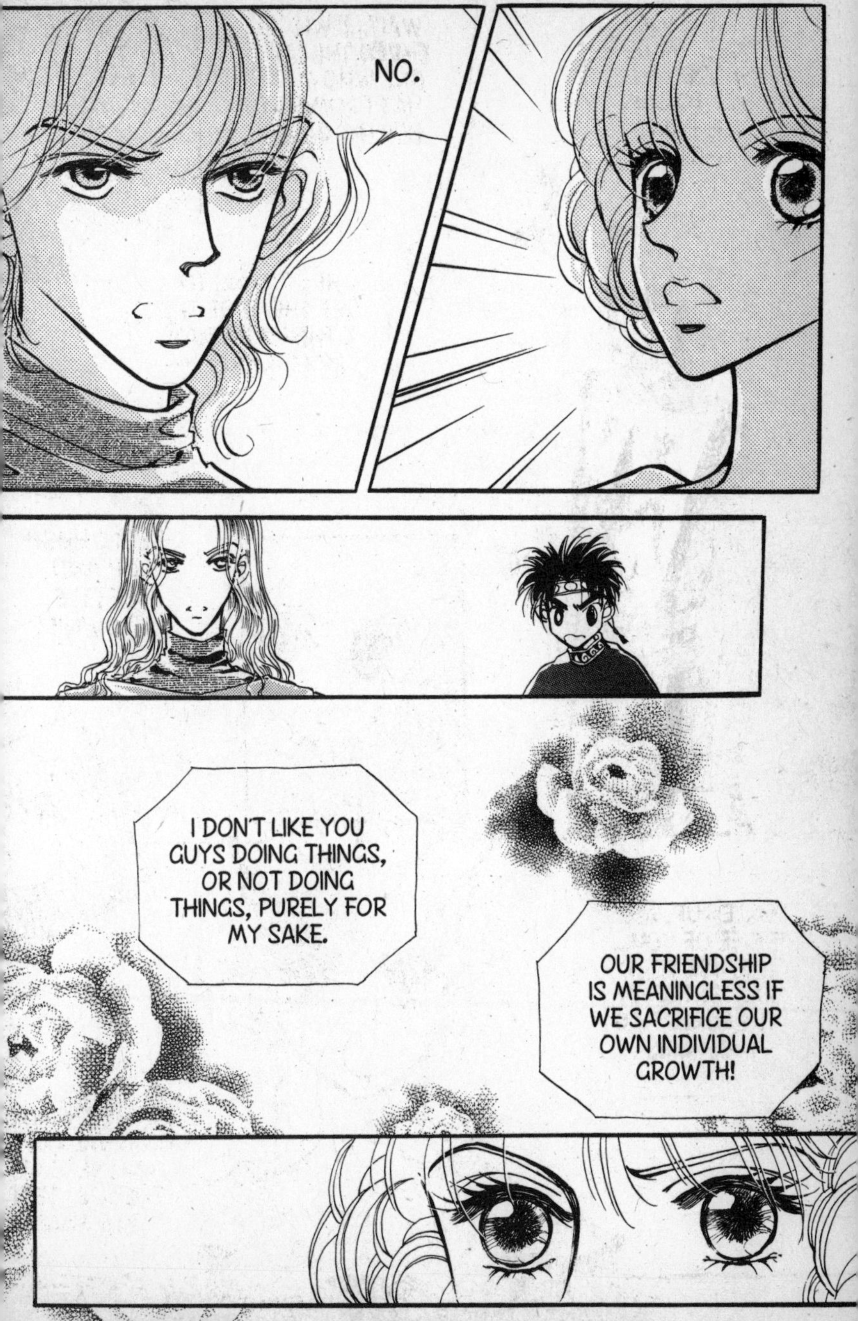
NO.
I DON'T LIKE YOU GUYS DOING THINGS, OR NOT DOING THINGS, PURELY FOR MY SAKE.
OUR FRIENDSHIP IS MEANINGLESS IF WE SACRIFICE OUR OWN INDIVIDUAL GROWTH!

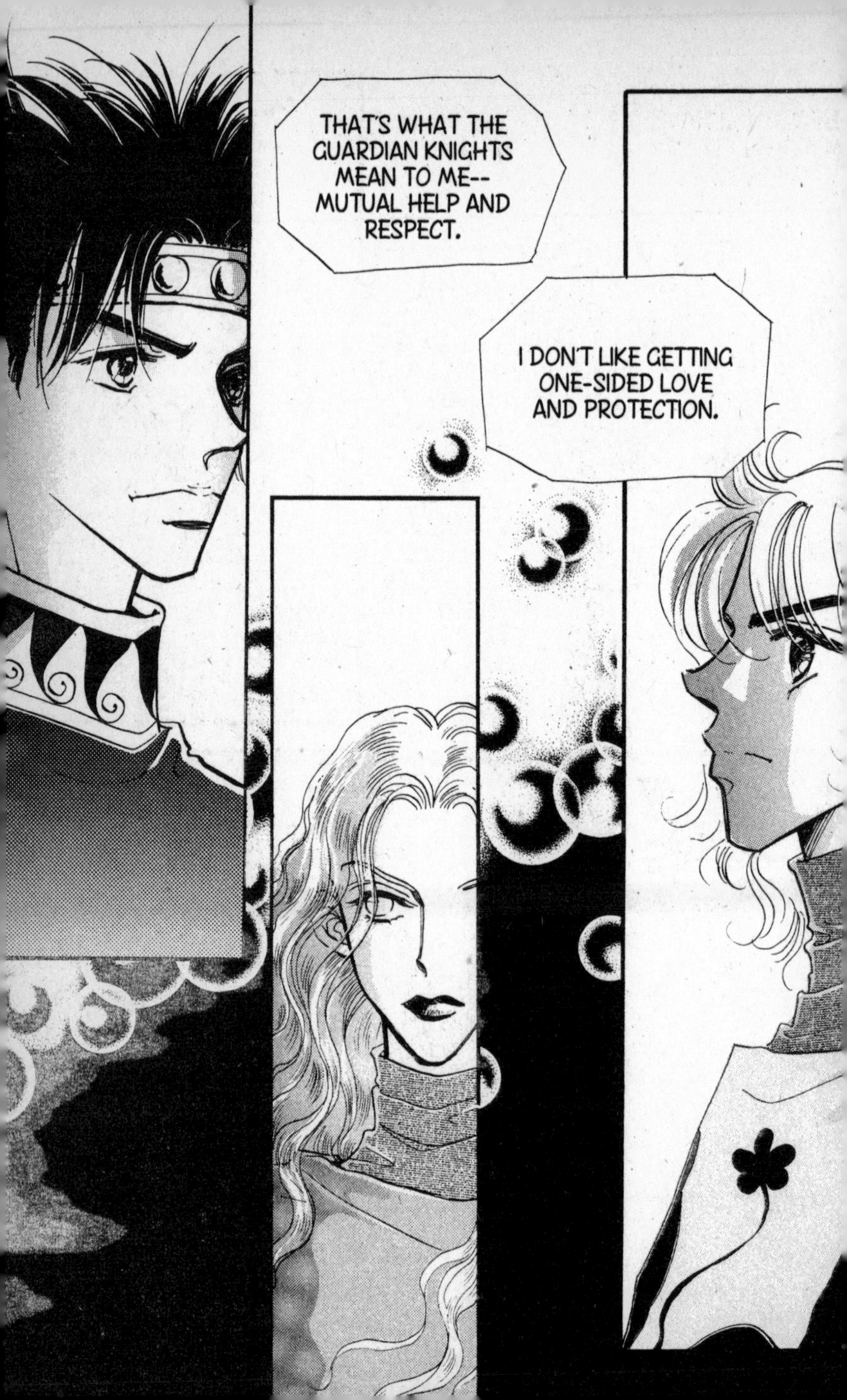
THAT'S WHAT THE GUARDIAN KNIGHTS MEAN TO ME-- MUTUAL HELP AND RESPECT.
I DON'T LIKE GETTING ONE-SIDED LOVE AND PROTECTION.

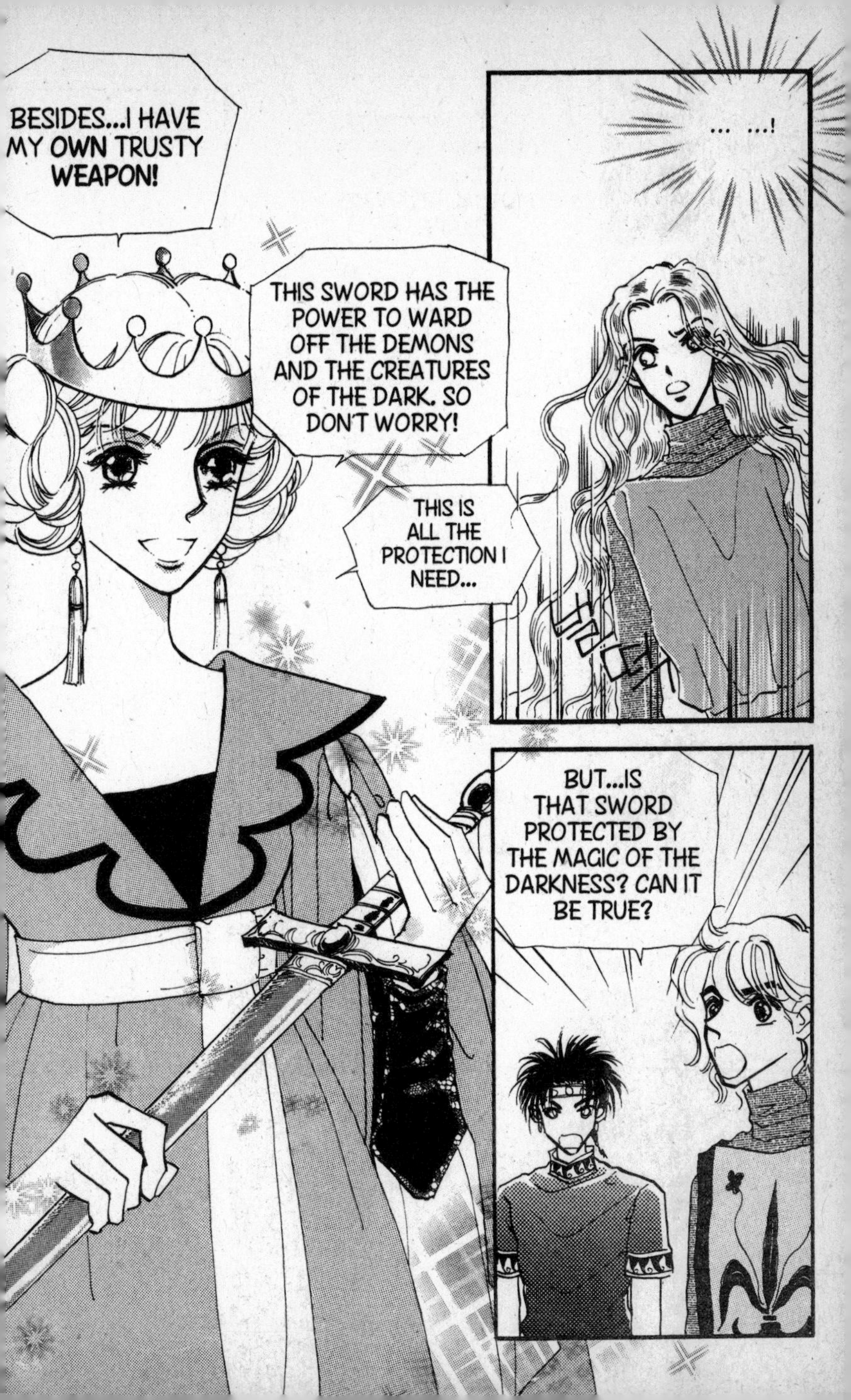
BESIDES...I HAVE MY OWN TRUSTY WEAPON!
THIS SWORD HAS THE POWER TO WARD OFF THE DEMONS AND THE CREATURES OF THE DARK. SO DON'T WORRY!
THIS IS ALL THE PROTECTION I NEED...
... ...!
BUT...IS THAT SWORD PROTECTED BY THE MAGIC OF THE DARKNESS? CAN IT BE TRUE?

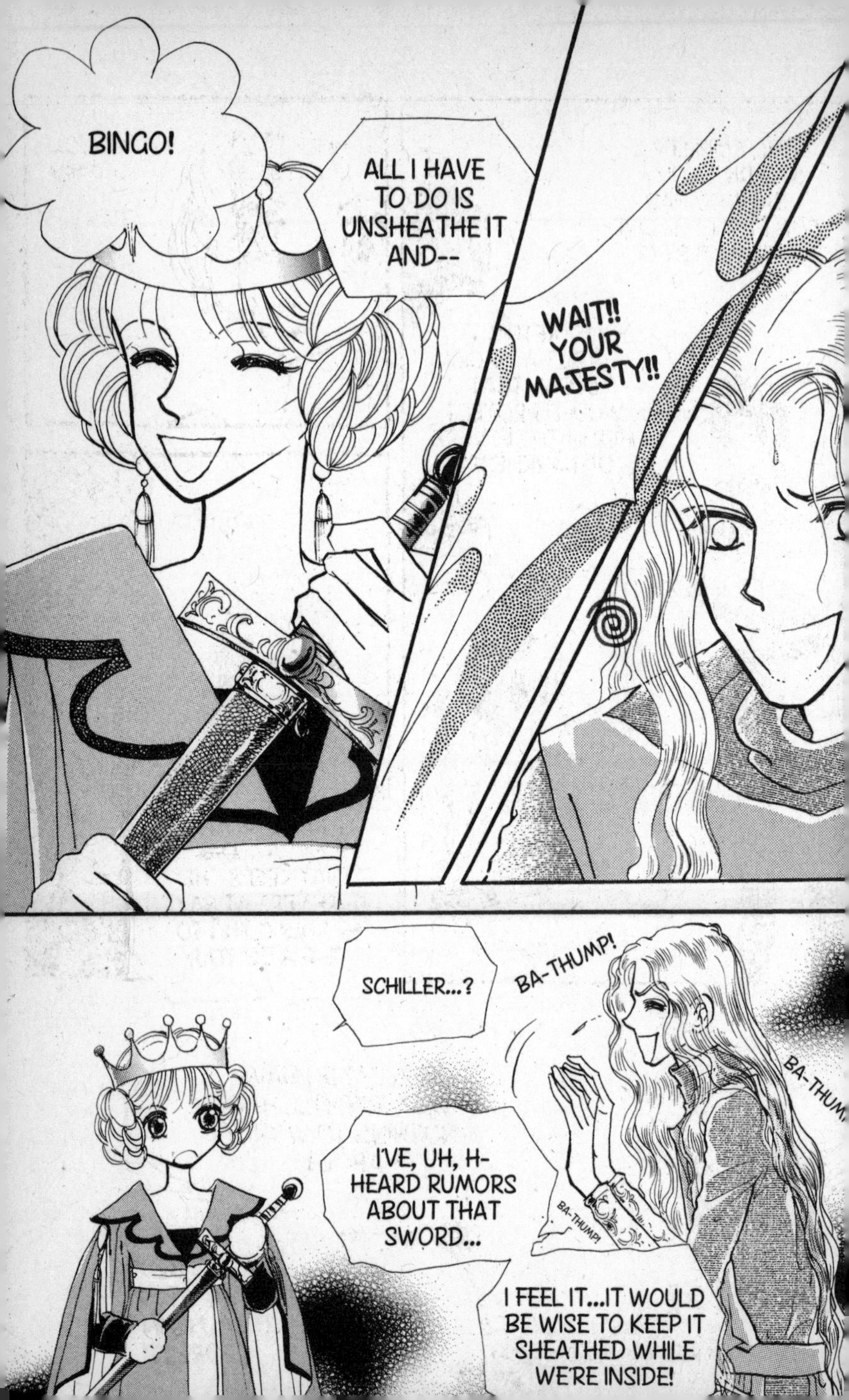
BINGO!
ALL I HAVE TO DO IS UNSHEATHE IT AND--
WAIT!! YOUR MAJESTY!!
SCHILLER...?
BA-THUMP!
BA-THUMP!
I'VE, UH, H-HEARD RUMORS ABOUT THAT SWORD...
BA-THUMP!
I FEEL IT...IT WOULD BE WISE TO KEEP IT SHEATHED WHILE WE'RE INSIDE!

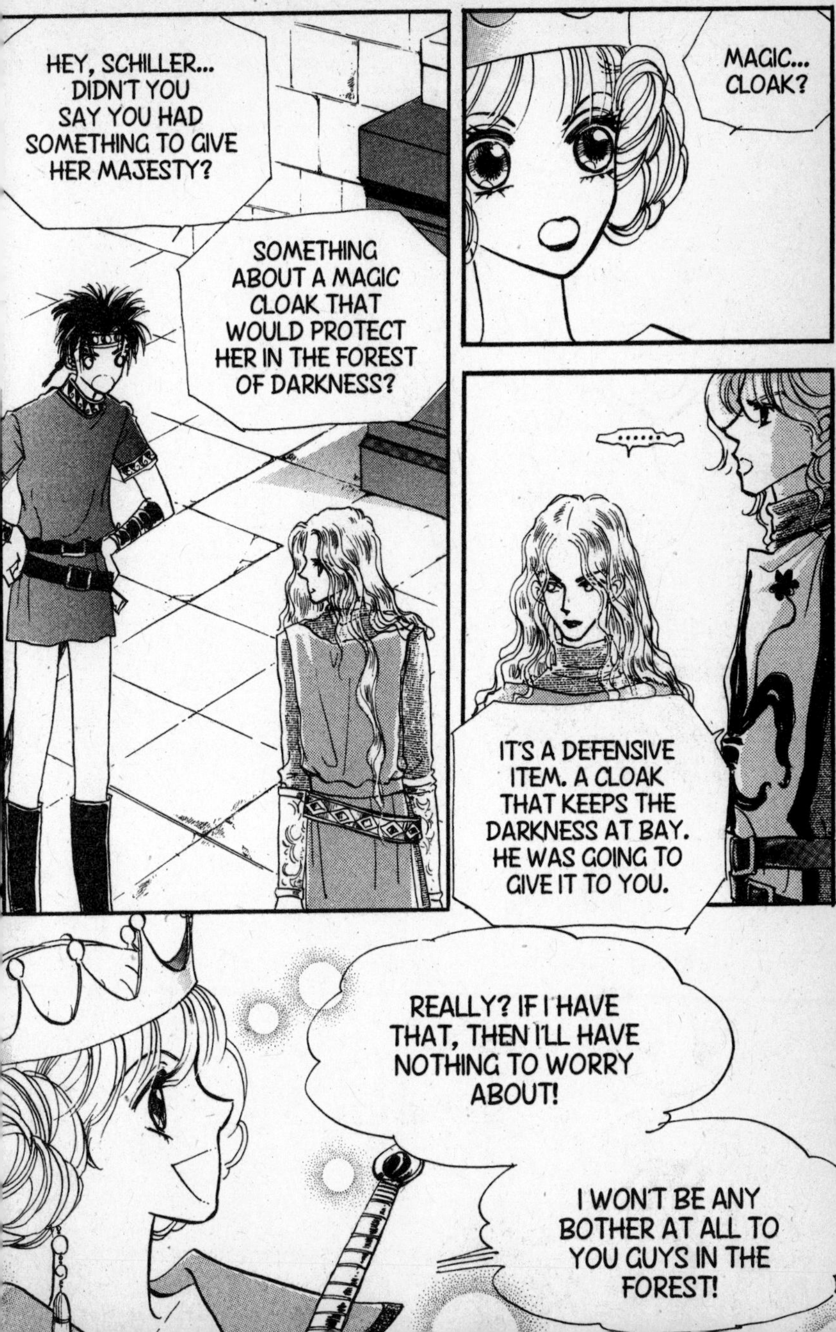
HEY, SCHILLER... DIDN'T YOU SAY YOU HAD SOMETHING TO GIVE HER MAJESTY?
SOMETHING ABOUT A MAGIC CLOAK THAT WOULD PROTECT HER IN THE FOREST OF DARKNESS?
MAGIC... CLOAK?
......
IT'S A DEFENSIVE ITEM. A CLOAK THAT KEEPS THE DARKNESS AT BAY. HE WAS GOING TO GIVE IT TO YOU.
REALLY? IF I HAVE THAT, THEN I'LL HAVE NOTHING TO WORRY ABOUT!
I WON'T BE ANY BOTHER AT ALL TO YOU GUYS IN THE FOREST!

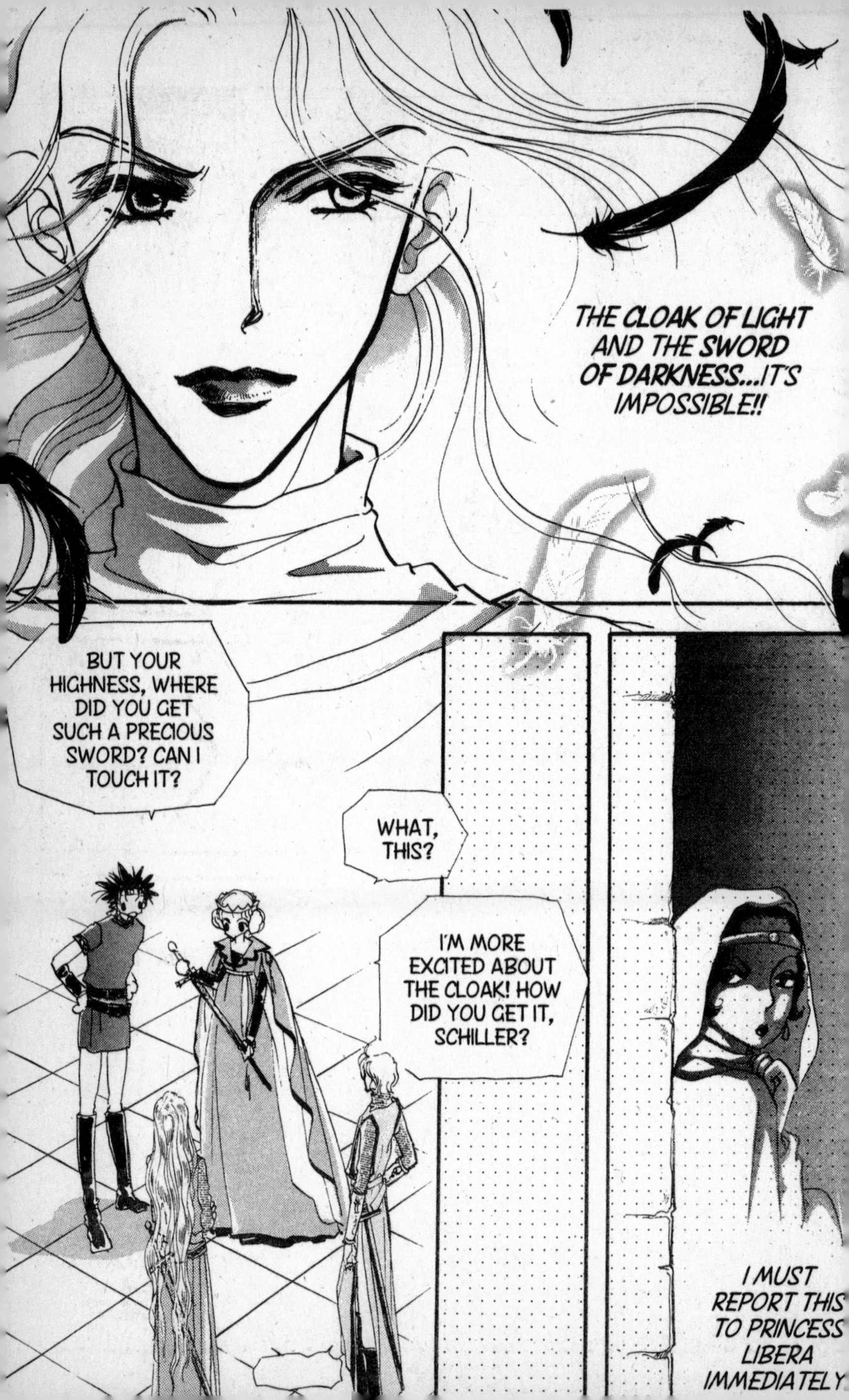
THE CLOAK OF LIGHT AND THE SWORD OF DARKNESS...IT'S IMPOSSIBLE!!
BUT YOUR HIGHNESS, WHERE DID YOU GET SUCH A PRECIOUS SWORD? CAN I TOUCH IT?
WHAT, THIS?
I'M MORE EXCITED ABOUT THE CLOAK! HOW DID YOU GET IT, SCHILLER?
I MUST REPORT THIS TO PRINCESS LIBERA IMMEDIATELY

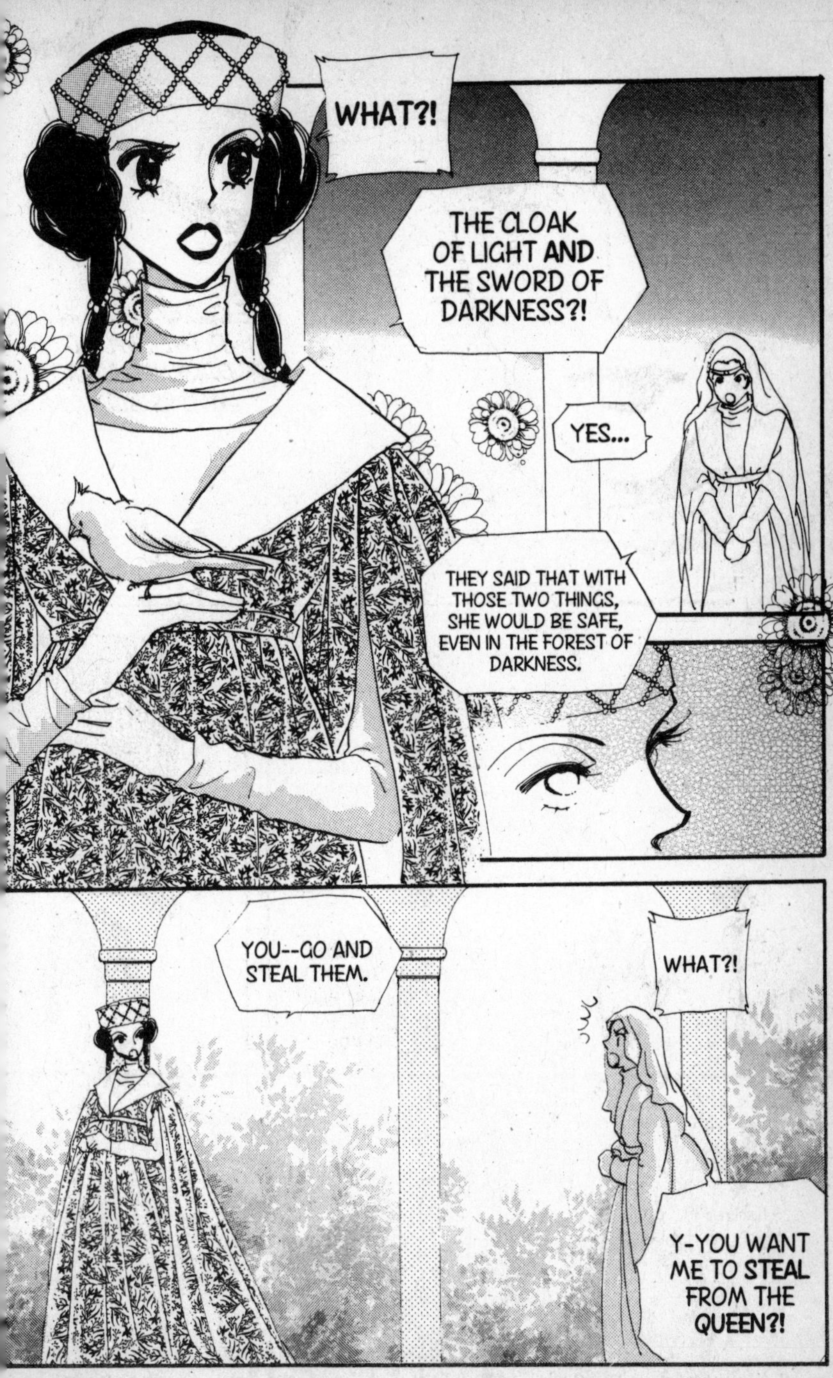
WHAT?!
THE CLOAK OF LIGHT AND THE SWORD OF DARKNESS?!
YES...
THEY SAID THAT WITH THOSE TWO THINGS, SHE WOULD BE SAFE, EVEN IN THE FOREST OF DARKNESS.
YOU--GO AND STEAL THEM.
WHAT?!
Y-YOU WANT ME TO STEAL FROM THE QUEEN?!

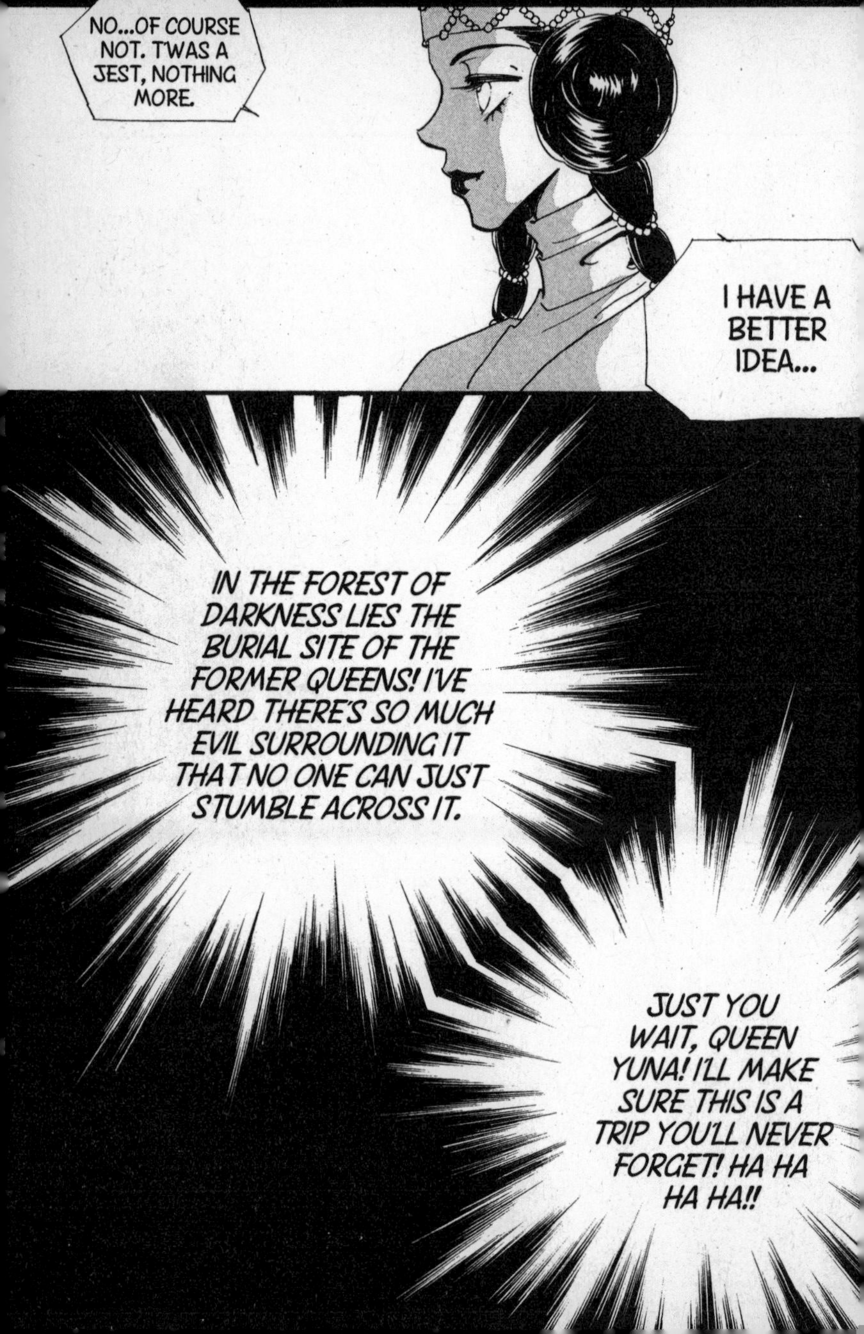
NO...OF COURSE NOT. TWAS A JEST, NOTHING MORE.
I HAVE A BETTER IDEA...
IN THE FOREST OF DARKNESS LIES THE BURIAL SITE OF THE FORMER QUEENS! I'VE HEARD THERE'S SO MUCH EVIL SURROUNDING IT THAT NO ONE CAN JUST STUMBLE ACROSS IT.
JUST YOU WAIT, QUEEN YUNA! I'LL MAKE SURE THIS IS A TRIP YOU'LL NEVER FORGET! HA HA HA HA!!

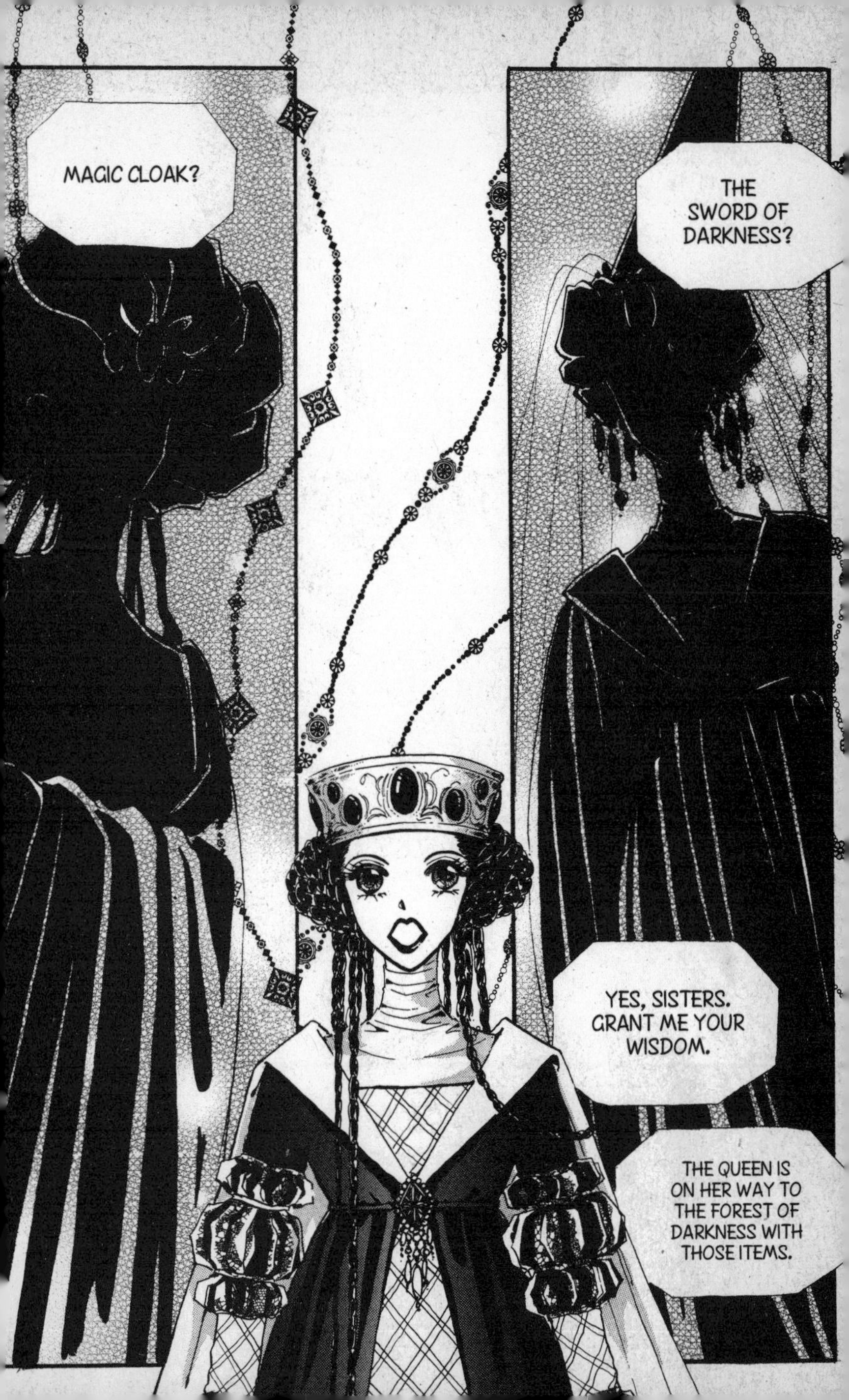
MAGIC CLOAK?
THE SWORD OF DARKNESS?
YES, SISTERS. GRANT ME YOUR WISDOM.
THE QUEEN IS ON HER WAY TO THE FOREST OF DARKNESS WITH THOSE ITEMS.

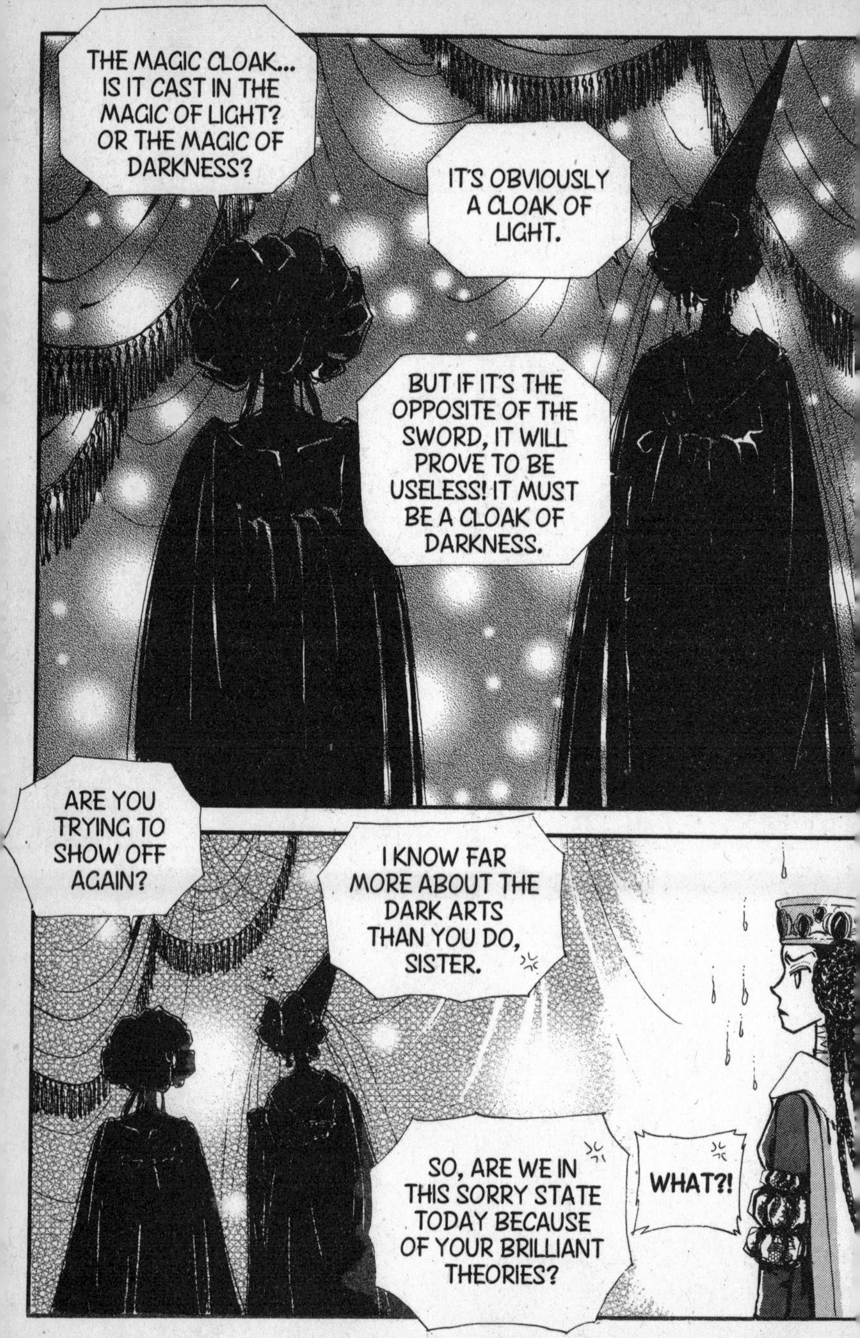
THE MAGIC CLOAK... IS IT CAST IN THE MAGIC OF LIGHT? OR THE MAGIC OF DARKNESS?
IT'S OBVIOUSLY A CLOAK OF LIGHT.
BUT IF IT'S THE OPPOSITE OF THE SWORD, IT WILL PROVE TO BE USELESS! IT MUST BE A CLOAK OF DARKNESS.
ARE YOU TRYING TO SHOW OFF AGAIN?
I KNOW FAR MORE ABOUT THE DARK ARTS THAN YOU DO, SISTER.
SO, ARE WE IN THIS SORRY STATE TODAY BECAUSE OF YOUR BRILLIANT THEORIES?
WHAT?!

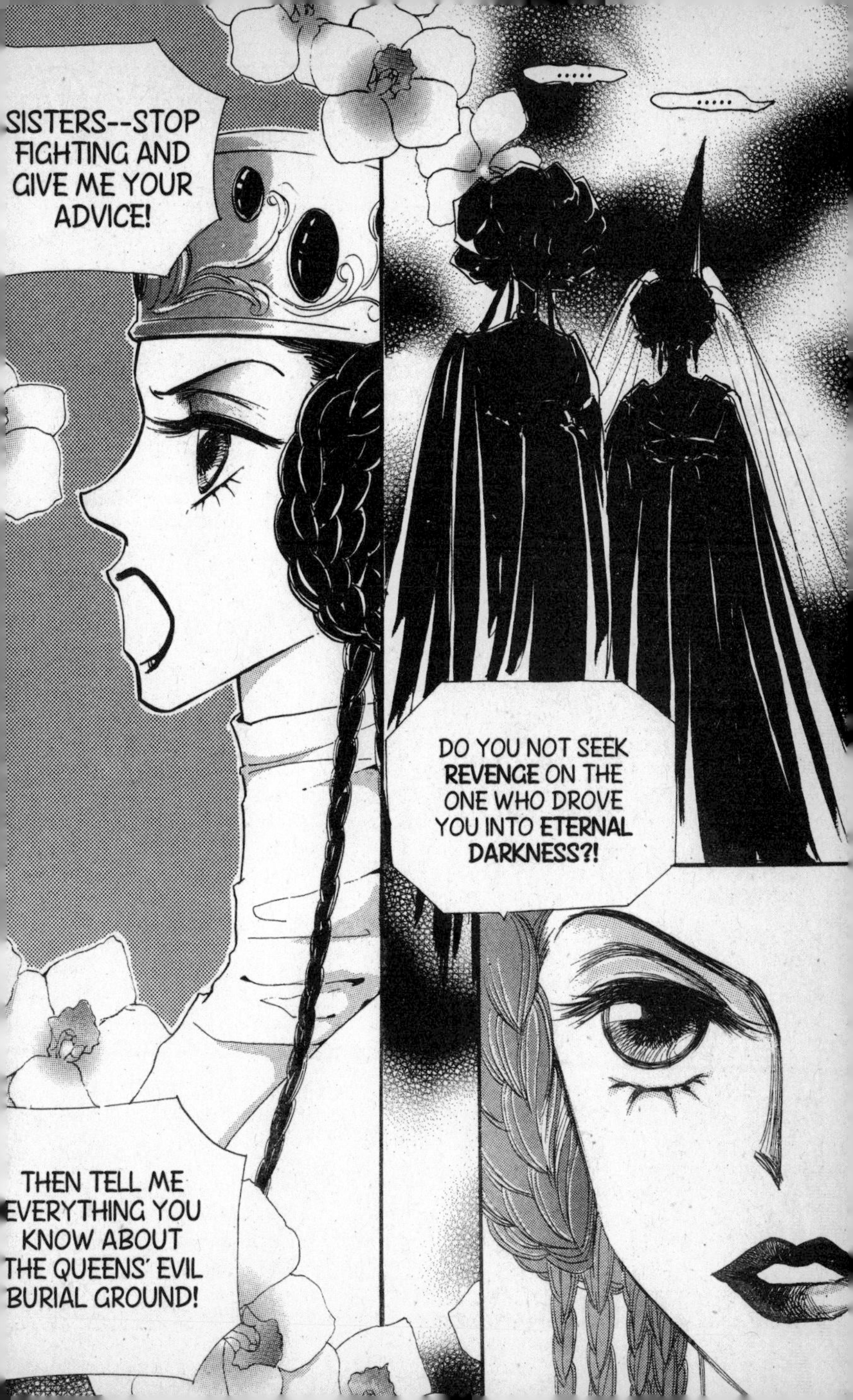
SISTERS--STOP FIGHTING AND GIVE ME YOUR ADVICE!
.....
.....
DO YOU NOT SEEK **REVENGE** ON THE ONE WHO DROVE YOU INTO **ETERNAL DARKNESS**?!
THEN TELL ME EVERYTHING YOU KNOW ABOUT THE QUEENS' EVIL BURIAL GROUND!

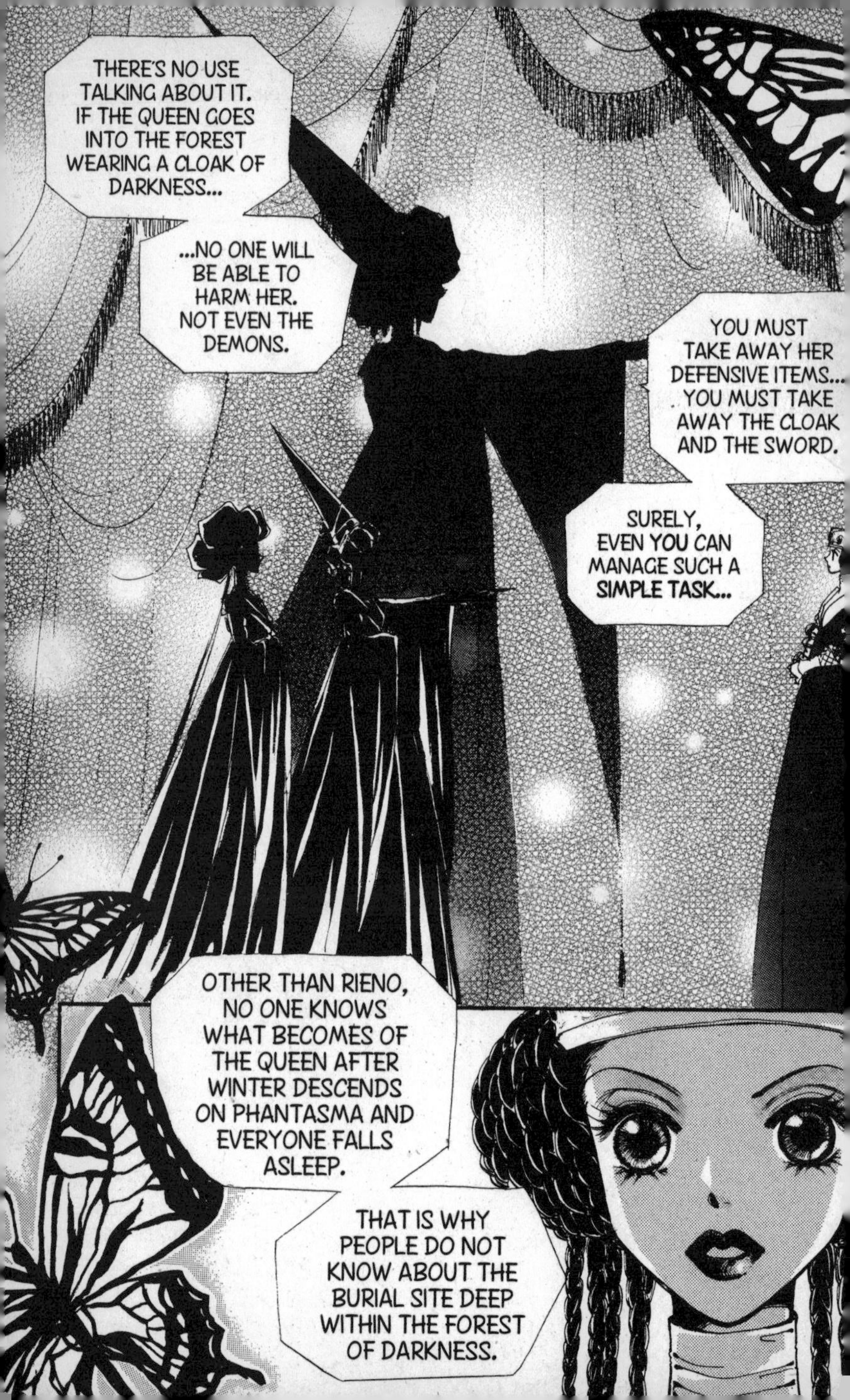
THERE'S NO USE TALKING ABOUT IT. IF THE QUEEN GOES INTO THE FOREST WEARING A CLOAK OF DARKNESS...
...NO ONE WILL BE ABLE TO HARM HER. NOT EVEN THE DEMONS.
YOU MUST TAKE AWAY HER DEFENSIVE ITEMS... YOU MUST TAKE AWAY THE CLOAK AND THE SWORD.
SURELY, EVEN YOU CAN MANAGE SUCH A SIMPLE TASK...
OTHER THAN RIENO, NO ONE KNOWS WHAT BECOMES OF THE QUEEN AFTER WINTER DESCENDS ON PHANTASMA AND EVERYONE FALLS ASLEEP.
THAT IS WHY PEOPLE DO NOT KNOW ABOUT THE BURIAL SITE DEEP WITHIN THE FOREST OF DARKNESS.

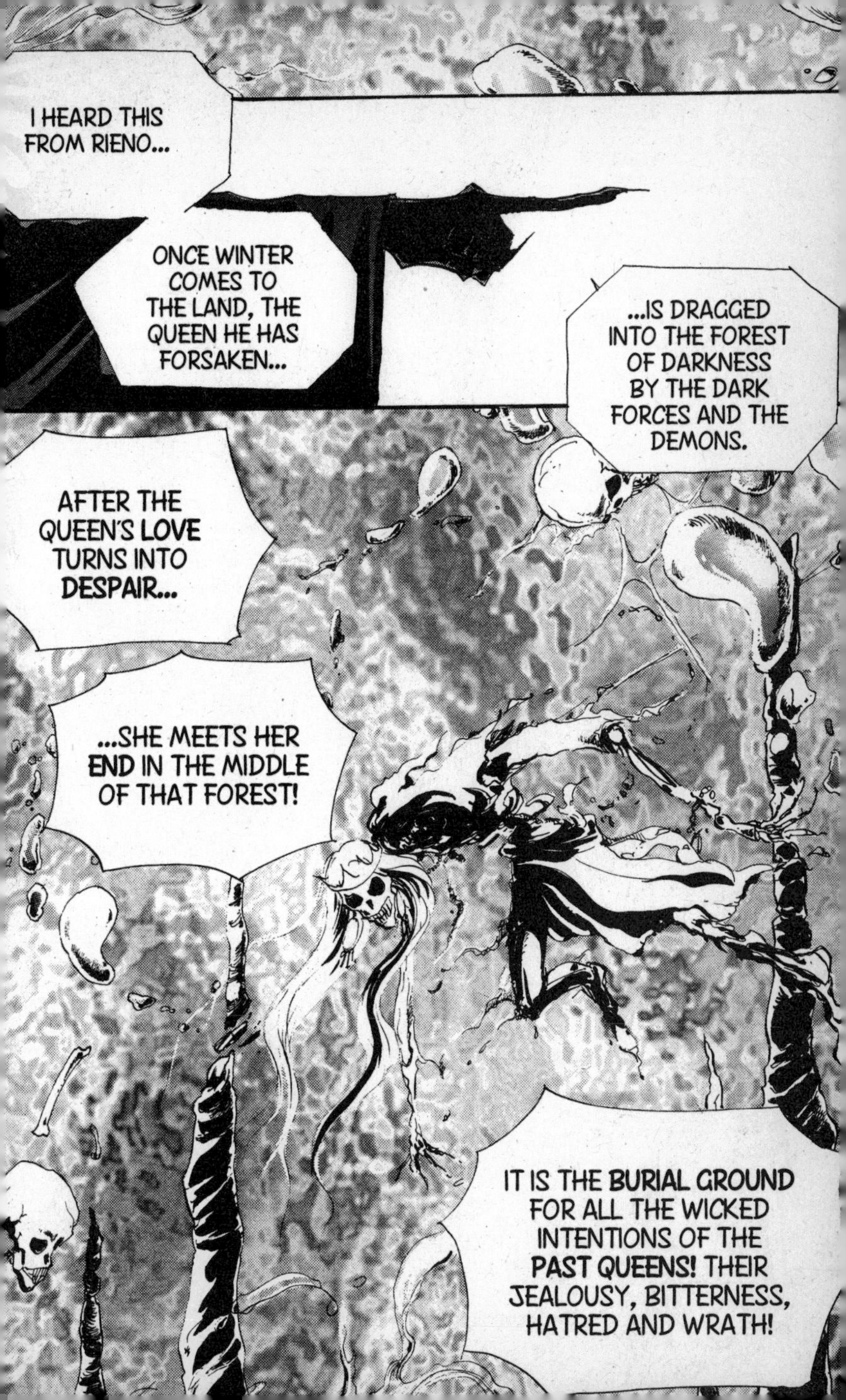
I HEARD THIS FROM RIENO...
ONCE WINTER COMES TO THE LAND, THE QUEEN HE HAS FORSAKEN...
...IS DRAGGED INTO THE FOREST OF DARKNESS BY THE DARK FORCES AND THE DEMONS.
AFTER THE QUEEN'S LOVE TURNS INTO DESPAIR...
...SHE MEETS HER END IN THE MIDDLE OF THAT FOREST!
IT IS THE BURIAL GROUND FOR ALL THE WICKED INTENTIONS OF THE PAST QUEENS! THEIR JEALOUSY, BITTERNESS, HATRED AND WRATH!

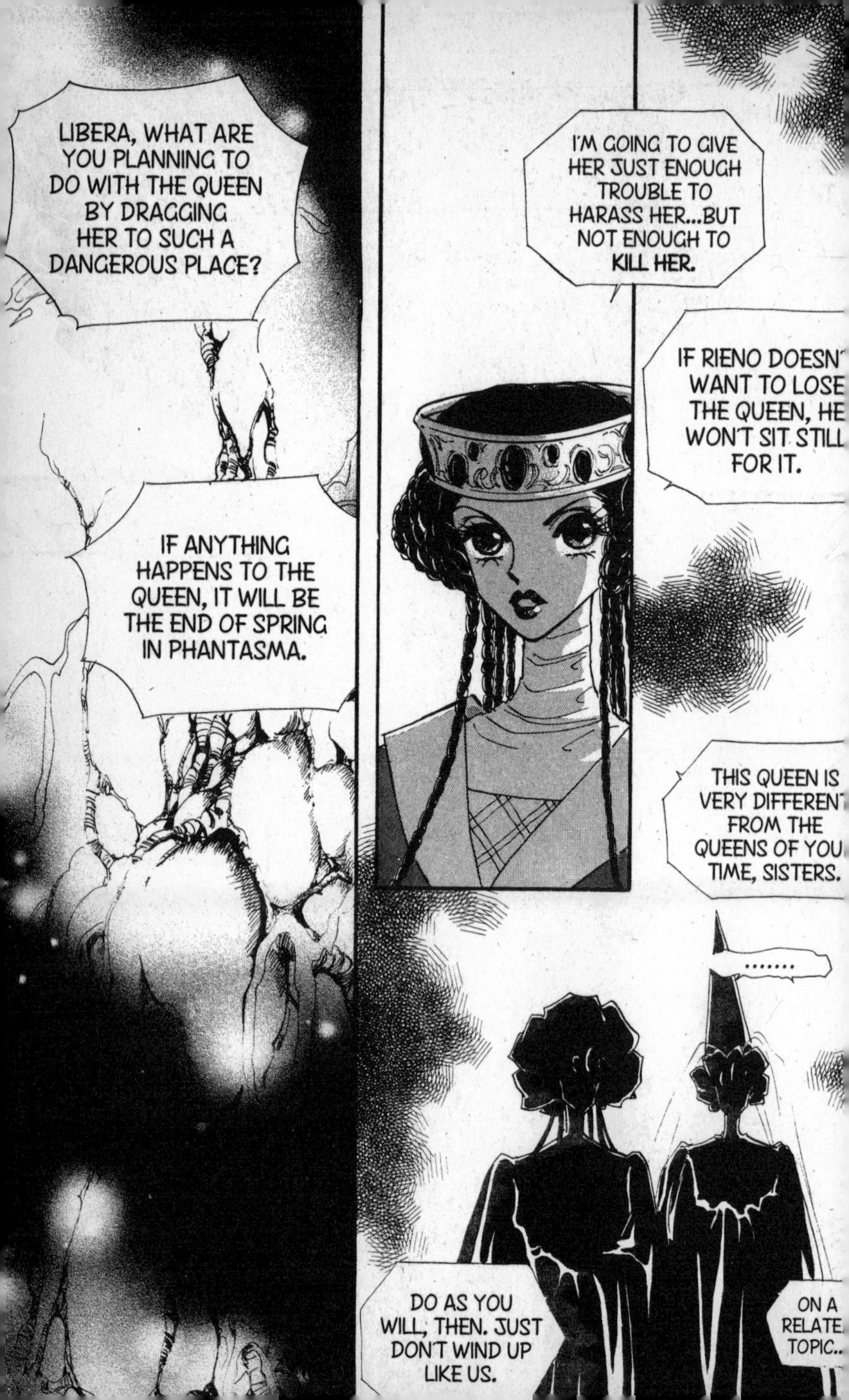
LIBERA, WHAT ARE YOU PLANNING TO DO WITH THE QUEEN BY DRAGGING HER TO SUCH A DANGEROUS PLACE?
IF ANYTHING HAPPENS TO THE QUEEN, IT WILL BE THE END OF SPRING IN PHANTASMA.
I'M GOING TO GIVE HER JUST ENOUGH TROUBLE TO HARASS HER...BUT NOT ENOUGH TO **KILL HER.**
IF RIENO DOESN' WANT TO LOSE THE QUEEN, HE WON'T SIT STILL FOR IT.
THIS QUEEN IS VERY DIFFEREN FROM THE QUEENS OF YOU TIME, SISTERS.
....
DO AS YOU WILL, THEN. JUST DON'T WIND UP LIKE US.
ON A RELATE TOPIC..

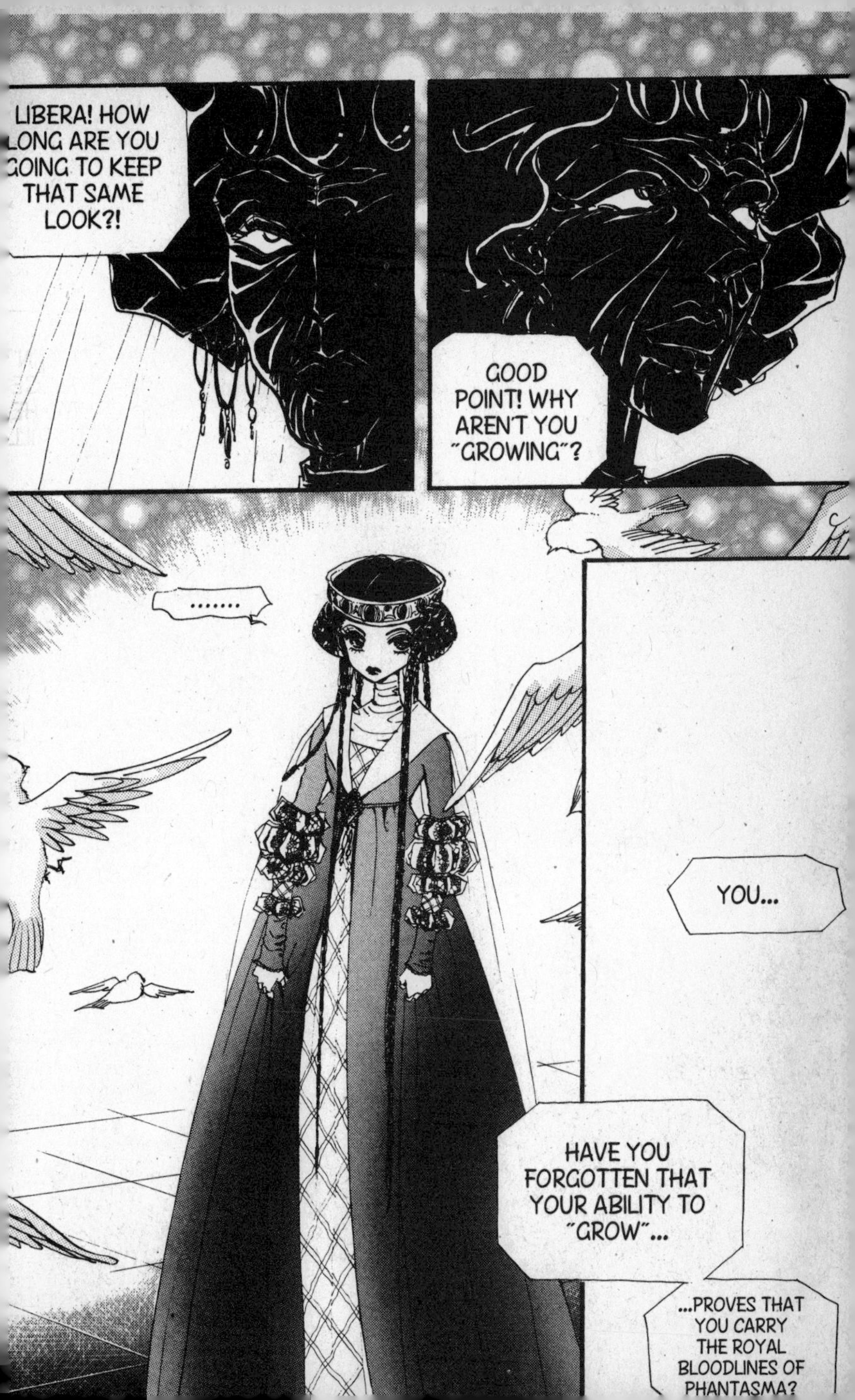
LIBERA! HOW LONG ARE YOU GOING TO KEEP THAT SAME LOOK?!
GOOD POINT! WHY AREN'T YOU "GROWING"?
....
YOU...
HAVE YOU FORGOTTEN THAT YOUR ABILITY TO "GROW"...
...PROVES THAT YOU CARRY THE ROYAL BLOODLINES OF PHANTASMA?

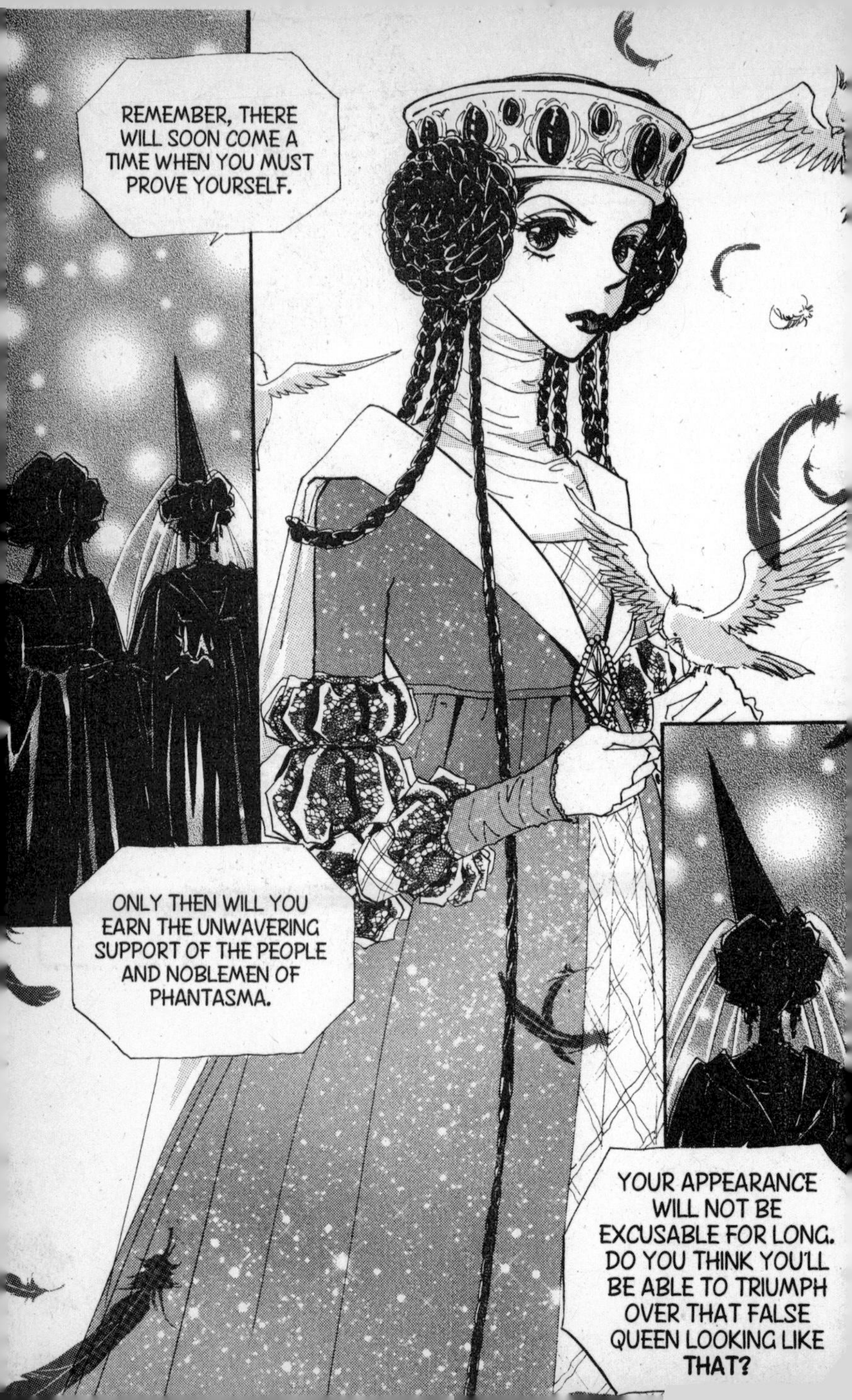
REMEMBER, THERE WILL SOON COME A TIME WHEN YOU MUST PROVE YOURSELF.
ONLY THEN WILL YOU EARN THE UNWAVERING SUPPORT OF THE PEOPLE AND NOBLEMEN OF PHANTASMA.
YOUR APPEARANCE WILL NOT BE EXCUSABLE FOR LONG. DO YOU THINK YOU'LL BE ABLE TO TRIUMPH OVER THAT FALSE QUEEN LOOKING LIKE THAT?

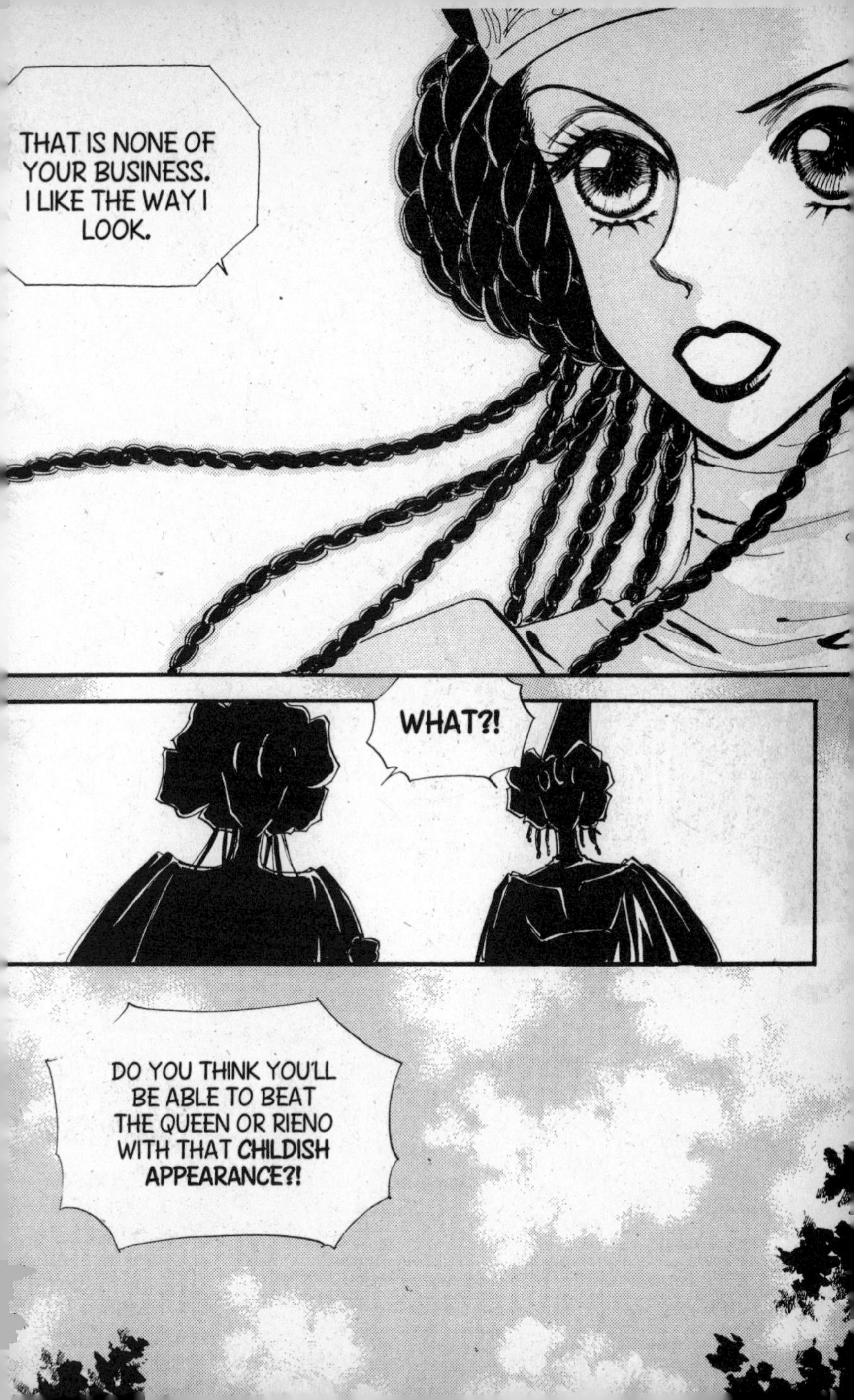
THAT IS NONE OF YOUR BUSINESS. I LIKE THE WAY I LOOK.
WHAT?!
DO YOU THINK YOU'LL BE ABLE TO BEAT THE QUEEN OR RIENO WITH THAT CHILDISH APPEARANCE?!

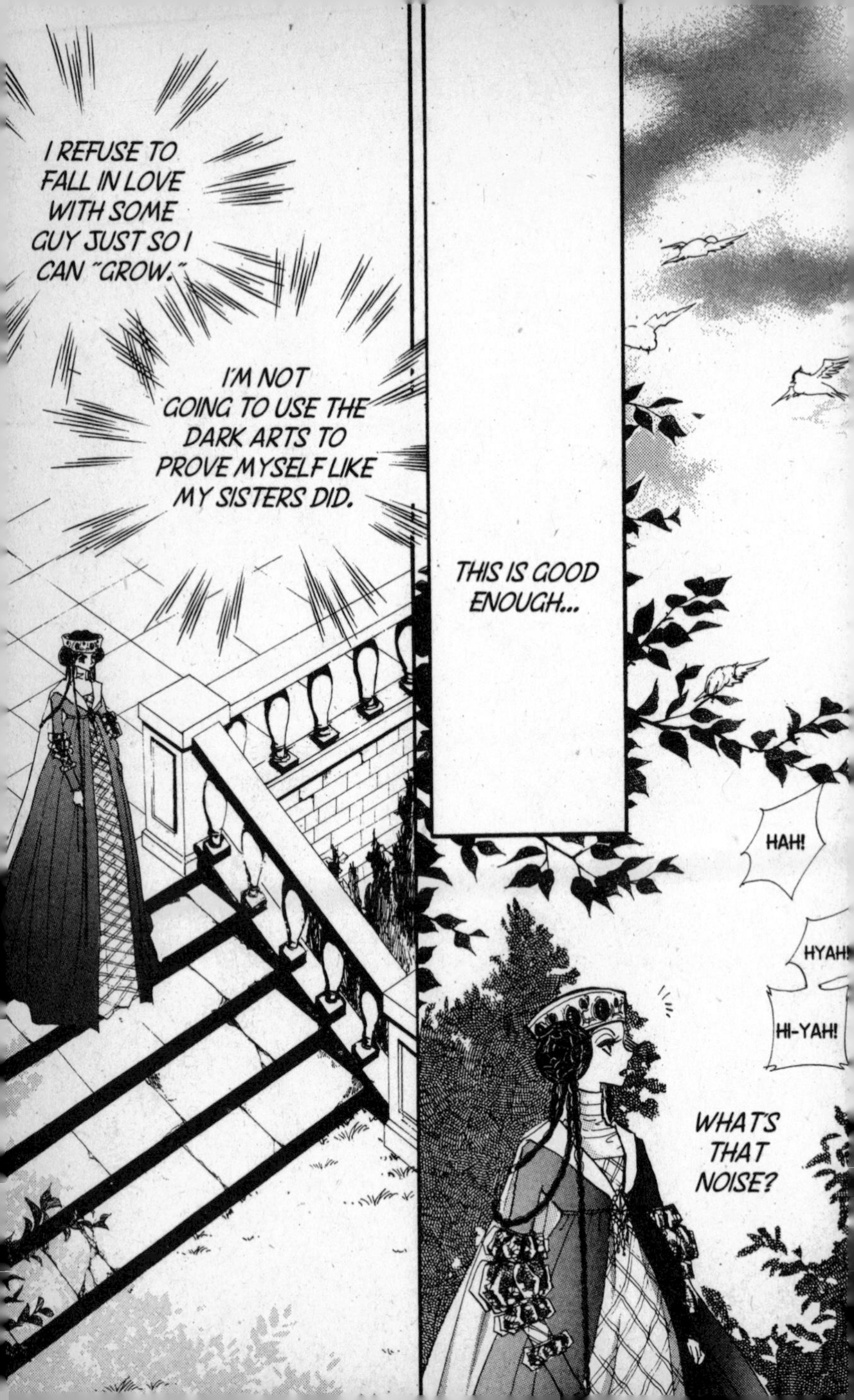
I REFUSE TO FALL IN LOVE WITH SOME GUY JUST SO I CAN "GROW."
I'M NOT GOING TO USE THE DARK ARTS TO PROVE MYSELF LIKE MY SISTERS DID.
THIS IS GOOD ENOUGH...
HAH!
HYAH
HI-YAH!
WHAT'S THAT NOISE?

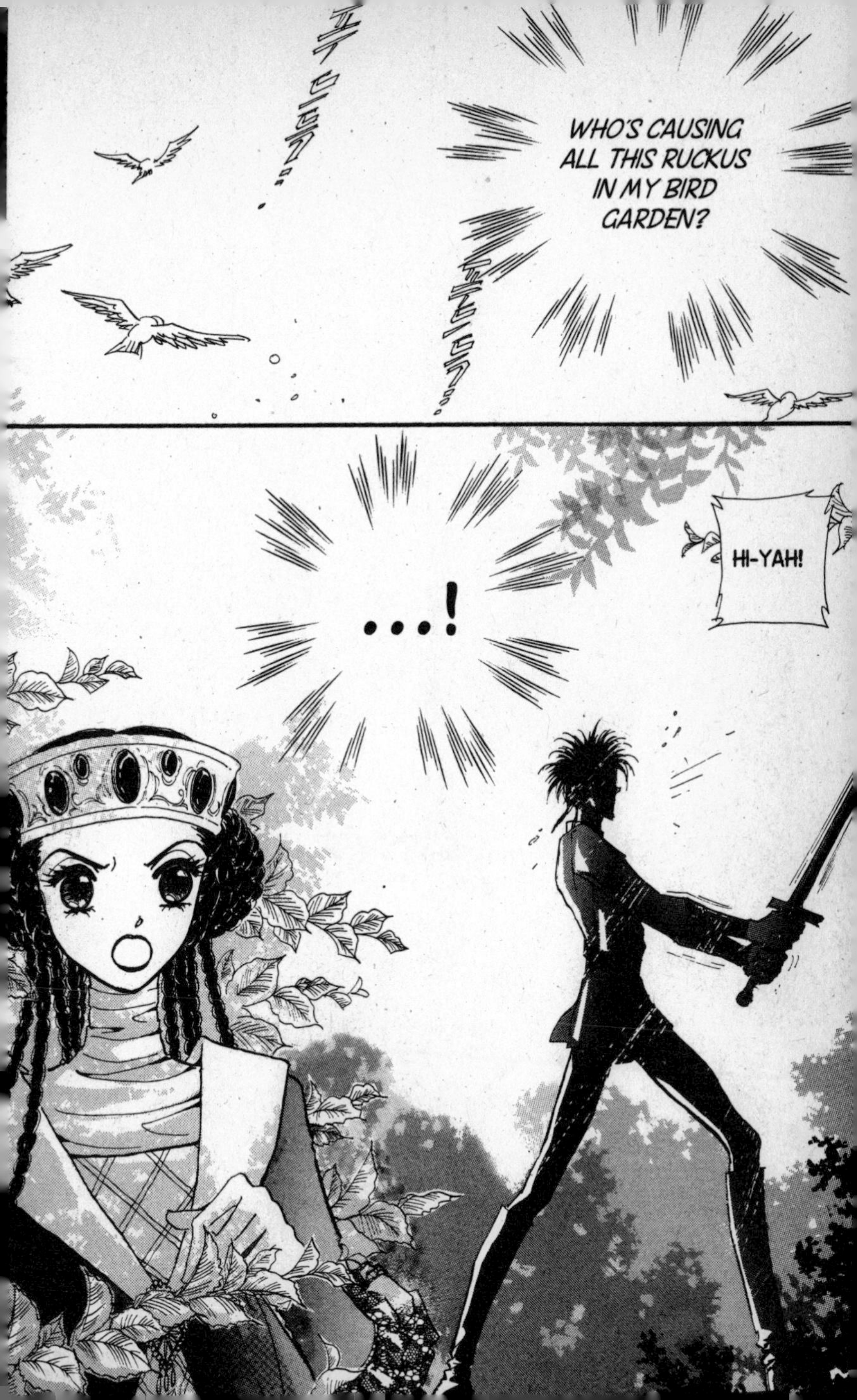
WHO'S CAUSING ALL THIS RUCKUS IN MY BIRD GARDEN?
...!
HI-YAH!

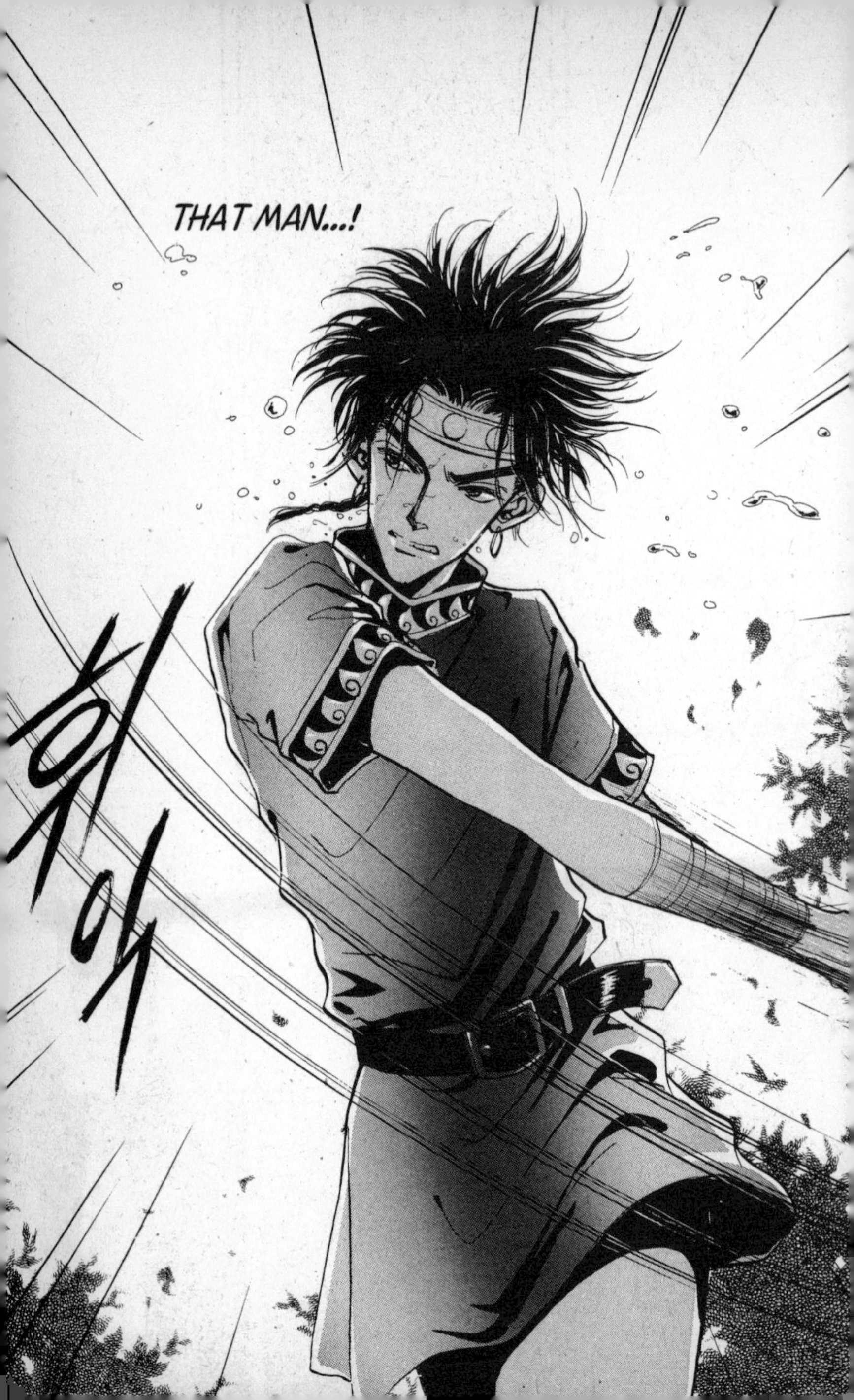
THAT MAN...!

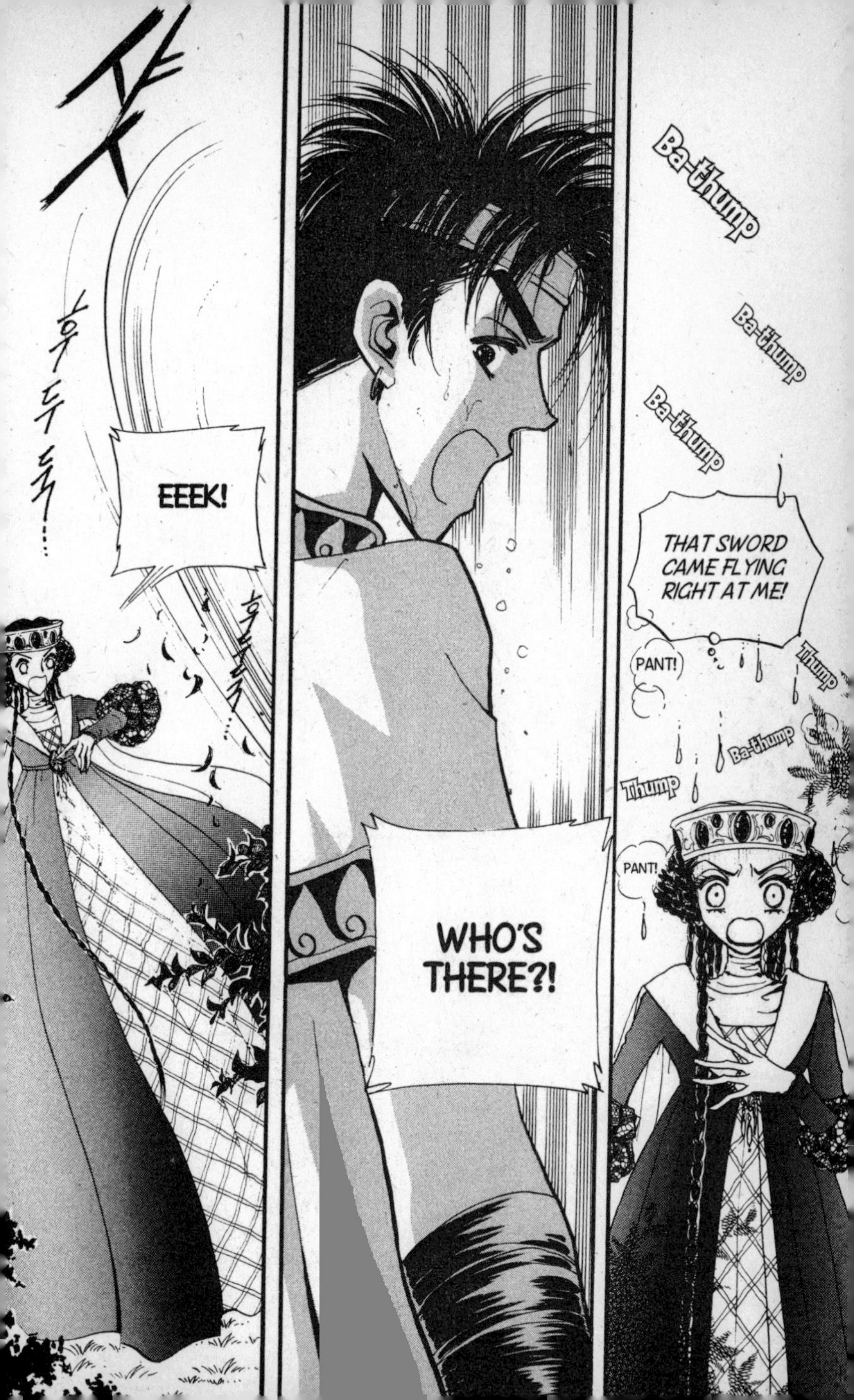
EEEK!
WHO'S THERE?!
Ba-thump
Ba-thump
Ba-thump
THAT SWORD CAME FLYING RIGHT AT ME!
PANT!
Thump
Ba-thump
Thump
PANT!

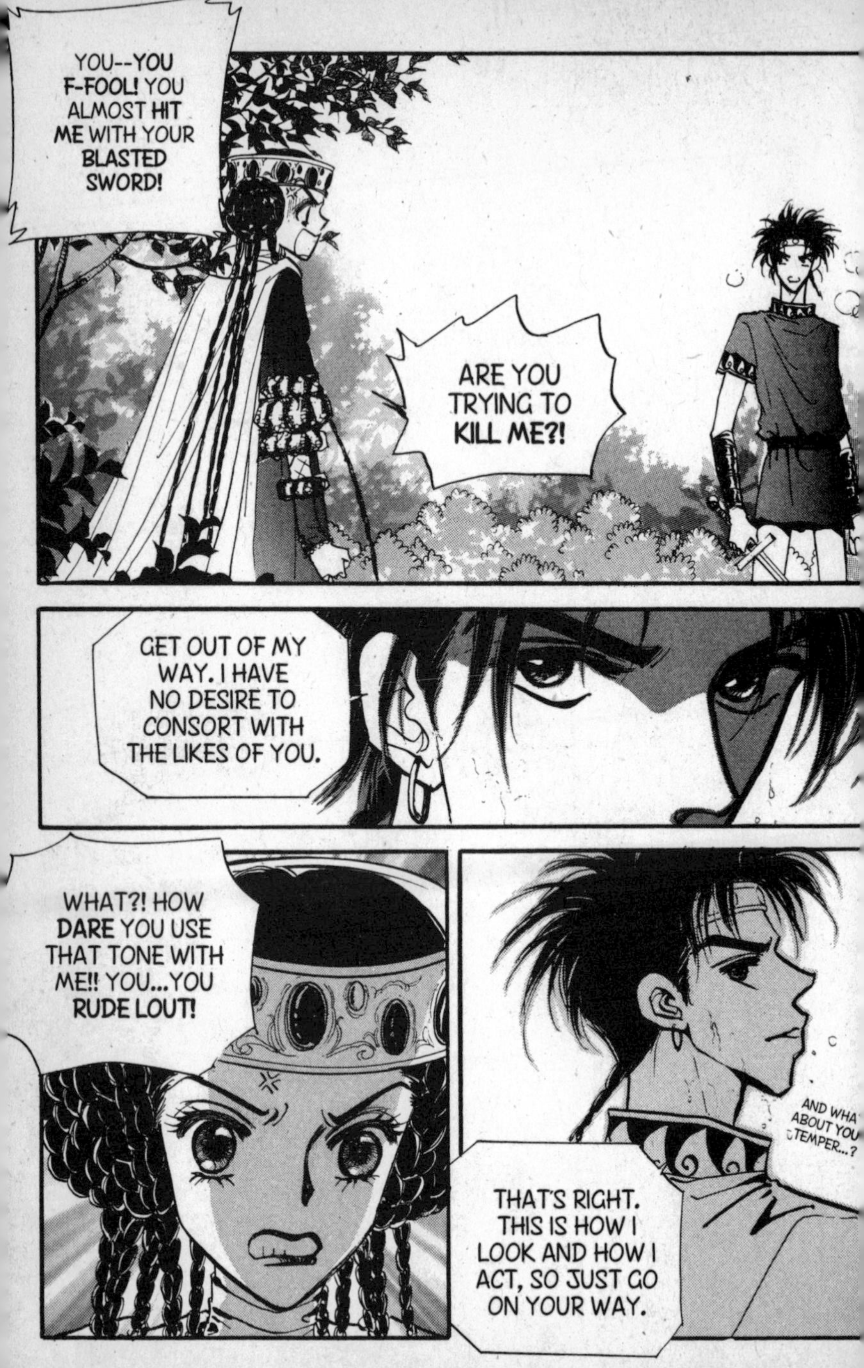
YOU--YOU F-FOOL! YOU ALMOST HIT ME WITH YOUR BLASTED SWORD!
ARE YOU TRYING TO KILL ME?!
GET OUT OF MY WAY. I HAVE NO DESIRE TO CONSORT WITH THE LIKES OF YOU.
WHAT?! HOW DARE YOU USE THAT TONE WITH ME!! YOU...YOU RUDE LOUT!
THAT'S RIGHT. THIS IS HOW I LOOK AND HOW I ACT, SO JUST GO ON YOUR WAY.
AND WHAT ABOUT YOUR TEMPER...?

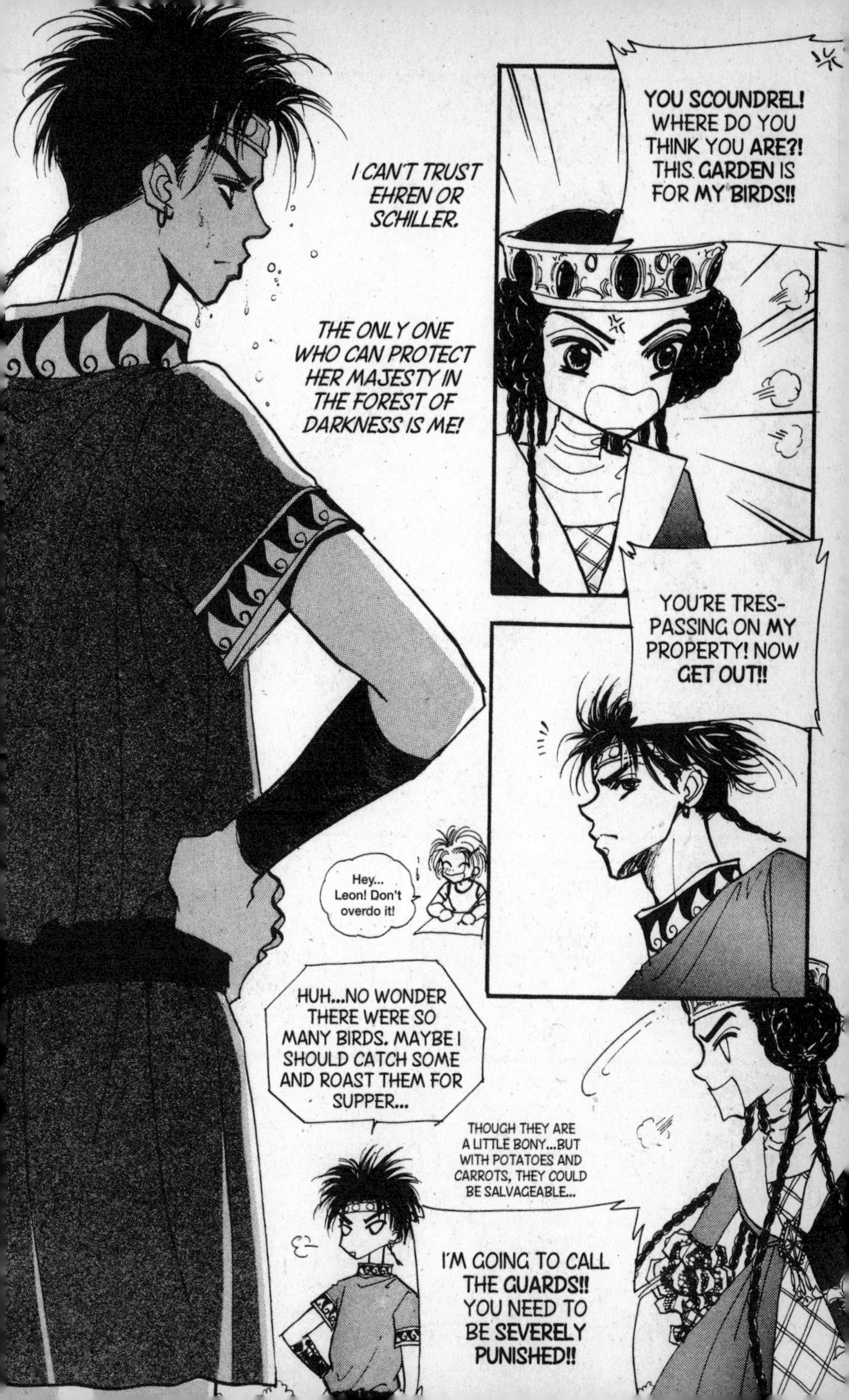
I CAN'T TRUST EHREN OR SCHILLER.
THE ONLY ONE WHO CAN PROTECT HER MAJESTY IN THE FOREST OF DARKNESS IS ME!
YOU SCOUNDREL! WHERE DO YOU THINK YOU ARE?! THIS GARDEN IS FOR MY BIRDS!!
YOU'RE TRES-PASSING ON MY PROPERTY! NOW GET OUT!!
Hey... Leon! Don't overdo it!
HUH...NO WONDER THERE WERE SO MANY BIRDS. MAYBE I SHOULD CATCH SOME AND ROAST THEM FOR SUPPER...
THOUGH THEY ARE A LITTLE BONY...BUT WITH POTATOES AND CARROTS, THEY COULD BE SALVAGEABLE...
I'M GOING TO CALL THE GUARDS!! YOU NEED TO BE SEVERELY PUNISHED!!

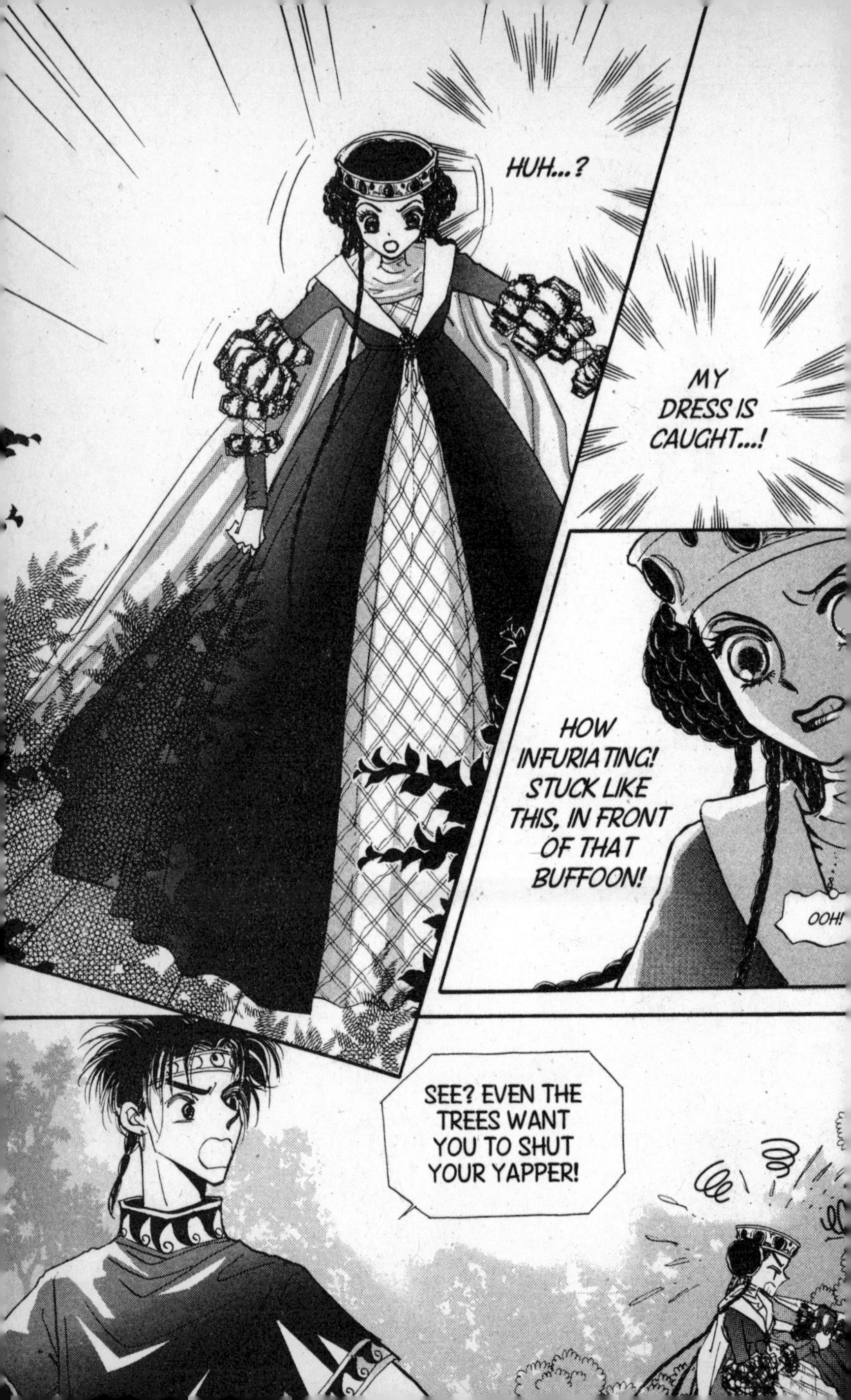
HUH...?
MY DRESS IS CAUGHT...!
HOW INFURIATING! STUCK LIKE THIS, IN FRONT OF THAT BUFFOON!
OOH!
SEE? EVEN THE TREES WANT YOU TO SHUT YOUR YAPPER!

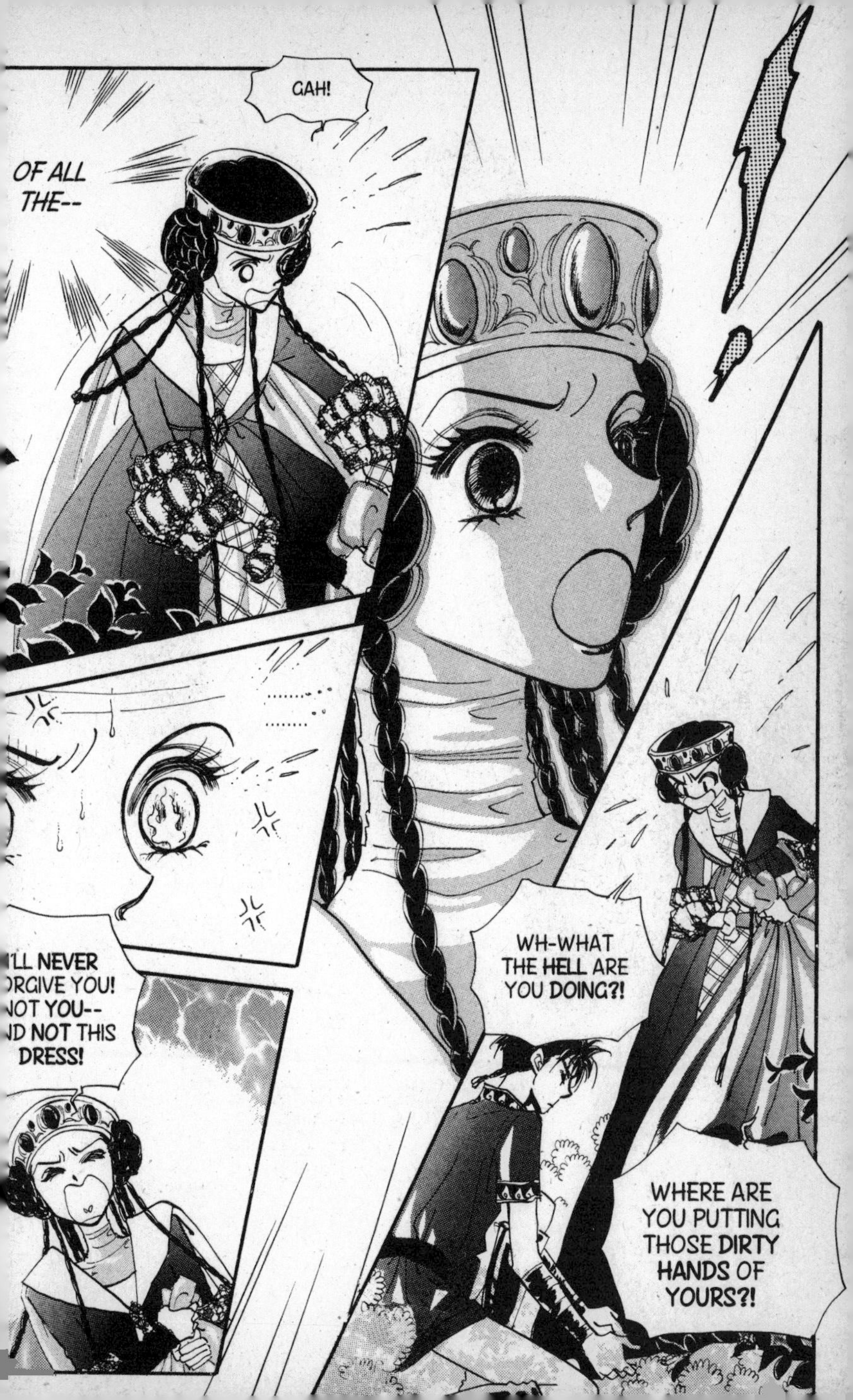

GAH!
OF ALL THE--
....
....
'LL NEVER ORGIVE YOU! NOT YOU-- ND NOT THIS DRESS!
WH-WHAT THE HELL ARE YOU DOING?!
WHERE ARE YOU PUTTING THOSE DIRTY HANDS OF YOURS?!

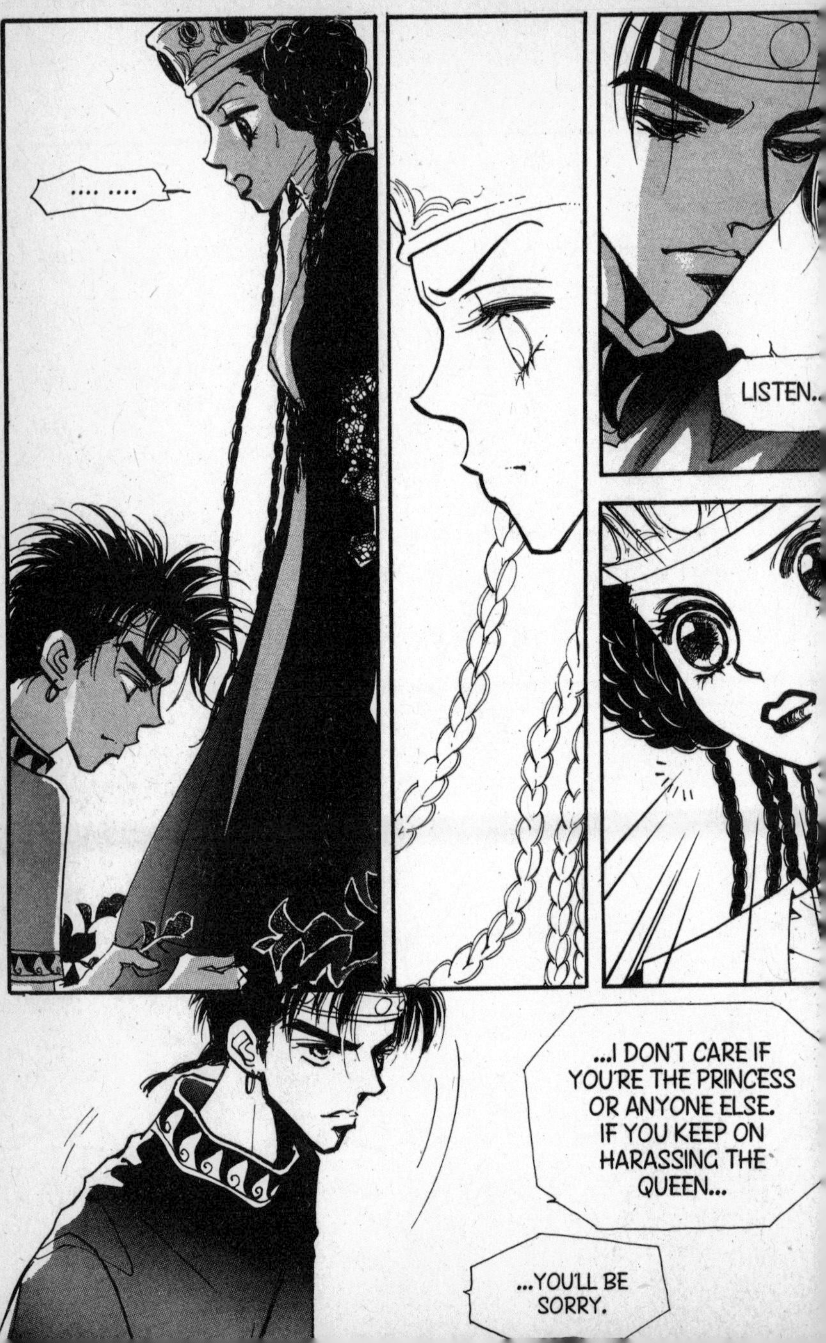
....
LISTEN...
...I DON'T CARE IF YOU'RE THE PRINCESS OR ANYONE ELSE. IF YOU KEEP ON HARASSING THE QUEEN...
...YOU'LL BE SORRY.

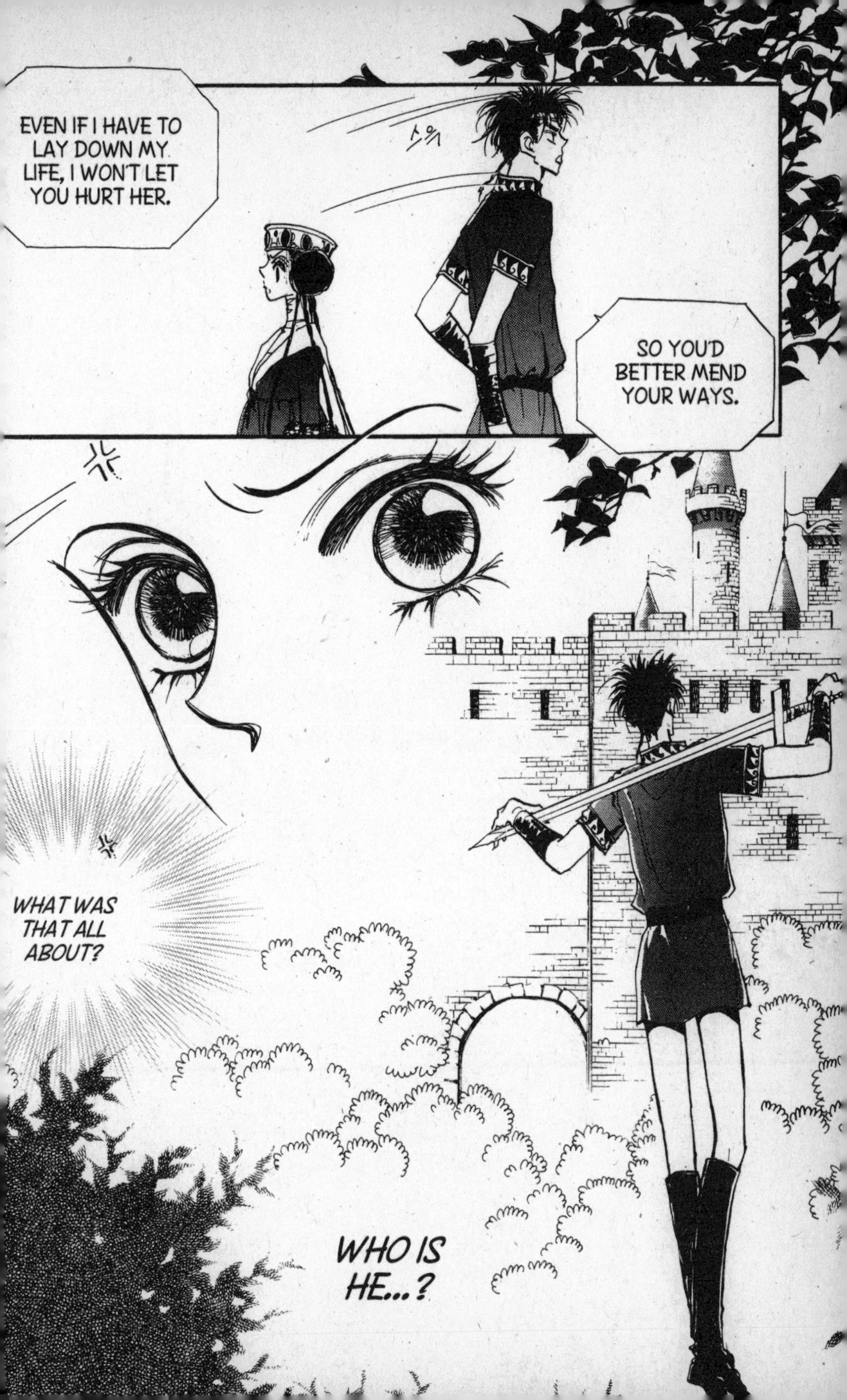
EVEN IF I HAVE TO LAY DOWN MY LIFE, I WON'T LET YOU HURT HER.
SO YOU'D BETTER MEND YOUR WAYS.
WHAT WAS THAT ALL ABOUT?
WHO IS HE...?

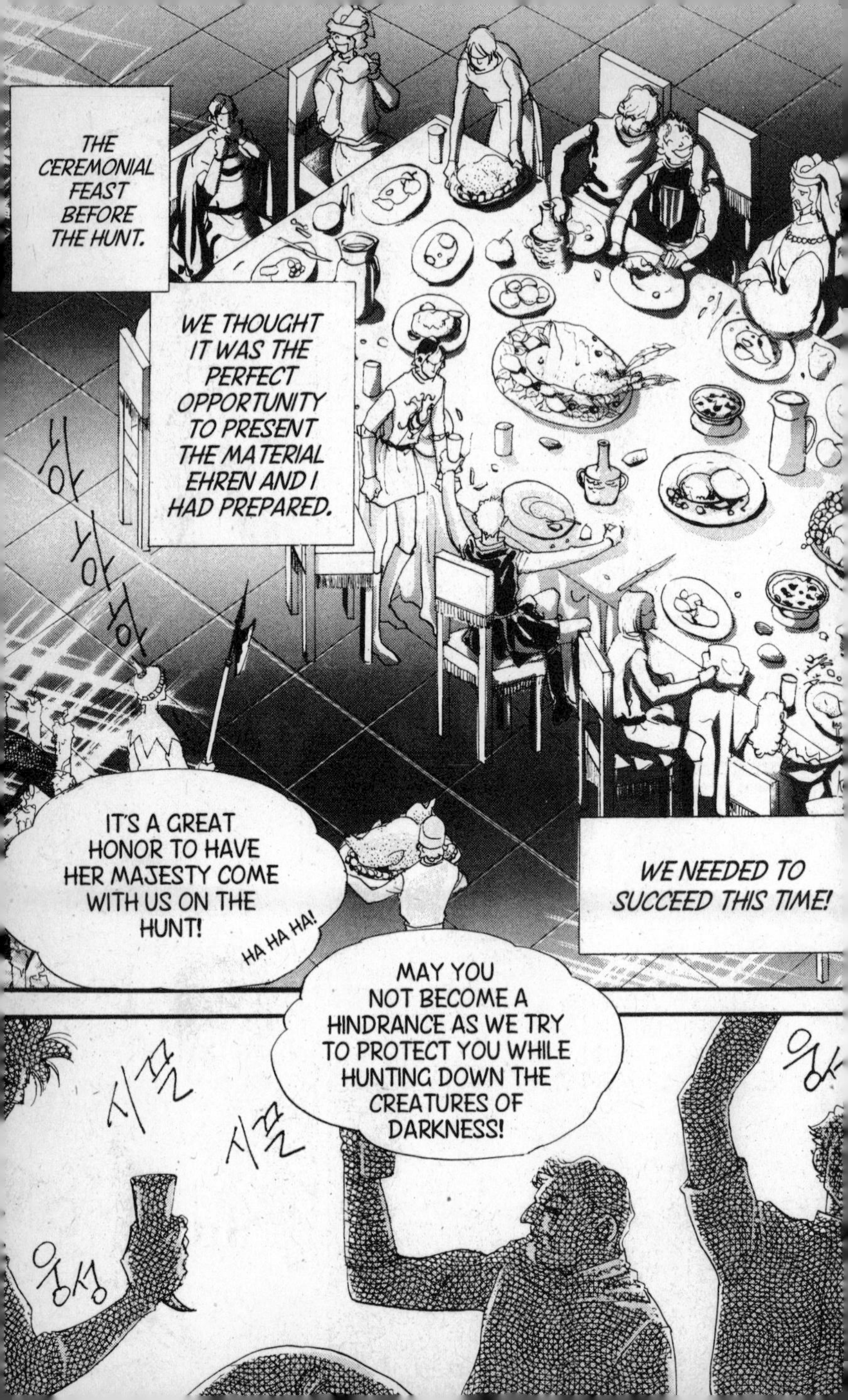
THE CEREMONIAL FEAST BEFORE THE HUNT.
WE THOUGHT IT WAS THE PERFECT OPPORTUNITY TO PRESENT THE MATERIAL EHREN AND I HAD PREPARED.
IT'S A GREAT HONOR TO HAVE HER MAJESTY COME WITH US ON THE HUNT!
HA HA HA!
WE NEEDED TO SUCCEED THIS TIME!
MAY YOU NOT BECOME A HINDRANCE AS WE TRY TO PROTECT YOU WHILE HUNTING DOWN THE CREATURES OF DARKNESS!

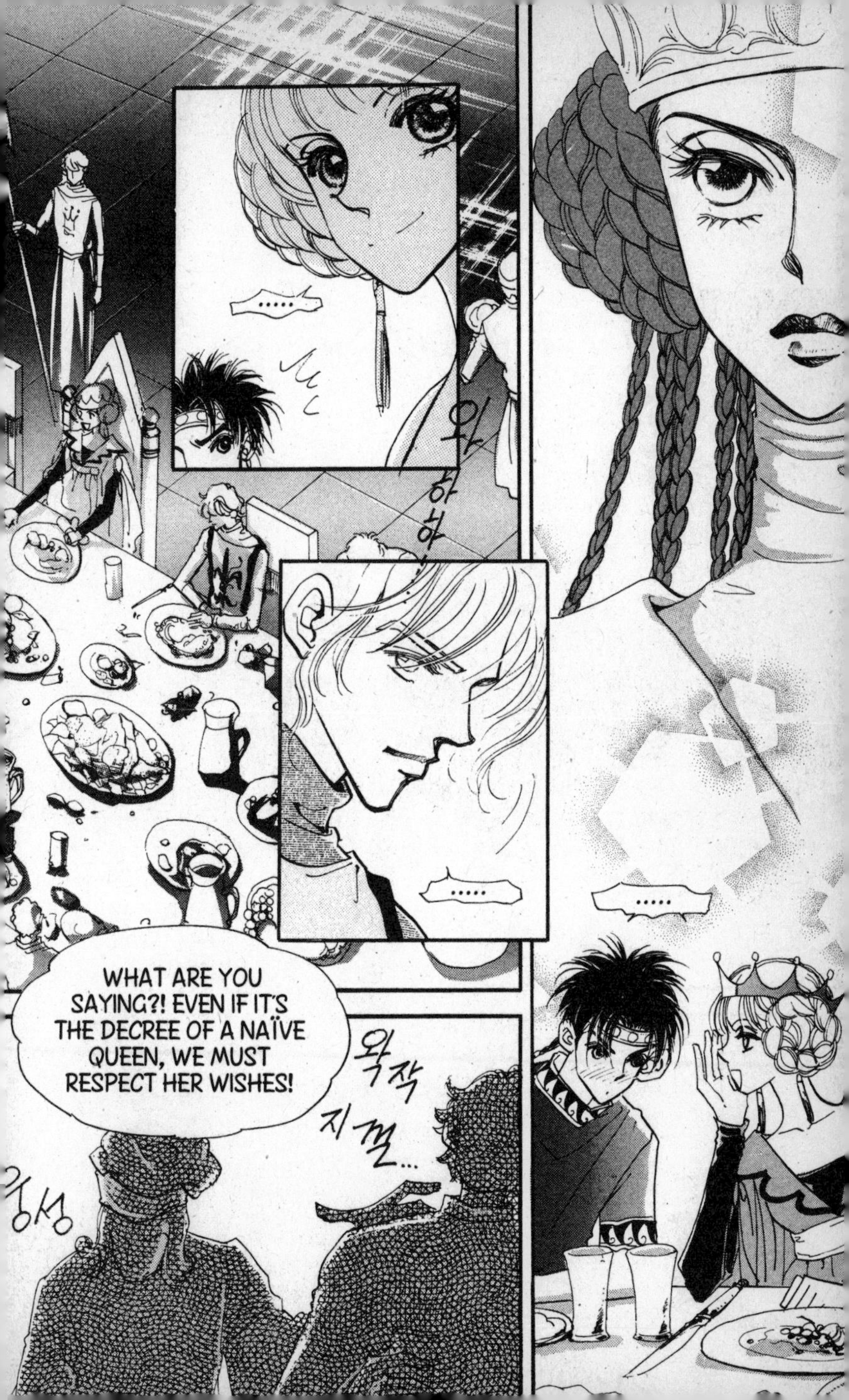
......
와하하
......
......
WHAT ARE YOU SAYING?! EVEN IF IT'S THE DECREE OF A NAÏVE QUEEN, WE MUST RESPECT HER WISHES!

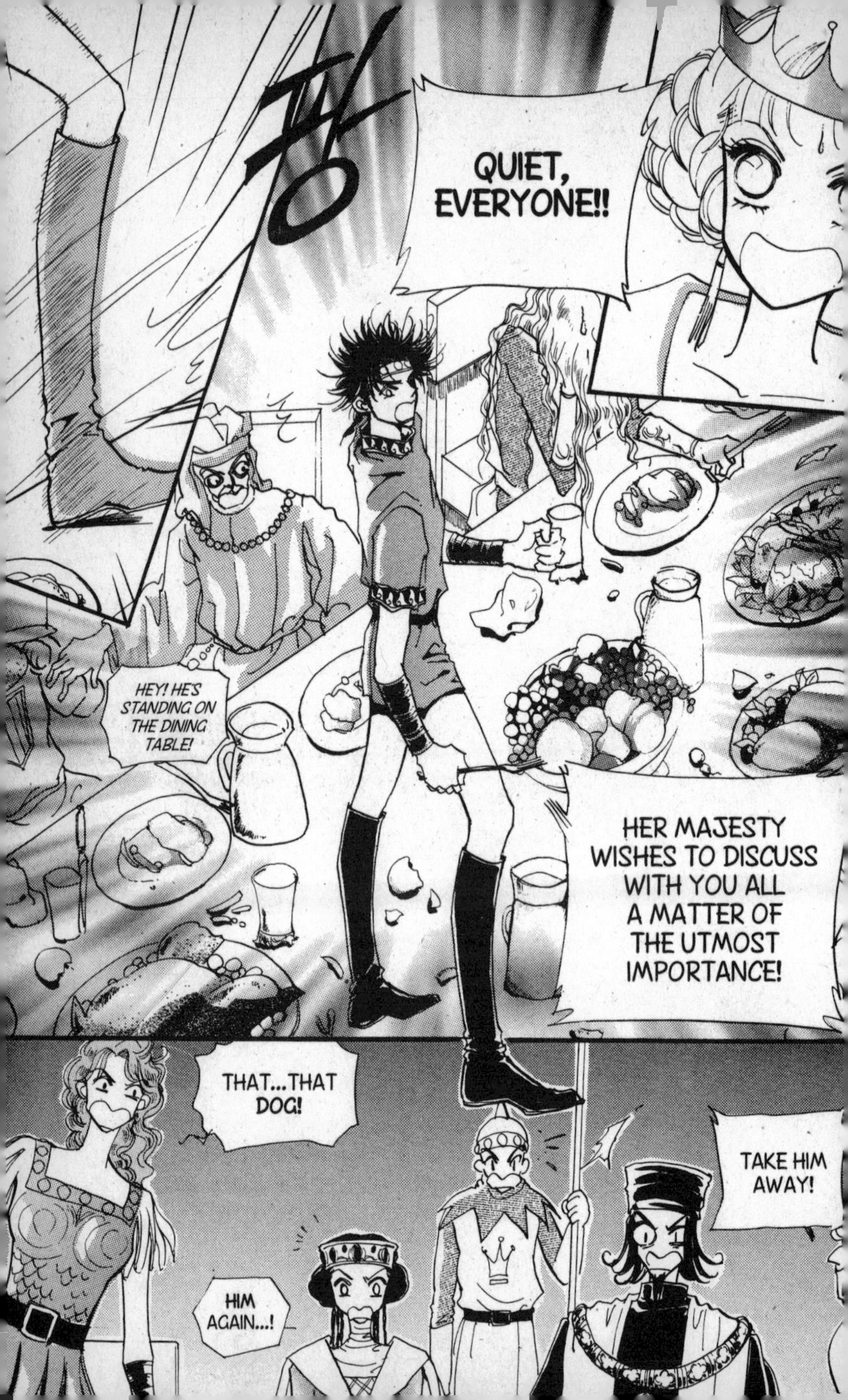
QUIET, EVERYONE!!
HER MAJESTY WISHES TO DISCUSS WITH YOU ALL A MATTER OF THE UTMOST IMPORTANCE!
HEY! HE'S STANDING ON THE DINING TABLE!
TAKE HIM AWAY!
THAT...THAT DOG!
HIM AGAIN...!

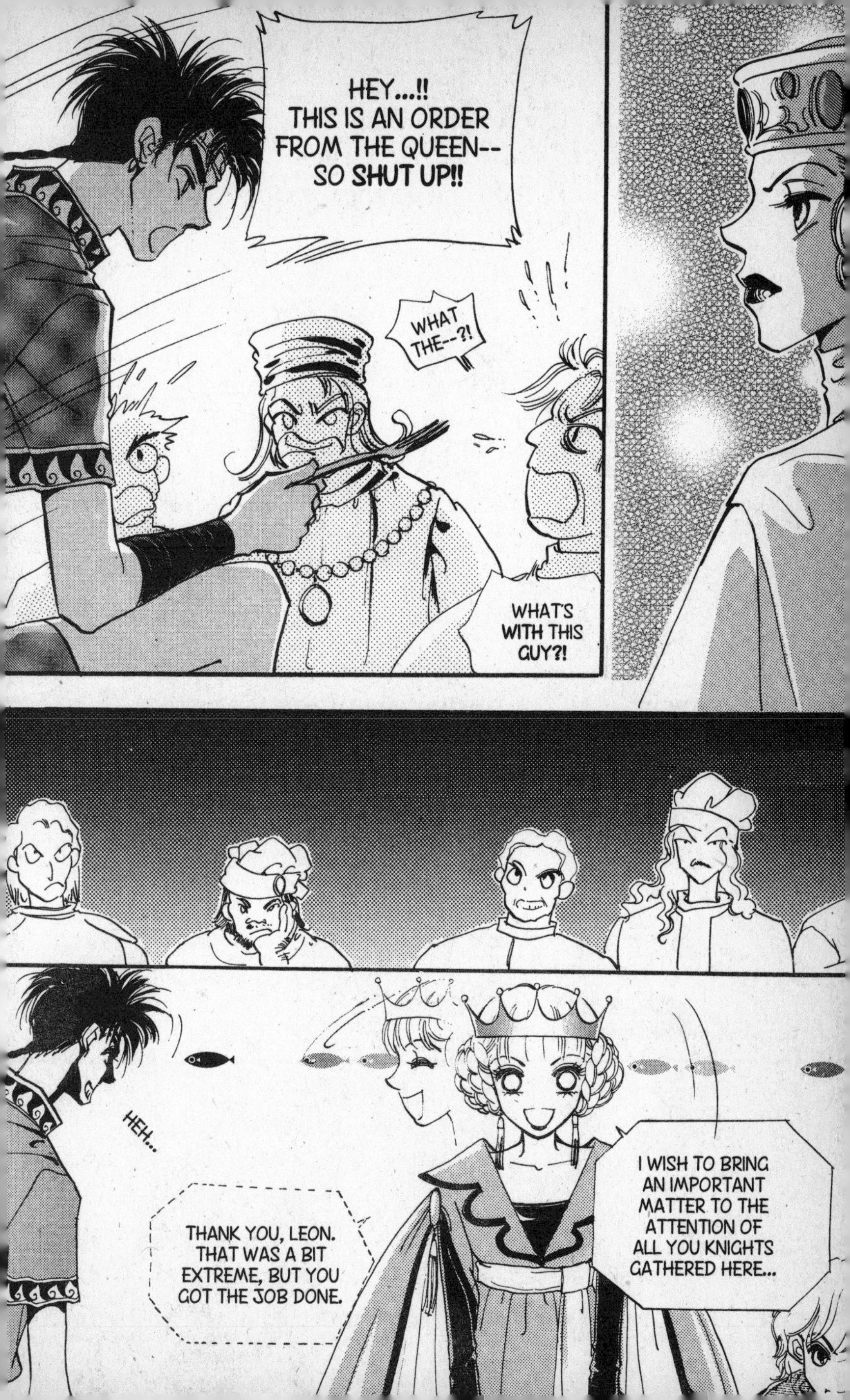
HEY...!! THIS IS AN ORDER FROM THE QUEEN-- SO SHUT UP!!
WHAT THE--?!
WHAT'S WITH THIS GUY?!
HEH...
THANK YOU, LEON. THAT WAS A BIT EXTREME, BUT YOU GOT THE JOB DONE.
I WISH TO BRING AN IMPORTANT MATTER TO THE ATTENTION OF ALL YOU KNIGHTS GATHERED HERE...

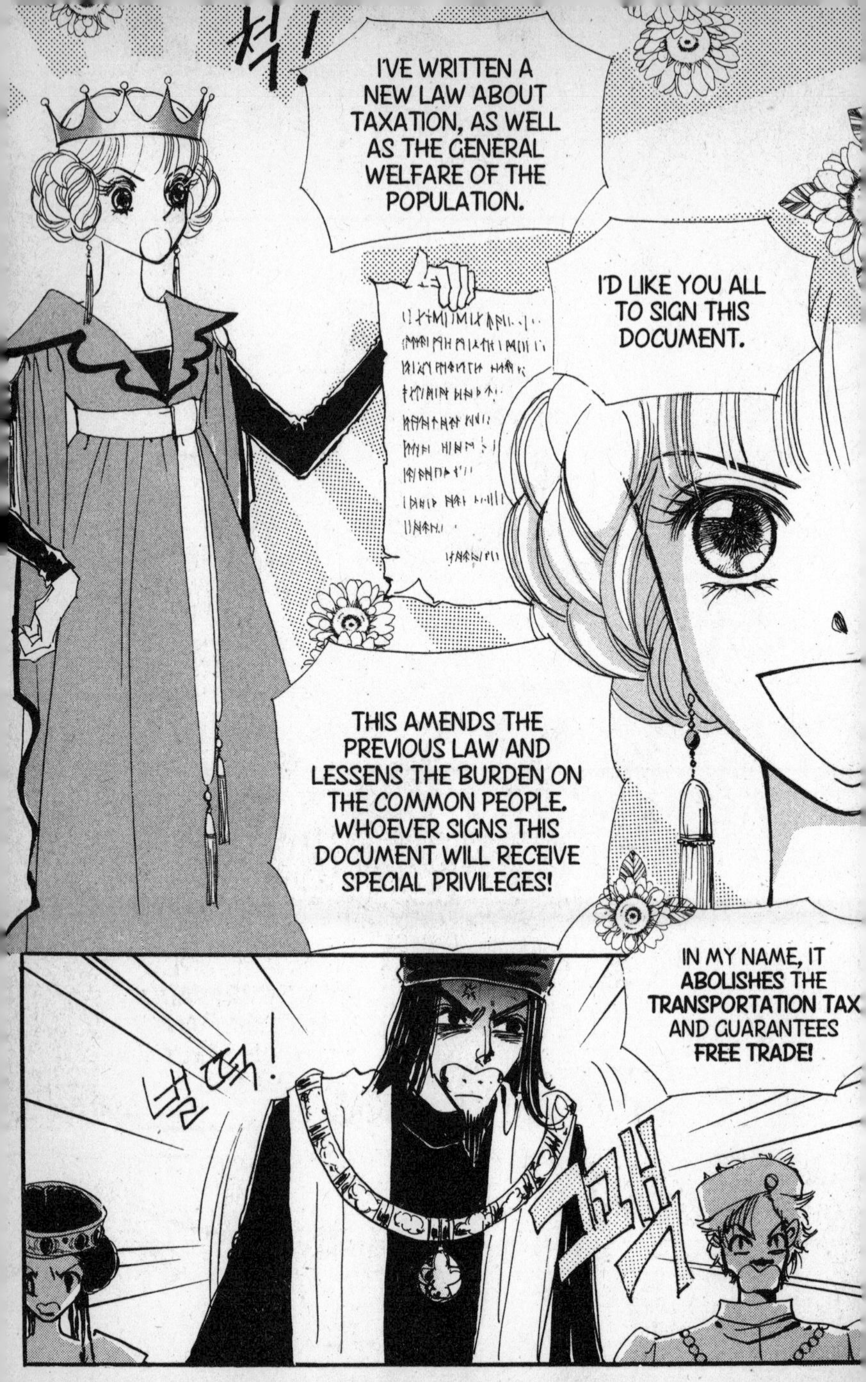
척!
I'VE WRITTEN A NEW LAW ABOUT TAXATION, AS WELL AS THE GENERAL WELFARE OF THE POPULATION.
I'D LIKE YOU ALL TO SIGN THIS DOCUMENT.
THIS AMENDS THE PREVIOUS LAW AND LESSENS THE BURDEN ON THE COMMON PEOPLE. WHOEVER SIGNS THIS DOCUMENT WILL RECEIVE SPECIAL PRIVILEGES!
IN MY NAME, IT ABOLISHES THE TRANSPORTATION TAX AND GUARANTEES FREE TRADE!
벌떡!

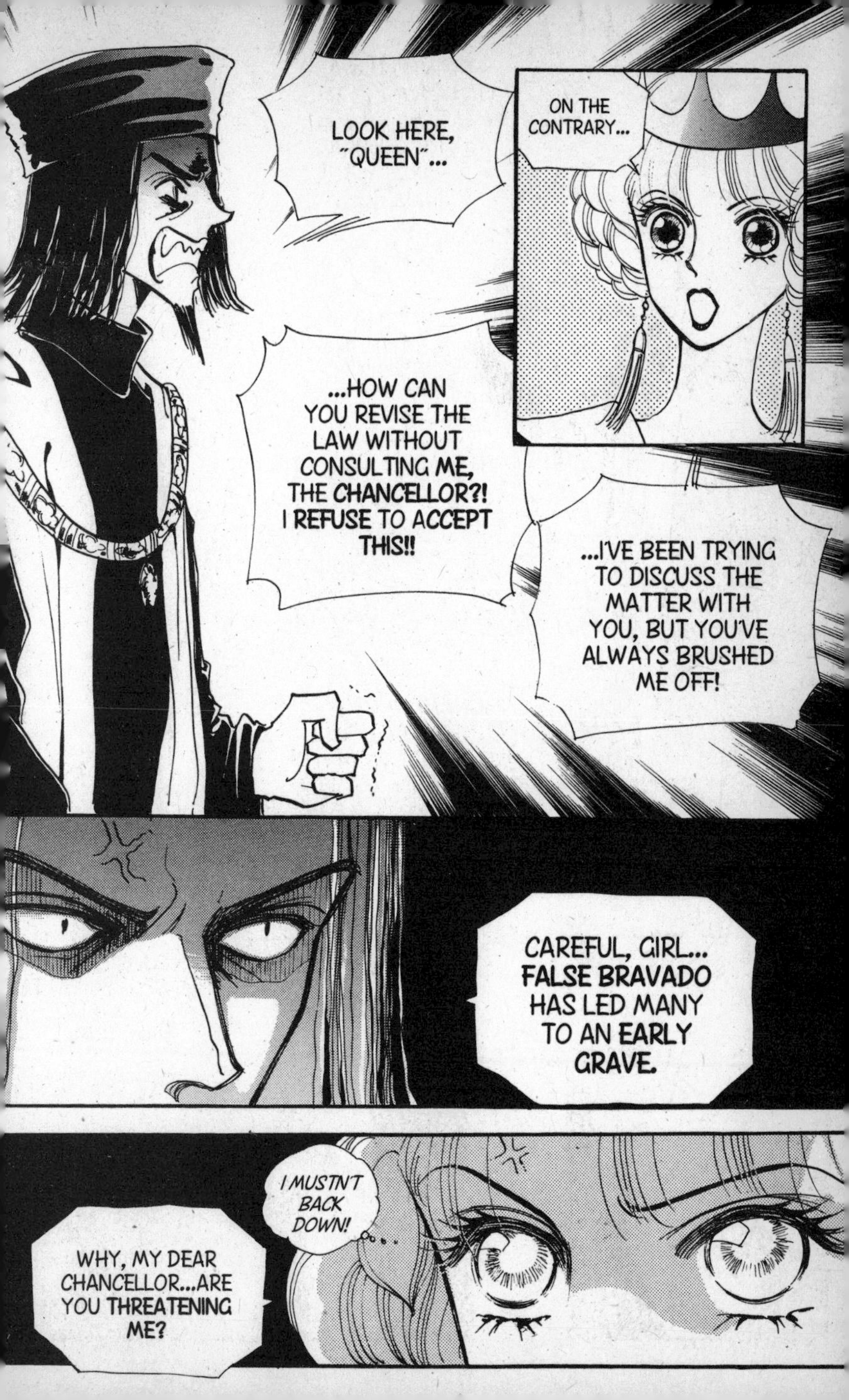
LOOK HERE, "QUEEN"...
ON THE CONTRARY...
...HOW CAN YOU REVISE THE LAW WITHOUT CONSULTING ME, THE CHANCELLOR?! I REFUSE TO ACCEPT THIS!!
...I'VE BEEN TRYING TO DISCUSS THE MATTER WITH YOU, BUT YOU'VE ALWAYS BRUSHED ME OFF!
CAREFUL, GIRL... FALSE BRAVADO HAS LED MANY TO AN EARLY GRAVE.
WHY, MY DEAR CHANCELLOR...ARE YOU THREATENING ME?
I MUSTN'T BACK DOWN!

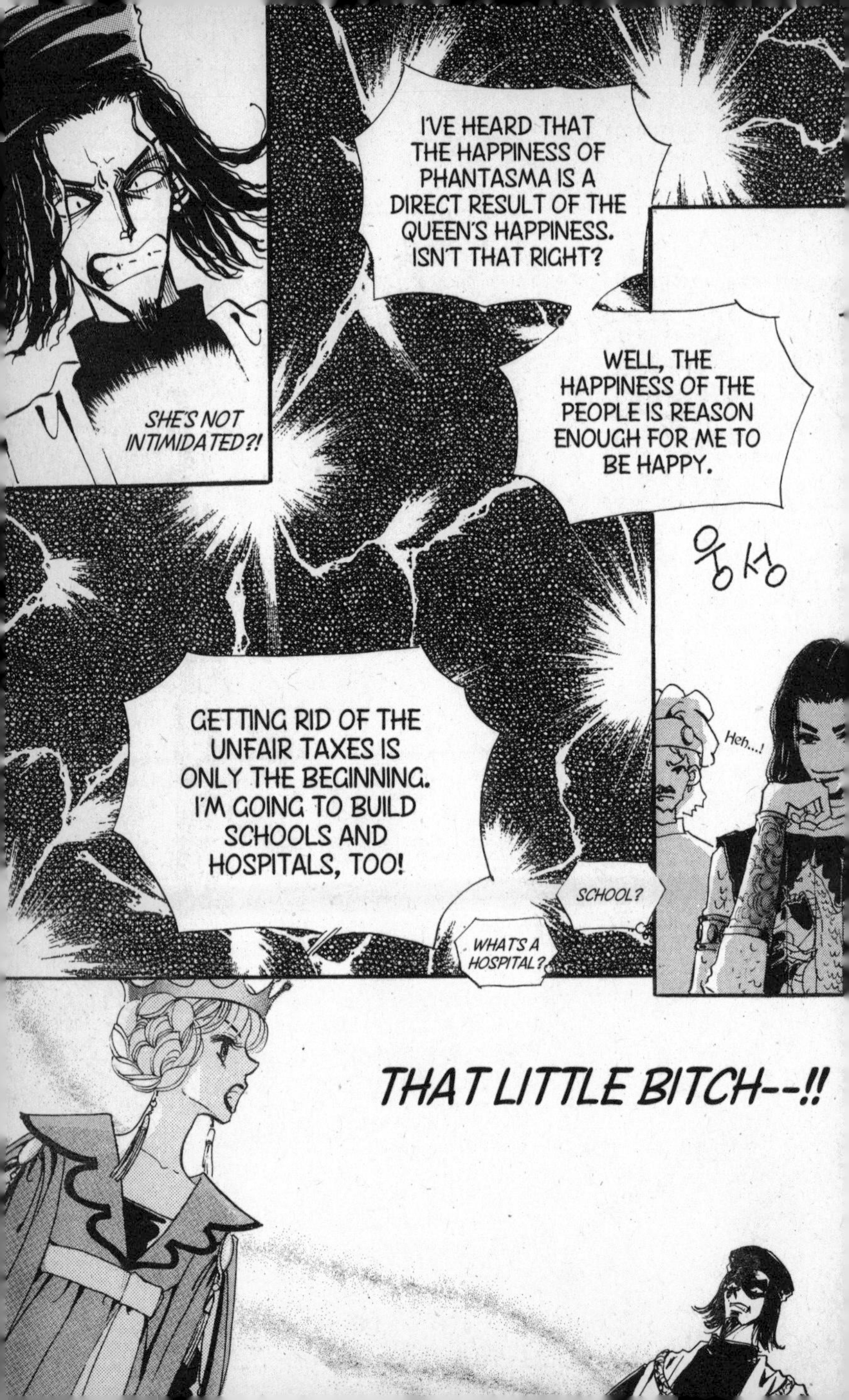
SHE'S NOT INTIMIDATED?!
I'VE HEARD THAT THE HAPPINESS OF PHANTASMA IS A DIRECT RESULT OF THE QUEEN'S HAPPINESS. ISN'T THAT RIGHT?
WELL, THE HAPPINESS OF THE PEOPLE IS REASON ENOUGH FOR ME TO BE HAPPY.
GETTING RID OF THE UNFAIR TAXES IS ONLY THE BEGINNING. I'M GOING TO BUILD SCHOOLS AND HOSPITALS, TOO!
SCHOOL?
WHATS A HOSPITAL?
웅성
Heh...!
THAT LITTLE BITCH--!!

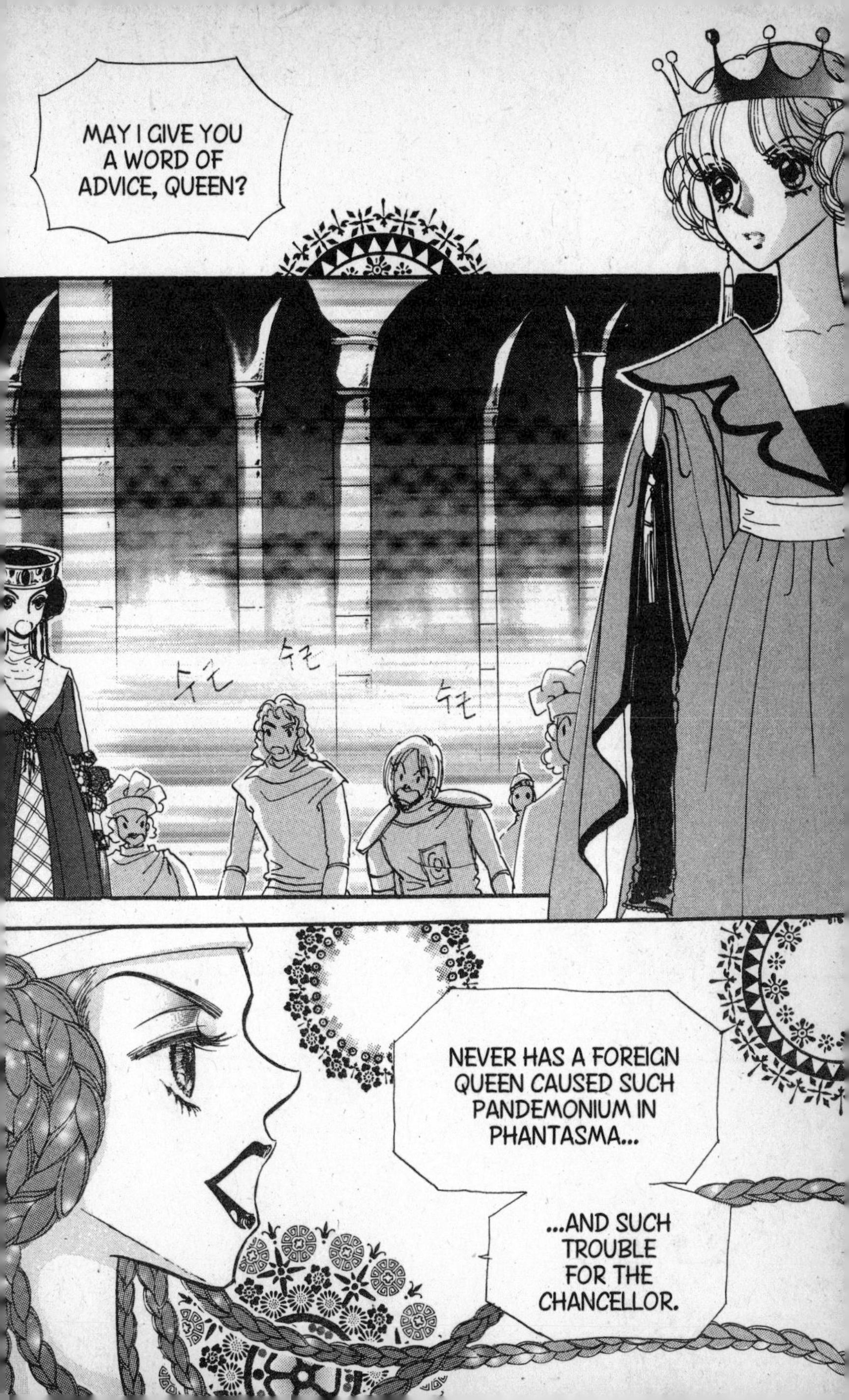
MAY I GIVE YOU A WORD OF ADVICE, QUEEN?
NEVER HAS A FOREIGN QUEEN CAUSED SUCH PANDEMONIUM IN PHANTASMA...
...AND SUCH TROUBLE FOR THE CHANCELLOR.

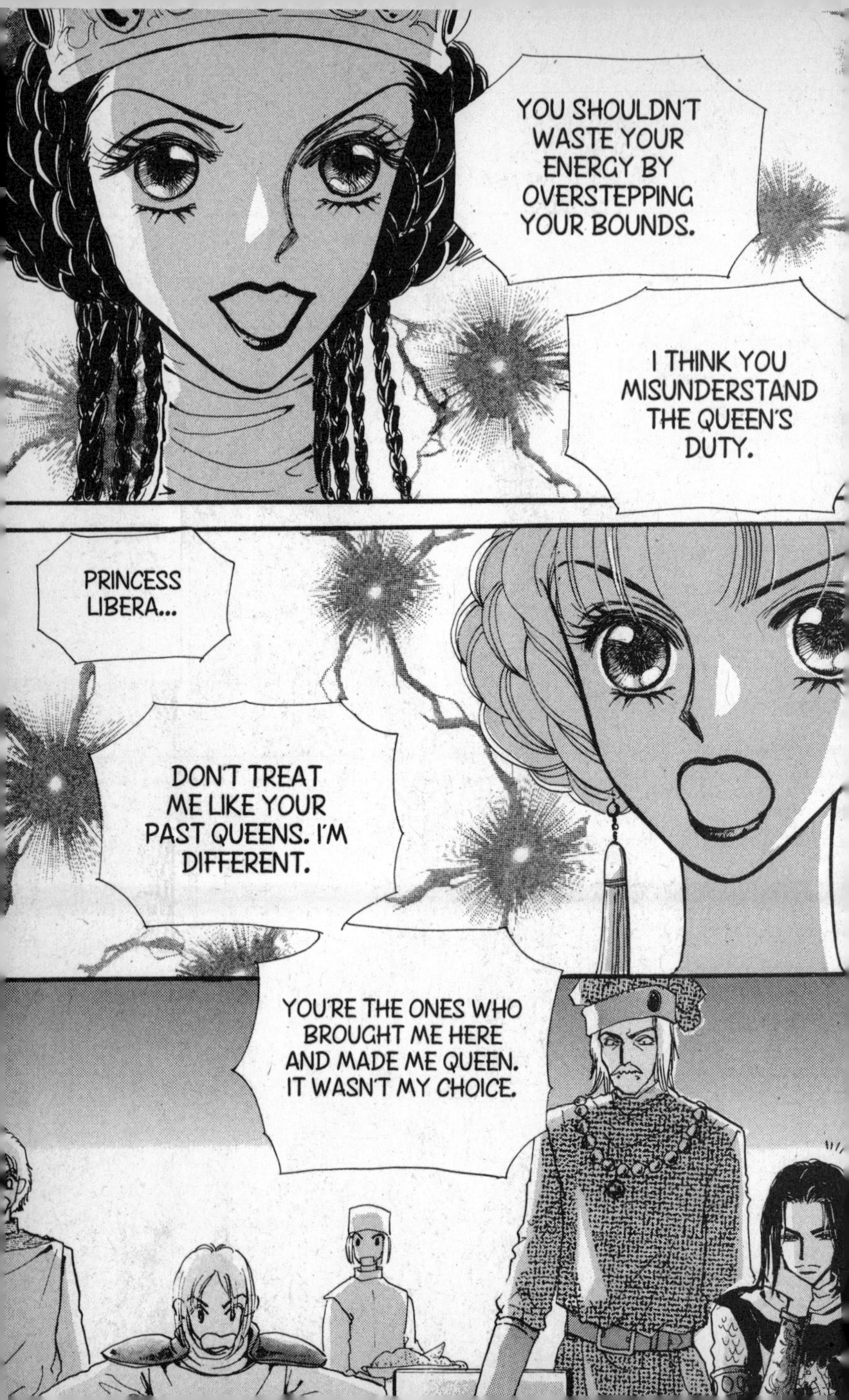

YOU SHOULDN'T WASTE YOUR ENERGY BY OVERSTEPPING YOUR BOUNDS.
I THINK YOU MISUNDERSTAND THE QUEEN'S DUTY.
PRINCESS LIBERA...
DON'T TREAT ME LIKE YOUR PAST QUEENS. I'M DIFFERENT.
YOU'RE THE ONES WHO BROUGHT ME HERE AND MADE ME QUEEN. IT WASN'T MY CHOICE.

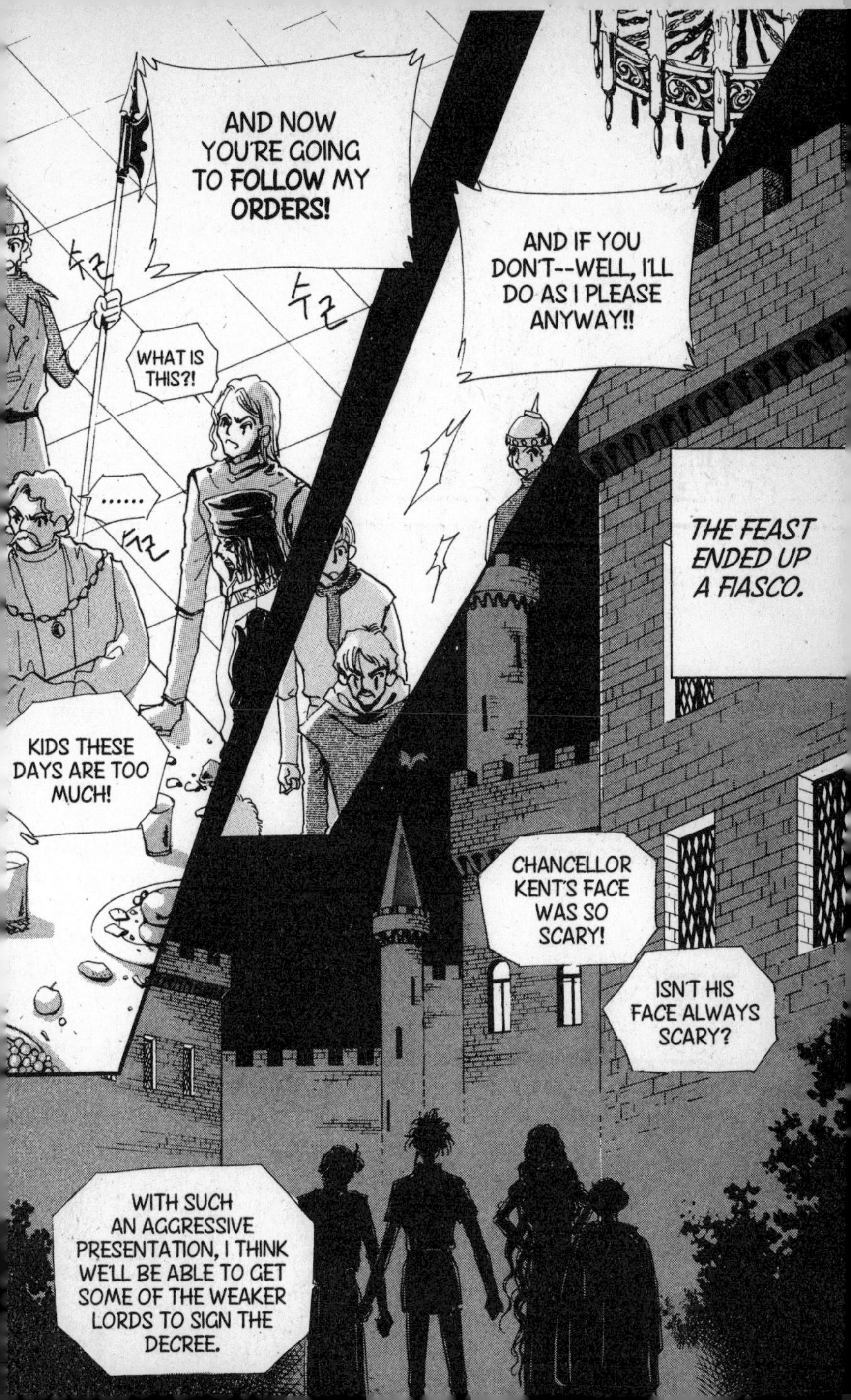
AND NOW YOU'RE GOING TO FOLLOW MY ORDERS!
수군
WHAT IS THIS?!
......
수군
KIDS THESE DAYS ARE TOO MUCH!
수군
AND IF YOU DON'T--WELL, I'LL DO AS I PLEASE ANYWAY!!
THE FEAST ENDED UP A FIASCO.
CHANCELLOR KENT'S FACE WAS SO SCARY!
ISN'T HIS FACE ALWAYS SCARY?
WITH SUCH AN AGGRESSIVE PRESENTATION, I THINK WE'LL BE ABLE TO GET SOME OF THE WEAKER LORDS TO SIGN THE DECREE.

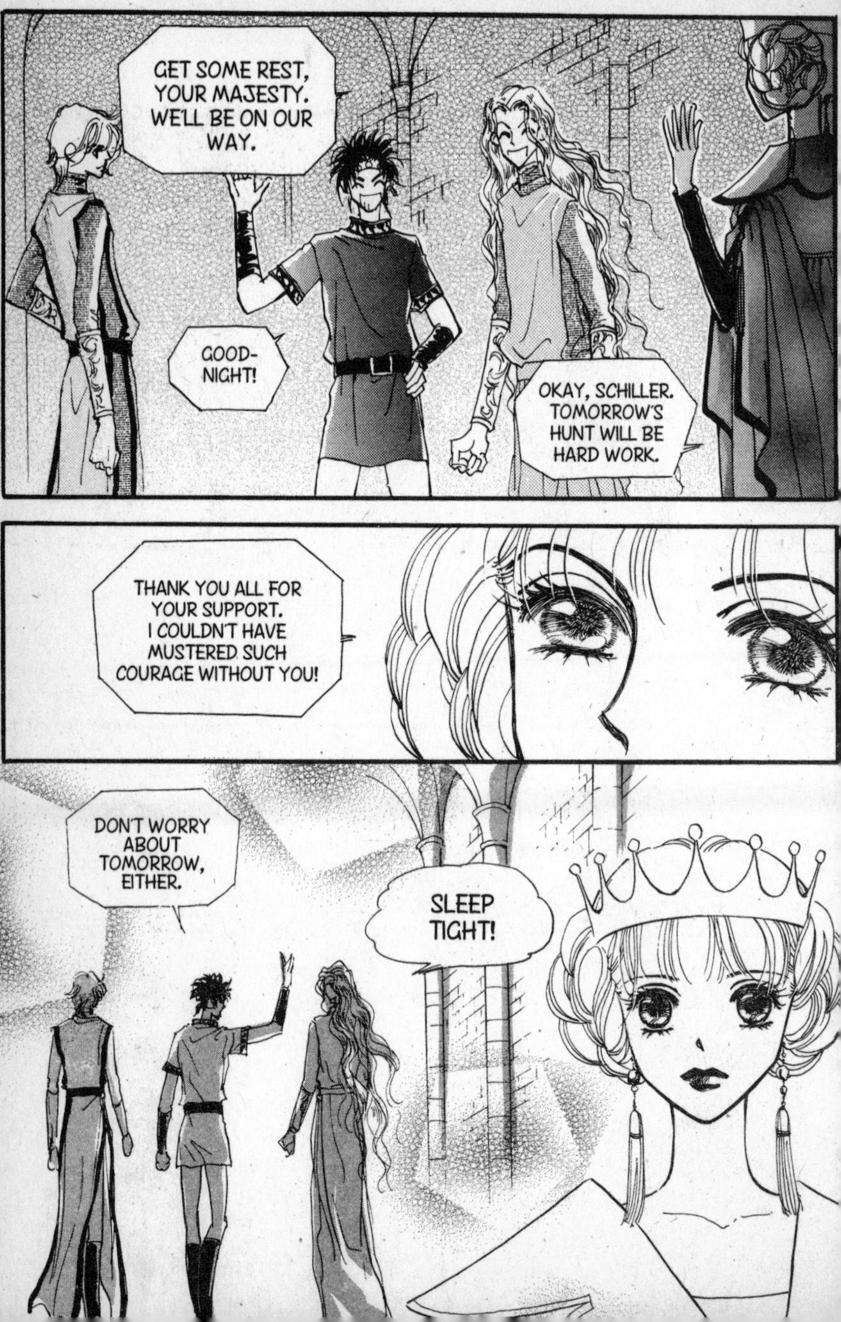
GET SOME REST, YOUR MAJESTY. WE'LL BE ON OUR WAY.
GOOD-NIGHT!
OKAY, SCHILLER. TOMORROW'S HUNT WILL BE HARD WORK.
THANK YOU ALL FOR YOUR SUPPORT. I COULDN'T HAVE MUSTERED SUCH COURAGE WITHOUT YOU!
DON'T WORRY ABOUT TOMORROW, EITHER.
SLEEP TIGHT!

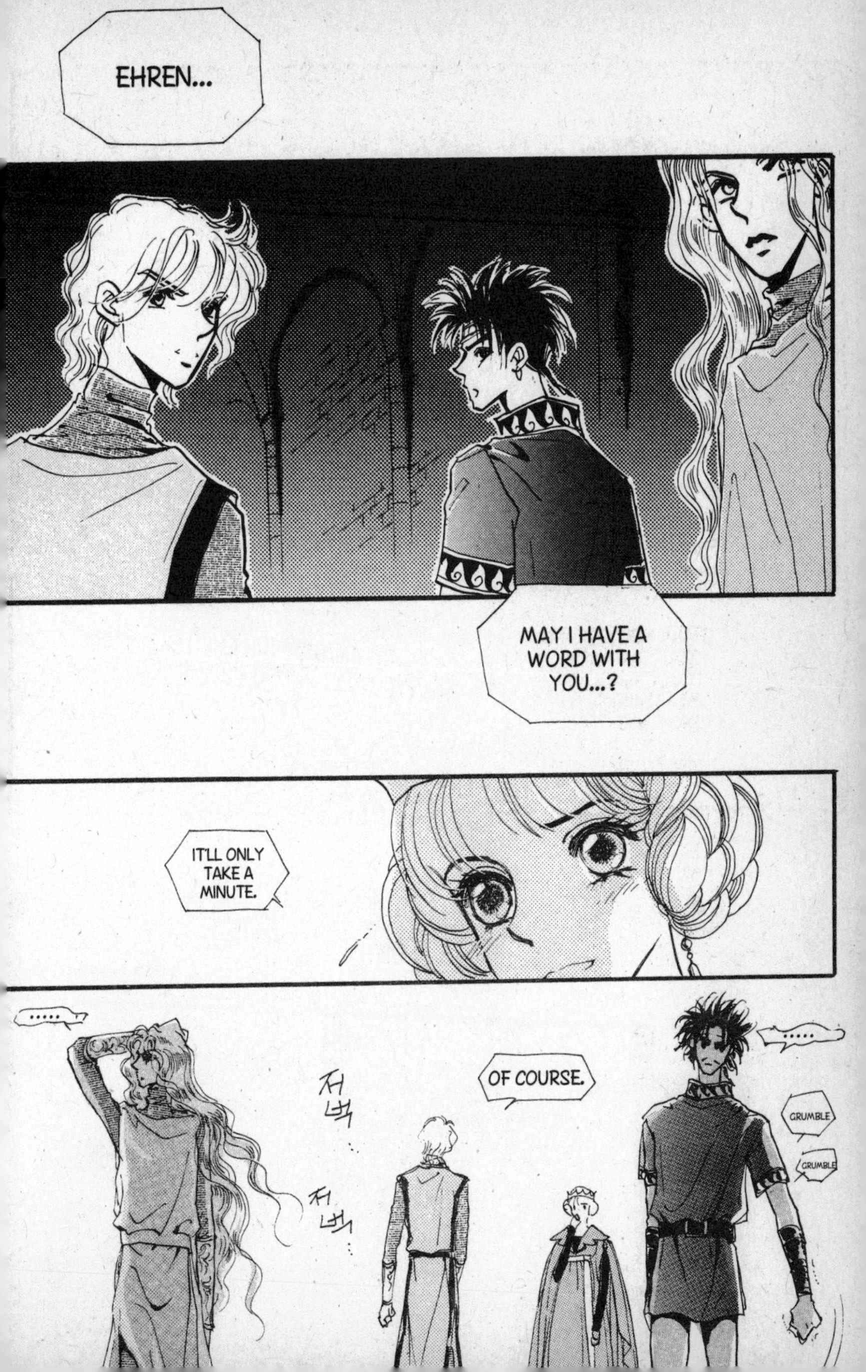
EHREN...
MAY I HAVE A WORD WITH YOU...?
IT'LL ONLY TAKE A MINUTE.
......
저벅...
저벅...
OF COURSE.
......
GRUMBLE
GRUMBLE

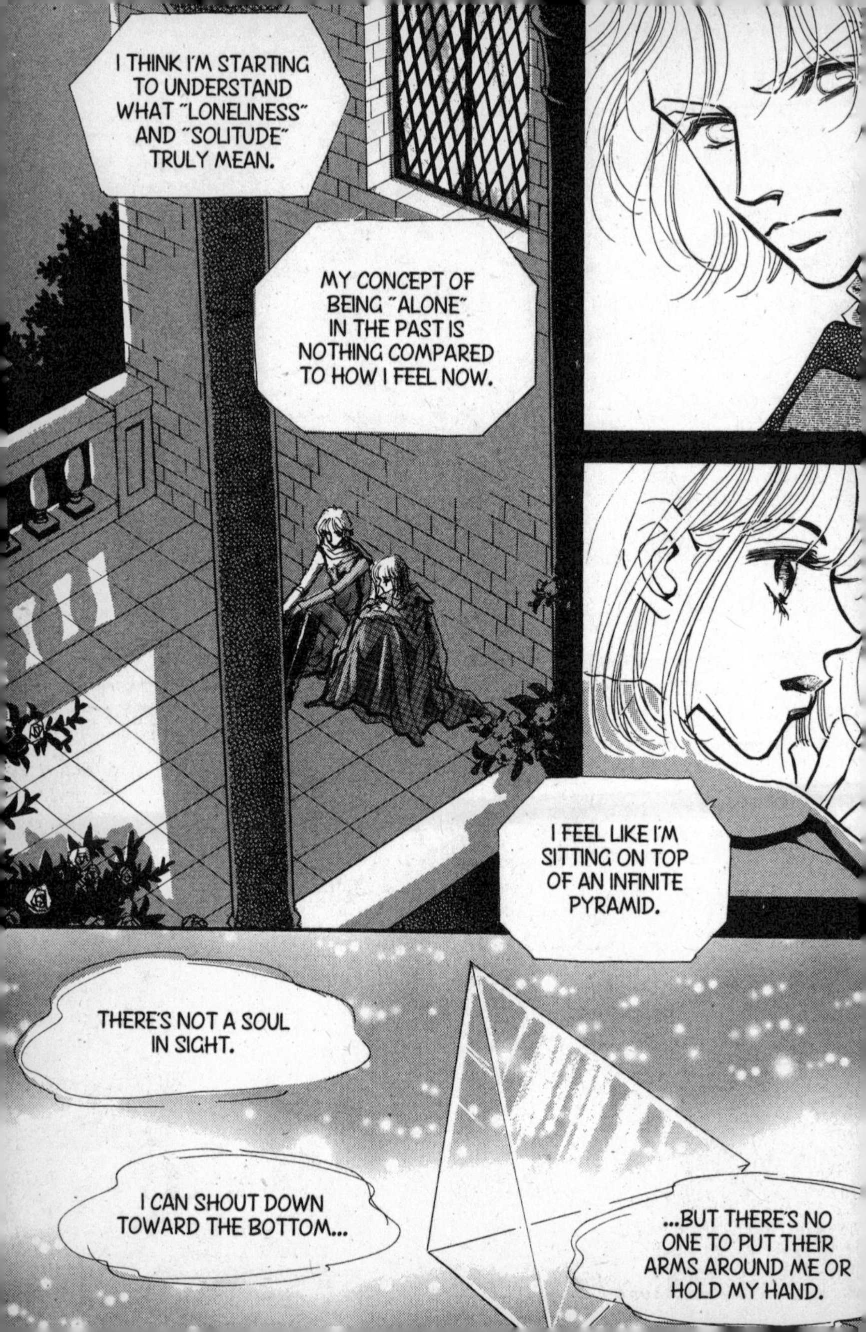
I THINK I'M STARTING TO UNDERSTAND WHAT "LONELINESS" AND "SOLITUDE" TRULY MEAN.
MY CONCEPT OF BEING "ALONE" IN THE PAST IS NOTHING COMPARED TO HOW I FEEL NOW.
I FEEL LIKE I'M SITTING ON TOP OF AN INFINITE PYRAMID.
THERE'S NOT A SOUL IN SIGHT.
I CAN SHOUT DOWN TOWARD THE BOTTOM...
...BUT THERE'S NO ONE TO PUT THEIR ARMS AROUND ME OR HOLD MY HAND.

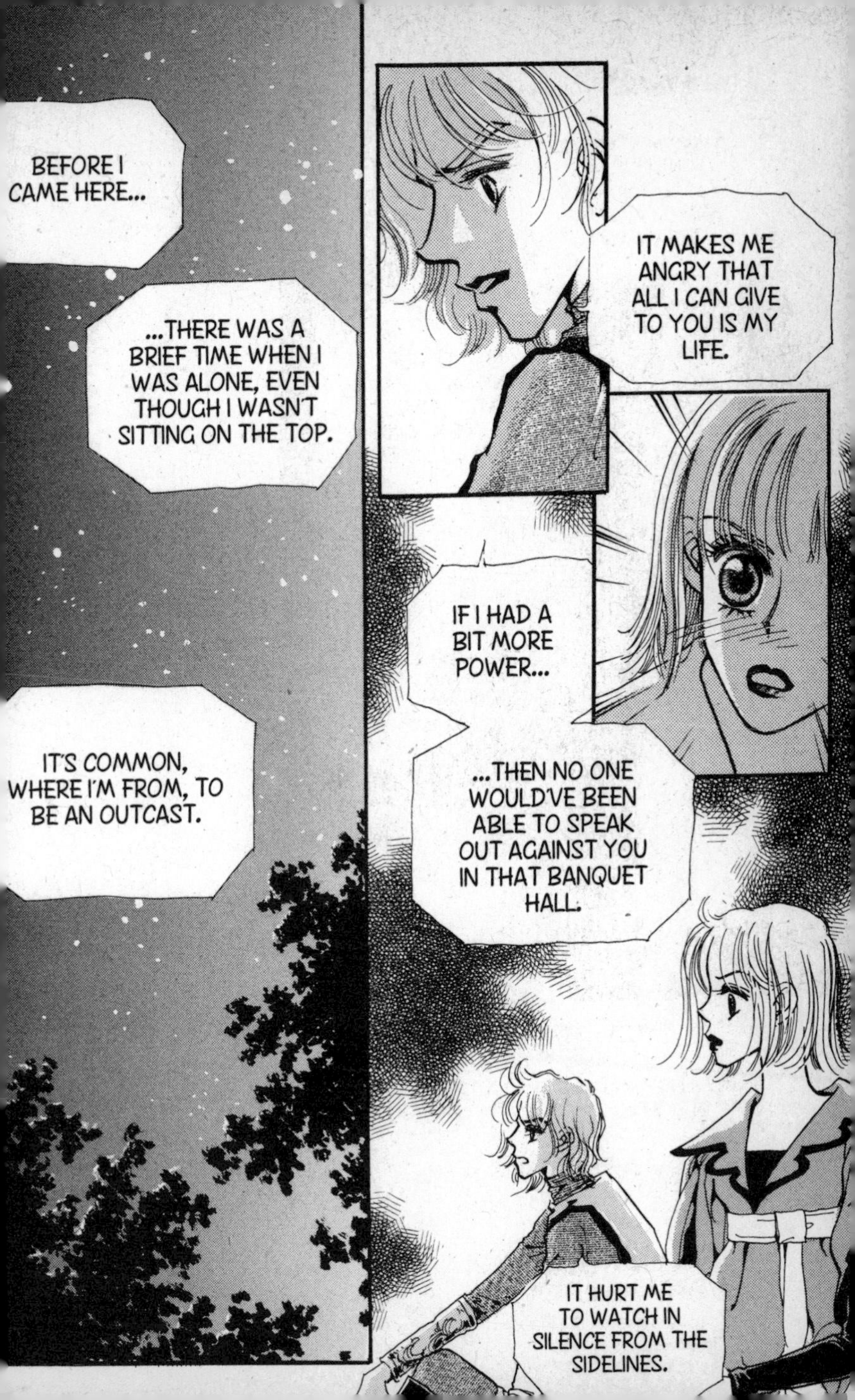
BEFORE I CAME HERE...
...THERE WAS A BRIEF TIME WHEN I WAS ALONE, EVEN THOUGH I WASN'T SITTING ON THE TOP.
IT'S COMMON, WHERE I'M FROM, TO BE AN OUTCAST.
IT MAKES ME ANGRY THAT ALL I CAN GIVE TO YOU IS MY LIFE.
IF I HAD A BIT MORE POWER...
...THEN NO ONE WOULD'VE BEEN ABLE TO SPEAK OUT AGAINST YOU IN THAT BANQUET HALL.
IT HURT ME TO WATCH IN SILENCE FROM THE SIDELINES.

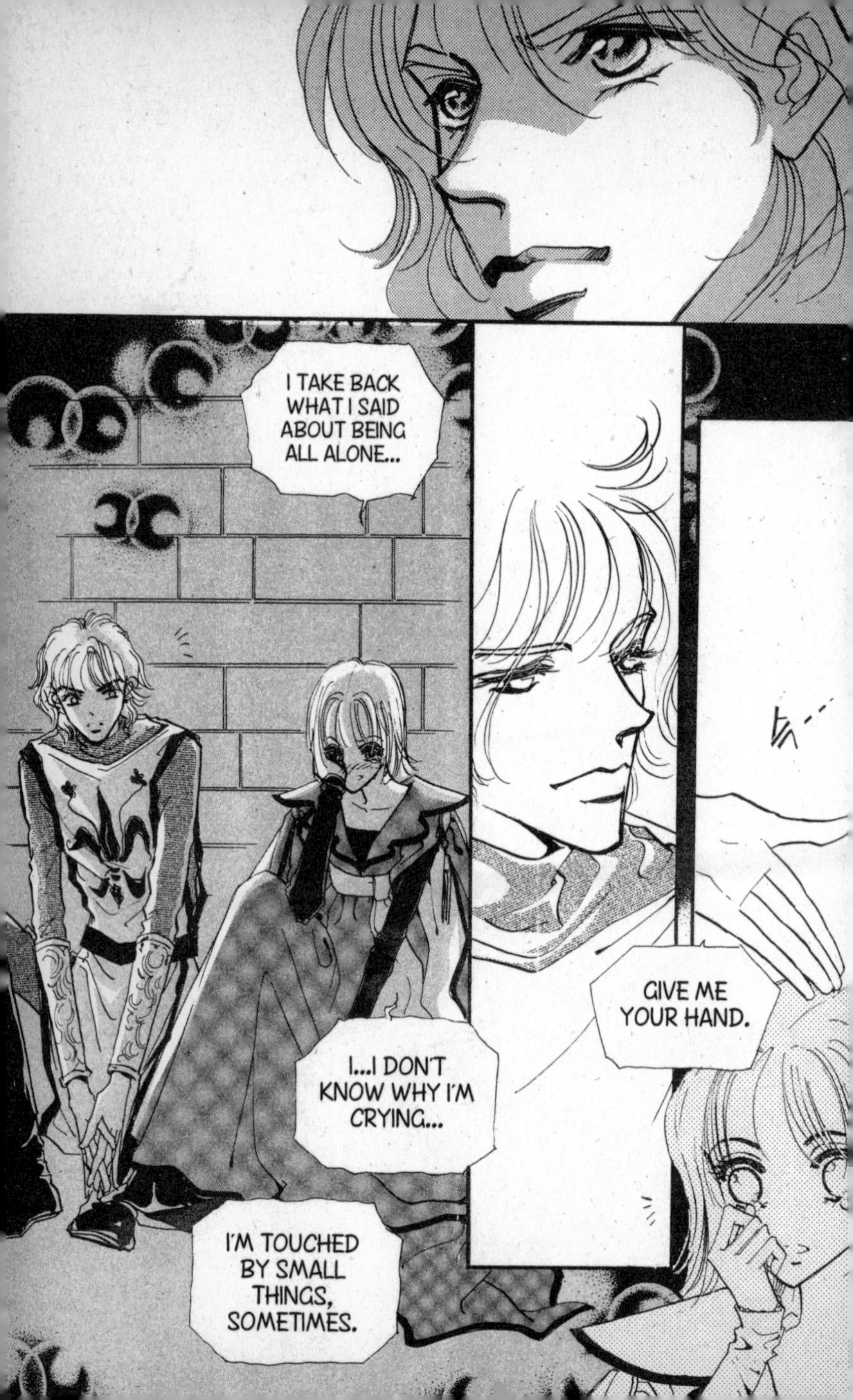
I TAKE BACK WHAT I SAID ABOUT BEING ALL ALONE...
I...I DON'T KNOW WHY I'M CRYING...
I'M TOUCHED BY SMALL THINGS, SOMETIMES.
GIVE ME YOUR HAND.

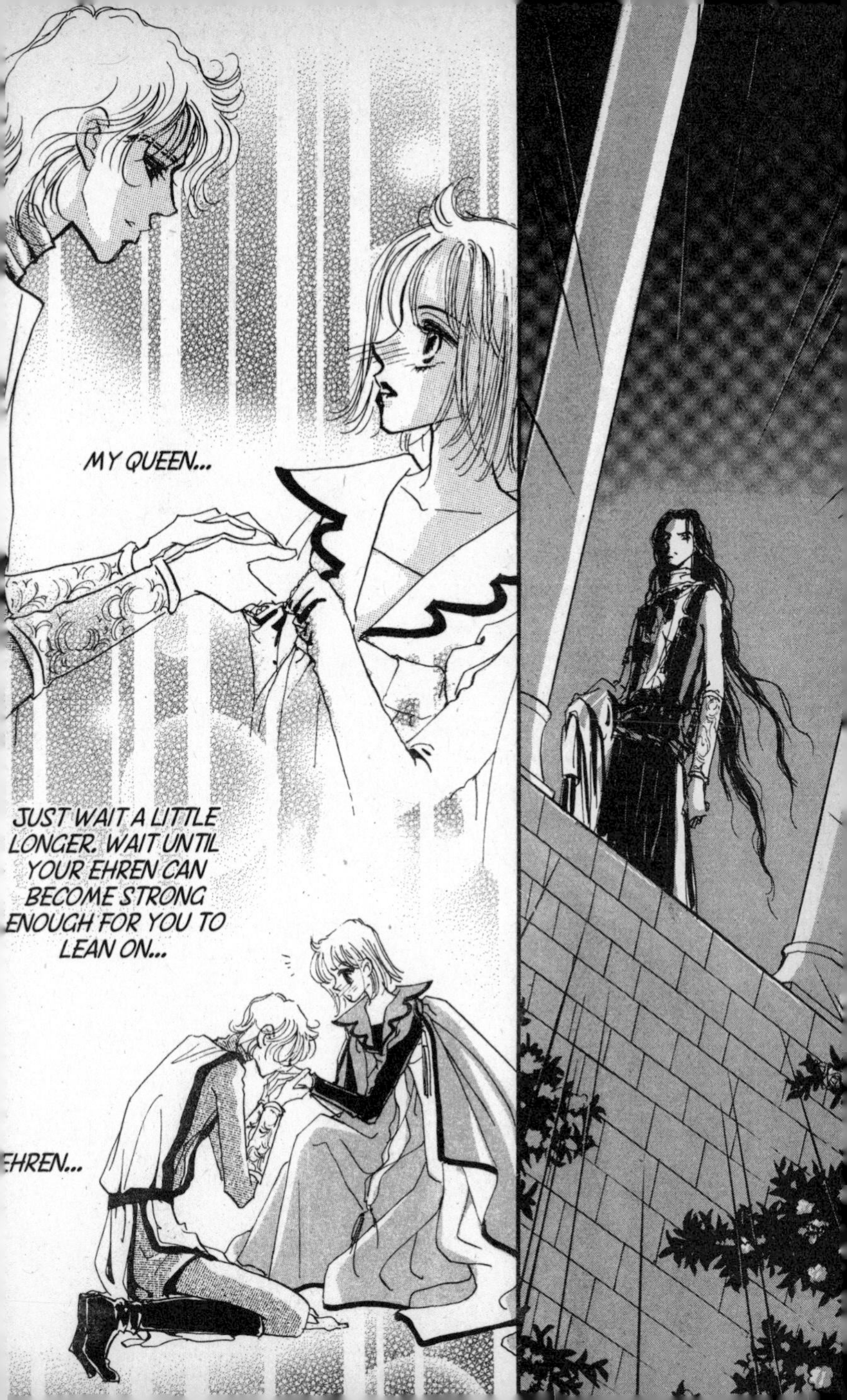
MY QUEEN...
JUST WAIT A LITTLE LONGER. WAIT UNTIL YOUR EHREN CAN BECOME STRONG ENOUGH FOR YOU TO LEAN ON...
HREN...

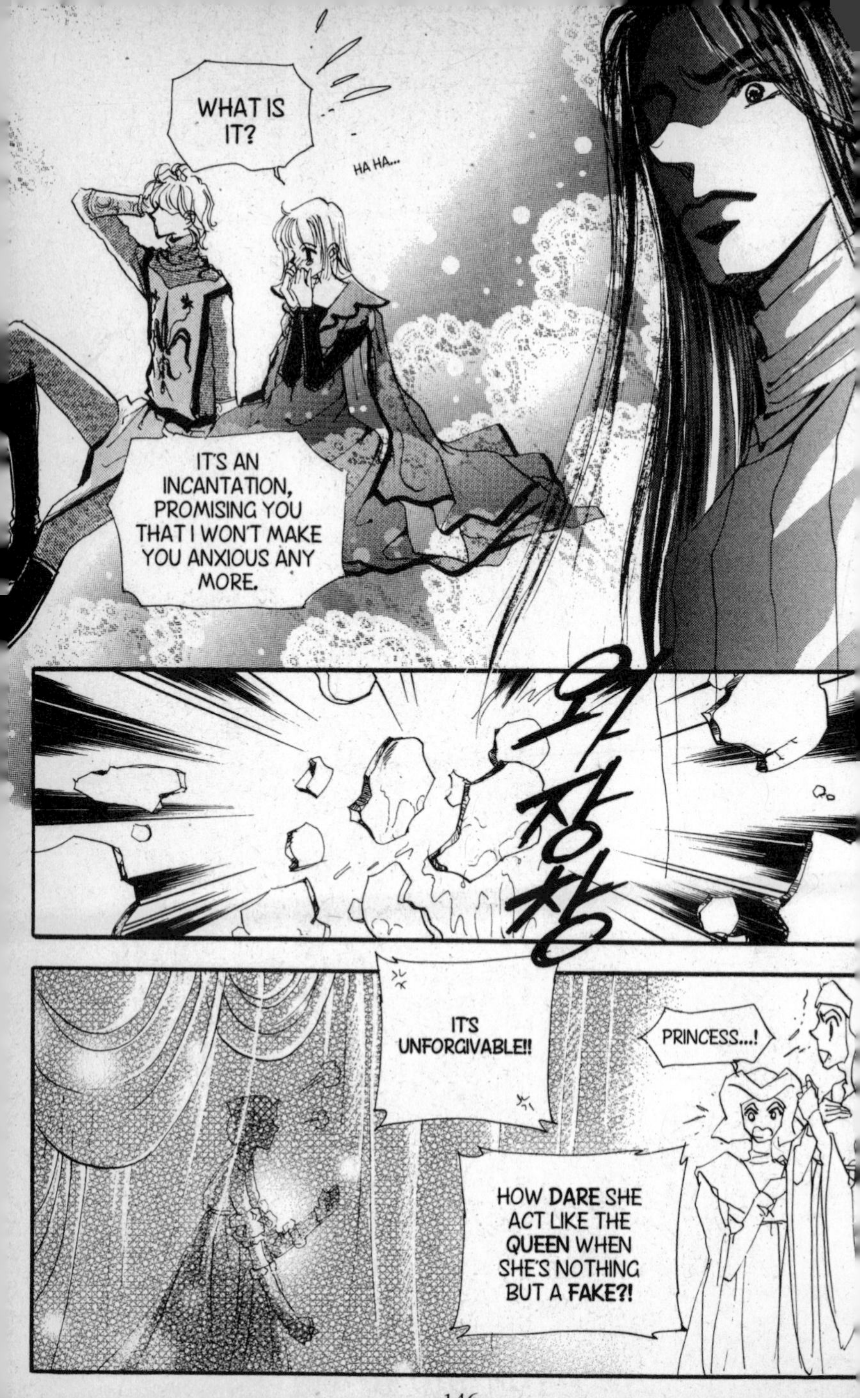
WHAT IS IT?
HA HA...
IT'S AN INCANTATION, PROMISING YOU THAT I WON'T MAKE YOU ANXIOUS ANY MORE.
와장창
IT'S UNFORGIVABLE!!
PRINCESS...!
HOW **DARE** SHE ACT LIKE THE **QUEEN** WHEN SHE'S NOTHING BUT A **FAKE?!**

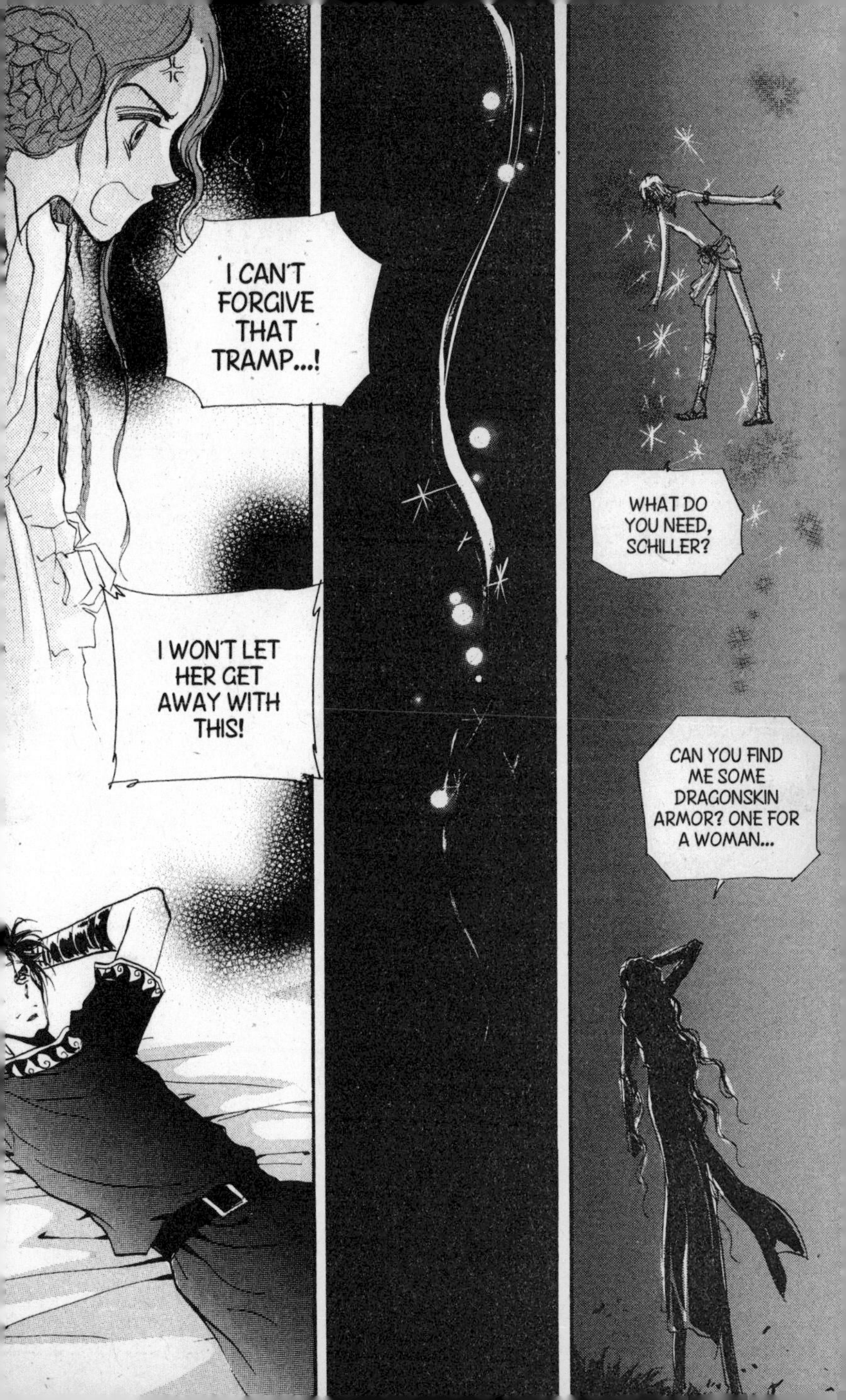
I CAN'T FORGIVE THAT TRAMP...!
I WON'T LET HER GET AWAY WITH THIS!
WHAT DO YOU NEED, SCHILLER?
CAN YOU FIND ME SOME DRAGONSKIN ARMOR? ONE FOR A WOMAN...

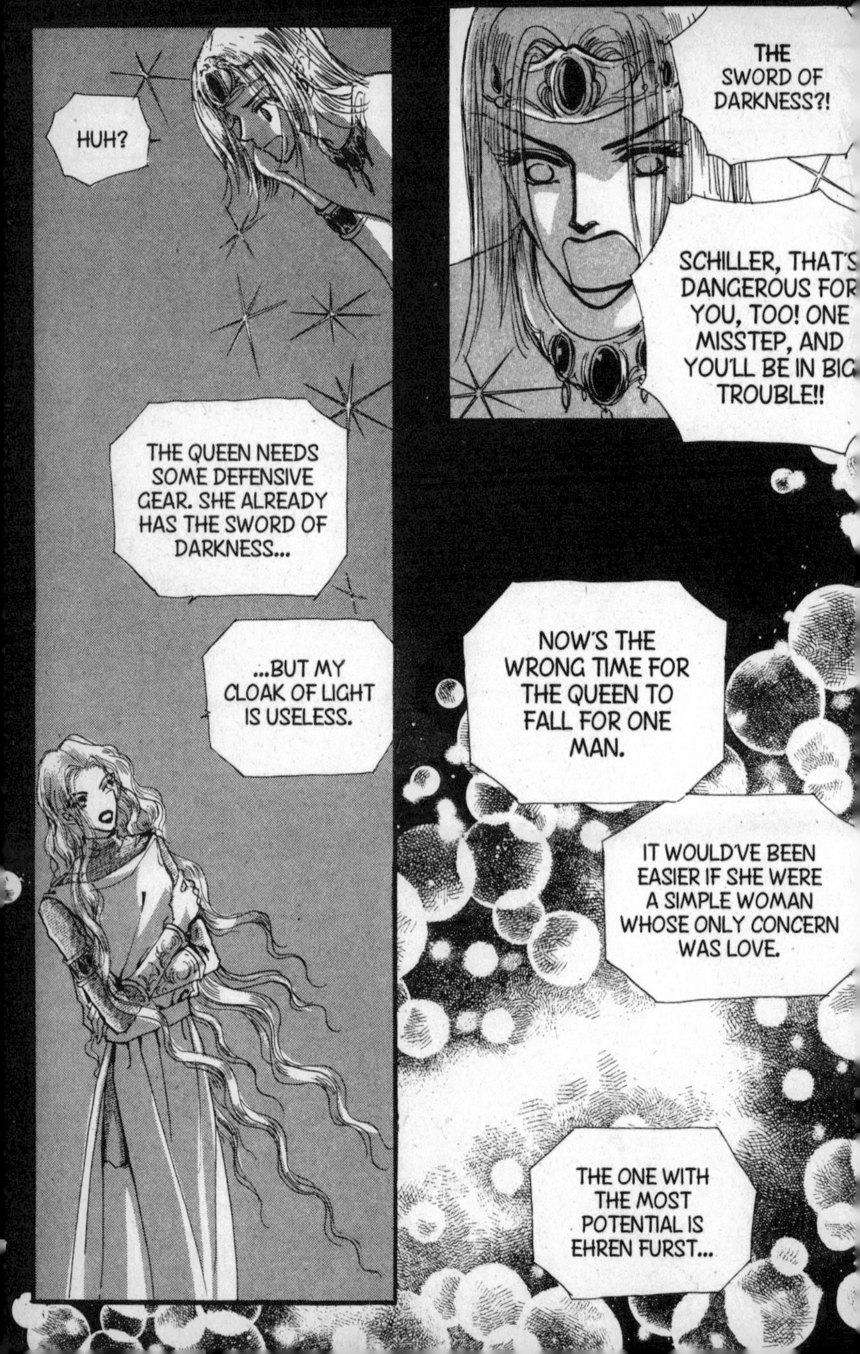
HUH?
THE QUEEN NEEDS SOME DEFENSIVE GEAR. SHE ALREADY HAS THE SWORD OF DARKNESS...
...BUT MY CLOAK OF LIGHT IS USELESS.
THE SWORD OF DARKNESS?!
SCHILLER, THAT'S DANGEROUS FOR YOU, TOO! ONE MISSTEP, AND YOU'LL BE IN BIG TROUBLE!!
NOW'S THE WRONG TIME FOR THE QUEEN TO FALL FOR ONE MAN.
IT WOULD'VE BEEN EASIER IF SHE WERE A SIMPLE WOMAN WHOSE ONLY CONCERN WAS LOVE.
THE ONE WITH THE MOST POTENTIAL IS EHREN FURST...

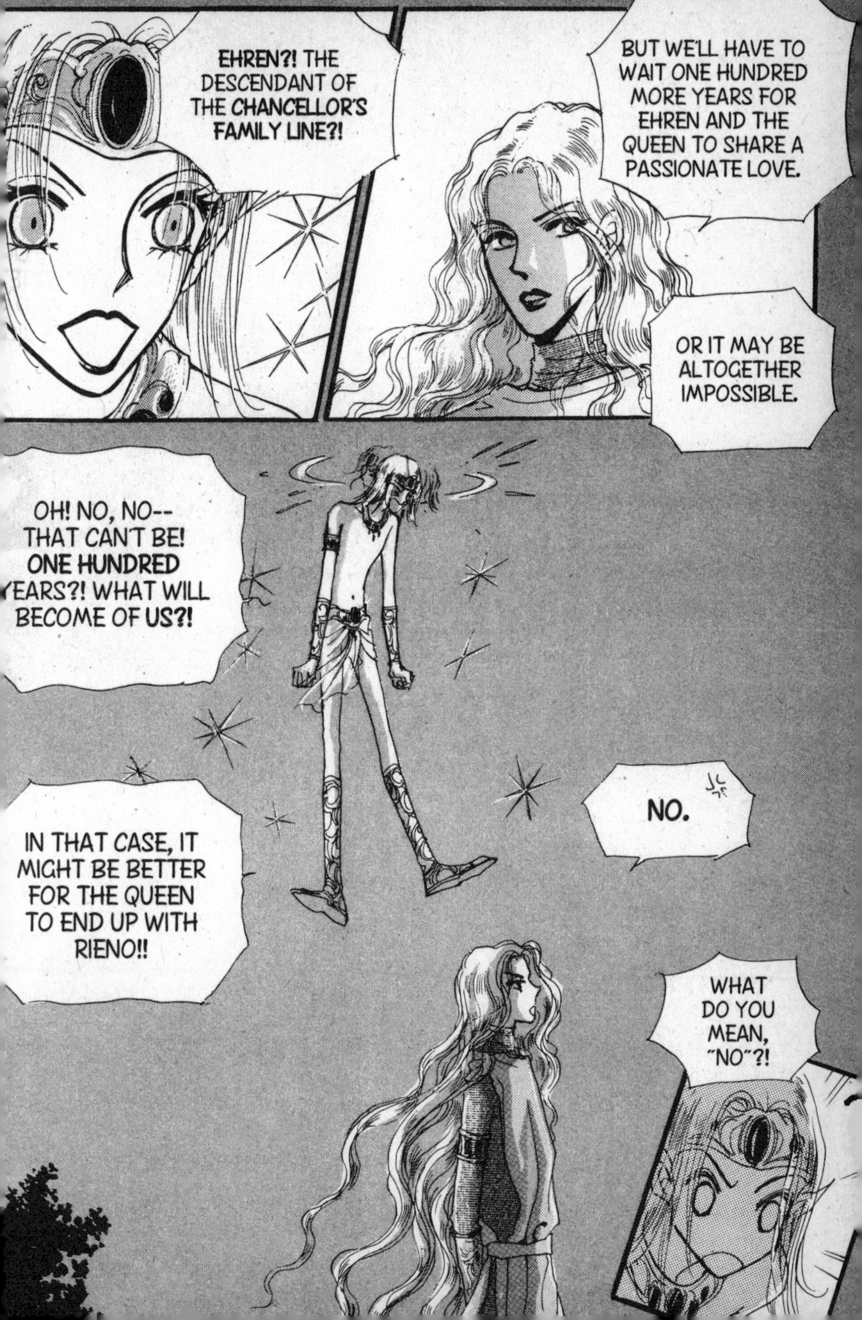
EHREN?! THE DESCENDANT OF THE CHANCELLOR'S FAMILY LINE?!
BUT WE'LL HAVE TO WAIT ONE HUNDRED MORE YEARS FOR EHREN AND THE QUEEN TO SHARE A PASSIONATE LOVE.
OR IT MAY BE ALTOGETHER IMPOSSIBLE.
OH! NO, NO-- THAT CAN'T BE! ONE HUNDRED YEARS?! WHAT WILL BECOME OF US?!
IN THAT CASE, IT MIGHT BE BETTER FOR THE QUEEN TO END UP WITH RIENO!!
NO.
WHAT DO YOU MEAN, "NO"?!

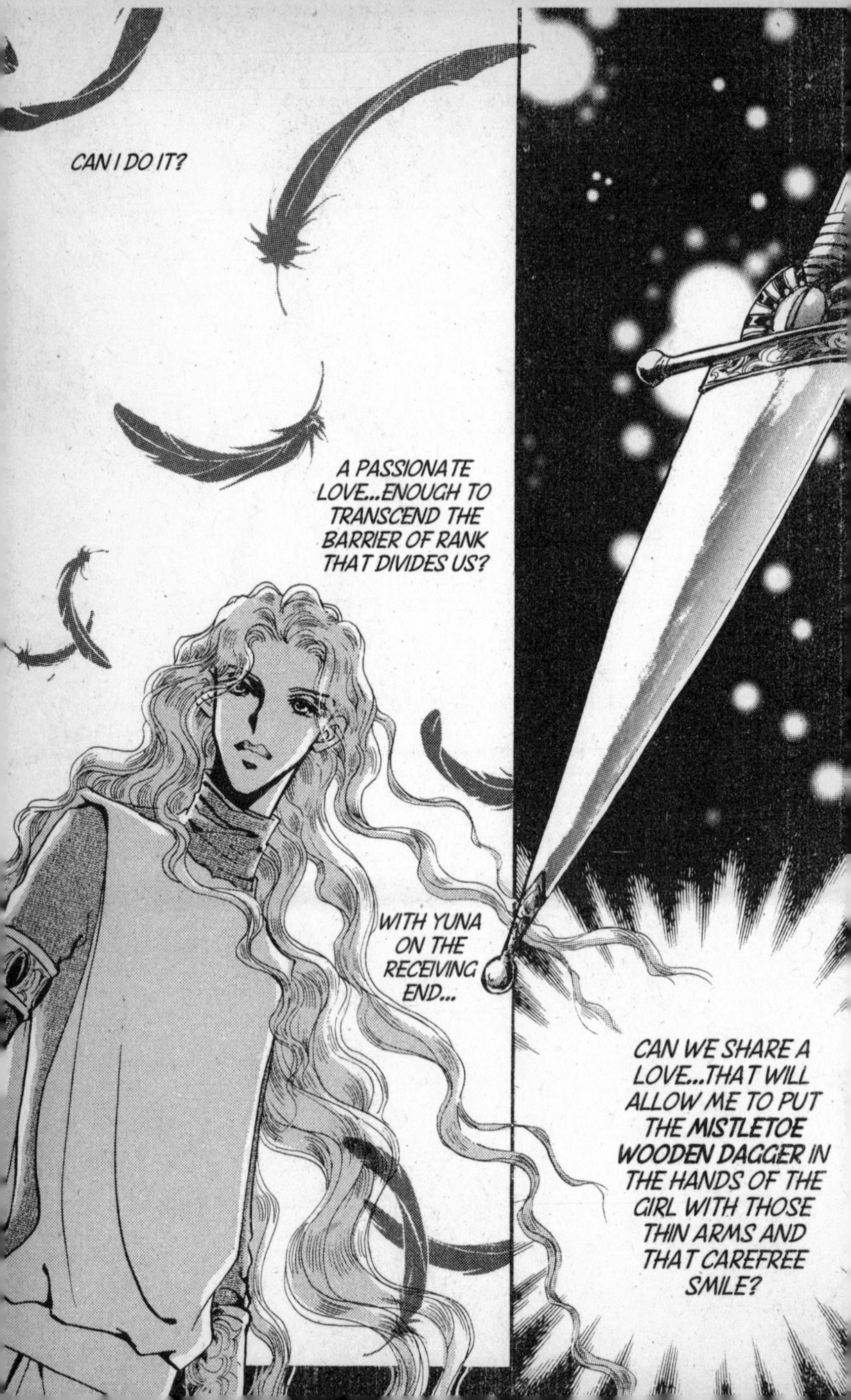
CAN I DO IT?
A PASSIONATE LOVE...ENOUGH TO TRANSCEND THE BARRIER OF RANK THAT DIVIDES US?
WITH YUNA ON THE RECEIVING END...
CAN WE SHARE A LOVE...THAT WILL ALLOW ME TO PUT THE **MISTLETOE WOODEN DAGGER** IN THE HANDS OF THE GIRL WITH THOSE THIN ARMS AND THAT CAREFREE SMILE?

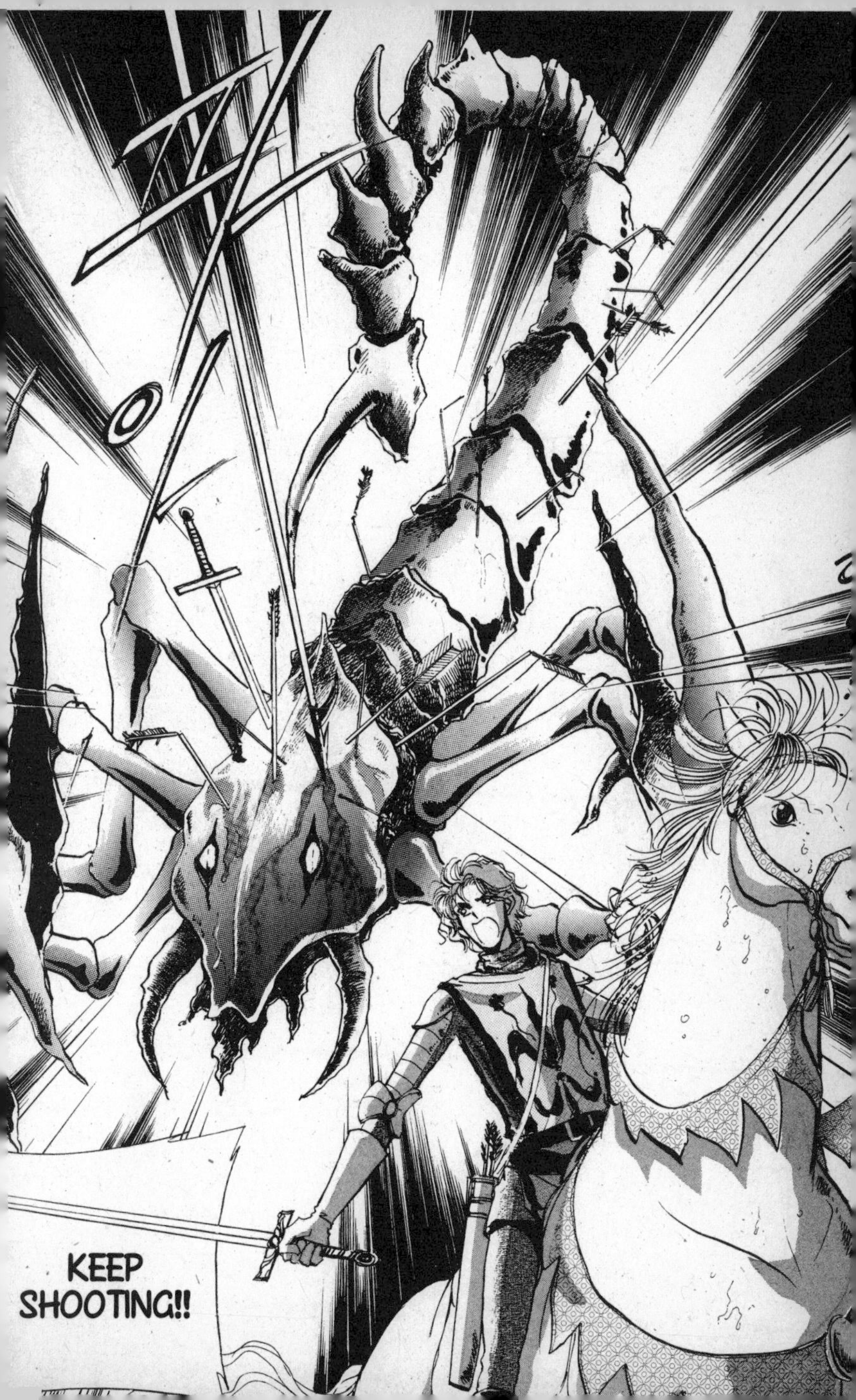
KEEP SHOOTING!!

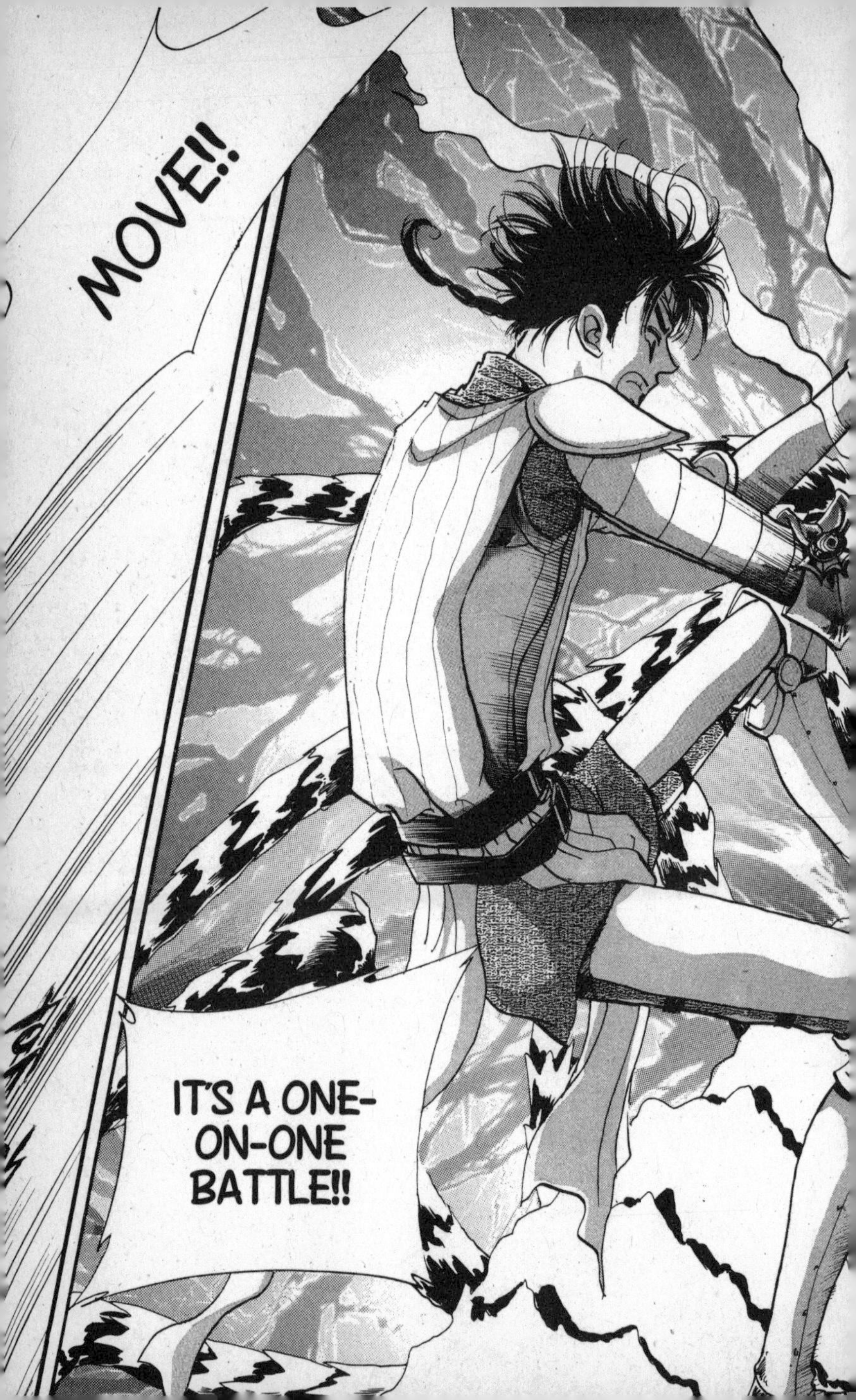
MOVE!!
IT'S A ONE-
ON-ONE
BATTLE!!

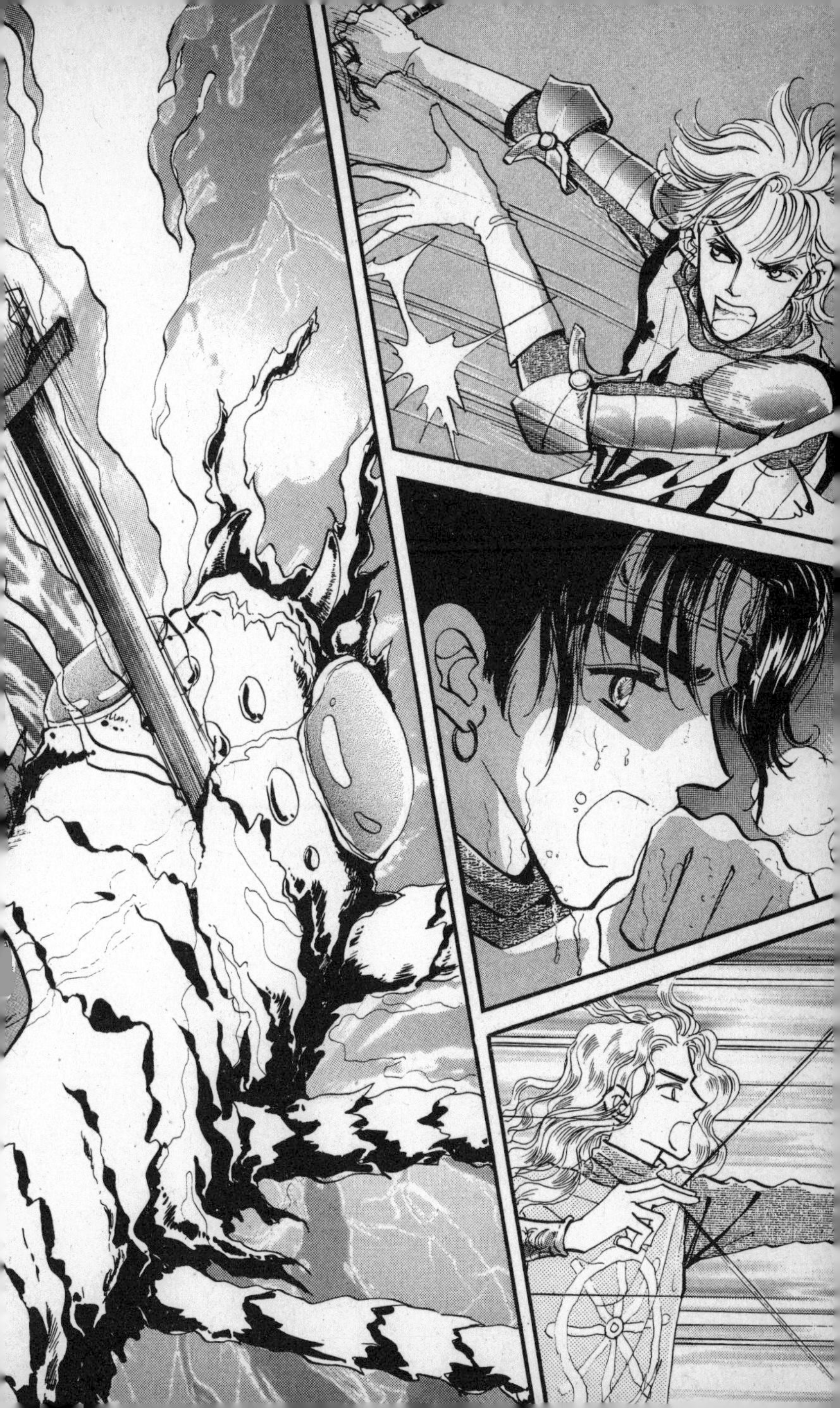

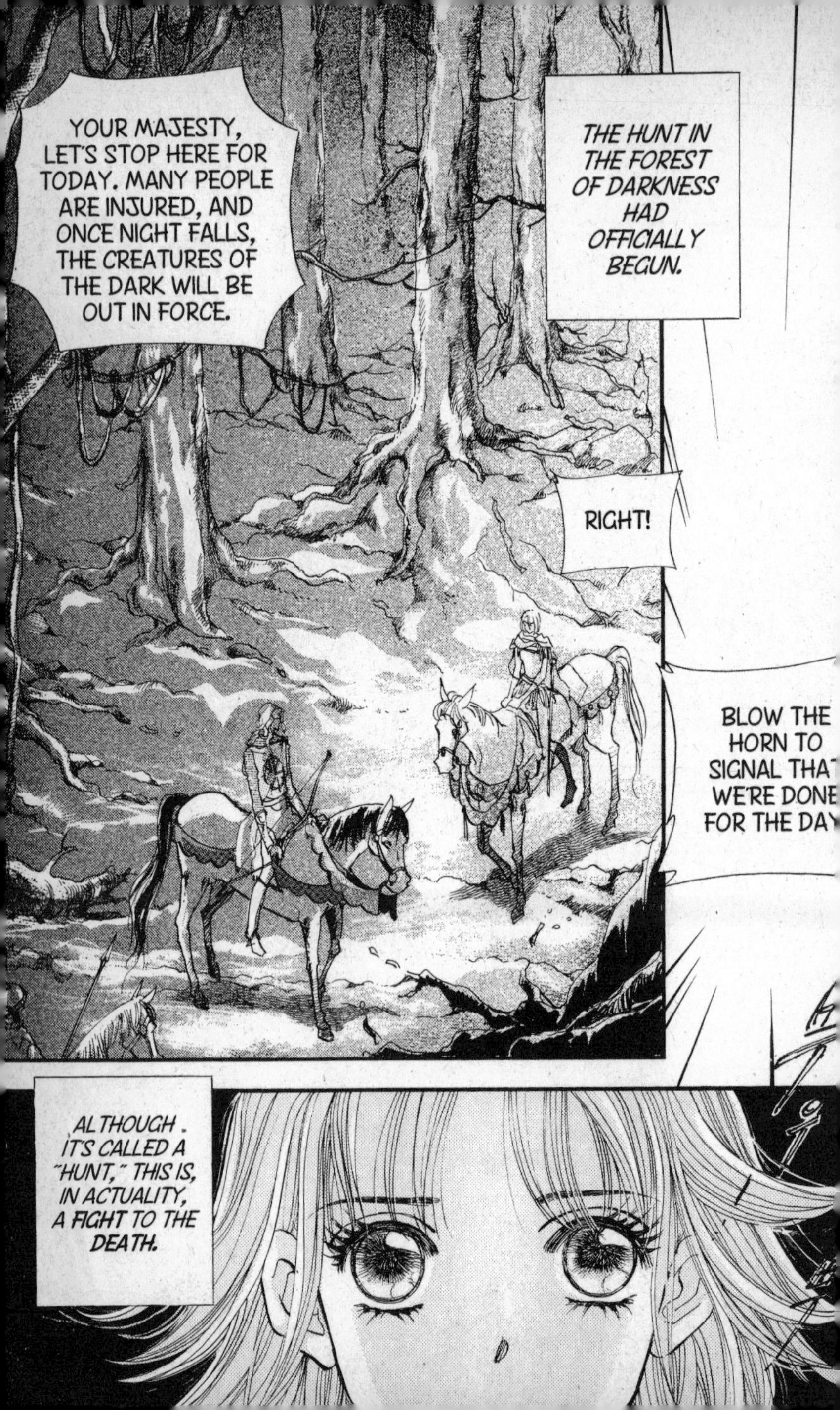
YOUR MAJESTY, LET'S STOP HERE FOR TODAY. MANY PEOPLE ARE INJURED, AND ONCE NIGHT FALLS, THE CREATURES OF THE DARK WILL BE OUT IN FORCE.
THE HUNT IN THE FOREST OF DARKNESS HAD OFFICIALLY BEGUN.
RIGHT!
BLOW THE HORN TO SIGNAL THAT WE'RE DONE FOR THE DAY
ALTHOUGH IT'S CALLED A "HUNT," THIS IS, IN ACTUALITY, A FIGHT TO THE DEATH.

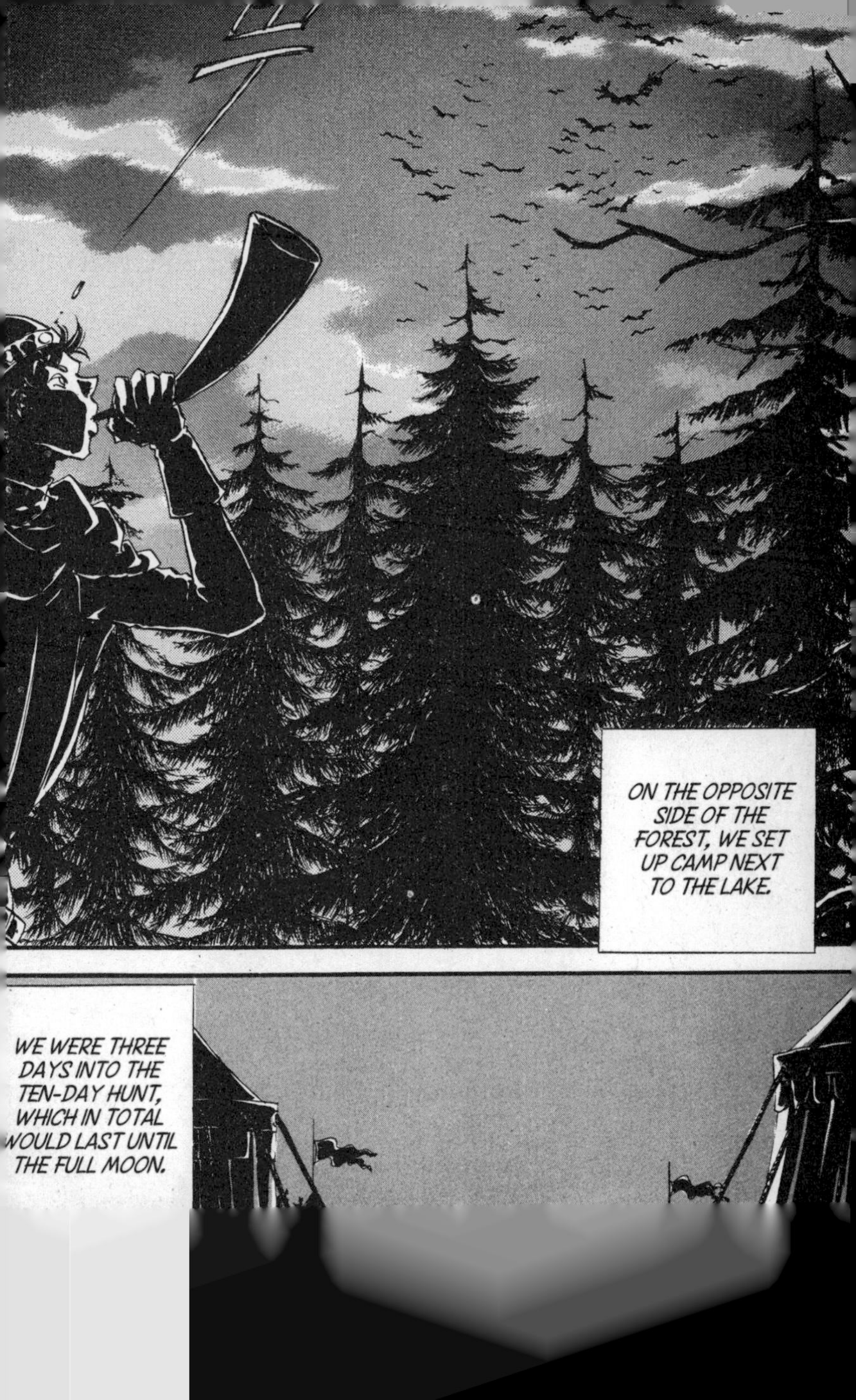
ON THE OPPOSITE SIDE OF THE FOREST, WE SET UP CAMP NEXT TO THE LAKE.
WE WERE THREE DAYS INTO THE TEN-DAY HUNT, WHICH IN TOTAL WOULD LAST UNTIL THE FULL MOON.

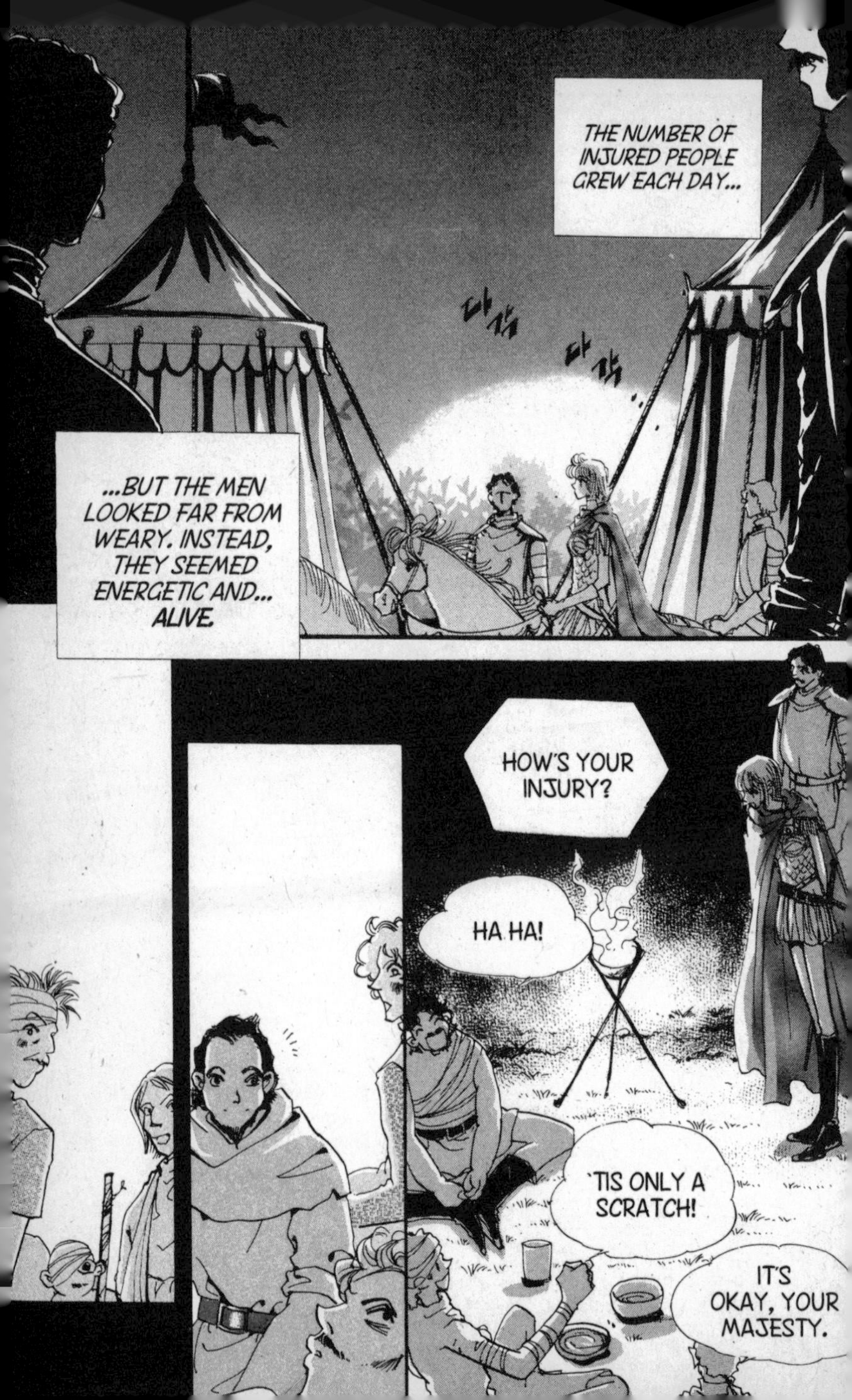
THE NUMBER OF INJURED PEOPLE GREW EACH DAY...
...BUT THE MEN LOOKED FAR FROM WEARY. INSTEAD, THEY SEEMED ENERGETIC AND... ALIVE.
HOW'S YOUR INJURY?
HA HA!
'TIS ONLY A SCRATCH!
IT'S OKAY, YOUR MAJESTY.

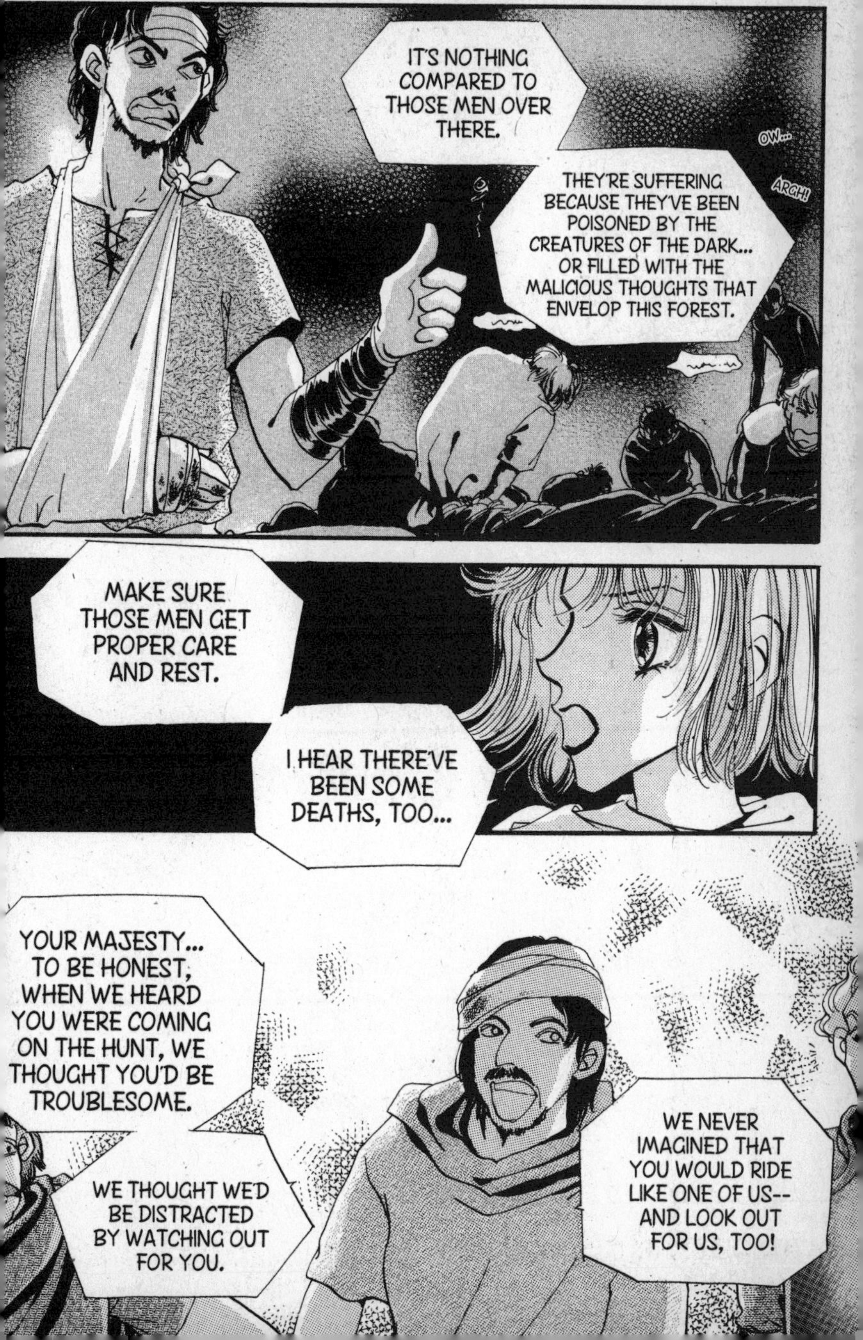
IT'S NOTHING COMPARED TO THOSE MEN OVER THERE.
OW...
ARGH!
THEY'RE SUFFERING BECAUSE THEY'VE BEEN POISONED BY THE CREATURES OF THE DARK... OR FILLED WITH THE MALICIOUS THOUGHTS THAT ENVELOP THIS FOREST.
MAKE SURE THOSE MEN GET PROPER CARE AND REST.
I HEAR THERE'VE BEEN SOME DEATHS, TOO...
YOUR MAJESTY... TO BE HONEST, WHEN WE HEARD YOU WERE COMING ON THE HUNT, WE THOUGHT YOU'D BE TROUBLESOME.
WE THOUGHT WE'D BE DISTRACTED BY WATCHING OUT FOR YOU.
WE NEVER IMAGINED THAT YOU WOULD RIDE LIKE ONE OF US-- AND LOOK OUT FOR US, TOO!

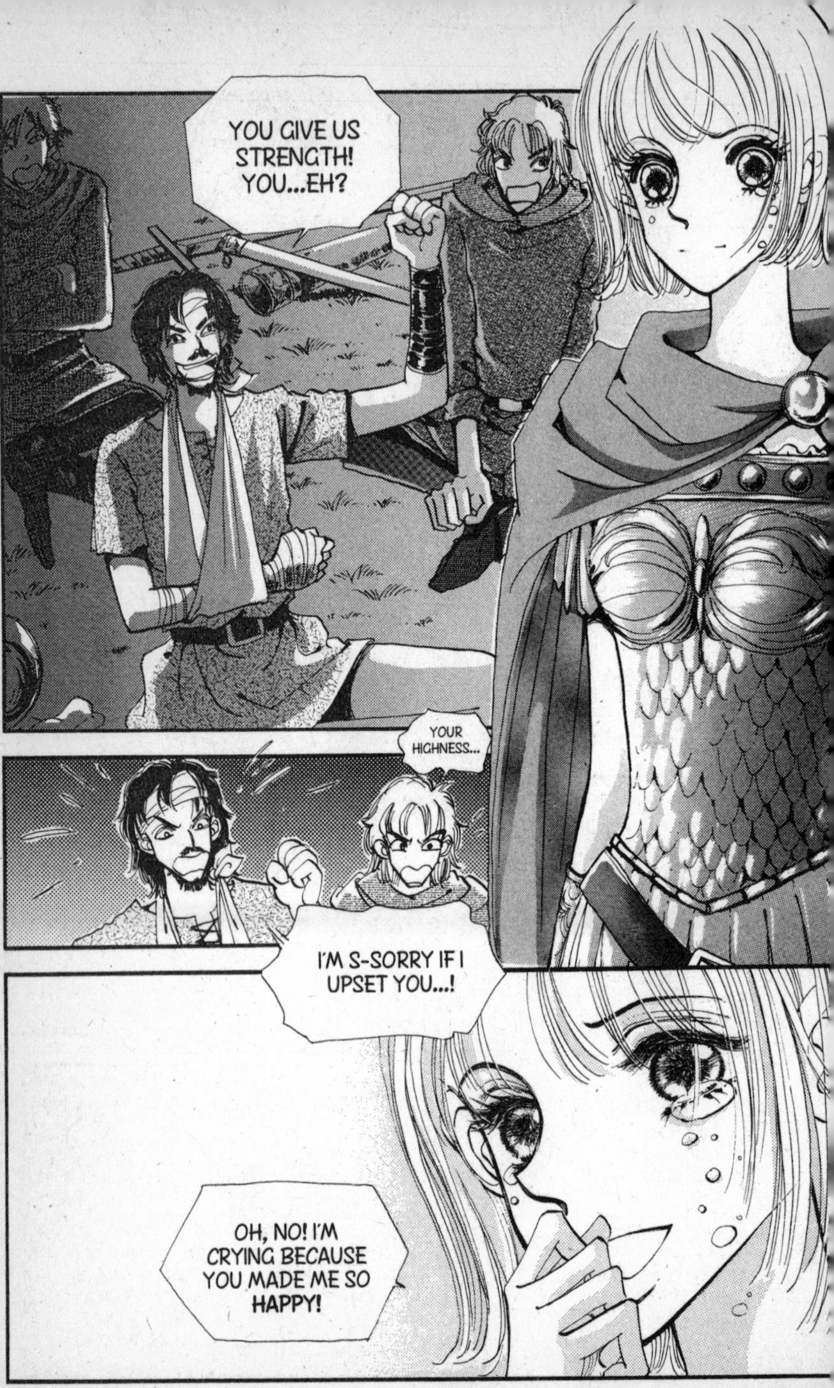
YOU GIVE US STRENGTH! YOU...EH?
YOUR HIGHNESS...
I'M S-SORRY IF I UPSET YOU...!
OH, NO! I'M CRYING BECAUSE YOU MADE ME SO HAPPY!

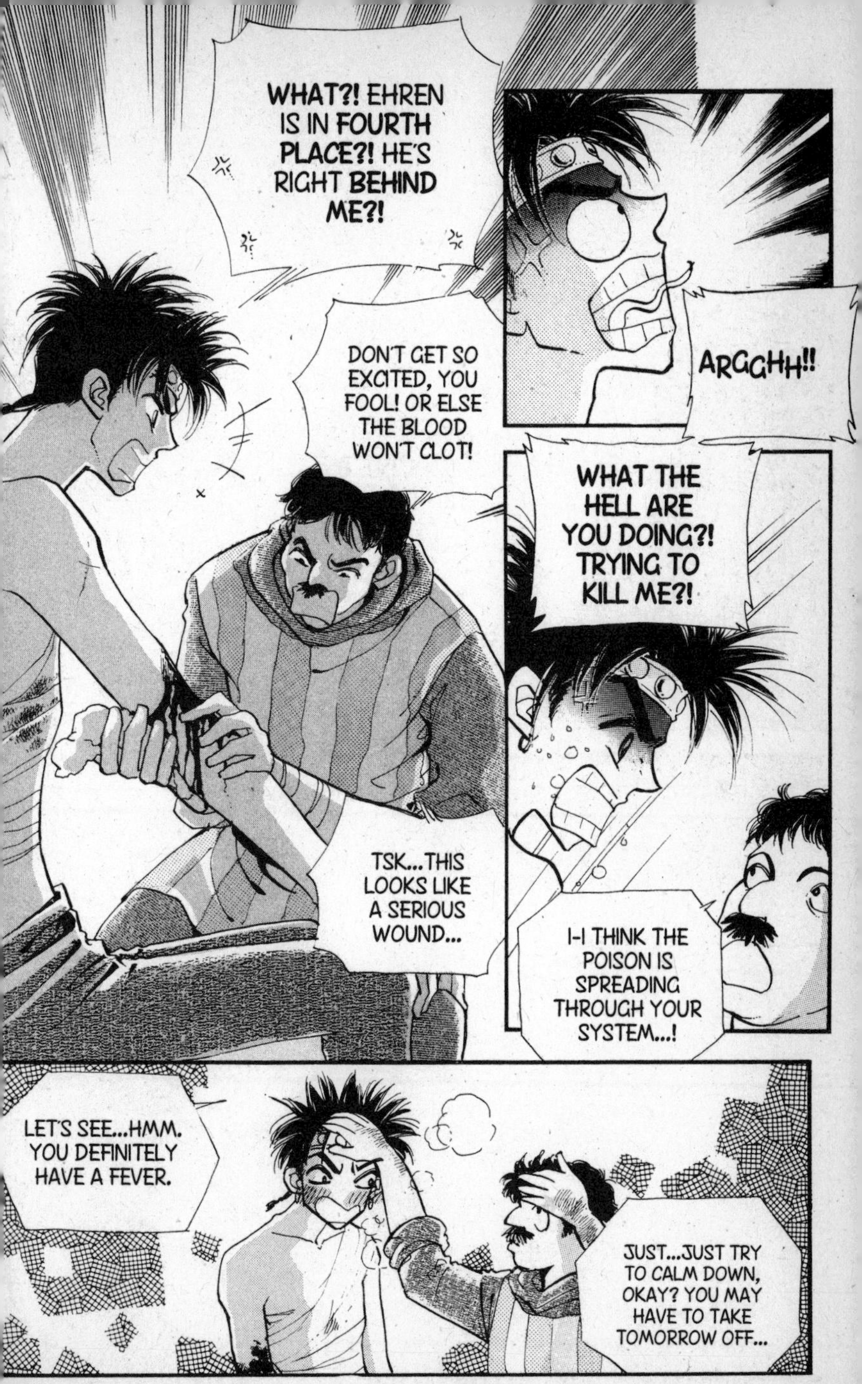
WHAT?! EHREN IS IN FOURTH PLACE?! HE'S RIGHT BEHIND ME?!
DON'T GET SO EXCITED, YOU FOOL! OR ELSE THE BLOOD WON'T CLOT!
TSK...THIS LOOKS LIKE A SERIOUS WOUND...
ARGGHH!!
WHAT THE HELL ARE YOU DOING?! TRYING TO KILL ME?!
I-I THINK THE POISON IS SPREADING THROUGH YOUR SYSTEM...!
LET'S SEE...HMM. YOU DEFINITELY HAVE A FEVER.
JUST...JUST TRY TO CALM DOWN, OKAY? YOU MAY HAVE TO TAKE TOMORROW OFF...

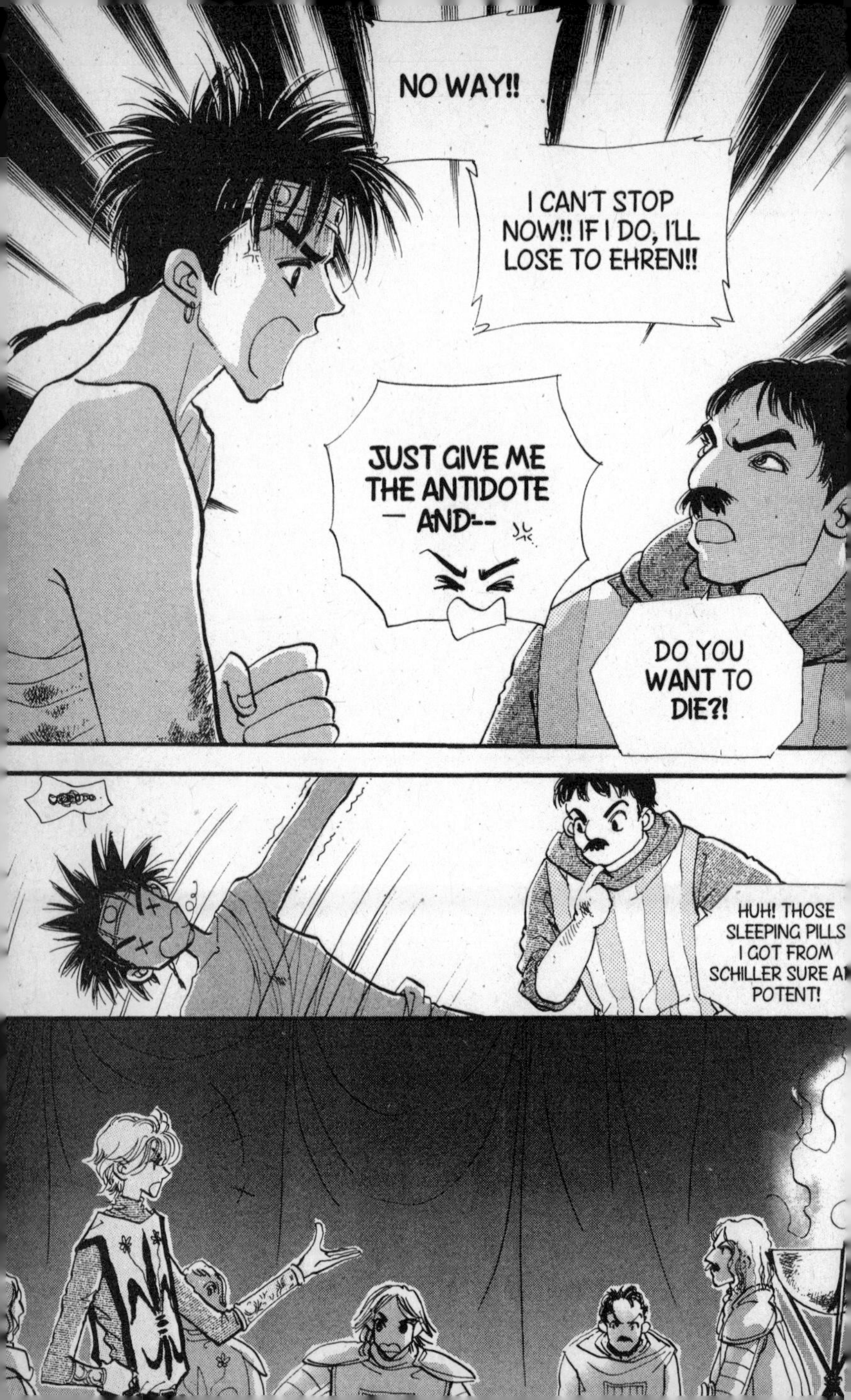
NO WAY!!
I CAN'T STOP NOW!! IF I DO, I'LL LOSE TO EHREN!!
JUST GIVE ME THE ANTIDOTE — AND--
DO YOU WANT TO DIE?!
HUH! THOSE SLEEPING PILLS I GOT FROM SCHILLER SURE A POTENT!

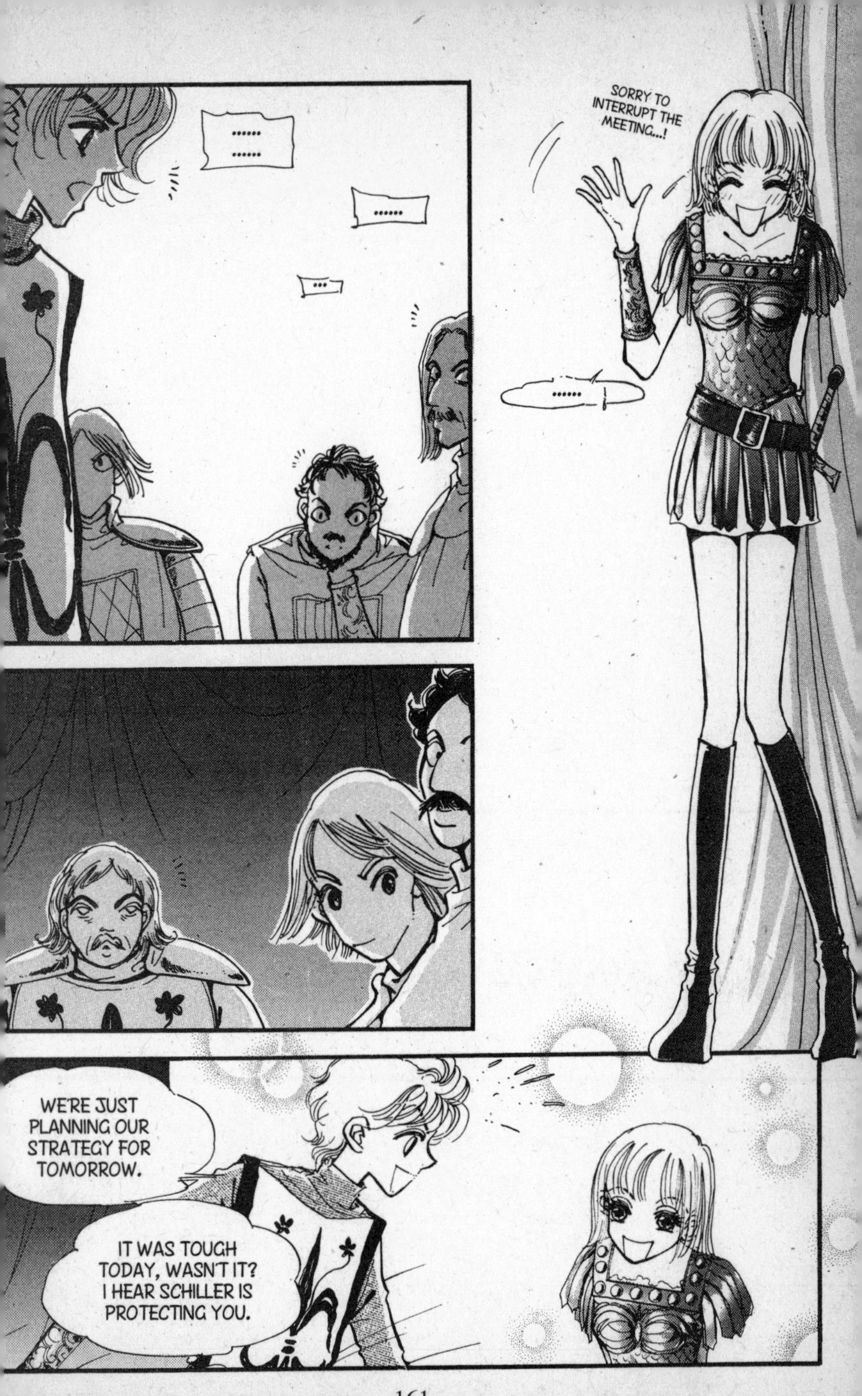
......
......
......
...
SORRY TO INTERRUPT THE MEETING...!
......
WE'RE JUST PLANNING OUR STRATEGY FOR TOMORROW.
IT WAS TOUGH TODAY, WASN'T IT? I HEAR SCHILLER IS PROTECTING YOU.

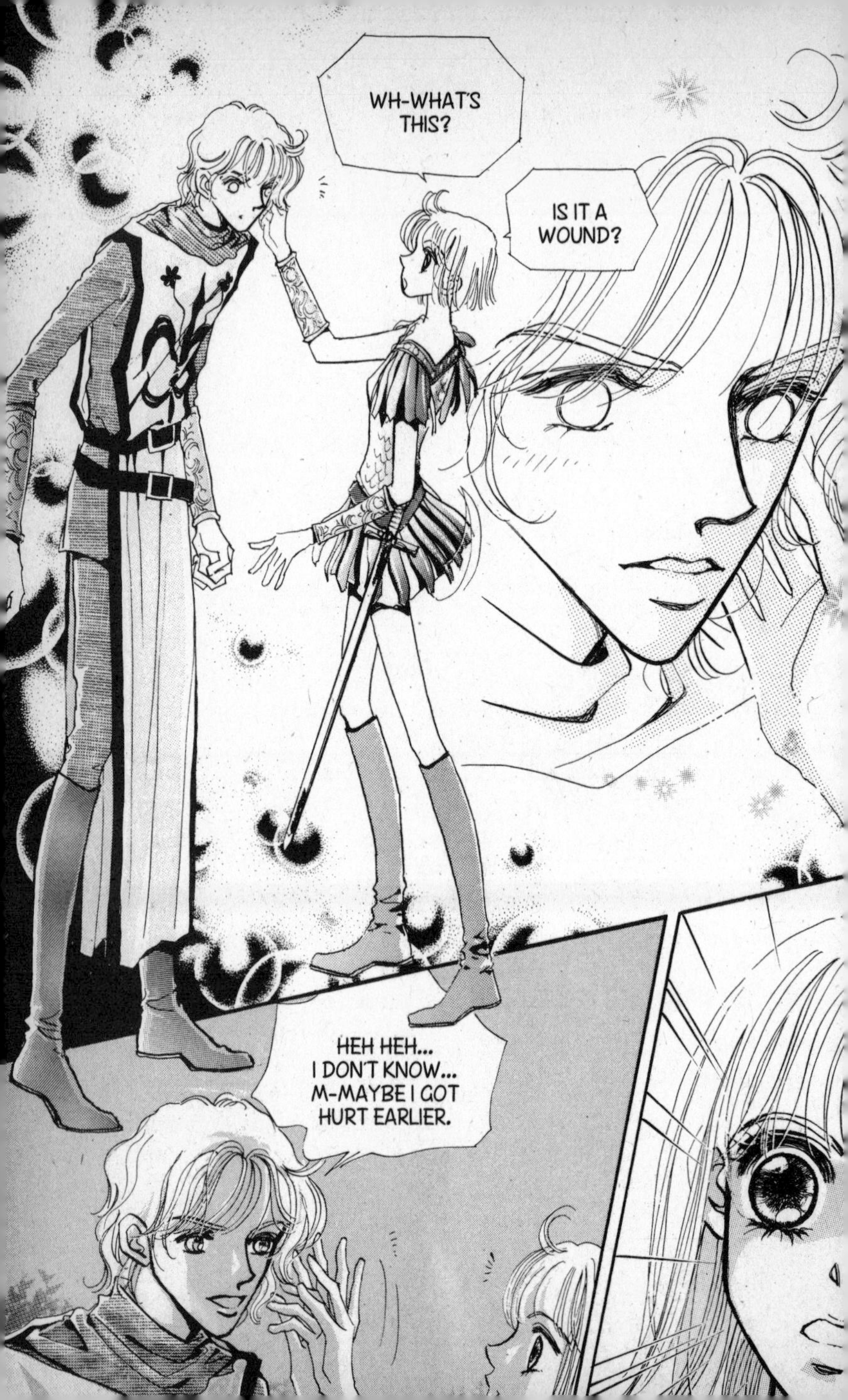
WH-WHAT'S THIS?
IS IT A WOUND?
HEH HEH... I DON'T KNOW... M-MAYBE I GOT HURT EARLIER.

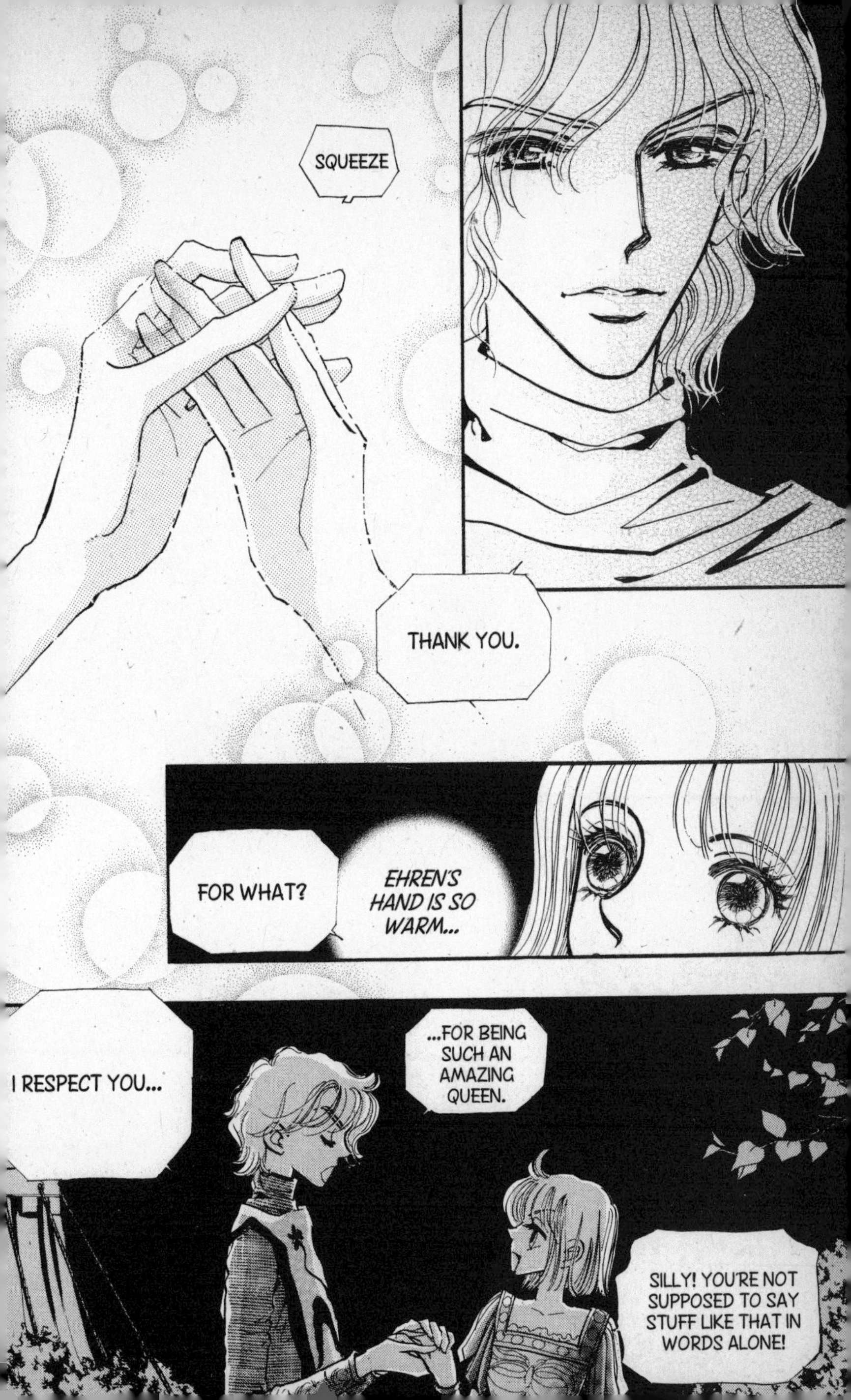
SQUEEZE
THANK YOU.
FOR WHAT?
EHREN'S HAND IS SO WARM...
I RESPECT YOU...
...FOR BEING SUCH AN AMAZING QUEEN.
SILLY! YOU'RE NOT SUPPOSED TO SAY STUFF LIKE THAT IN WORDS ALONE!

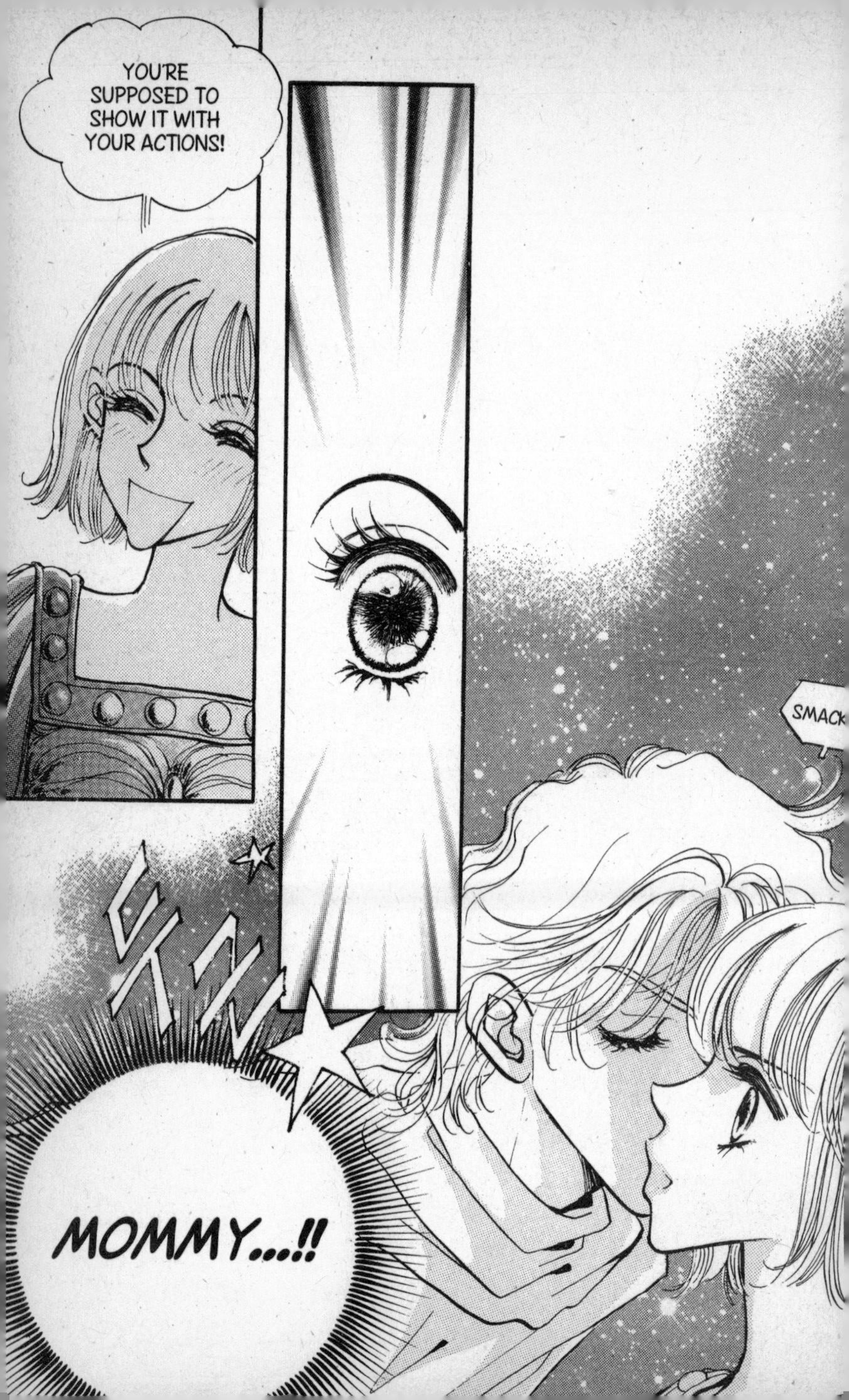
YOU'RE SUPPOSED TO SHOW IT WITH YOUR ACTIONS!
SMACK
MOMMY...!!

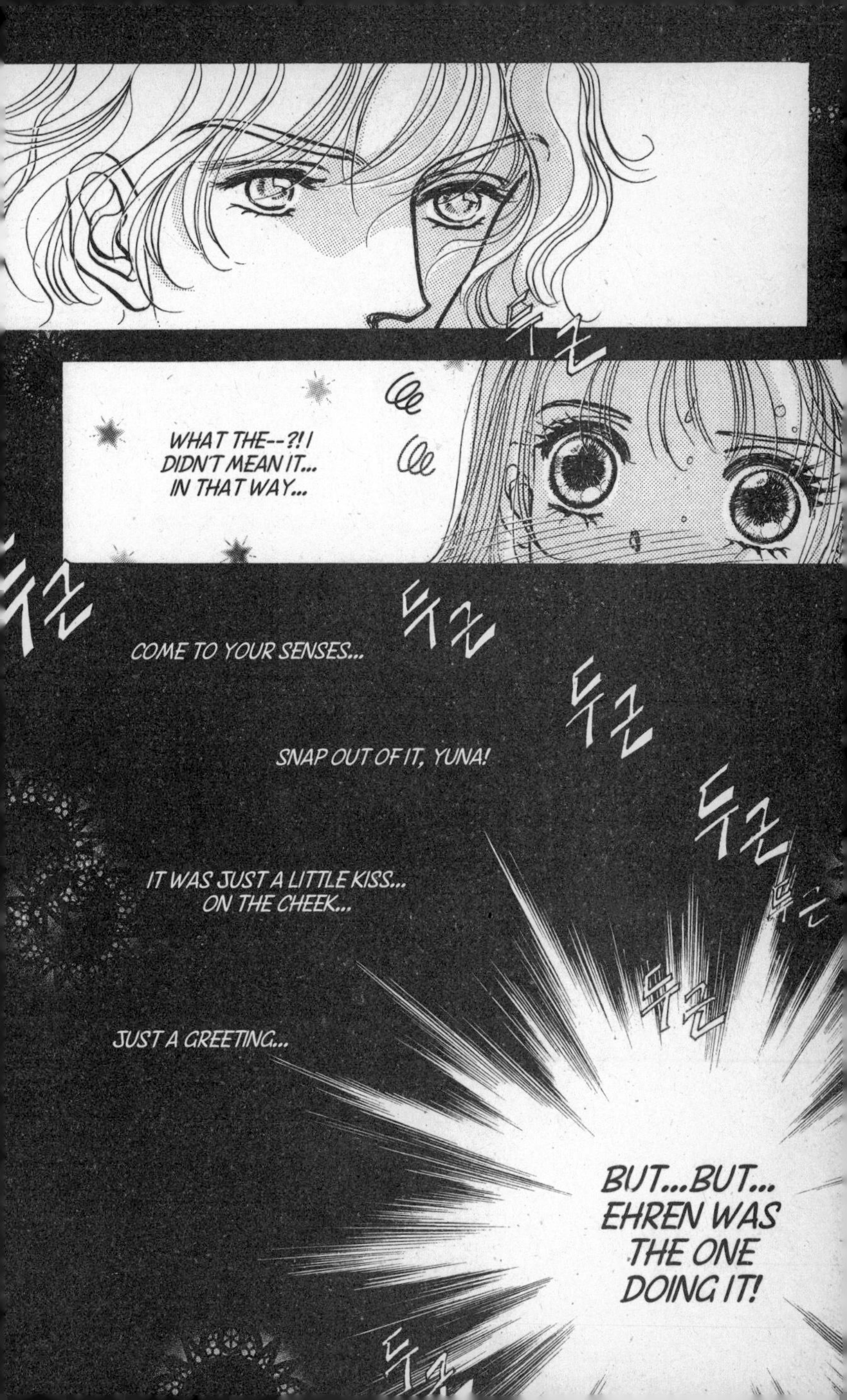
두근
WHAT THE--?! I DIDN'T MEAN IT... IN THAT WAY...
두근
두근
COME TO YOUR SENSES...
두근
SNAP OUT OF IT, YUNA!
두근
IT WAS JUST A LITTLE KISS... ON THE CHEEK...
두근
두근
JUST A GREETING...
BUT...BUT... EHREN WAS THE ONE DOING IT!

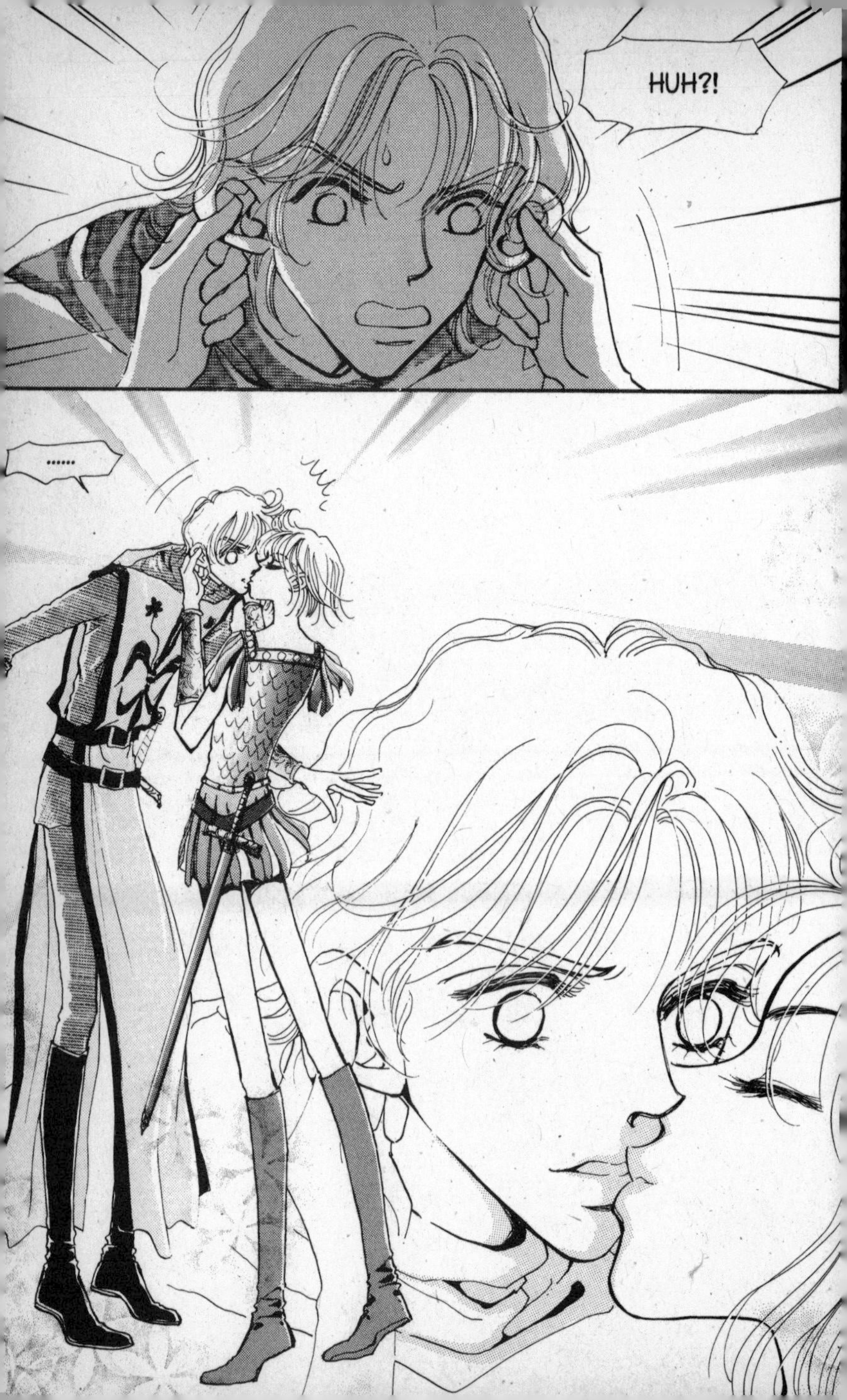
HUH?!
......

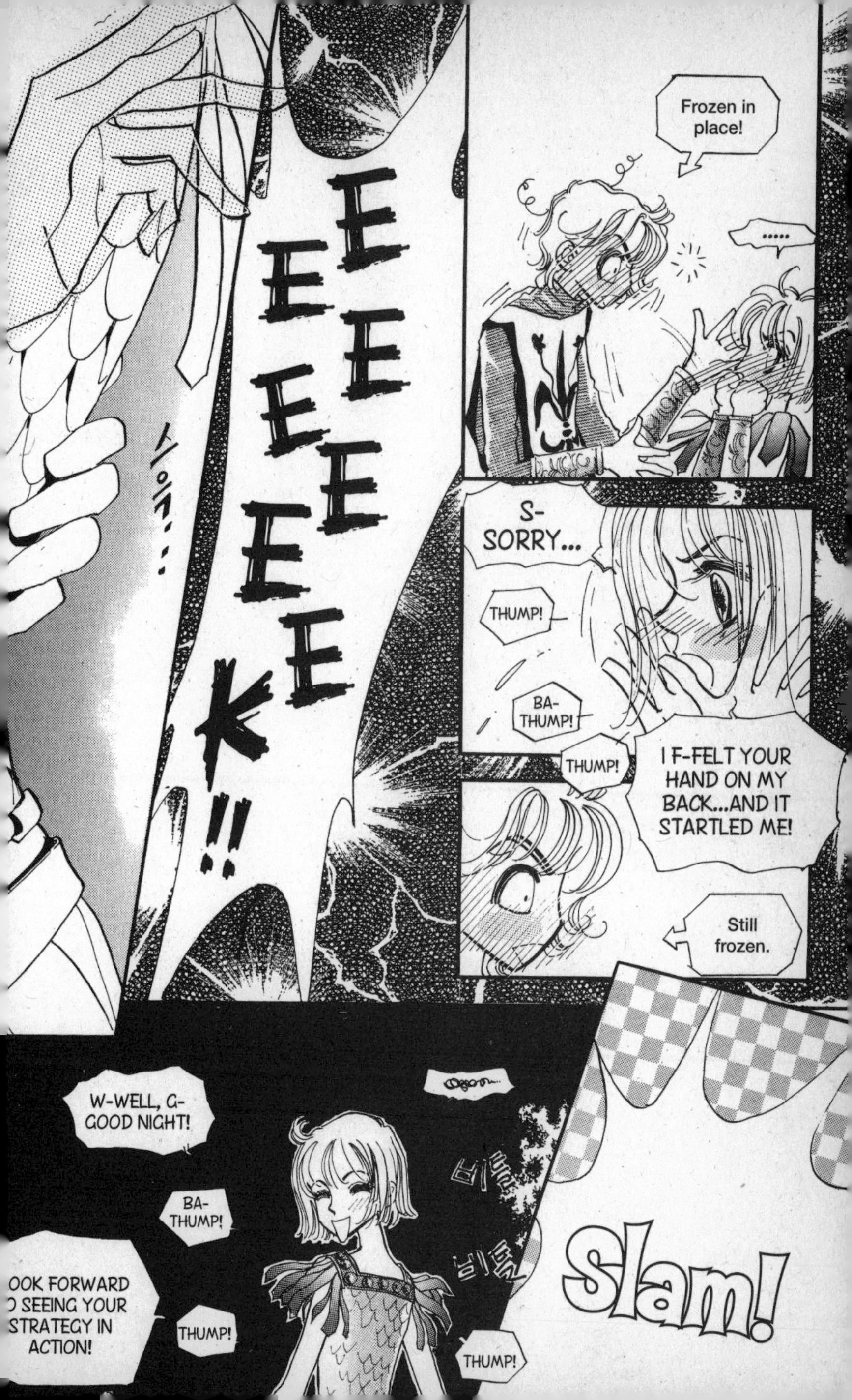

EEEEEEEK!!
Frozen in place!
......
S-SORRY...
THUMP!
BA-THUMP!
THUMP!
I F-FELT YOUR HAND ON MY BACK...AND IT STARTLED ME!
Still frozen.
W-WELL, G-GOOD NIGHT!
BA-THUMP!
OOK FORWARD O SEEING YOUR STRATEGY IN ACTION!
THUMP!
THUMP!
Slam!

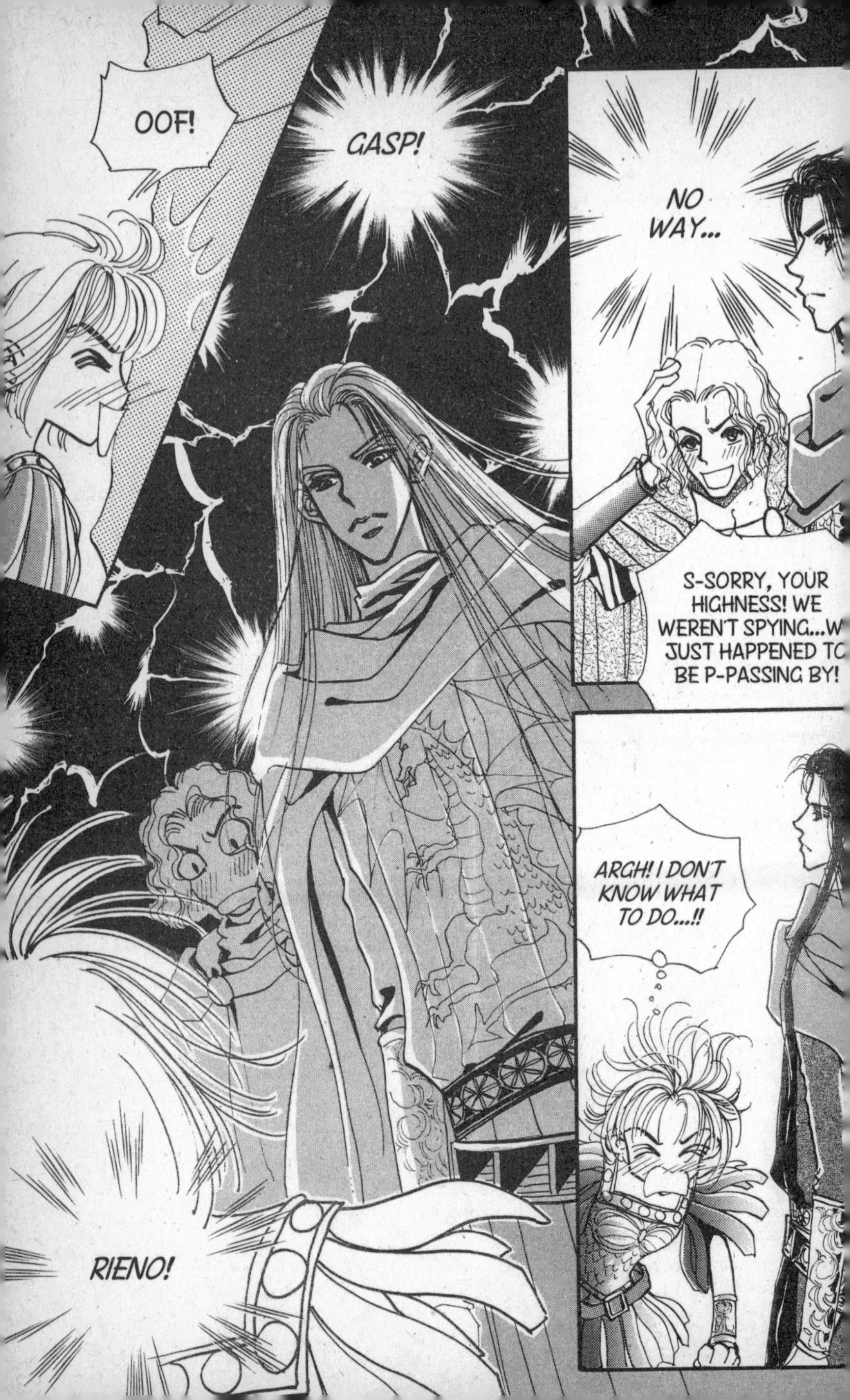
OOF!
GASP!
RIENO!
NO WAY...
S-SORRY, YOUR HIGHNESS! WE WEREN'T SPYING...W JUST HAPPENED TC BE P-PASSING BY!
ARGH! I DON'T KNOW WHAT TO DO...!!

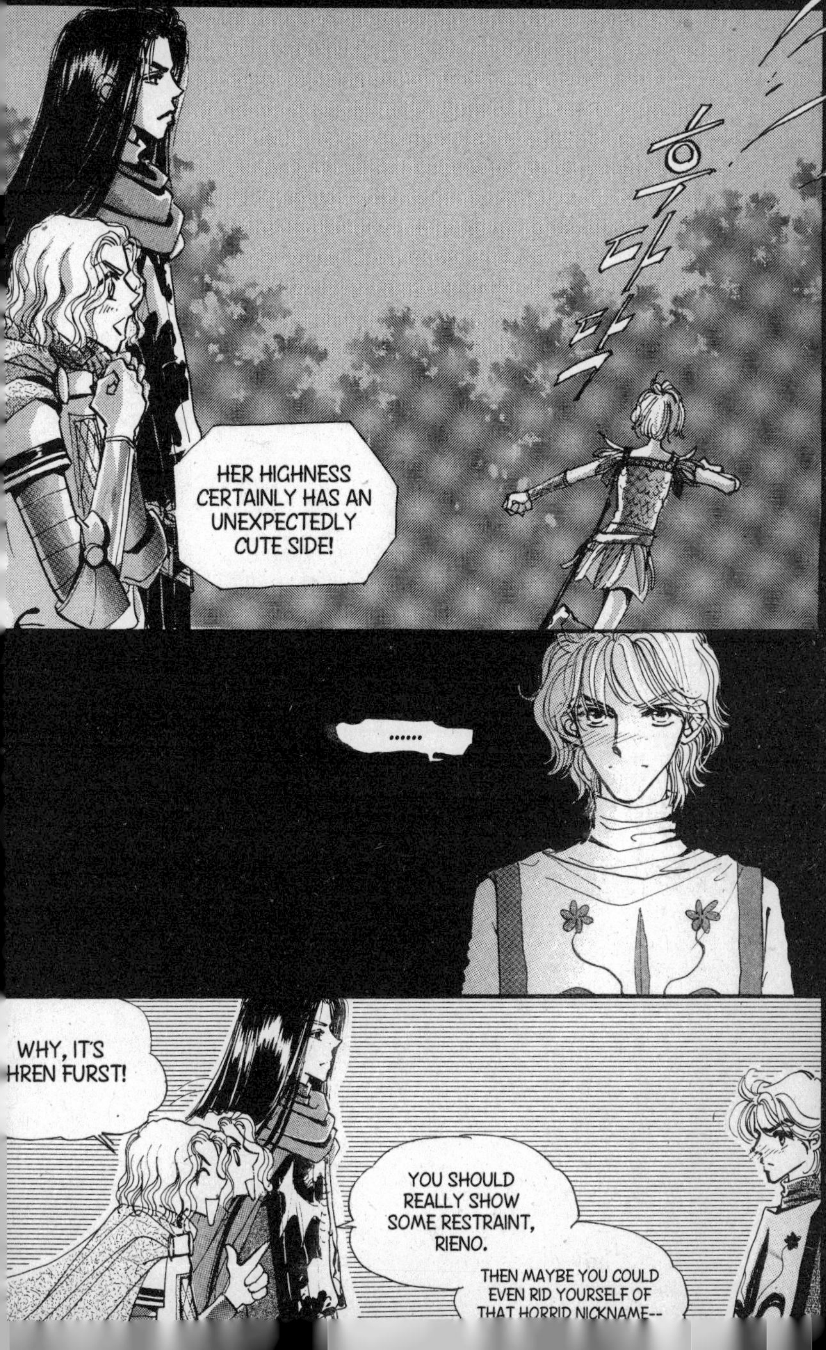
후다닥
HER HIGHNESS CERTAINLY HAS AN UNEXPECTEDLY CUTE SIDE!
......
WHY, IT'S
HREN FURST!
YOU SHOULD REALLY SHOW SOME RESTRAINT, RIENO.
THEN MAYBE YOU COULD EVEN RID YOURSELF OF THAT HORRID NICKNAME--

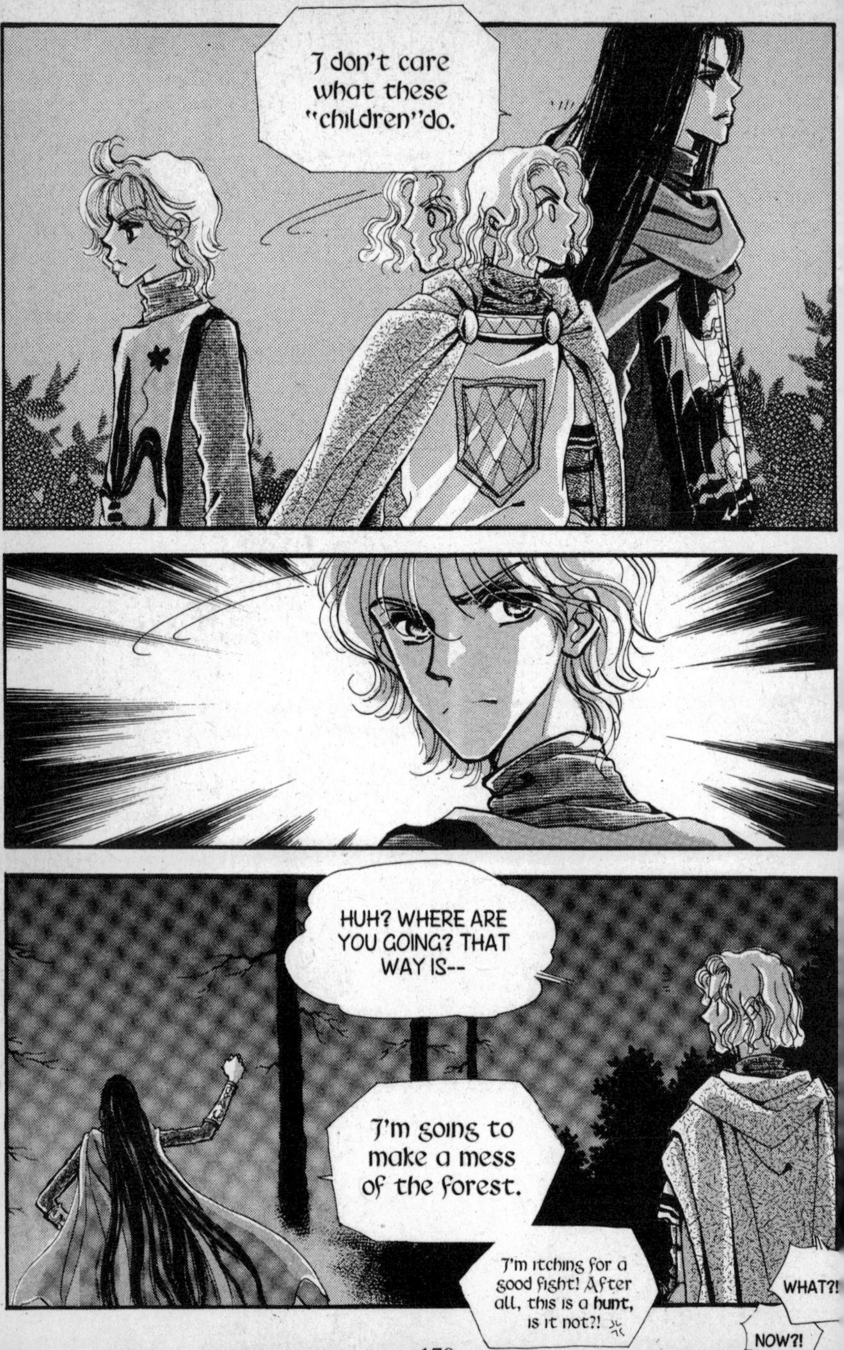
I don't care what these "children" do.
HUH? WHERE ARE YOU GOING? THAT WAY IS--
I'm going to make a mess of the forest.
I'm itching for a good fight! After all, this is a **hunt**, is it not?!
WHAT?!
NOW?!

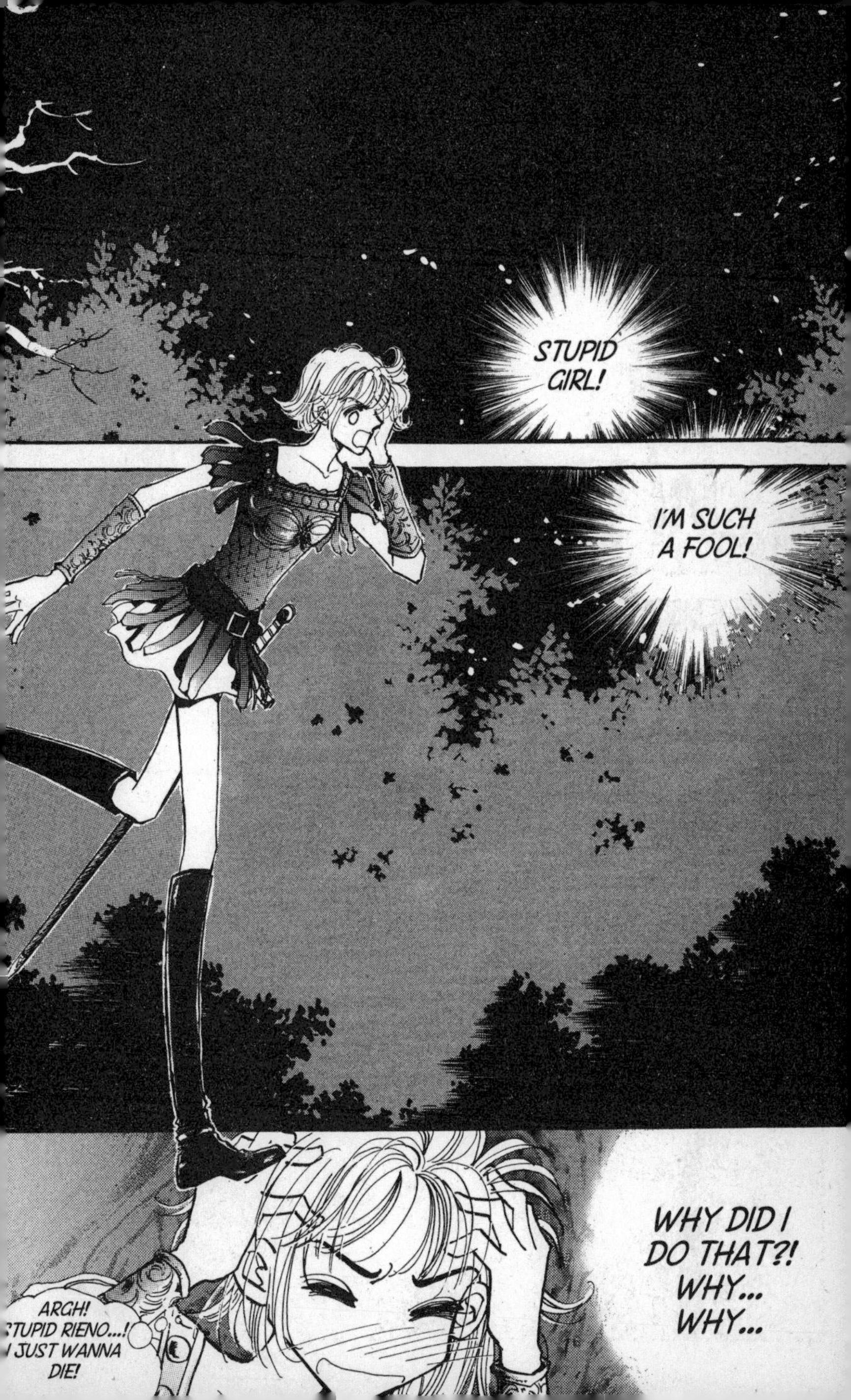
STUPID GIRL!
I'M SUCH A FOOL!
ARGH! STUPID RIENO...! I JUST WANNA DIE!
WHY DID I DO THAT?! WHY... WHY...

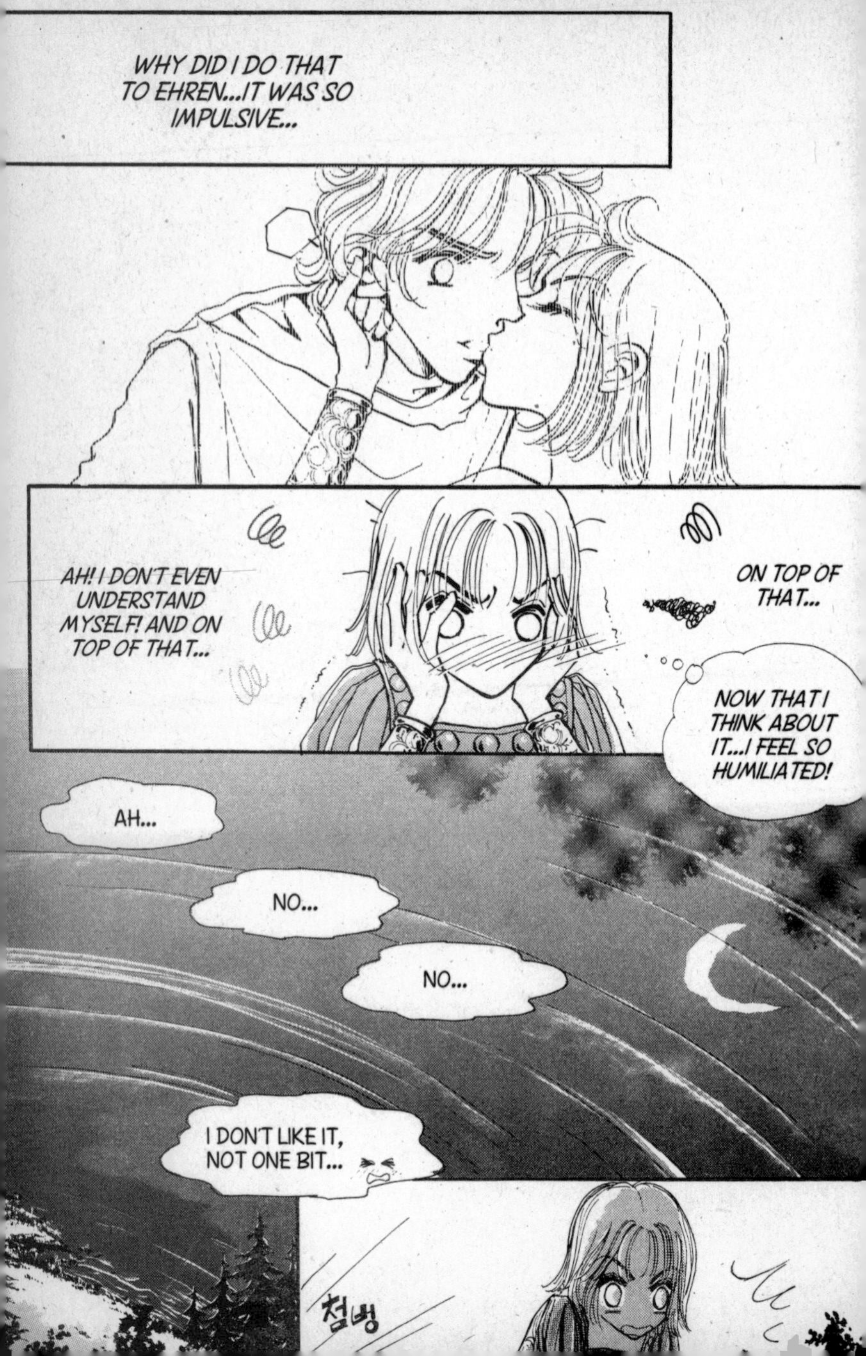
WHY DID I DO THAT TO EHREN...IT WAS SO IMPULSIVE...
AH! I DON'T EVEN UNDERSTAND MYSELF! AND ON TOP OF THAT...
ON TOP OF THAT...
NOW THAT I THINK ABOUT IT...I FEEL SO HUMILIATED!
AH...
NO...
NO...
I DON'T LIKE IT, NOT ONE BIT...
첨벙

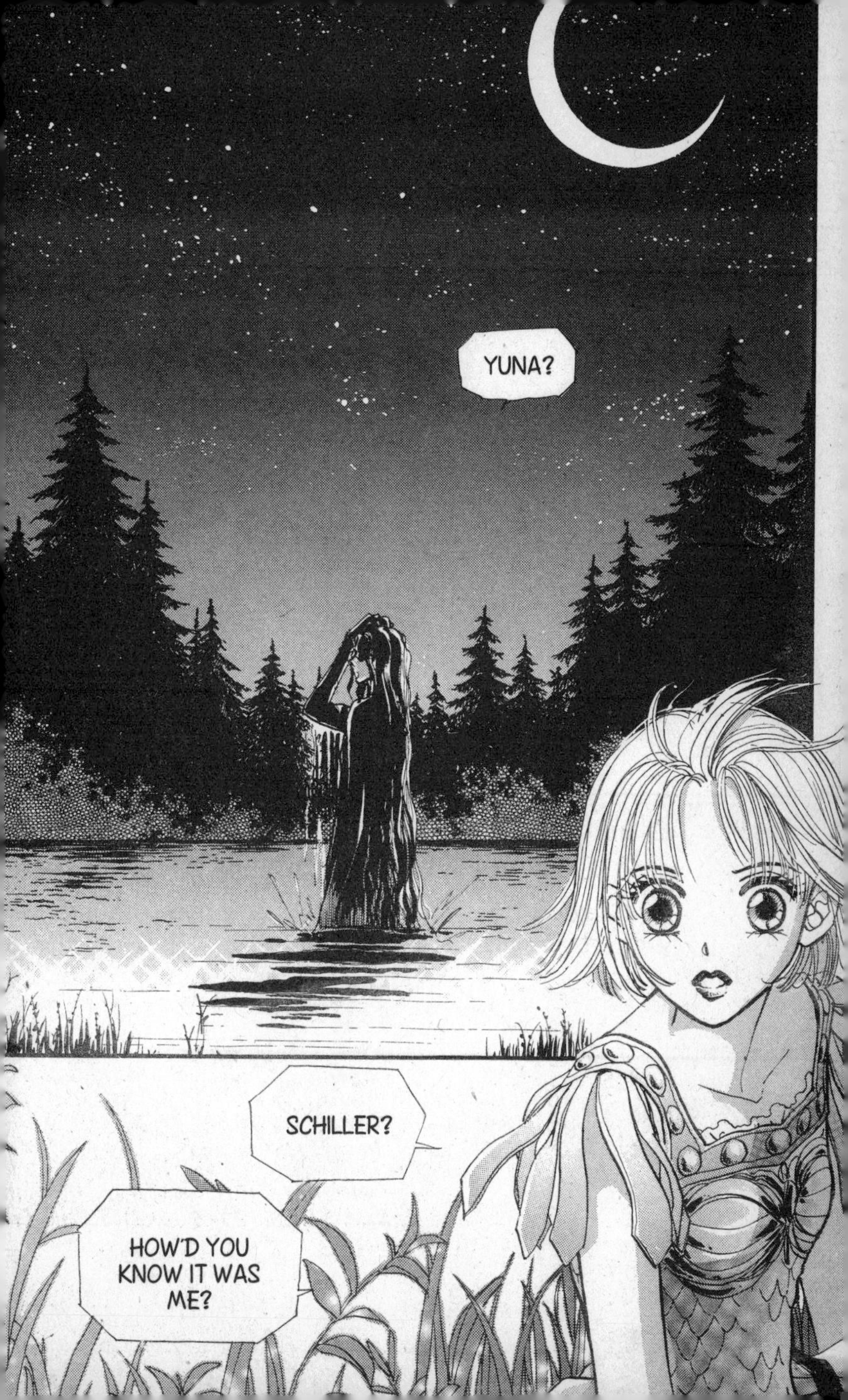
YUNA?
SCHILLER?
HOW'D YOU KNOW IT WAS ME?

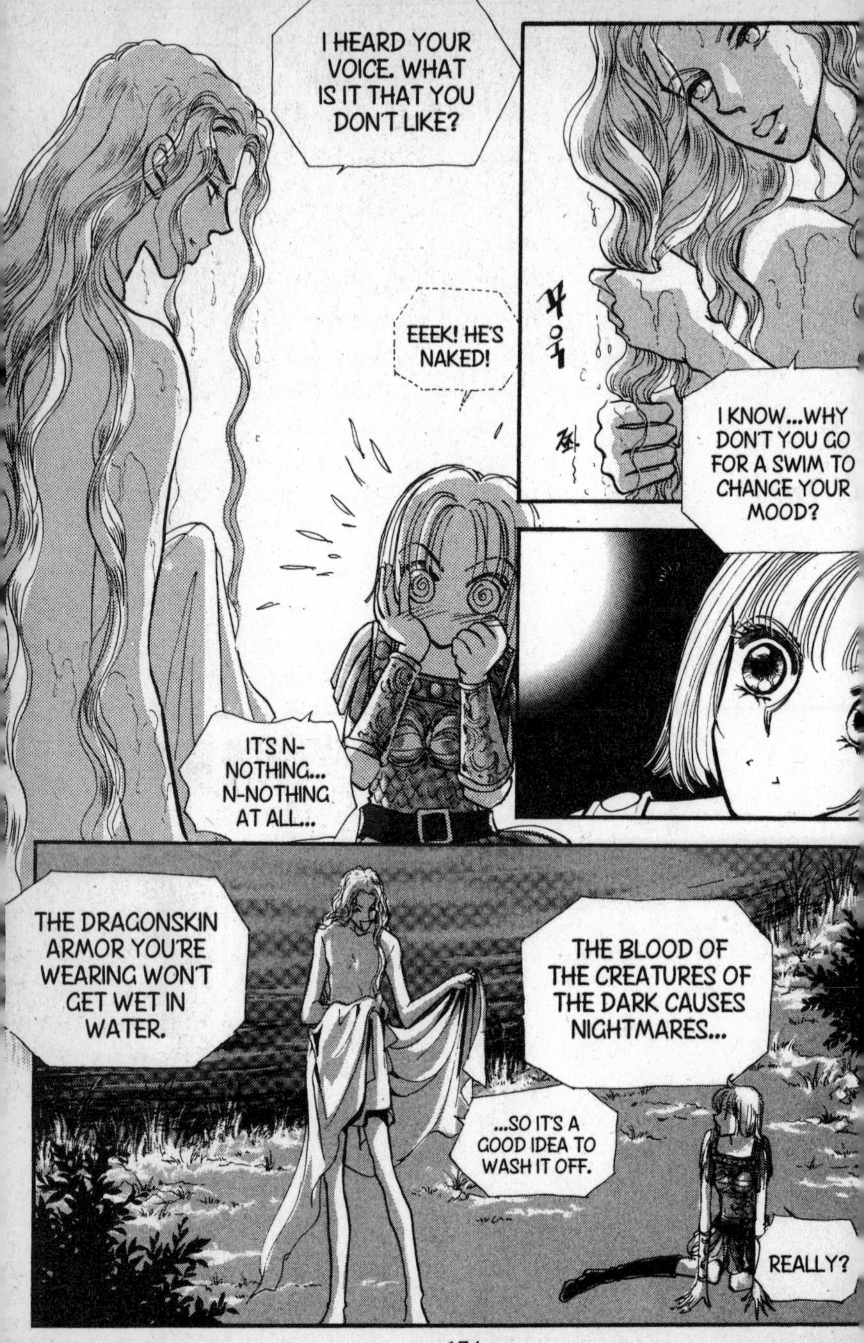
I HEARD YOUR VOICE. WHAT IS IT THAT YOU DON'T LIKE?
EEEK! HE'S NAKED!
IT'S N-NOTHING... N-NOTHING AT ALL...
I KNOW...WHY DON'T YOU GO FOR A SWIM TO CHANGE YOUR MOOD?
THE DRAGONSKIN ARMOR YOU'RE WEARING WON'T GET WET IN WATER.
THE BLOOD OF THE CREATURES OF THE DARK CAUSES NIGHTMARES...
...SO IT'S A GOOD IDEA TO WASH IT OFF.
REALLY?

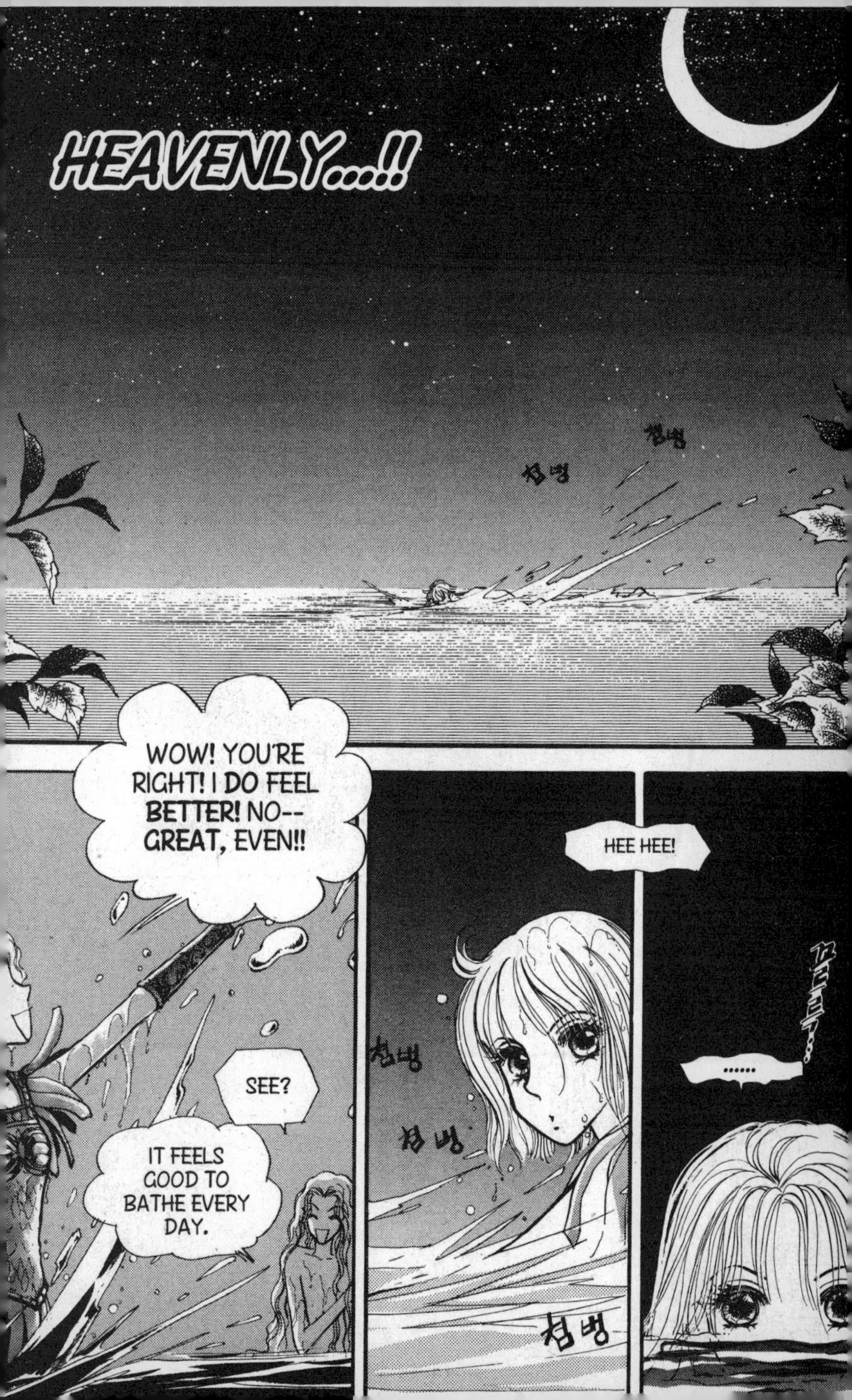

HEAVENLY...!!
첨벙
첨벙
WOW! YOU'RE RIGHT! I DO FEEL BETTER! NO-- GREAT, EVEN!!
SEE?
IT FEELS GOOD TO BATHE EVERY DAY.
첨벙
첨벙
첨벙
HEE HEE!
......

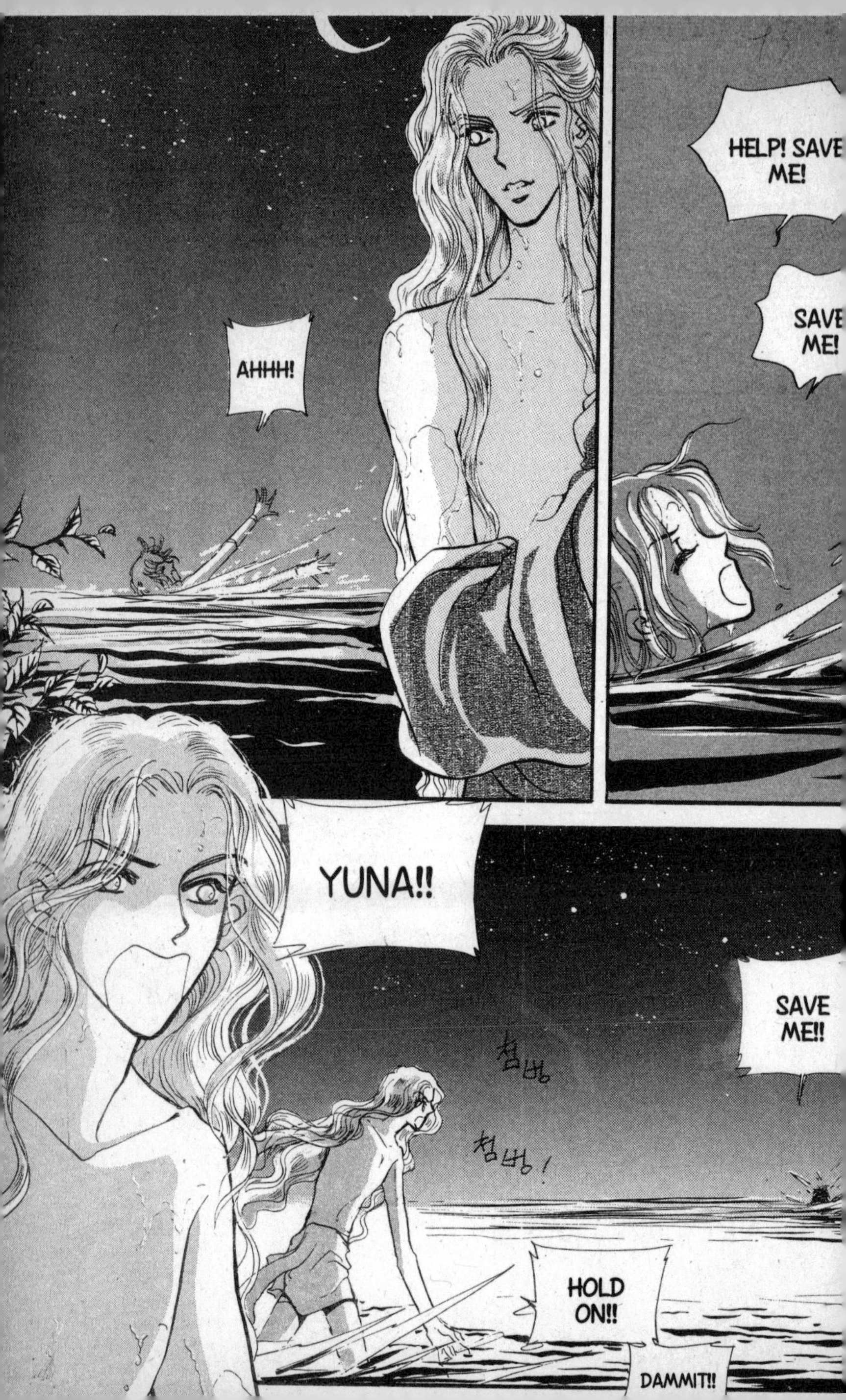
AHHH!
HELP! SAVE ME!
SAVE ME!
YUNA!!
SAVE ME!!
첨벙
첨벙!
HOLD ON!!
DAMMIT!!

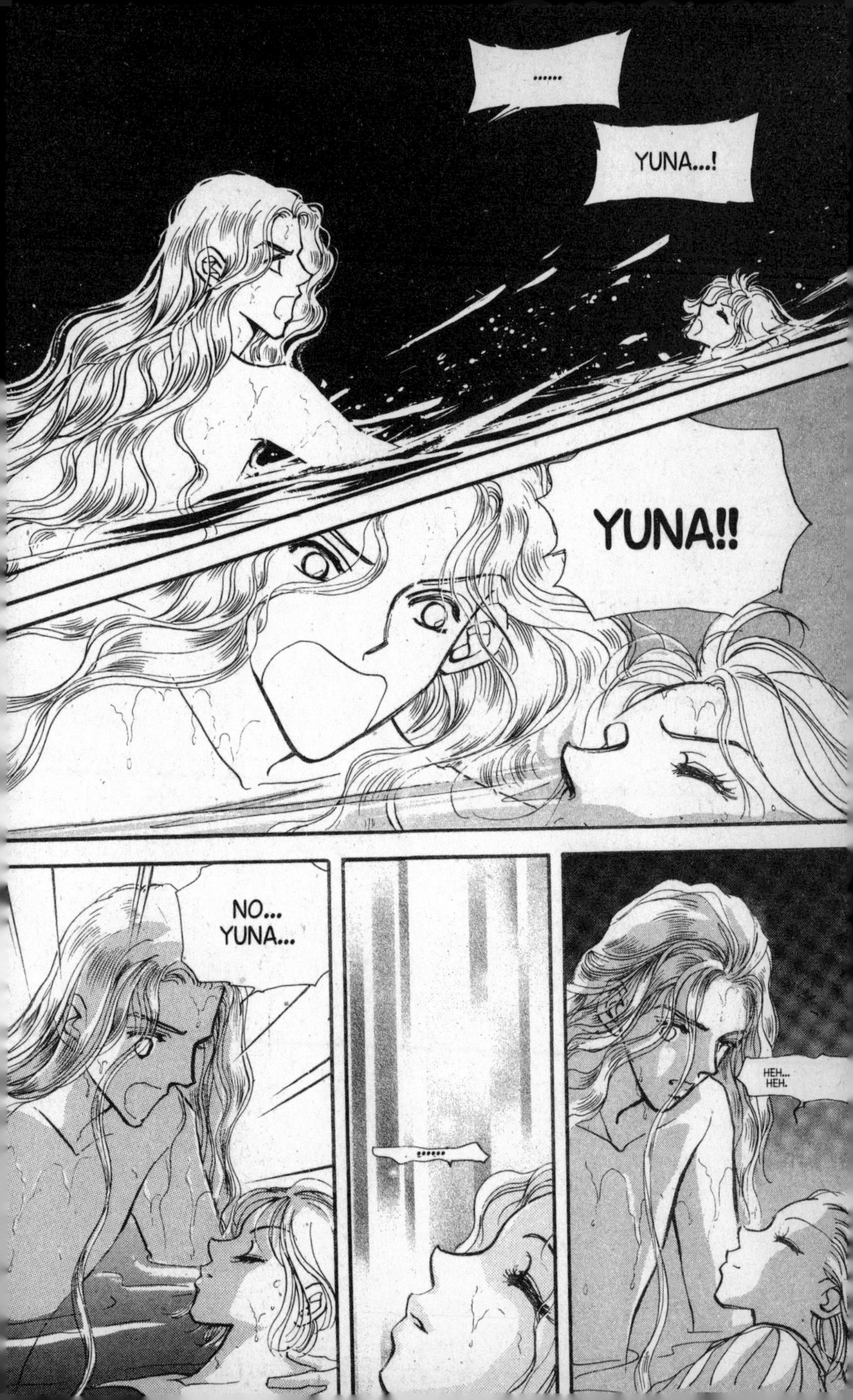
......
YUNA...!
YUNA!!
NO... YUNA...
......
HEH... HEH.

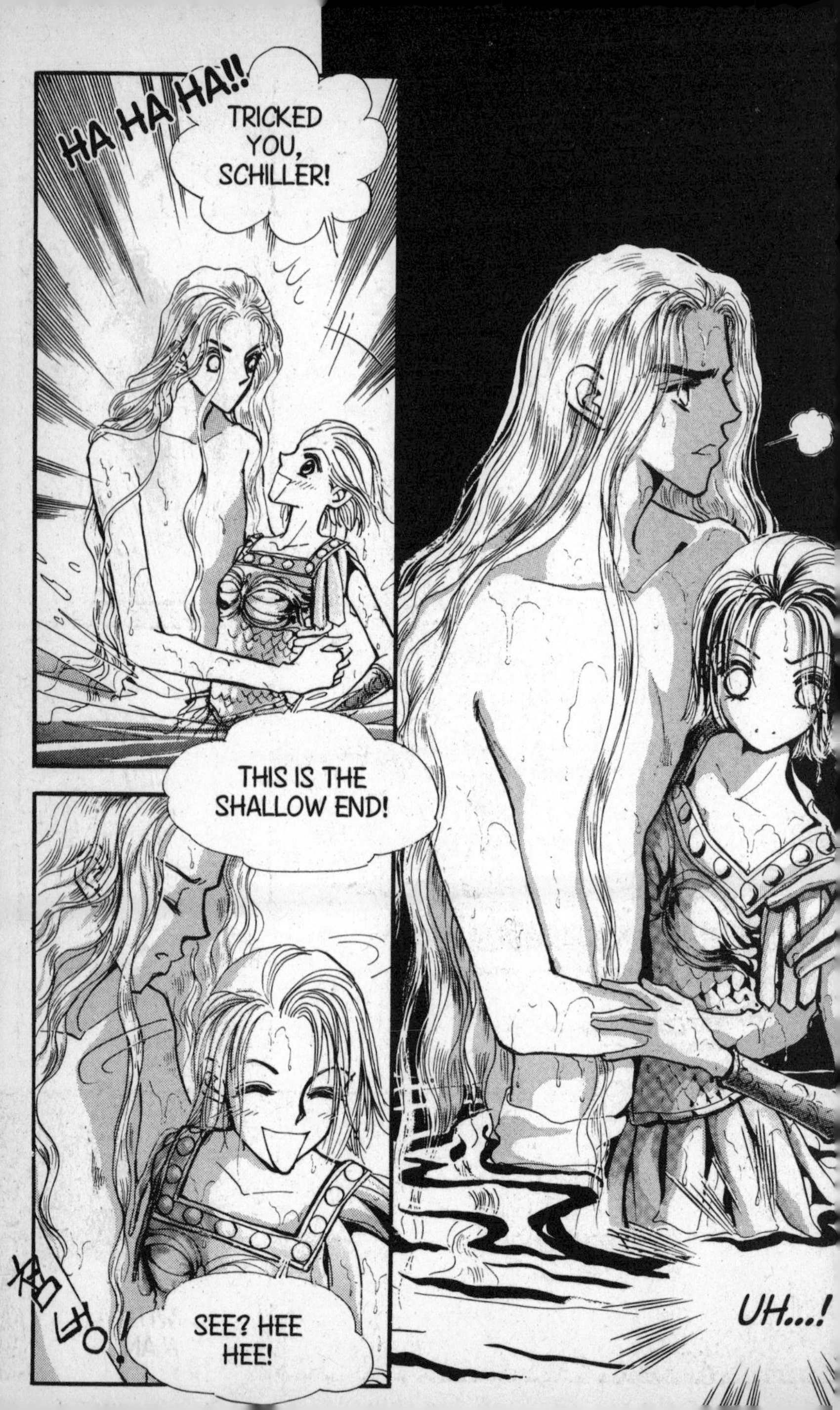
HA HA HA!!
TRICKED YOU, SCHILLER!
THIS IS THE SHALLOW END!
SEE? HEE HEE!
UH...!

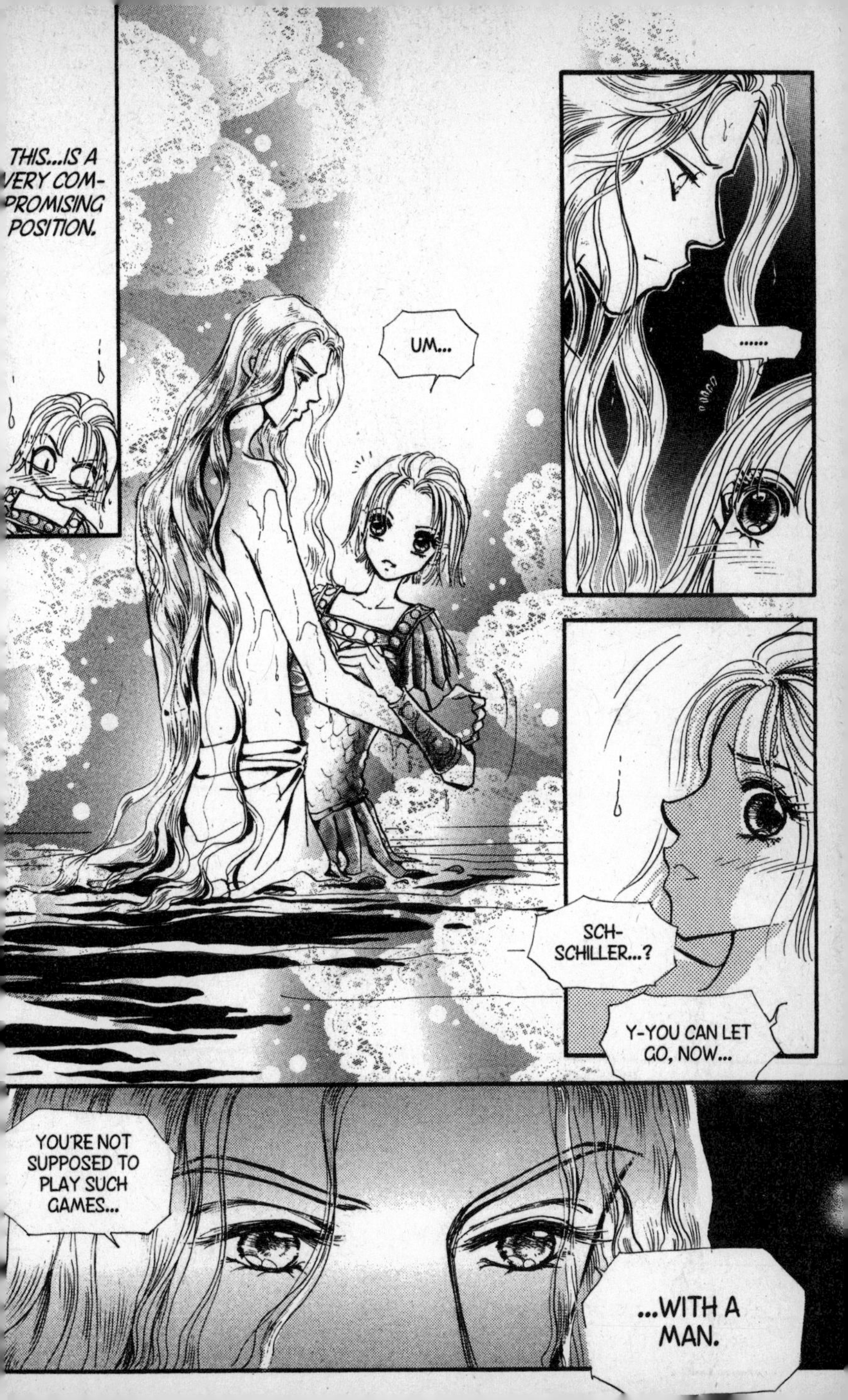
THIS...IS A VERY COM-PROMISING POSITION.
UM...
......
SCH-SCHILLER...?
Y-YOU CAN LET GO, NOW...
YOU'RE NOT SUPPOSED TO PLAY SUCH GAMES...
...WITH A MAN.

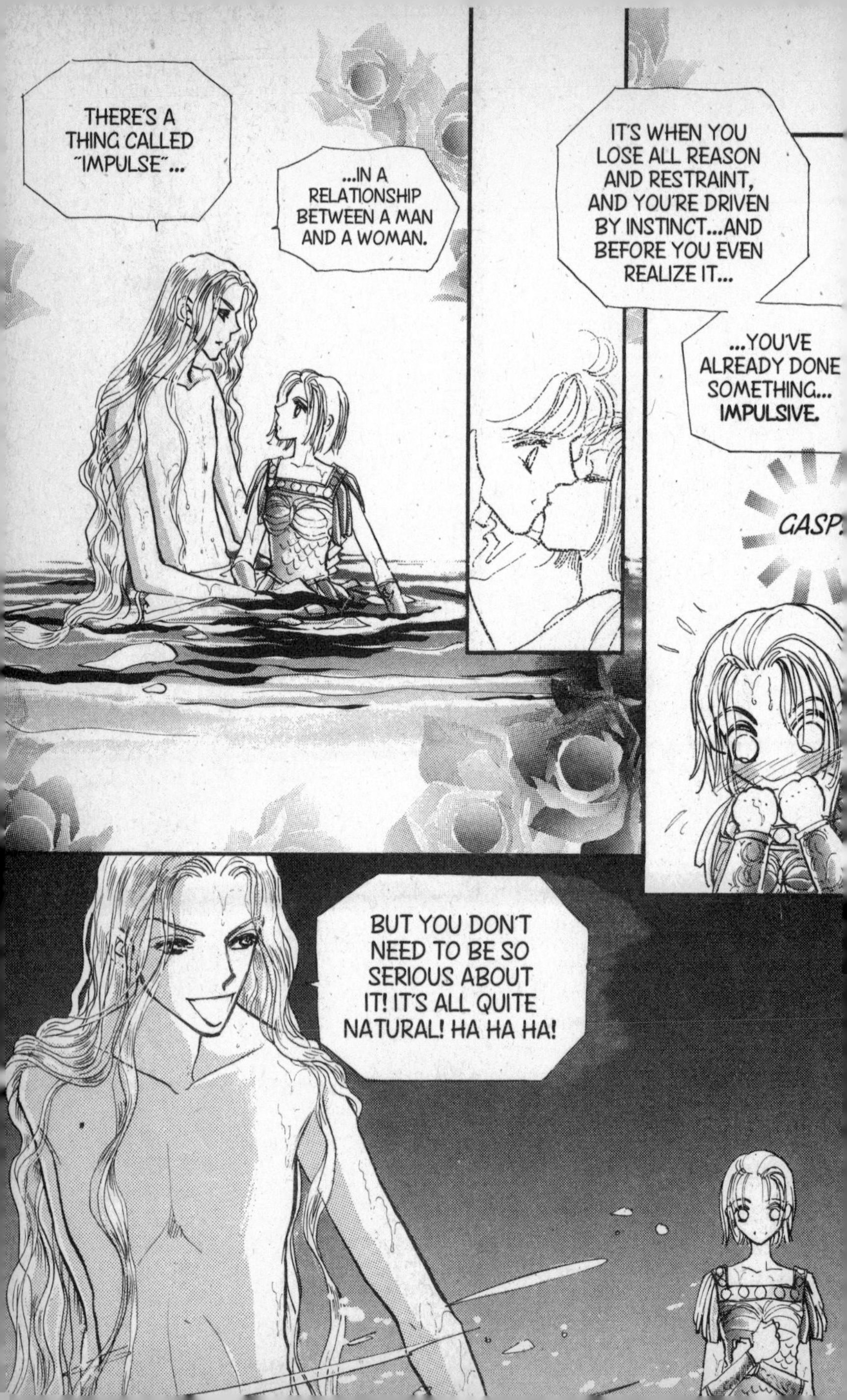
THERE'S A THING CALLED "IMPULSE"...
...IN A RELATIONSHIP BETWEEN A MAN AND A WOMAN.
IT'S WHEN YOU LOSE ALL REASON AND RESTRAINT, AND YOU'RE DRIVEN BY INSTINCT...AND BEFORE YOU EVEN REALIZE IT...
...YOU'VE ALREADY DONE SOMETHING... IMPULSIVE.
GASP!
BUT YOU DON'T NEED TO BE SO SERIOUS ABOUT IT! IT'S ALL QUITE NATURAL! HA HA HA!

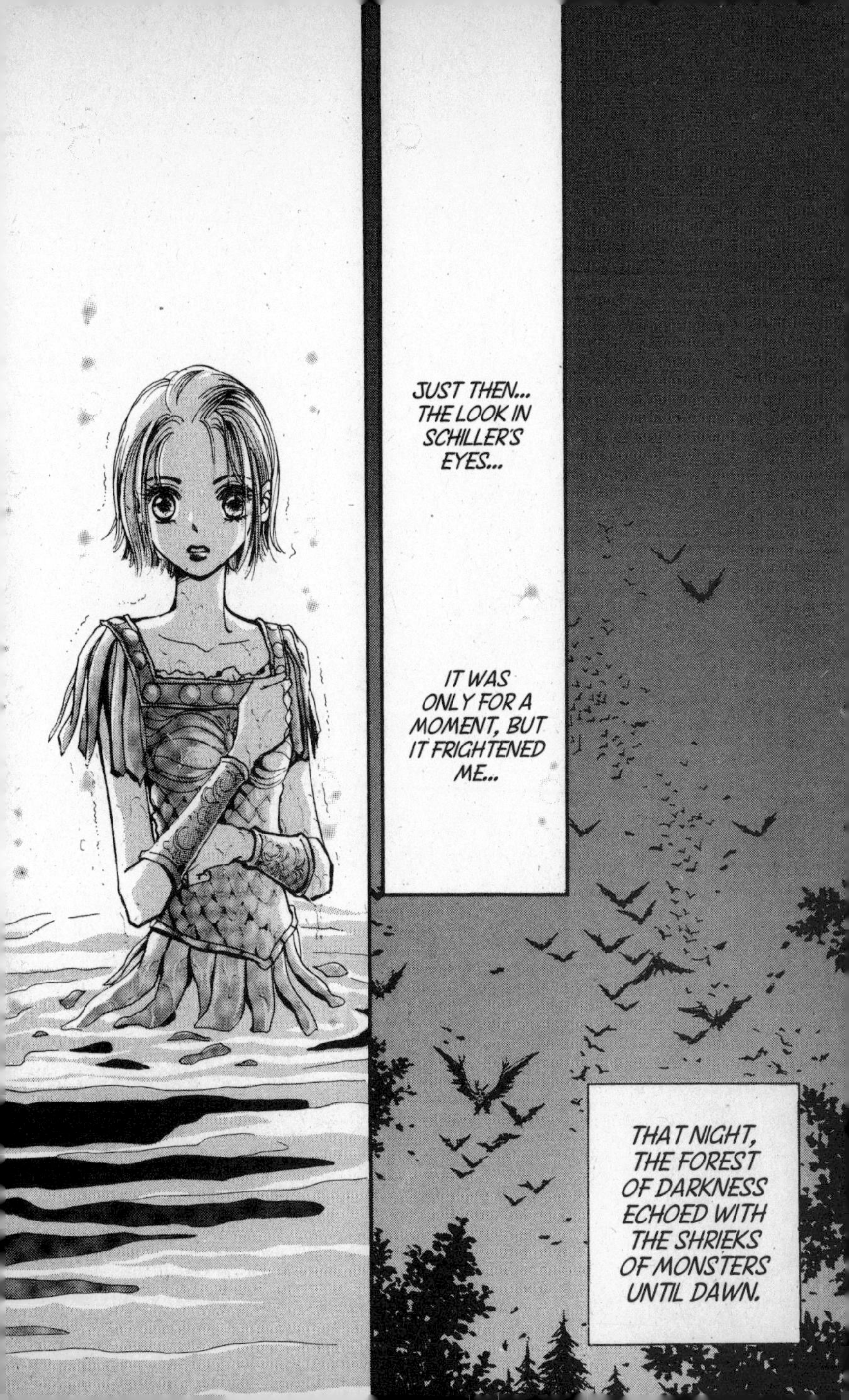
JUST THEN... THE LOOK IN SCHILLER'S EYES...
IT WAS ONLY FOR A MOMENT, BUT IT FRIGHTENED ME...
THAT NIGHT, THE FOREST OF DARKNESS ECHOED WITH THE SHRIEKS OF MONSTERS UNTIL DAWN.

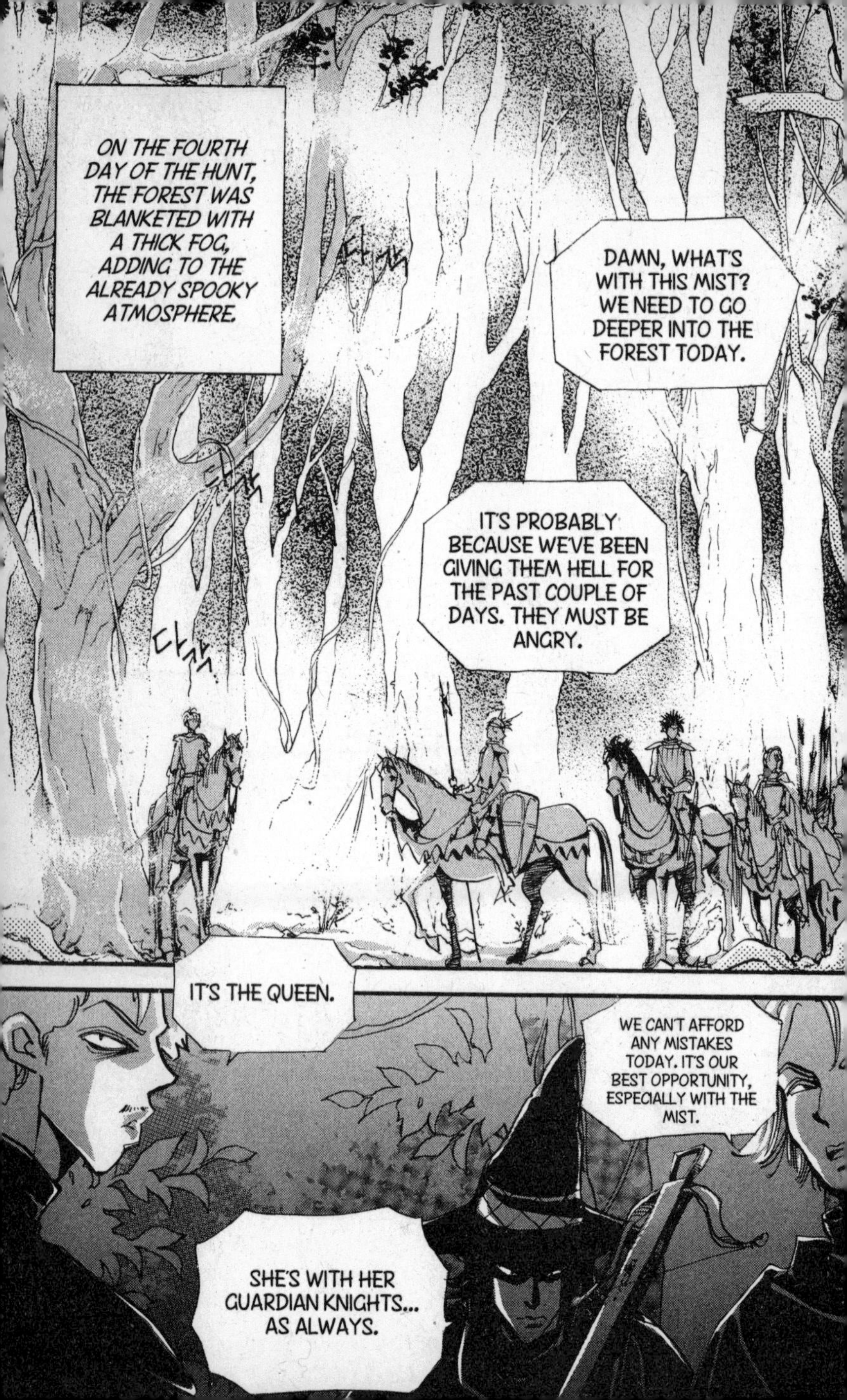
ON THE FOURTH DAY OF THE HUNT, THE FOREST WAS BLANKETED WITH A THICK FOG, ADDING TO THE ALREADY SPOOKY ATMOSPHERE.
DAMN, WHAT'S WITH THIS MIST? WE NEED TO GO DEEPER INTO THE FOREST TODAY.
IT'S PROBABLY BECAUSE WE'VE BEEN GIVING THEM HELL FOR THE PAST COUPLE OF DAYS. THEY MUST BE ANGRY.
IT'S THE QUEEN.
WE CAN'T AFFORD ANY MISTAKES TODAY. IT'S OUR BEST OPPORTUNITY, ESPECIALLY WITH THE MIST.
SHE'S WITH HER GUARDIAN KNIGHTS... AS ALWAYS.

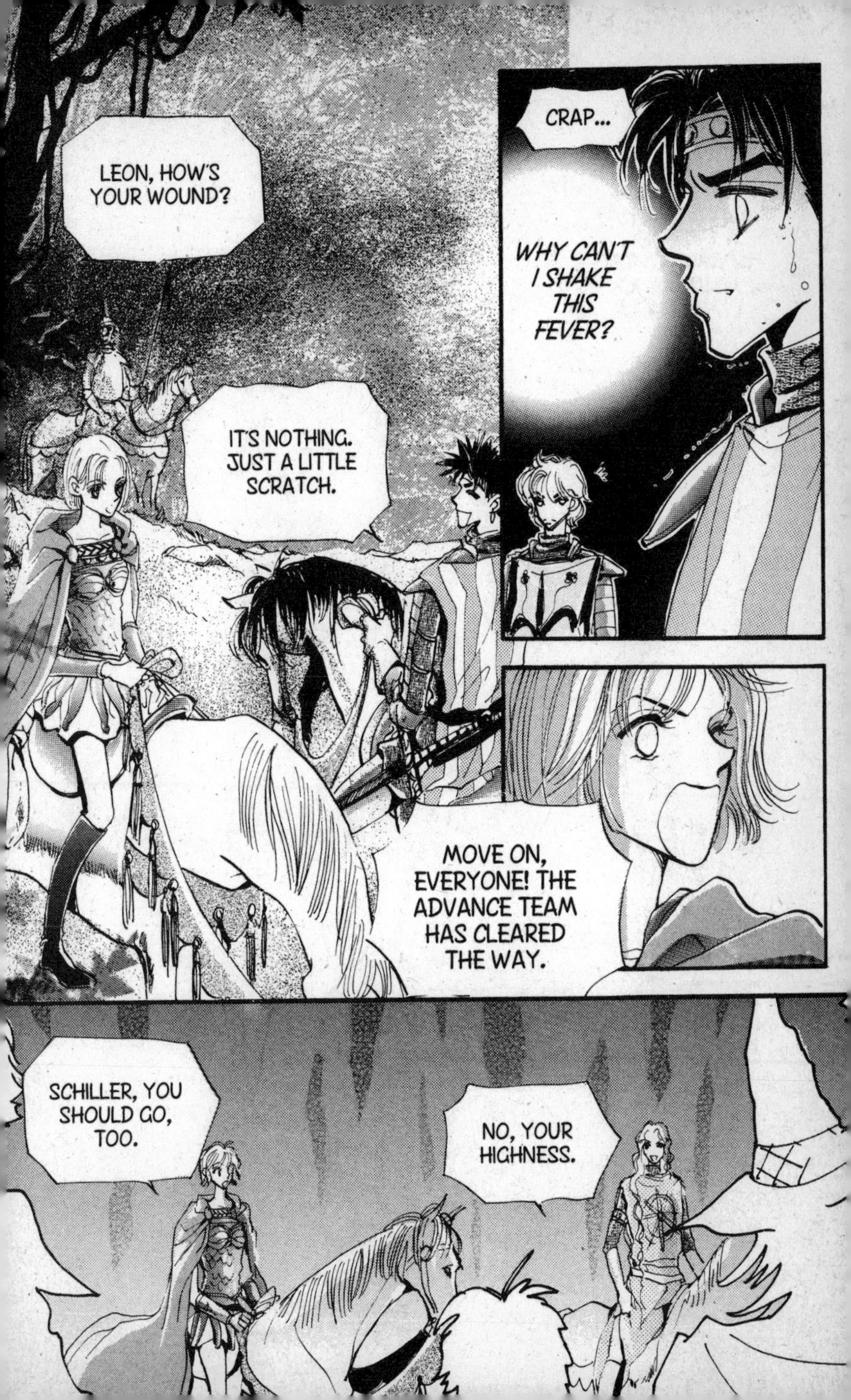
LEON, HOW'S YOUR WOUND?
IT'S NOTHING. JUST A LITTLE SCRATCH.
CRAP...
WHY CAN'T I SHAKE THIS FEVER?
MOVE ON, EVERYONE! THE ADVANCE TEAM HAS CLEARED THE WAY.
SCHILLER, YOU SHOULD GO, TOO.
NO, YOUR HIGHNESS.

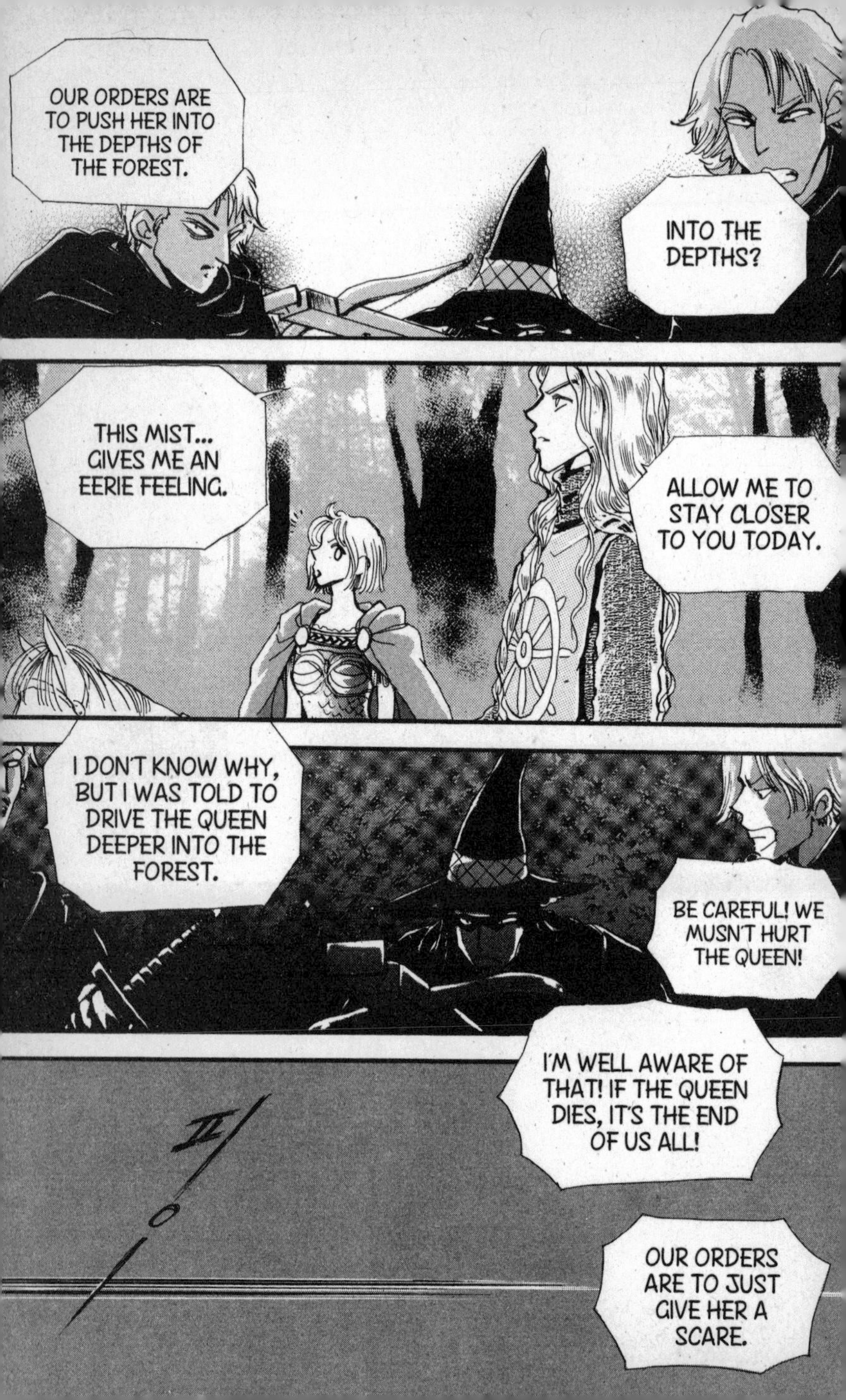
OUR ORDERS ARE TO PUSH HER INTO THE DEPTHS OF THE FOREST.
INTO THE DEPTHS?
THIS MIST... GIVES ME AN EERIE FEELING.
ALLOW ME TO STAY CLOSER TO YOU TODAY.
I DON'T KNOW WHY, BUT I WAS TOLD TO DRIVE THE QUEEN DEEPER INTO THE FOREST.
BE CAREFUL! WE MUSN'T HURT THE QUEEN!
I'M WELL AWARE OF THAT! IF THE QUEEN DIES, IT'S THE END OF US ALL!
OUR ORDERS ARE TO JUST GIVE HER A SCARE.

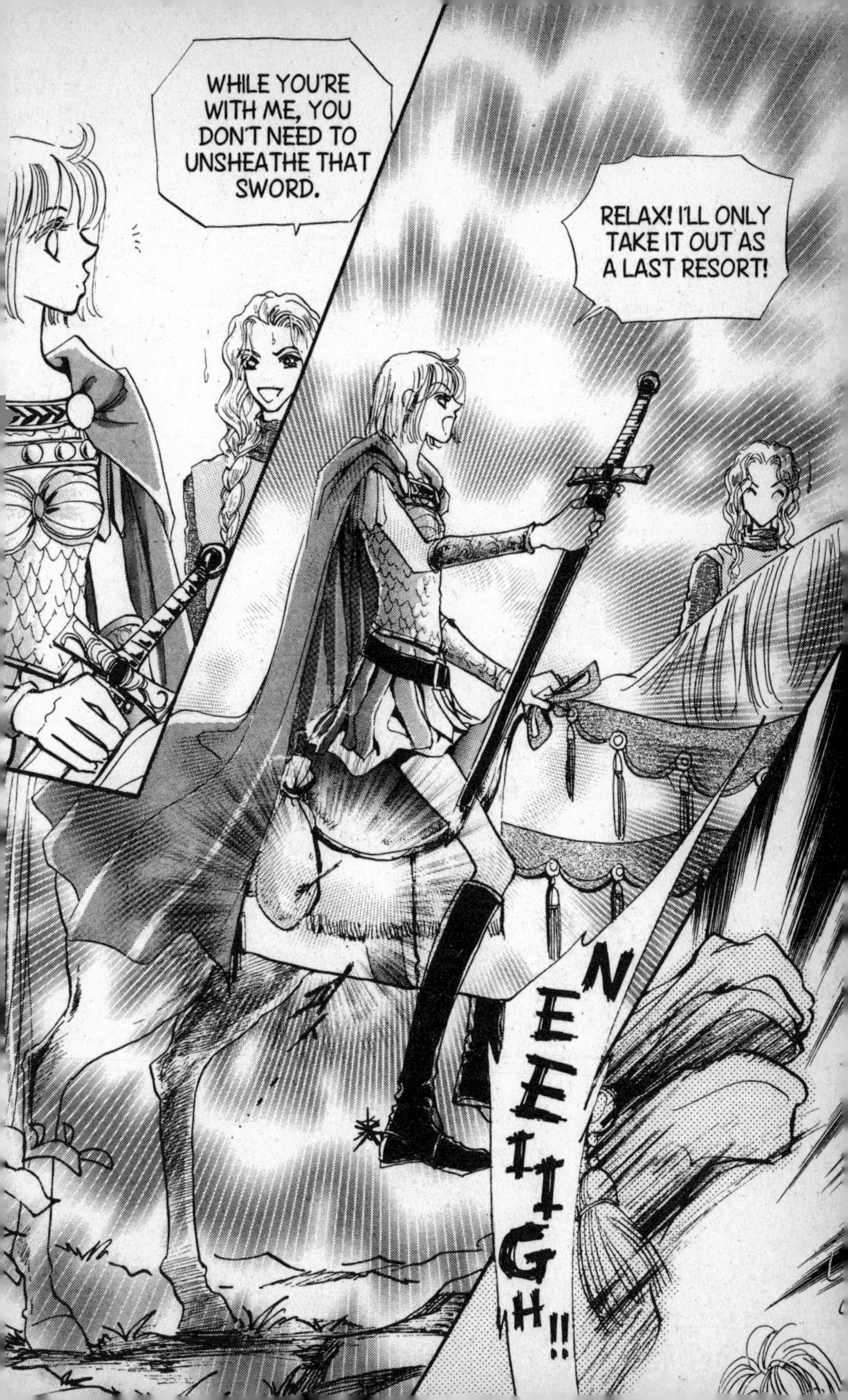
WHILE YOU'RE WITH ME, YOU DON'T NEED TO UNSHEATHE THAT SWORD.
RELAX! I'LL ONLY TAKE IT OUT AS A LAST RESORT!
NEEEIIGH!!

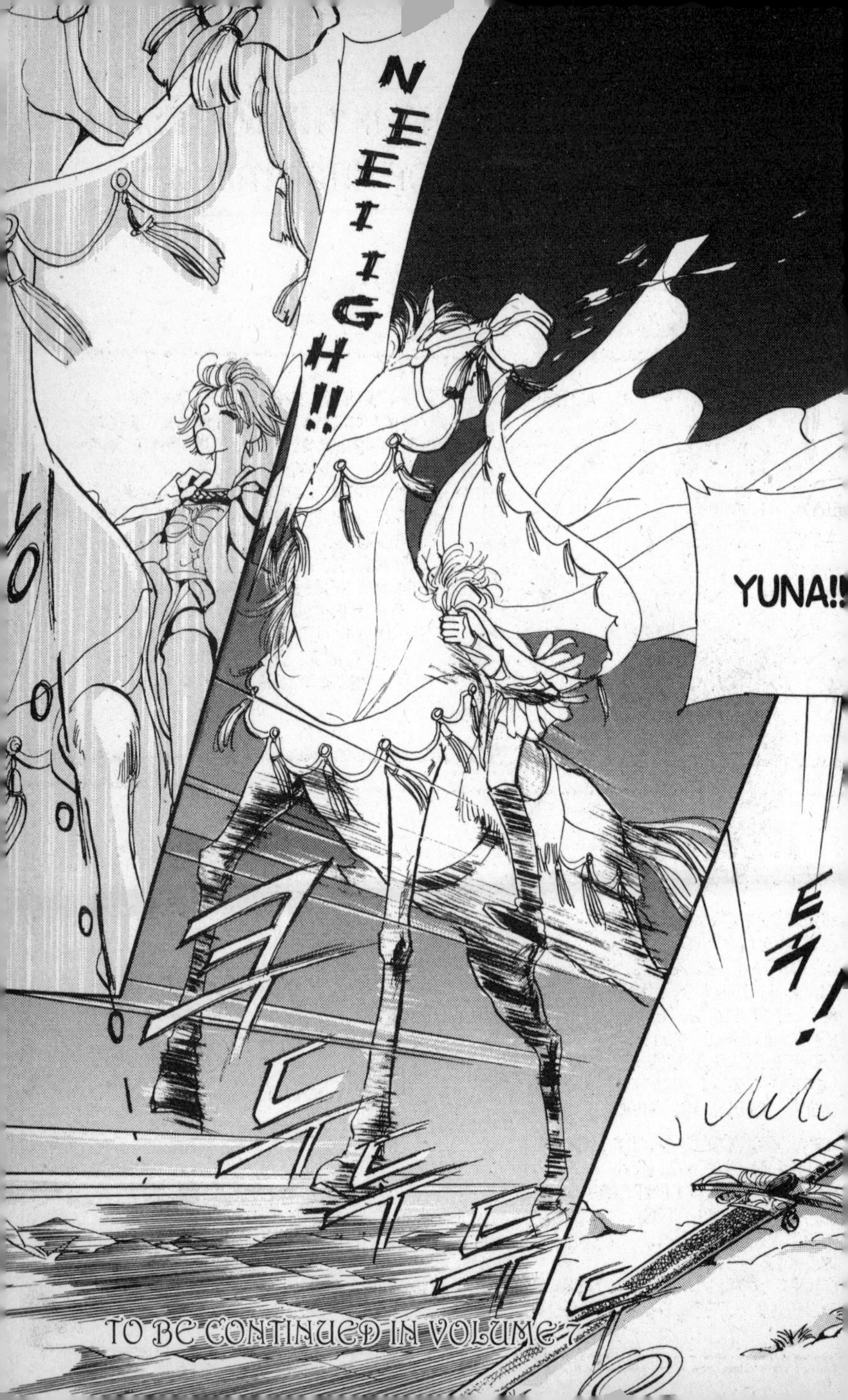
NEEIIGH!!
YUNA!!

TO BE CONTINUED IN VOLUME 7

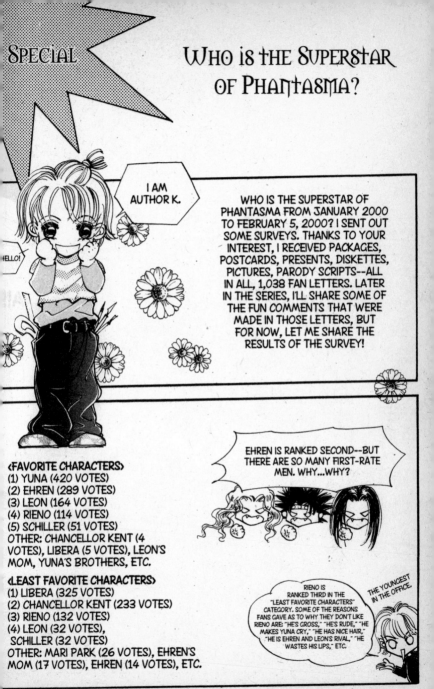

SPECIAL

WHO IS THE SUPERSTAR OF PHANTASMA?

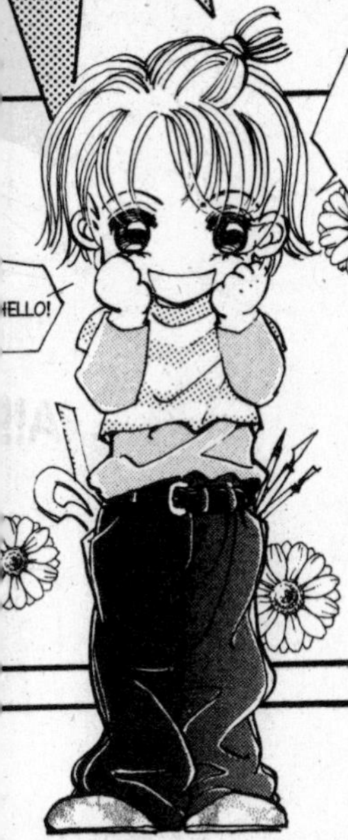
I AM AUTHOR K.
HELLO!

WHO IS THE SUPERSTAR OF PHANTASMA FROM JANUARY 2000 TO FEBRUARY 5, 2000? I SENT OUT SOME SURVEYS. THANKS TO YOUR INTEREST, I RECEIVED PACKAGES, POSTCARDS, PRESENTS, DISKETTES, PICTURES, PARODY SCRIPTS--ALL IN ALL, 1,038 FAN LETTERS. LATER IN THE SERIES, I'LL SHARE SOME OF THE FUN COMMENTS THAT WERE MADE IN THOSE LETTERS, BUT FOR NOW, LET ME SHARE THE RESULTS OF THE SURVEY!

‹FAVORITE CHARACTERS›

(1) YUNA (420 VOTES)
(2) EHREN (289 VOTES)
(3) LEON (164 VOTES)
(4) RIENO (114 VOTES)
(5) SCHILLER (51 VOTES)
OTHER: CHANCELLOR KENT (4 VOTES), LIBERA (5 VOTES), LEON'S MOM, YUNA'S BROTHERS, ETC.

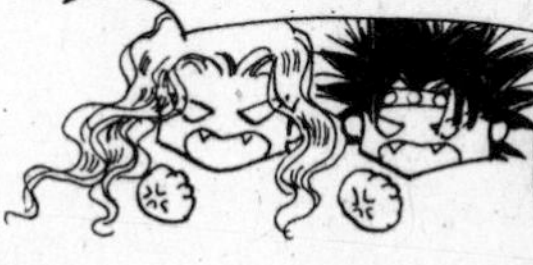
EHREN IS RANKED SECOND--BUT THERE ARE SO MANY FIRST-RATE MEN. WHY...WHY?

‹LEAST FAVORITE CHARACTERS›

(1) LIBERA (325 VOTES)
(2) CHANCELLOR KENT (233 VOTES)
(3) RIENO (132 VOTES)
(4) LEON (32 VOTES),
SCHILLER (32 VOTES)
OTHER: MARI PARK (26 VOTES), EHREN'S MOM (17 VOTES), EHREN (14 VOTES), ETC.

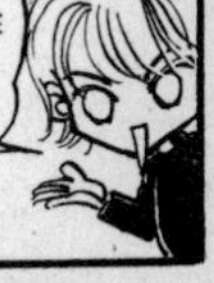
RIENO IS RANKED THIRD IN THE "LEAST FAVORITE CHARACTERS" CATEGORY. SOME OF THE REASONS FANS GAVE AS TO WHY THEY DON'T LIKE RIENO ARE: "HE'S GROSS," "HE'S RUDE," "HE MAKES YUNA CRY," "HE HAS NICE HAIR," "HE IS EHREN AND LEON'S RIVAL," "HE WASTES HIS LIPS," ETC.
THE YOUNGEST IN THE OFFICE.

The drawings in the background were taken from the ideas of fans. The above picture was sent in by So Young Han in Dae Jun.

⟨BEST COUPLE⟩
(1) YUNA & EHREN (318 VOTES)
(2) YUNA & RIENO (110 VOTES)
(3) YUNA & LEON (92 VOTES)
(4) LEON & SCHILLER (29 VOTES)
(5) LIBERA & CHANCELLOR KENT (25 VOTES)
OTHER: LEON & EVA (12 VOTES), LEON &
LIBERA (8 VOTES), YUNA & SCHILLER
(29 VOTES), YUNA & KAHYUN
(5 VOTES), ETC.

BY A LANDSLIDE.

I'M NOT COMPLAINING.

"Felt strange to begin with" couple

DARN IT! RANKED SECOND JUST BECAUSE I HAVEN'T APPEARED AS MUCH!

YUNA...!

SHOULD I PLAY THE BRIDE? HONEY...?

LEON... SCHILLER...

YOU BOYS LOOK SO GOOD TOGETHER!

I'M EMBAR-RASSED!

FANS OF EHREN AND LEON... WATCH OUT!

Overcoming the massive barrier...

⟨WORST COUPLE⟩
(1) LIBERA & RIENO (27 VOTES)
(2) LIBERA & LEON (19 VOTES)
(3) LIBERA & EHREN (15 VOTES)
(4) LIBERA & KENT (14 VOTES)
(5) YUNA & RIENO (11 VOTES)
(6) EHREN & LEON (6 VOTES)
OTHER: EHREN & YUNA, LEON &
YUNA, LEON & SCHILLER, YUNA &
SCHILLER, ETC.

ACK! WHY THE HELL AM I PAIRED WITH THAT OLD MAN? CHANGE ME!

Libera & Kent Divine Punishment

A COUPLE?! JUST KILL ME NOW...

GOODBYE, WORLD...

WHERE ARE YOU GOING, LEON?

Ehren & Leon

All the background gags were suggested by readers. I simply drew the thoughts and comments of our readers. These ideas came from: Su Won Lee from Seoul SongMa Gu, Eun Hae Park from Kyung Ki region, Yu Sun Yang from Seoul, and Yu Na Kim from Jun Nam.

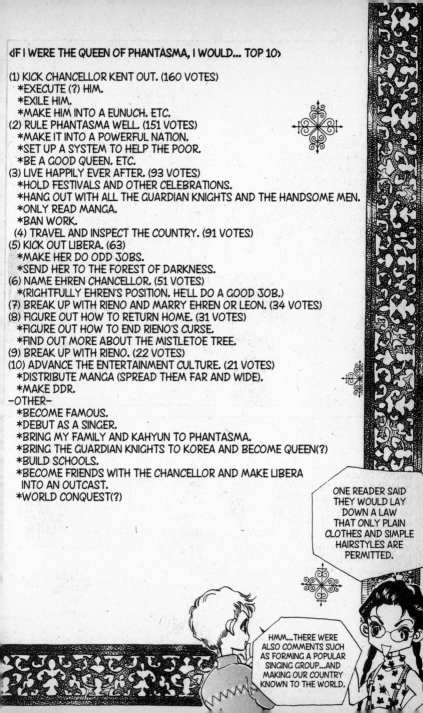

≪IF I WERE THE QUEEN OF PHANTASMA, I WOULD... TOP 10≫

(1) KICK CHANCELLOR KENT OUT. (160 VOTES)
  *EXECUTE (?) HIM.
  *EXILE HIM.
  *MAKE HIM INTO A EUNUCH. ETC.
(2) RULE PHANTASMA WELL. (151 VOTES)
  *MAKE IT INTO A POWERFUL NATION.
  *SET UP A SYSTEM TO HELP THE POOR.
  *BE A GOOD QUEEN. ETC.
(3) LIVE HAPPILY EVER AFTER. (93 VOTES)
  *HOLD FESTIVALS AND OTHER CELEBRATIONS.
  *HANG OUT WITH ALL THE GUARDIAN KNIGHTS AND THE HANDSOME MEN.
  *ONLY READ MANGA.
  *BAN WORK.
 (4) TRAVEL AND INSPECT THE COUNTRY. (91 VOTES)
(5) KICK OUT LIBERA. (63)
  *MAKE HER DO ODD JOBS.
  *SEND HER TO THE FOREST OF DARKNESS.
(6) NAME EHREN CHANCELLOR. (51 VOTES)
  *(RIGHTFULLY EHREN'S POSITION. HE'LL DO A GOOD JOB.)
(7) BREAK UP WITH RIENO AND MARRY EHREN OR LEON. (34 VOTES)
(8) FIGURE OUT HOW TO RETURN HOME. (31 VOTES)
  *FIGURE OUT HOW TO END RIENO'S CURSE.
  *FIND OUT MORE ABOUT THE MISTLETOE TREE.
(9) BREAK UP WITH RIENO. (22 VOTES)
(10) ADVANCE THE ENTERTAINMENT CULTURE. (21 VOTES)
  *DISTRIBUTE MANGA (SPREAD THEM FAR AND WIDE).
  *MAKE DDR.
-OTHER-
  *BECOME FAMOUS.
  *DEBUT AS A SINGER.
  *BRING MY FAMILY AND KAHYUN TO PHANTASMA.
  *BRING THE GUARDIAN KNIGHTS TO KOREA AND BECOME QUEEN(?)
  *BUILD SCHOOLS.
  *BECOME FRIENDS WITH THE CHANCELLOR AND MAKE LIBERA
   INTO AN OUTCAST.
  *WORLD CONQUEST(?)

ONE READER SAID THEY WOULD LAY DOWN A LAW THAT ONLY PLAIN CLOTHES AND SIMPLE HAIRSTYLES ARE PERMITTED.

HMM...THERE WERE ALSO COMMENTS SUCH AS FORMING A POPULAR SINGING GROUP...AND MAKING OUR COUNTRY KNOWN TO THE WORLD.

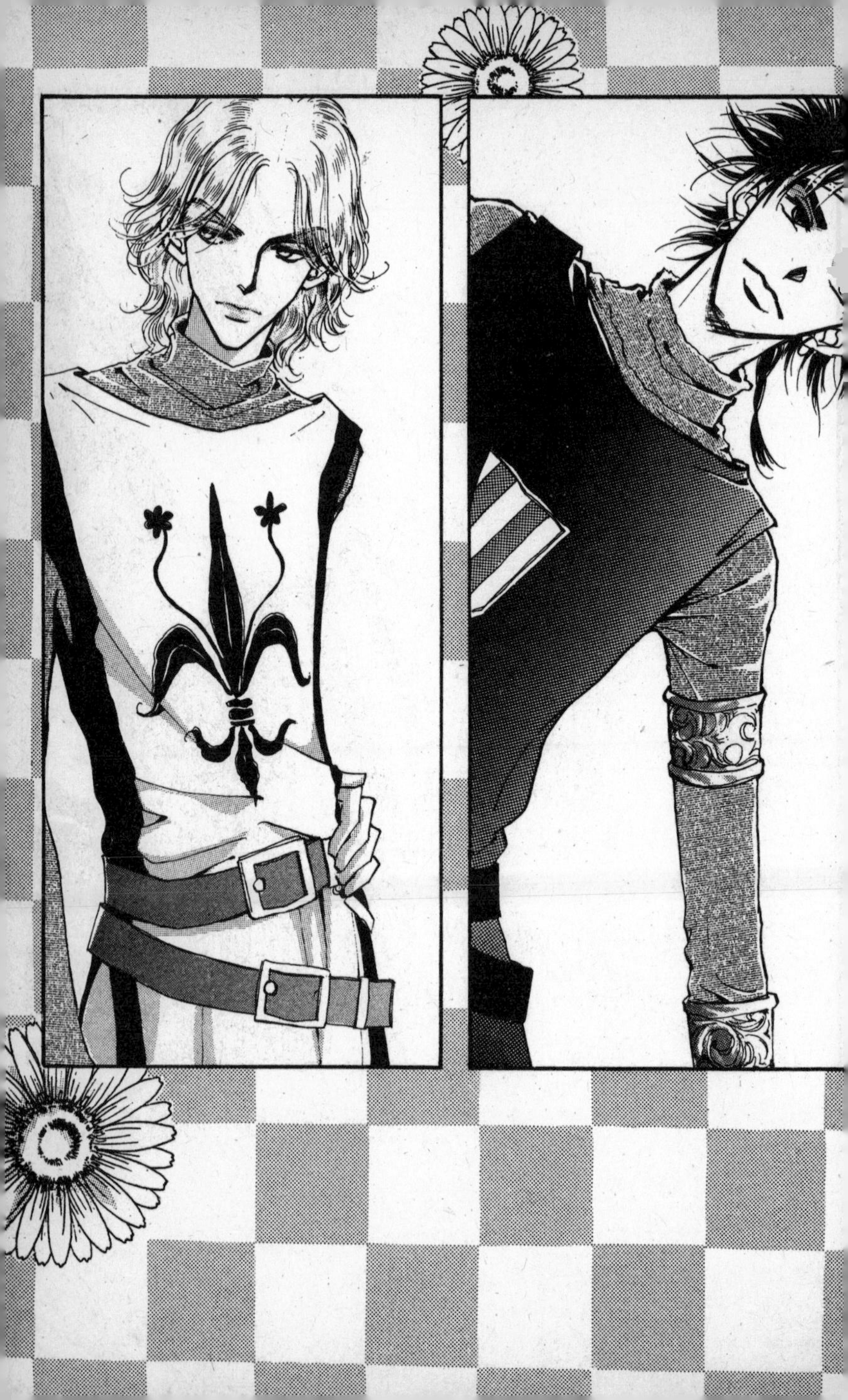

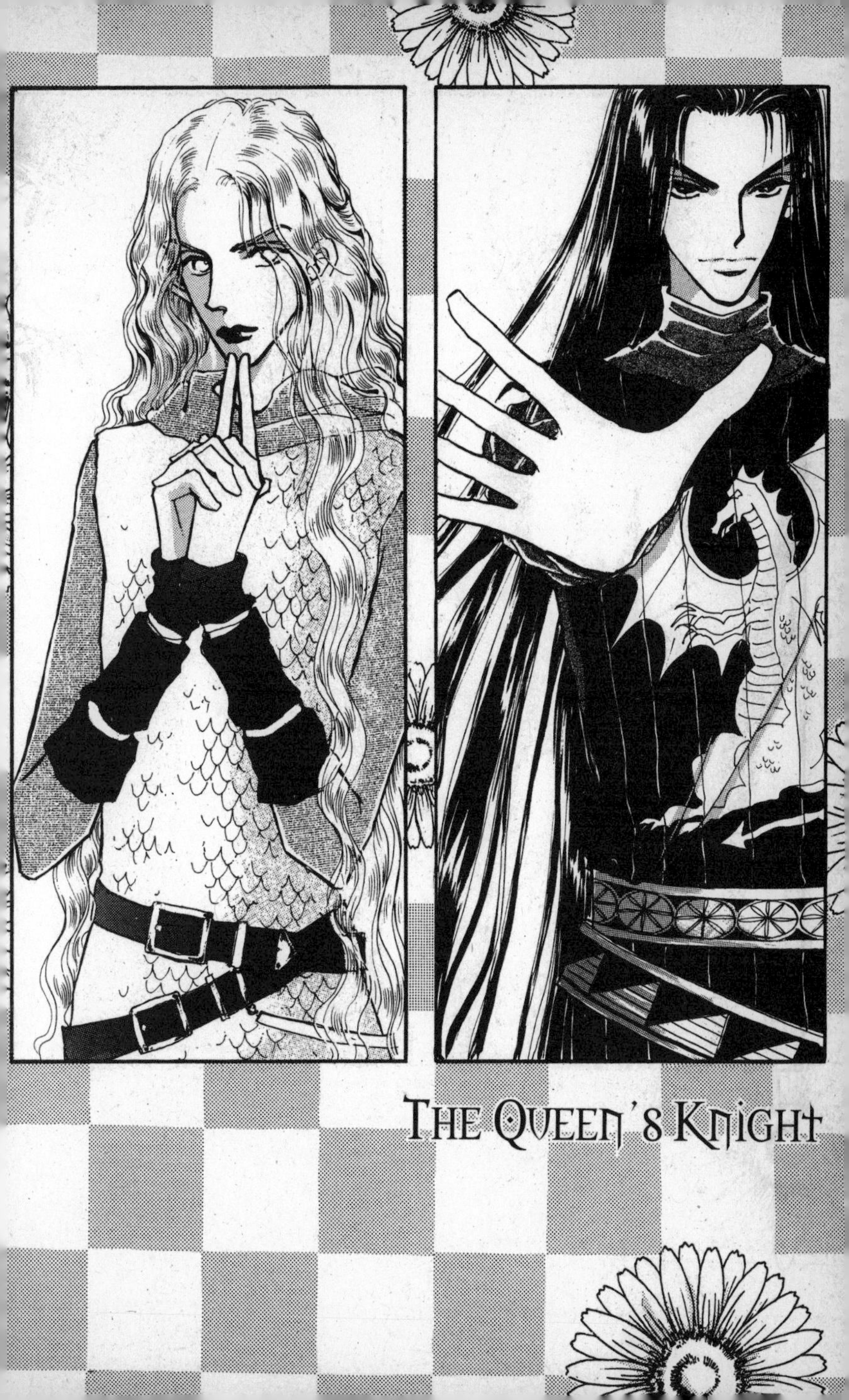
THE QUEEN'S KNIGHT

In the Next Volume of...

The Queen's Knight

The chase is on as the knights desperately pursue Yuna into the depths of the Forest of Darkness...where her only chance of surviving may rest on Rieno's shoulders. Later, Yuna is pressured by Chancellor Kent to reveal the identity of the person she is in love with. Ehren, however, comes up with a temporary solution that works the other knights into a jealous frenzy!

Coming Soon!

DRAMACON™

Sometimes even two's a crowd.

When Christie settles in the Artist Alley of her first-ever anime convention, she only sees it as an opportunity to promote the comic she has started with her boyfriend. But conventions are never what you expect, and soon a whirlwind of events sweeps Christie off her feet and changes her life. Who is the mysterious cosplayer who won't even take off his sunglasses indoors? What do you do when you fall in love with a guy who is going to be miles away from you in just a couple of days?

CREATED BY SVETLANA CHMAKOVA!

"YOU CAN'T AVOID FALLING UNDER ITS CHARM." -IGN.COM

READ AN ENTIRE CHAPTER ONLINE FOR FREE:
WWW.TOKYOPOP.COM/MANGAONLINE

TOKYOPOP MANGA SUPPLEMENT

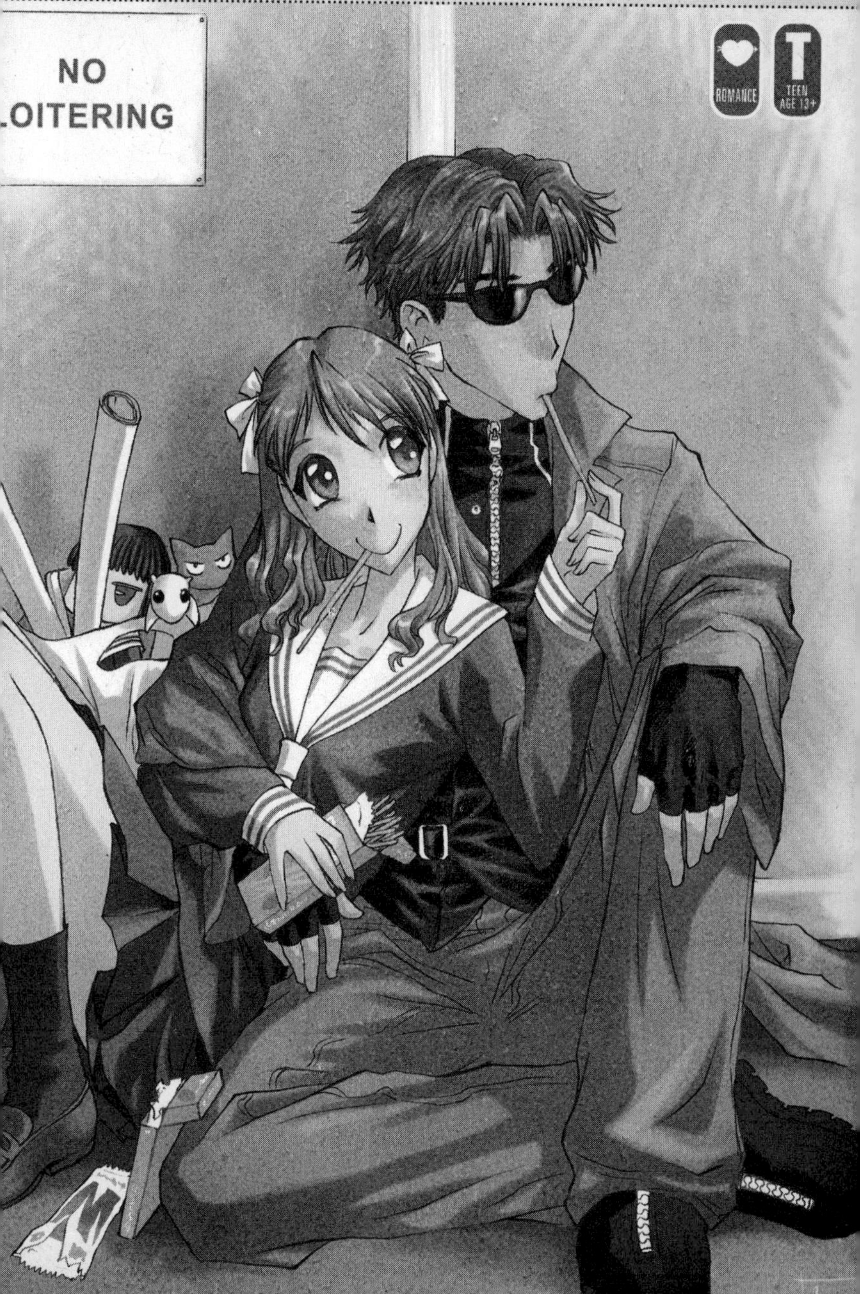
NO
OITERING
ROMANCE
T
TEEN
AGE 13+

TOKYOPOP MANGA SUPPLEMENT

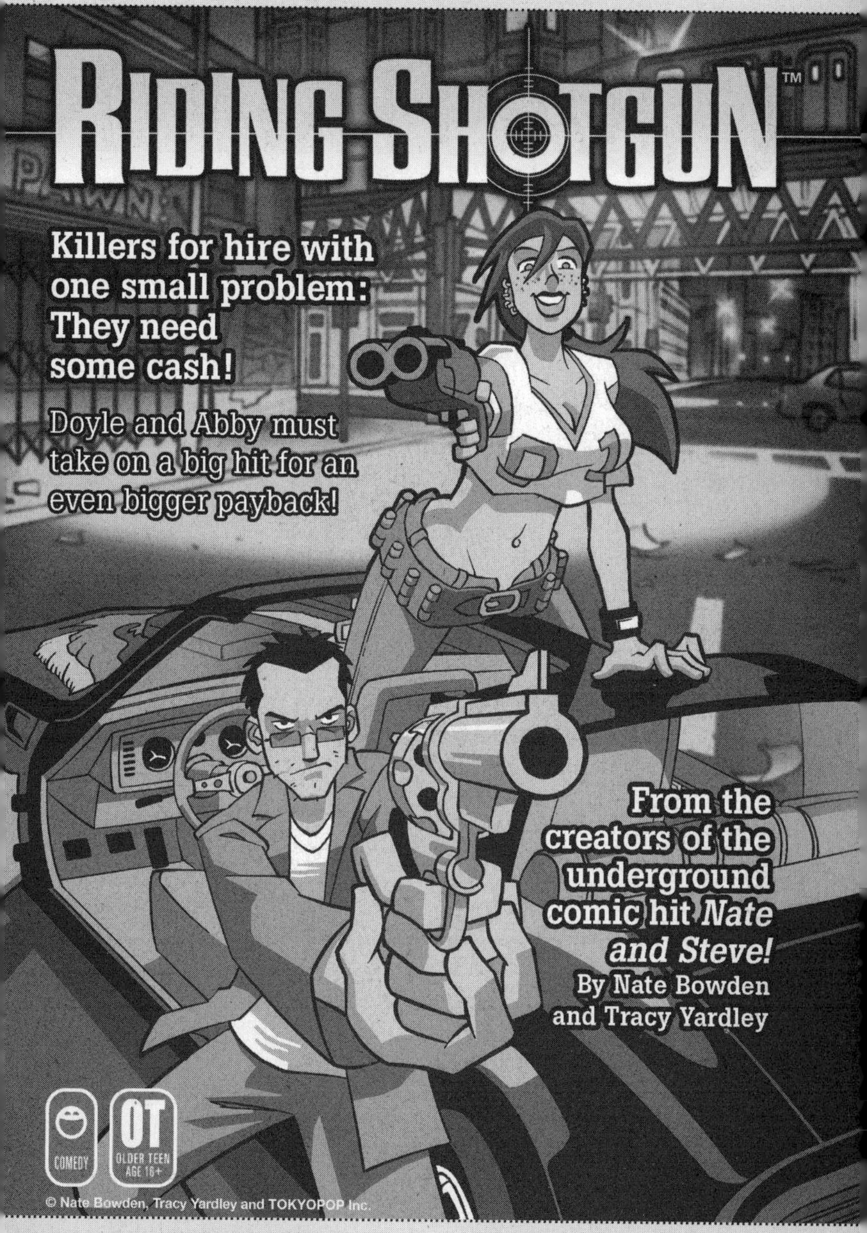
RIDING SHOTGUN™
Killers for hire with one small problem: They need some cash!
Doyle and Abby must take on a big hit for an even bigger payback!
From the creators of the underground comic hit *Nate and Steve!*
By Nate Bowden and Tracy Yardley
COMEDY
OT
OLDER TEEN AGE 16+
© Nate Bowden, Tracy Yardley and TOKYOPOP Inc.

EAD A CHAPTER ONLINE FOR FREE: WWW.TOKYOPOP.COM/MANGAONLINE

SHOWCASE

TOKYOPOP MANGA SUPPLEMENT

OTOGI ZOSHI
TOKYOPOP
Narumi Seto
1

OTOGI ZOSHI

BY NARUMI SETO

An all-out samurai battle to retrieve the Magatama, the legendary gem that is said to hold the power to save the world!

ACTION | T TEEN AGE 13+

Hot new prequel to the hit anime!

STRAWBERRY MARSHMALLOW

BY BARASUI

Cute girls do cute things...in *very* cute ways.

A sweet slice of delight that launched the delicious anime series!

COMEDY | T TEEN AGE 13+

STRAWBERRY
MARSHMALLOW
TOKYOPOP
BARASUI
1

CREATED BY:
SANAMI MATOH
ONE WAY
TOKYOPOP
TRASH

TRASH

BY SANAMI MATOH

When your uncle is the biggest mob boss in New York, it's hard to stay out of the family business!

COMEDY

... the creator of the fan-favorite ...

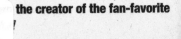